D1156906

Law and Politics in the Supreme Court

MARTIN SHAPIRO

LAW AND POLITICS IN THE SUPREME COURT

NEW APPROACHES TO POLITICAL JURISPRUDENCE

THE FREE PRESS OF GLENCOE
COLLIER-MACMILLAN LIMITED, LONDON

Printed in the United States of America

For information, address:
The Free Press of Glencoe
A Division of The Macmillan Company
The Crowell-Collier Publishing Company
60 Fifth Avenue, New York, N.Y. 10011

Collier-Macmillan Canada, Ltd., Toronto, Ontario

Designed by Sidney Solomon

Library of Congress Catalog Card Number: 64-23078

To my mother and father

Preface

I THINK it was Sorel who said that he always wrote by reading, that is, by reacting to the ideas of others. I am certainly very conscious of the elements of reaction, or rather of opposition, in this book. The one truly moving episode of my graduate education was hearing Learned Hand deliver the Holmes Lectures, and my thinking about the Supreme Court has been largely an attempt to grapple with the ideas of Hand, Justice Frankfurter, and Professor Wechsler. It is the proper job of a preface to thank those who have helped the author, and my first thanks must surely go to the intellectual leaders who created a body of thought about the Court that I view as fundamentally incorrect and immensely challenging.

If much of this book represents a reaction to notions of judicial modesty and judicial neutrality, even more of it represents a revolt against the traditional approach to the Supreme Court through the study of history and Constitutional law. I was fortunate to have received much of my graduate training under Professor Robert McCloskey, whose scholarship is one of the high points of that tradition and whose scholarly toleration has smoothed many paths. It is always good to fight with the best—particularly if they forbear to flatten you.

More than is frequently realized, political scientists arrive at their intellectual positions as a result of the varied and often strange, or at least random, patterns of courses with which they are connected. As a graduate student at Harvard University, I worked in both Professor McCloskey's Constitutional law classes and in the American National Government course taught by Arthur Maass and Don Price, whose views on American government have undoubtedly helped me to place the Supreme Court in the context of national politics. Along these lines I should also thank the members of the Department of Government at Harvard and of the Department of Political Science at Stanford University for allowing me to break out of the standard Constitutional law framework and to place courses with such anomalous titles as American Judicial Government and The American Court System in their catalogues. As to my more general intellectual indebtedness to the members of the Harvard faculty, it has become customary to make such acknowledgments in the preface to one's published dissertation, and hopefully I shall eventually avail myself of that proper place.

Some of the materials in this book appeared in preliminary form in *The George Washington, Southern California,* and *Vanderbilt law reviews,* and *Kentucky Law Journal,* which have kindly given me permission to incorporate them here.

It is also appropriate to thank here the army of nameless desk workers at the Harvard Law Library who supply their customers' wants cheerfully and efficiently in spite of their complete disinterest in the materials they handle. My special thanks are due to Mrs. Gretchen Gillen of the Stanford Law Library, who has treated an interloper from political science with a degree of efficiency and personal concern that is simply extraordinary.

The typist on this project was Mrs. Harold Small, who has the blessed ability to type without asking a lot of questions that interrupt the author as he dashes to finish chapter three while she is typing chapter two. The expense of preparing the manuscript was covered by a Supplementary Research Grant from the office of the Dean of the Graduate School at Stanford.

Heinz Eulau, in his dual capacity as helpful colleague and formidable reader for The Free Press, has read the entire manuscript and assures me that my errors are my own. My wife took what time she could spare from her own scholarly work to provide me with occasional editorial assistance.

As the first chapter of this book serves as introduction, I shall limit my introductory remarks here to pointing out that Chapter 1 establishes some propositions about the nature of the Supreme Court and the way it ought to be studied and that each of the later chapters seeks to support and apply these propositions to some facet of the Court's work.

limit my introductory remarks to pointing out that Chapter 1 elaborates some philosophical ideas about the nature of the Supreme Court and the way it ought to be studied and that each of the later chapters seeks to support and apply these propositions to some facet of the Court's work.

CONTENTS

Law and Politics in the Supreme Court

1

The Supreme Court as Political Agency

¶ Political *versus* Constitutional Court

THE SUPREME COURT is an agency of American government. So are the Interstate Commerce Commission and the House Rules Committee. The taxpayer who descends on Washington to have his tax status altered may turn to the Internal Revenue Service, the House Ways and Means Committee, the Supreme Court, or his own congressman. The businessman who is worried about government regulation of his enterprise may deal with the Department of Commerce, the Supreme Court, one of a half-dozen regulatory agencies, the Justice Department, and the President himself. The labor union seeking freedom from government curbs on the strike weapon begins with the Supreme Court, the Secretary of Labor, the Justice Department, Senator Humphrey, or a Congressional investigating committee. The Chamber of Commerce president who wants a new yacht basin for his community may visit a Senate committee or the Corps of Engineers—but probably not the Supreme Court.

These examples could be multiplied endlessly, but the point is simple enough. For those who want something from government—and the purpose of government is after all to satisfy people's wants—Washington is a place where specific agencies or individuals can do specific things for specific people. For some people, the Bureau of the Budget is more helpful and thus more important than the Secretary of the Treasury. For others, the Senate Foreign Relations Committee is more helpful than the Supreme Court.

The Negro, for instance, may seek desegregation. He receives some help from the Supreme Court (the school desegregation decisions), from the President (establishment of a high-level committee on discrimination by federal contractors), from the Secretary of Defense (desegregation of armed forces), from Congress as a whole (civil rights legislation), and from individual congressmen or committees (the Powell Amendment, investigations of discrimination, approval of Negro appointments to high office). The Attorney General may give him support in litigation, and the I.C.C. may order the desegregation of bus depots.

Clearly, in order to accomplish all that one wants, or to keep others from accomplishing too much, co-operation or conflict among several agencies is necessary. One cannot say that the power, importance, or function of a given agency is X. Nor can one even say that the power, importance, or function of one agency *vis-à-vis* another is X. Different agencies have different powers and functions at different times for different people, depending on the constellation of other political forces surrounding the particular problem.[1]

It is therefore impossible to speak in the abstract of the power or function of the Supreme Court. The Supreme Court, like other agencies, has different powers and different functions depending upon who wants it to do what, when, and in conjunction with or opposition to what other agencies or political forces. If a final answer can ever be offered to the question, What is the role of the Supreme Court? it will be achieved by correlating various powers and functions in specific areas, rather than by a general examination of the nature of the Court.

But our fascination with the Supreme Court as a unique phenomenon of American history, and with the constitutional format that establishes it as one of the three separate and coequal branches of national government, tends to thrust the Court out of the context of interrelated committees and commissions, services and bureaus in which we examine most problems of American government. THE Supreme Court, a thing apart, at most related only to THE Congress, THE President, or even THE people, becomes the focus of attention as soon as the nine men add their voices to those of the 999 others who are interested in any given governmental operation.

This tendency to view the Court as a unique and relatively isolated body is largely the result of its power of judicial review. The power to declare acts of Congress and the state legislatures unconstitutional, which makes the Supreme Court so different from the highest courts of most other nations, has willy-nilly become the principal concern of most students of our judiciary. The consequences are, first of all, continued emphasis on the Court *v.* the Congress. For judicial review seems to present a dramatic clash between two monolithic and coequal forces; the command of the legislature *versus* the constitutional fiat of the judiciary. Second, preoccupation with review has meant that both lawyers and political scientists who make the study of the Court their life's work teach courses, not on the Supreme Court, but on constitutional law. For academic purposes, "Supreme Court" and "Constitutional law" are almost interchangeable terms. Students are almost inevitably exposed first to the Supreme Court as Constitutional Court.

The business of the Court beyond judicial review is not entirely neglected by the law schools and political science faculties. It may be found, by diligent searching, in courses and texts on administrative law, taxation, patents, government regulation of industry, and so forth. But the search must be diligent, and the treasure is necessarily scattered and incomplete. For if the student of Constitutional law is prone to see the Court in the largest capital letters, the students of many other sectors of law and government are likely to see it as a largely peripheral and intermittent factor. These scholars, each of whom deals with the very limited fragment of the Court's work that touches his domain, look to the students of the Court *per se* to put the pieces back together again. But the students of the Court are likely to be too preoccupied with Constitutional law, that is, with judicial review, to do the job.

Finally, the Court's retreat in the 1937–42 period has considerably aggravated the myopia brought on by preoccupation with judicial review. Before 1937, much of the Court's work in matters of economics and business regulation was either carried on in specifically Constitutional terms or at least weighted with strong Constitutional overtones. To put it bluntly, there was always the risk that the Court would drag in the Constitution to overthrow legislation or administrative action it did not like. Students of the Constitutional Supreme Court therefore maintained a careful watch over its economic decisions, for in this area the Court was always on the verge of Constitutional judgments.

With the "switch in time" the Court translated its economic activities from judicial review to statutory interpretation. The Constitution largely disappeared from business- and labor-regulation decisions, and with that disappearance and the concurrent increase in the Court's concern for the Bill of Rights, the observer of Court *qua* Constitution tended to become entirely occupied with what was left of the Court's Constitutional business.

The civil-rights jurisdiction of the Court is an important, perhaps its most important, jurisdiction, but preoccupation with this area to the exclusion of others is doubly distorting. It is in the civil-rights area that the Supreme Court is most likely to appear as the lonely champion raising its hand against the excesses of the other branches and the states. Conversely, it is in other categories like labor and tax law that the most intimate and continuous interaction, both co-operative and competitive, between the Court and other agencies of government is most evident. The vision of a Constitutional Court set apart determines the subject matter for investigation, and the choice of subject matter confirms the vision.

The distortion occurs not only when the Constitutional observer abandons economic for civil-liberties litigation but even within economic fields. When the Constitutional filter is applied, taxation is reduced to intergovernmental tax immunity and state taxation of interstate commerce, labor regulation to the questions of whether or not picketing is speech and union action is state action, rate-and-service regulation to the sporadic eruption of procedural due-process problems.

No one would attempt to understand the House Appropriations Committee solely on the basis of its appropriations for office supplies and foreign aid—or the Department of Agriculture on its fish-hatchery and tobacco price-support programs alone. Nor can the Supreme Court's participation in the life of the nation be understood solely by studying the almost random pattern of decisions in which Constitutional factors incidentally play a part.

The point is not that no one should pay attention to judicial review or that "Constitutional law" is a tag to be avoided. Review is important, and the way political and legal subject matter is divided is a matter of convenience rather than abstract rule. The law schools have found it convenient to slice off Constitutional law as a chunk that, like contracts or administrative law, has sufficient internal coherence for separate presentation. There seems to be no good reason to question the judgment of the schools, especially when lawyers in the Anglo-American tradition have always insisted that the law is a living body, a true system in which each part affects every other, so that dissection is purely for analytical purposes.

The primary concern of the law schools is law, however, not the structure and behavior of governmental bodies. Dissections that help to illuminate the law often tend to obscure the nature of even those agencies that operate in legal settings. The problem of subdivision is therefore particularly acute in political science departments. In a recent compendium on the study of politics,[2] one commentator argued that public law had entered political science at the time that, and only because, the law schools were paying no attention to the subject. Now that the law schools are active in the field, Professor Morgenthau would be happy to give the whole job back to them.[3] Another commentator argued that public law is an essential field of political science, which has fallen into some disrepute among political scientists because it has been too much associated with the courts.[4]

The point here is again, not that public law is or is not a convenient subdivision of political science, but that political scientists have generally focused their attention, favorable or unfavorable, on law rather than on courts. If the study of public law has been obscured, as Professor Sherwood insists, by its association with the courts, so the study of the courts has been obscured by viewing them entirely through the medium of law.

Indeed, if political scientists actually studied and taught public law, the problem would not be so serious. But in political science curricula, we almost invariably find Constitutional law, administrative law, and international law. "Public law" is little more than a convenient general heading for cataloguing purposes. The

Supreme Court is naturally presented in the context of Constitutional law, just as in the law schools the Supreme Court becomes the Constitutional Supreme Court.

This vision of the Constitutional Supreme Court has been reinforced by the conventional mode of teaching and writing about Constitutional law through historical exposition. The same method has generally been used for the Supreme Court, and the two tend to be mixed up. Somehow what emerges is the Constitutional history of the Supreme Court or the history of the Constitutional Court. Because of its dramatic Constitutional history, a history so different from those of courts in other lands, the Court tends to become (and I intend no invidious analogy) our "peculiar institution." Peculiar, not only in the sense of being unique—but in the sense of being separate from and larger than life.

I do not argue that the Supreme Court is not unique or that its historic role as interpreter of the Constitution is not important but rather that total preoccupation with its Constitutional role yields a picture both too large and too small. The picture is too large when the Court looms as a sort of historical presence, apart from and overlooking the rest of American government. It is too small when the historically and presently very significant non-Constitutional business of the Court is ignored. And it is historically deceptive when, through a history of judicial review, the Court is presented as involved in a sort of continuous war with Congress and the President. Paradoxically, it is the tendency to look at too little of the Court—its Constitutional business alone—that makes the Court seem so big, a separate and equal "branch" of government marching through American history waving the huge club of judicial review.

We return to the proposition that the difficulty of examining the Supreme Court through Constitutional law or public law or Constitutional history is that such an approach tends to obscure the nature of the Court as one governmental agency among many. In the last few years, a body of scholarship has begun to develop that seeks to take the Court out of the context of law and place it in the context of politics, to treat the Supreme Court as an agency of government. It is this movement that I call the "new" or "political" jurisprudence.

¶ Political Jurisprudence

It is advisable to issue a few disclaimers at the beginning. First, while much of the work to be described has been done by political scientists rather than by lawyers, there is no need to dispute which are the "best" or "proper" students of the courts. It is natural for political scientists to look at the Supreme Court in the context of politics, at courts rather than at law.[5] On the other hand, lawyers, both as principal clients and sole source of personnel for the judiciary, have always been students of courts and judges, as well as of law. They have adopted techniques and outlooks from sociology and economics to improve their understanding of their own profession, and they will undoubtedly also adopt those of political science.

If it is better to avoid the feuds between lawyers and political scientists, it is best to avoid the feuds among political scientists themselves. Some work on courts has been done by so-called "group theorists," some by the most *avant garde* behaviorists, some by more traditionally oriented political scientists. At this point, there is no sense in trying to award laurels in the academic race. All techniques for examining the Court in a political context are worth attention.

Simply choosing to focus on the Supreme Court, however, plunges us into academic battle. For in recent years the tendency in political science has been to argue that power, political behavior, or the decision-making process, rather than governmental institutions, should be the focal point of study. Nevertheless, books on Congress, the Presidency, and, for that matter, the Forestry Service continue to be written. Surely to examine legal relations among the formal structures of government is not enough. But I do not think that we must abandon the study of institutions altogether. Instead, examination of institutions can be conducted in terms of the powers they wield, the behavior of their personnel, and their places in the various decisional processes.

It is clear from this discussion that "political" scholarship directed at the Court has been neither entirely consistent nor completely articulated. It is not my purpose to iron out or explain away the inconsistencies or describe a unified body of thought where none exists. Nor am I attempting a catalogue of all the work done in this area.[6] I hope only to show that a new approach to the study of courts is in the making and to sketch the broad outlines of that approach and its possible usefulness in understanding the Supreme Court.

Professor David Truman has been a catalyst for this new jurisprudence. It may be argued that his brief section on the judiciary in *The Governmental Process*[7] is little more than an assertion that courts can be just as conveniently handled within his system of analysis as other government bodies can. Truman attempts to analyze all government in terms of the influence and interactions of interest groups, measuring influence largely in terms of "access." He admits that there is little of the kind of direct access to the courts that pressure groups have to legislative bodies. The Supreme Court is after all not subject to the same types of pressure as the Congress. He emphasizes indirect access through such means as influencing the selection of judges. Indeed he defines judicial politics as interest-group politics largely in terms of widespread expectations about judicial behavior—like the belief in judicial impartiality—which are "interests" held by "potential" (unorganized) groups of which judges are aware and by which they govern themselves. In one sense, this approach is an attempt to force widely held social values into the mold of group politics that he has constructed. But we need not decide here whether or not all political behavior can and must be understood in terms of group pressures.[8] Truman does mention that organized groups do gain direct access to the courts by engaging in litigation, and he emphasizes that litigation, like war, is the conduct of politics by other means.

Furthermore, Truman's rather general suggestions about group access to the courts have been followed up in terms of both pressure-group lobbying and the "constituency" of the Court.[9] Lobbying techniques like the *amicus* brief, the test case, and the writing of law-review articles favorable to certain causes have been described, and the long-range judicial campaigns of such groups as the N.A.A.C.P. have been analyzed. Attacks on the Supreme Court by Senator Jenner, *et al.,* quickened the search for the Court's constituency. The crucial question became not, Is the Court interpreting the Constitution "correctly"? but, Are the Court's post-1937 interpretations undermining its old support in the business community? If so, are the new interpretations attracting a new constituency among the northern, urban, minority-group-oriented liberals?

Particular attention has been paid to the bar as a group that has constant access to the Court through the arguments and briefs of its members, their academic and polemic writing, and their recruitment as justices.[10] Lawyers are no longer viewed simply as contestants before an impartial referee or as officers of the Court. They form a constellation of political forces that play upon a political agency.

Indeed the whole discussion of lobbying and constituency inevitably leads to the question of whether or not the Court is a "clientele" agency. This expression is usually associated with those regulatory agencies that have become spokesmen for the interests they were established to regulate. It has often been argued that the I.C.C. has served as a clientele agency for the railroads. The Court has, of course, always been viewed as a spokesman for upholding "The Constitution" against the hostile sentiments of the moment. If, however, the Court is visualized as caught in reciprocal relations of service and support with various special interests or constituencies, then the concept of clientele agency may be applicable to the Supreme Court, as well as to the I.C.C.

If group, constituency, and clientele have become key concepts of contemporary political thought, power is often its principal preoccupation. This preoccupation has led to attempts to assess the power rather than simply the legitimacy of the Court. Professor Dahl, who has done some of the pioneering work on the concept of power, has attempted to treat the Court in the context of its position *vis-à-vis* the other power-holders in government.[11] The "political" attacks on the Court in the late '30s and early '50s have inspired considerable commentary, much of which inevitably, and some deliberately, describes and evaluates the political power of the Court in terms of its ability to protect itself in the clinches.[12]

Perhaps the titles of two recent works best illustrate this new preoccupation with the "power court." One is *The Supreme Court: Vehicle of Revealed Truth or Power Group*.[13] And the author's reply to his own question is definitely not "revealed truth." The other book is entitled *The Uses of Power*[14] and contains a chapter on the Supreme Court's supervision of such police practices as search and seizure. Even more indicative of the new jurisprudence is the second book's recognition of the Supreme Court's activities as comparable to the House Rules Committee's delay of an aid-to-education bill, the F.C.C.'s decision on granting a TV channel, and a Pennsylvania fight between railroaders and truckers—a fight, incidentally, in which the railroads thrust with a public-relations firm and the truckers parried with the Supreme Court.[15] Of course, the question of the Court's power is not new. It is at least as old as the Federalist Papers. But its treatment as political power, comparable and related to the power of the Chairman of the House Rules Committee; the police chief of Long Beach, California; and the Democratic Party is very different from the hoary debate over the Constitutional powers of the three great branches of American national government.

This preoccupation with power has also led to, or has perhaps simply been the reciprocal of, the breakdown in the classic Constitutional view that the legislature makes law, the executive administers it, and the courts decide individual cases under it. As we have become aware that legislators, bureaucrats, and judges all perform functions traditionally assigned to one another, the notion of separation of powers has been replaced or modified by the notion of process. That is, our principal concern has been to discover, apart from formal Constitutional shibboleths, precisely who does what, when, and how in the sequence of activities that leads to a governmental decision, action, or program.

Thus *The Legal Process,*[16] a recent introductory text for law students, deals with courts, legislatures, and administrative agencies as mutually interacting parts of the same process. Indeed, the subtitle of the work is *An Introduction to Decision Making By Judicial, Legislative, Executive and Administrative Agencies,* and one of the key sections is labeled "The Judge as Policy Maker." Jack Peltason's *Federal Courts in the Federal System,*[17] Victor Rosenblum's *Law As a Political Instrument,*[18] and Robert Dahl's "Decision-Making in a Democracy: The Supreme Court as a National Policy-Maker"[19] are pioneering efforts to fit the Court into the processes of politics. The case-study technique of examining a piece of litigation in the context of the entire problem in which it arose serves the same purpose.[20]

In fact, much of the work on "process" has been done in terms of the "decision" or "policy-making process." As a pole vaulter's function is to pole vault, so a governmental officer's function is to decide. This observation can hardly be news to even the most traditional interpreter of the judiciary, for surely it has always been recognized that what a judge does is decide. We generally speak of court "decisions."

The notion of policy- or decision-making does, however, provide some new approaches to the study of the Supreme Court. In the first place, studies of the policy-making process tend to be conducted in terms of particular areas: foreign policy, agricultural policy, defense policy. This approach leads us away from broad generalizations about the role of Congress or the Presidency or the Supreme Court in American government and into the problem of exactly what parts certain agencies of government, including the Supreme Court, play in a particular area of policy-making and the extent to which their roles change from area to area.[21] The function of the Supreme Court in the hierarchy of courts has also begun to receive some attention in terms of the political relationships between superior and subordinate in a highly bureaucratized governmental structure.[22]

Focus on decision-making has also dramatized the fact that the "final" decisions of government are compounded of the partial decisions of its component parts. This phenomenon is particularly evident in the actions of legislatures and electorates, where decisions that bills pass or that X rather than Y be President obviously result from aggregates of the votes of individual members. Voting studies that describe and analyze how each component's decision contributes to the final decision, the relation of each component to every other, and the shifting pattern of votes from issue to issue have proliferated.

Supreme Court justices, of course, vote, and their individual votes determine the general outcomes of the cases. Their votes, or more precisely the internal alignments or arrangements of their votes, shift from case to case. The opinions of the justices in individual cases also add up to a kind of over-all record for the term, in the way that the sum of a given Congress's legislative decisions allows us to generalize about its legislative behavior.[23]

It is not surprising therefore that the same voting analysis techniques that have been used to describe how legislatures and electorates arrive at decisions have now been applied to the Supreme Court. Much of this statistical analysis is strictly descriptive, an attempt to show the relation of one Justice's votes to another's, the presence of blocs, the possibility that certain Justices vacillate, or the direction in which the Court is moving on particular issues.[24]

Certain kinds of case contain a number of factors whose arrangement and weighting determine the Court's decision. For instance, in so-called "fair trial cases," the Court considers the defendant's intelligence and previous experience, his treatment within and without the courtroom, public sentiment surrounding the trial, prejudicial statements by the judge and prosecution, and so forth. These factors can be statistically compared in order to describe how many and what relationship among factors must be present for a finding of an unfair trial.[25] Statistics are also used to describe the Court's workload or to measure its tendency to decide in favor of certain litigants over others (individuals over government, business over labor, and so forth).

Behind the gross description of voting patterns, however, lies an attempt to understand the motivation of judges. The foundation of behavioral psychology is the proposition that we may discover the way men think by observing how they behave. One, perhaps the crucial, aspect of a justice's behavior is how he votes. The study of his voting may therefore tell us how he thinks. Two basic techniques have been used in this approach. In the first, the level of agreement between each possible pair of Justices is recorded, and those Justices with the highest level of agreement, in terms of voting the same way in the same cases, are grouped. Justices belonging to the same bloc, that is, voting together in a relatively large number of cases, are assumed to share a common attitude around which the bloc clusters. A group of Justices who constantly vote for the individual and against the government in civil-rights cases may be described as having a procivil-rights attitude.[26] The other basic method is scalogram analysis, which also measures behavior on the basis of votes with or against the majority. If certain cases "scale," that is, show symmetrical voting patterns among the Justices, then it is assumed that voting on those cases was determined by a single attitude dimension, for instance, sentiment toward labor unions or business.[27]

The general assumption of both group and scale analysis has been that attitudes toward the various socioeconomic and political interests presented by the cases are an important factor in determining at least some of the decisions of some of the Justices.[28] Attitudinal-statistical research has not only sought to isolate and measure attitudes toward social values like freedom of speech or free enterprise, but it has also sought to measure the Justices' attitudes toward other government agencies and toward the Court itself, that is, toward judicial self-restraint, spheres of competence, and so forth.[29]

Judicial attitudes can also be examined from the point of view of judicial biography. Of course, there have always been biographies of individual justices, but they have usually been aimed, like other biographies, at describing wise and famous men, rather than at explaining why the Supreme Court has taken the political steps it has taken. More recently, judicial biographies have attempted specifically to relate off-the-bench experience to on-the-bench performance.[30] "Collective biography"[31] has also become a very active field. If materials on the demographic characteristics and economic and political experiences of judges can be correlated with their voting behavior, inferences can be drawn concerning the effects of attitudes derived from particular social backgrounds on judicial decisions.[32]

Parallel to attitudinal research and using much of the same data is an approach that treats the Court as a small group and subjects it to the general modes of analysis and measurement that psychologists and sociologists have devised for examining such groups. The nine Justices then become the subject of studies in small-group psychology, which aim at discovering patterns of leadership, deference, and so forth.[33] The role of the Chief Justice as political leader has been described,[34] and attempts have been made to assess the relative power and influence of the Justices *vis-à-vis* one another.[35] While much of bloc analysis is aimed at identifying operative political attitudes, it can also be employed to chart the group politics of the court itself. The existence of relatively firm blocs may ensure the power of "swing Justices" and the need for compromise in order to gain a majority. Conversely, it may explain the intransigent and absolutist opinions of Justices caught in a minority bloc that has no hope of gaining a majority and therefore no motivation to compromise.

Also closely related to attitudinal studies are some research results that may be labeled crudely "behavioral." Although statistics may demonstrate that Justice X always votes probusiness, they offer no proof that he does so because he allows strongly probusiness sentiments to shape his decisions. Indeed, there is a kind of basic circularity in statistical approaches to the problem of judicial attitudes. Consistency in voting behavior is used to infer the attitude, and then the attitude is used to explain the consistency. This circularity can be at least partially broken by seeking for information on attitudes in materials other than voting records[36] or by manipulating the case samples to reduce the possibility of incursions by stray variables. Even with their circularity, however, statistical studies are useful to political jurisprudence. If we find that Justice X or, more important, Justices X, Y, Z, A, and B always vote prolabor, we may still not have learned why, but we have discovered something about the impact of the Supreme Court on labor policy and the nature of its relations with other labor policy-makers. A simple description of what happened, that is, who won, may be quite useful in assessing the political role of the Supreme Court.

The statistical, and more generally the behavioral, approach to the Supreme Court has become one of the most extensive and controversial areas of the new jurisprudence. We need not concern ourselves at this point with the methodological correctness or the economy (the ratio of scholarly input to useful output) of this approach. What is important in terms of a developing political jurisprudence is the underlying view of judges and law from which the behavioral approach springs and which it in turn tends to foster. First, it is *behavior* that is being examined, *not law*. The judge is viewed as a political actor, his decisions constitute his behavior, and that behavior is examined in the same way as the behavior of other political actors. Secondly, it is not the legal rhetoric but the actual vote on the case that becomes the center of attention. To be sure, the real reason for this concentration on voting may be simply that votes are easier to quantify than the logic and rhetoric of opinions. Nevertheless, the focus shifts from words to results, from legal language to political events. The whole behavioral approach to the Supreme Court becomes itself one of the forces pulling the Court out of its sheltered legal haven into the mainstream of political analysis.

The new jurisprudence, which I have chosen to call "political jurisprudence," is composed of many strands, but it is basically an attempt to treat the Supreme Court as one government agency among many—as part of the American political process, rather than as a unique body of impervious legal technicians above and beyond the political struggle. Such a jurisprudence is not, of course, an abrupt leap forward (or backward). Its roots lie in two earlier jurisprudential philosophies, judicial realism and sociological jurisprudence. The realists approached judges and courts with a kind of systematic skepticism. They attacked the judicial myth of impartial decisions by logical deduction from established first principles and urged students to look at what courts did, not what they said. Their emphasis was on the facts and the decision, rather than on the rhetoric, of any given case. The judge was portrayed as a human being with normal human emotions and prejudices who, in many instances at least, reached his decisions on the basis of his personal reactions to the facts and then sought for legal language to justify his choices.

Sociological jurisprudence viewed law as a social instrument and law-making as the balancing and reconciliation of potentially conflicting social interests. To be sure, the legislature was the principal social engineer. But the law-making, as opposed to law-discovering, functions of judges had become apparent to most legal scholars even before the realists stripped away the remainder of the judicial myth. The judge too was viewed as sociologist, social engineer, balancer of interets.

It would be easy—a little too easy—to say that political jurisprudence is simply the culmination of these two movements. The realists tell us to look at what judges do, not what they say. The sociological jurists tell us that what they do is to balance social interests. Behold the political court and the judge as political actor. Both tell us that law is not a matter of fixed principles but of the psychologically and sociologically determined reactions of judges to the world around them and of their attempts to shape that world. Political jurisprudence also views the judge as politician acting upon and being acted upon by other political forces.

Political jurisprudence, however, also owes a very particular debt to students of the Supreme Court. The Supreme Court, after all, always has been considered as more than simply a court. It is one of the three branches of government that, under the checks and balances concept, were meant to interact. Judicial review has always been recognized as, in some sense, a political power. Students of the Supreme Court in the context of Constitutional law, although tending to distort and to isolate the Court within the framework of government, have at least understood that the Court is part of government. Modern scholars who have taken the Court for their province, most particularly Professors Corwin and Pritchett, have, at least since the 1930s, paid considerable attention to the Court's political power. The growth of political science as a discipline also naturally led to attempts to integrate the Court into the whole framework of government.

Furthermore, the Supreme Court has in recent years served as the focus for a great debate over judicial modesty *versus* judicial activism. The main argument of the modest has been that judicial review inevitably involves policy-making of the sort normally undertaken by the "political" branches and that in a democracy such activity should be left to the elected officials of government. The Court therefore should be extremely sparing in its use of the review power. The modest have been very successful at convincing the scholarly public that judicial review is a political function and that the Court, in declaring statutes unconstitutional, is doing something strikingly similar to what legislatures and executives do. But, after a period of dominance, modesty has ultimately failed to convince the Court or the bulk of its constituency that it should give up review. The result of the most important body of thought and writing about courts to appear in recent decades has been to emphasize anew the political potential of the Supreme Court without substantially diminishing that potential.

It is little wonder then that the Supreme Court should be the point at which sociological jurisprudence, judicial realism, and political science come together and that study of the Supreme Court has so far been the principle vehicle for political jurisprudence. The Supreme Court is the first political court of the nation and the first to be examined in political terms.

It is also little wonder then that political jurisprudence has received its most serious attack to date from scholars who oppose the concept of a political Supreme Court.

¶ The Challenge to Political Jurisprudence: Neutral Principles and Legal Standards

In the last few years, there has been a flurry of scholarly activity centered about the need for "neutral principles" or "standards" or "reason" in the Supreme Court and more particularly in Constitutional adjudication.[37] The call for neutral principles in its mildest form is a plea for reasoned elaboration rather than *ipse dixits* in Supreme Court opinions.[38] There has been particular objection to handling important questions through *per curiam* decisions, which simply state the results with no explanation of how or why the Court arrived at them except Delphic citations of a few precedents.[39] Nor have the commentators been pleased with full opinions that fail to canvass all the relevant issues and to refute the objections of opponents.[40] Too often the majority and the dissenters have engaged in separate monologues, rather than in dialogue. This failure to meet, let alone to agree, on the issues indicates that the Justices have not sufficiently exploited their opportunities for consultation. Proper consultation would allow them to compose rather than publicize many of their differences and to arrive at the reasoned solutions that the give and take of their collective wisdom could provide.[41] Thus, it is argued, both the majority and the dissenters have often missed or mishandled the crucial legal issues.[42]

So far so good. Everyone is against sin and for a good argument. Not even the most rigorous legal realist prefers a badly written, illogical, incomplete opinion to a clear and learned discourse. But the proponents of "standards" do not mean by "reason" simply the rationalization of the Court's decisions in terms of the logic and rhetoric of the law.[43] For them, "reasoned elaboration" refers not only to the style and shape of the decision but, more important, to the mode of arriving at it. The Supreme Court must reach its decisions by a process of reasoned conclusion from general principles.[44]

The call for general principles, in its mildest form, is a plea to the Court to decide cases on something less eccentric than personal sympathies for the parties to the particular litigation.[45] Again there can be little objection. Not even Justice Frankfurter's famous *khadi* dispensing justice under a tree would be performing satisfactorily if he always decided for the pretty blonde against the wizened crone. This approach, however, soon blossoms into a broad attack on result-oriented jurisprudence, not only in terms of what happens to the particular litigants, but also in terms of general social, political, and economic results.[46] The judge should not be swayed by the possible consequences of his decision. He must content himself with the reasonable application of general principles to particular facts. Proponents of reason do not argue that the judge may not look beyond the case before him. Indeed, the insistence that the judge must take the long view is the hallmark of the proponents of standards.[47] But the long view is not to encompass the practical consequences of his decision but only the long-run viability of the standard he enunciates.[48] In other words, his chief concern should not be whether or not a given decision will for the next twenty years facilitate or hinder the rise of the Negro to a position of equality; it should be whether the standard of equality he enunciates today will, in the next twenty years, support him in the path of logic and consistency or lead him into the temptation of irrationality.[49] Is the standard he enunciates today sufficiently general and rational to be applicable to the cases that will come before him tomorrow?

It is here that the notion of neutral principles enters. The judge must be neutral in the sense of bringing to his task of adjudication no predisposition toward any given social or political result except reason and consistency. He must deal impartially with the conflicting social interests represented by the litigants before him.[50] It has even been argued that the Justices' sole task is to keep the grounds clear for the struggle between interests (business and labor, white and black, for example) and simply record the results reached on the economic and political battlefronts.[51] The ideal seems to be a disinterested, nonpartisan, apolitical judiciary, one that brings no political or economc preferences or values to the bench.

If the judge is not to decide cases on the basis of choice between social interests—or, put another way, between political policies—how is he to decide them? By standards of course, but these standards are not to be generalizations of the judge's own values or policy preferences. What, then, should the standards and their sources be? These questions constitute the crux of the entire discussion. The plea for neutral principles is not a new tendency in jurisprudential thought but a very old one wrapped in a newer vocabulary. Despite occasional bows to modern concepts of the judge as law-maker and human being, the proponents of standards have before them the old vision of the Court as law-discoverer rather than as law-maker. Neutral principles or standards are really the objective and eternal rules embedded in a "Blackstonian" body of law and the Constitution, which the judge discovers and applies to the case before him. When the defenders of neutral principles speak of a judge motivated by reason rather than will,[52] they visualize the common-law judge who did not command (make law) but simply discovered, by deductive and analogical reasoning, which of the great verities of the common law controlled the particular set of facts before him. Since the common law itself was the embodiment of reason and was applied by a purely reasonable process, there was no need of, nor could there be any room for, judicial prejudice, fiat, or preference.

Karl Llewellyn, in one of his last works, offered a peculiar variation on this search for objective standards.[53] Llewellyn, of course, had been one of the principal leaders of the legal realists, who had done so much to destroy the judicial myth. He later tried to put it back together again. While admitting that the judges make law, in the sense of filling the gaps between statutes and precedents, he argued that their discretion is not principally a matter of preference or valuation. Instead, the judge is limited and directed by the great traditions of the common law. His task, like that of the great common-law judges, is to discover

> appropriate, natural rules . . . right law. This is a natural law which is real, not imaginary; it is not what reason can recognize in the nature of man and of the life conditions of the time and

> place; it is thus not eternal nor changeless nor everywhere the same, but is indwelling in the very circumstances of life. The highest task of law-giving consists in uncovering and implementing this immanent law.[54]

Appellate courts do not choose between alternative social policies; they discern the underlying and objective legal principles that govern given fact situations.

This search for legal standards, which the Justices are to discover by the process of collective legal reasoning, is little more than the lawyers' nostalgia for the legal view of the Court and the legal modes of discourse that prevailed before the advent of the political view of the Court and political modes of discourse. Constant references to what "first-rate" lawyers, that is, experts in legal technology, think of the Court reflect this basic urge to lift the Justices out of the vulgarity of politics and public policy and restore them to their rightful places in the closed circle of those who are learned and immersed in the law. Curiously enough, even the style in which the debate is conducted indicates this nostalgia for law with a capital "L." The proponents of reasoned standards write in measured and learned prose and use the concepts and conventions of the "first-rate" lawyers and the law reviews. Their opponents tend to write either in straightforward English (often bordering on journalese) or in the new jargon of the social sciences, as if to suggest that the Supreme Court is not a topic only for lawyers' lawyers but for anyone interested in politics.

For these reasons, the movement toward neutral principles or standards must be viewed as a response to, and the principal intellectual opponent of, the new political jurisprudence. The opposition is not absolute, but the basic message of the standard-bearers is that the Supreme Court must be viewed not as a "naked power organ" but as one of the "courts of law."[55]

Naturally enough, rebuttal of the "neutral principles" concept begins by re-emphasizing more recent thinking about the nature of the judicial process, which the proponents of standards have soft-pedaled. The critics of neutral principles repeatedly emphasize that cases reaching the Supreme Court are the "trouble" or "pathological" or "no-law" cases. It is precisely because no readily ascertainable legal rule satisfactorily disposes of the issue that appeal reaches the highest court. Frequently there is no law to be discovered, and the Court must make its own law by balancing the interests of the competing parties.[56]

Of course, the proponents of standards admit that courts must often balance interests.[57] They want the Court to act as an impartial or neutral balancer. The antineutrality commentators reply that choice between interests in a given case is impossible unless the judge has some scale of preferences or goals.[58] The use of the term "balance" is deceptive because it implies that the judge, like a laboratory balance, stands rigidly between the two interests and brings his arm down on the weightier side. A laboratory scale is impartial because advance agreement has been reached both on a standard of measure (grams, for example) and on the quality or characteristic (gravitational attraction) to be deemed decisive in choice. If a choice is made between two apples by putting them on opposite sides of a balance, it has been decided in advance that weight, rather than volume or color or sweetness, is the preferred quality.

Social interests do not lend themselves to a single accepted standard of measure. They have several characteristics, some of which may be considered relevant, others not. It is difficult for the judge to be neutral because he has no exact or even nearly exact scale of measurement like grams or ounces with which to balance. Personal prejudices are likely to creep into his inexact measurings. And, in another sense it is impossible for the judge to be neutral: Unless he has some pre-established hierarchy of values or social goals, some pre-established standards of relevance, how can he determine which characteristics of the interests before him to balance?

Because of the vagueness of social measurement, it must frequently happen that two social interests of roughly equal weight—in terms of the number of individuals involved, for example—come before the Court. These interests may be in conflict because the social goals they seek to achieve are in conflict. Then the Court must make a decision not only between parties but between goals as well. Judicial choice between social interests implies—indeed requires—social preferences. In the "no-law" case the judge is, therefore, inevitably legislating his preferences.[59]

Those who oppose "standards" argue that since valuation is inevitable, it is better to recognize it and take up discussion of what values the Court should further, rather than to ignore the problem by flight into fictitious neutrality. Real neutrality might be possible for a judiciary that operated within and bowed to a society where a real harmony of interests and values prevailed, but the "trouble case" shows that such harmony does not always exist.[60] A court that must decide between litigants must decide between the values they represent. Professors Miller and Howell therefore insist that the principal duty of the Supreme Court is to develop and freely acknowledge a system of values.[61]

Thurman Arnold has put this antineutralist argument in its most extreme form.[62] Against Professor Hart's plea for more collective judgment and compromise of differences by the Supreme Court, he argues that Constitutional decisions hinge on the political and social preferences of the Justices. Since these preferences are probably strongly held and relatively fixed, neither compromise nor further enlightenment is likely to arise from extended debate in the conference room.

Dean Griswold replies that Arnold is simply incorrect, that when students of the law forgather, the product of their collective wisdom is sounder and more acceptable to each than any of their original notions.[63] This issue is one of several on which the scholarly contestants, like the judges about whom some of them complain, simply do not find common ground. Dean Griswold asserts that a group of legal scholars can arrive at correct collective solutions to legal problems. Judge Arnold insists that each member of a group of politicians goes his own way when it comes to making law. Both may be right. The issue again is whether the Supreme Court is a group of legal scholars or a group of politicians.

It is at this point that the rebuttal enters, and indeed becomes a principal example of, political jurisprudence. Professors Miller and Howell note that the "pathological" case that typically reaches the Supreme Court is pathological precisely because no successful solution is provided by other government agencies.[64] Professors Mueller and Schwartz note that, in the difficult Constitutional cases, the Court can never be "neutral." The very taking of jurisdiction puts it in potential conflict with the legislature whose decision the Court is about to review.[65] The Court is therefore operating within the context of intergovernmental relations.

The general armament of political jurisprudence is mustered by the antineutrals. Society is an interacting set of power relations. The courts deal with social problems. "The Judicial area is, thus, a political battleground. . . . The role, then, of the Supreme Court in an age of positive government must be that of an active participant in government. . . ."[66] If the Court is a part of positive government, its actions, like those of other governmental agencies, must be judged, not on the basis of some internal or inherent rationality, but by their results. Miller and Howell suggest a teleological jurisprudence concerned with the social consequences of judicial decisions.[67] Professor Bickel wants principled decisions, in the sense of selecting social values and working toward their future fulfillment.[68] In short, by emphasizing the concept of a political court over that of the court of law, it is possible to justify the very result-oriented analysis of the Supreme Court that is so distasteful to the "first rate lawyer."

"Teleological" jurisprudence implies broad, long range, social results. It does not suggest that *bête noire* of the believers in principled adjudication: decision according to the identity of the particular litigants. Too much is often made, however, of separating particular litigants from the legal or valuational problems they represent. It is the town drunk not the town banker who will raise, in case after case, the issue of police brutality. The litigant who attacks racially discriminatory practices will generally be a Negro and his courtroom opponent a white Protestant American. Separation of litigant from cause tends to mark another flight to that fictional land where legal issues present themselves as abstractions from social and political situations. If, indeed, the Court is one of several agencies to which various groups go for help, there is no more reason for the Court than for other governmental agencies to ignore the identities of the groups. A legislative committee, while hearing rival bills on their merits, still wants to know which came from the American Federation of Labor–Congress of Industrial Organizations and which from United States Steel. A teleological jurisprudence must take into account effects on particular litigants as well as general social results. At the very least, the former will probably be indicative of the latter.

On the whole, then, the opponents of standards favor a political, result-oriented, law-making court, in opposition to the neutralists' apolitical, logic-oriented, law-discovering judiciary.

¶ Neutralists, Antineutralists, and the Political Supreme Court

When all is said and done, the two sides fail to convince each other or uncommitted observers because, curiously enough, the antistandards commentators do not really see the actual position of the Court in politics, and it is precisely that position which is at the root of the neutralists' nostalgic yearning for a return to an older "legal" view. While the debate is confined to the nature of legal reasoning and how, if at all, "neutral" should be defined,[69] the major problem—and unfortunately it is a problem rather than a premise—is how many and how bold the Court's decisions should be. The decisive issues are those related to the tag "judicial modesty." How strong is the Court? What are the sources of its power? To what extent can it challenge other agencies of government?

In all the excitement over the concept of neutral principles, it is frequently forgotten that Professor Wechsler delivered the lectures that introduced the concept as a reply to Learned Hand's eloquent plea for judicial abdication of most of the power of judicial review.[70] The notion of neutral principles was designed to provide some basis for judicial activism in the face of a long-term, concerted effort by Judge Hand, Justice Frankfurter, and their allies to limit severely or even to eliminate the Supreme Court's power to declare statutes unconstitutional.

Wechsler, Hart, *et al.,* attempted to prepare defenses for the Court on two fronts. First, the Justices had been subject to attack by both the lower courts and the bar. The neutralists, acutely aware of the political fact that the Supreme Court's relations with lower courts—particularly state courts—are based not on command but on influence, argued that carefully reasoned and consistent opinions are essential to healthy intercourt relations.[71] That higher courts should give clear and consistent instructions may be looked upon as a moral imperative of justice. That is not the point here. The Supreme Court depends on the lower courts for the administration of its policies. While the Court's language is one of command, the state courts in particular have so many means of delay and avoidance at their disposal that the "mandates" of the Supreme Court are often little more than requests. The Court's power is therefore determined to an important degree by the co-operation it can elicit from these lower courts. As in all interagency relations, the technically subordinate agencies are likely to be more co-operative when their "superiors" act to make their lives easier rather than more difficult. Lower courts do not like to be reversed. Their role is easiest when they know precisely how the issues before them are likely to be treated on appeal. It is for this reason that unclear opinions, *ipse dixits,* and multiple opinions make the lower courts unhappy. Neutral principles, in the sense of standards that will be applied uniformly in case after case, reasoned explanation of precisely how the Supreme Court reaches its decisions, and clearly enunciated majority views are therefore, no matter what their abstract validity or philosophic feasibility, politically powerful weapons for the Supreme Court.

It may be that consistency is the virtue of small minds and that the lower-court judges are wrong in demanding it or, as Llewellyn has suggested, are often looking for the wrong kind.[72] Nevertheless, as long as its institutional power rests on the largely voluntary co-operation of subordinates, the Court must please those subordinates no matter how jurisprudentially backward they may be. Although the language may be that of moral or legal imperatives, it is clearly this political fact that lies behind much of the pleading for standards. Whether or not internal consistency is logically or philosophically compatible with the new goal-oriented jurisprudence, it is politically compatible; indeed it is politically essential. The Supreme Court must have the support of the lower courts to reach its goals, whatever they may be. If consistency is an effective tool for recruiting such support, then consistency there must be.

The lower-court judges are not only subordinates to be wooed but also, together with the bar, important opinion leaders. Americans are intrigued by expertise. If they want to know whether or not a bridge is sound, they ask an engineer. If they want to know whether or not a court is any good, they are likely to ask judges and lawyers—thus the concern among proponents of standards with the increasing restlessness of the "first-rate lawyers" toward recent Supreme Court pronouncements. All of the cutting things that Judge Arnold says about first-rate lawyers as running dogs of the corporations, entranced by the formalistic stupidities of law, may be true. But they will not change the political fact that the Court is stronger for having these opinion leaders on its side.

This notion of the bench and bar as opinion leaders leads to the second front: the general public. The judicial myth of impartiality and nondiscretionary application of "correct" legal maxims has lost much of its force in the United States. Since this myth is the principal support of judicial activity, Judge Hand counseled retreat from those areas, particularly decisions on the constitutionality of legislation, where the most damage was likely to be done to what remained of judicial prestige.[73] The judge, wrapping what little was left of his black robe of impersonality around him, was to retire to those fields of law where his policy preferences were least likely to be evident.

If the judicial myth on which the power of the Court rests has diminished in appeal, then there are two possible courses. The one is, as Judge Hand suggested, to retreat in order to preserve what remains. The other is to hold one's ground and attempt to repair the damage. The second is, in effect, what the protagonists of standards seek to do. Neutral principles or standards demand that the judge avoid sympathy for particular citizens' social and political preferences, and any arbitrary and unreasoned position on legal issues. Cases are to be decided on the basis of consistently applied standards to be found within the law itself. Differences within the Court are to be ironed out in chambers, not proclaimed on decision days. In short, what is demanded is the traditional myth of the impersonal, nonpolitical, law-finding judge whose decisions are the results of the inexorable logic of the law and not of his own preferences and discretion.

The objection of the standards enthusiasts to *ad hoc* or *ipse dixit* opinions without reasoned elaboration is that the Court's opponents may counter with opposite *ad hoc* opinions.[74] And one *ad hoc* is as good as another. Underlying this position is the feeling that once the Court's opponent, particularly the lay opponent, is lured from simple statements of preference into the "artificial reason of the law," the black robes surely must win.

Professors Miller and Howell have denounced this attempt to rebuild the myth as a jurisprudence of nondisclosure or "squid" tactics—the attempt to avoid discovery by emitting clouds of black ink.[75] But surely this attitude is a strange one for those who purport to stress the political dimensions of the Court. The distinction between what the Court tells the public about its activities and what scholars tell one another must be held firmly in mind. The politician is not usually asked to speak the language of political science or condemned for not doing so. Suicide is no more moral in political than in personal life. It would be fantastic indeed if the Supreme Court, in the name of sound scholarship, were to disavow publicly the myth upon which its power rests.

In the long run and as a matter of general education, it might be best if everyone were told the truth, the whole truth, and nothing but the truth, assuming for a moment that what the anti-standardists have to say is such a truth. But politics is the art of the possible here and now. Insofar as the standardists' writings are to be taken as counsel to the Court on how its opinions should be written, they seem to constitute sound political advice.[76] Even within the scholarly world, the plea for standards cannot be dismissed as obscurantism. Analogies with the physical scientist's search for truth will not do.[77] Atoms are not affected by what scholars write about them. Courts and judges are. If the myth of the Court is destroyed in the law schools, the Court loses power. Surely it is important to teach this truth, perhaps a more important truth than that of the discretionary role of judges.

Other critics of Wechsler meet the real issues more squarely when they argue that the standards approach might lead to complete judicial passivity.[78] If the Supreme Court can act only when it is able to formulate a standard that will yield defensible results in all future imaginable cases, it may be unable to act at all. Such standards are hard to find. Let us take as an example the seemingly clear standard that the state may not segregate persons on the basis of race. Does that mean that the state may not assign its Negro plain-clothes detectives to Negro neighborhoods and its white detectives to white neighborhoods? There seem to be few standards indeed that are always applicable, particularly as the troublesome case—the case that typically reaches the Court—is likely to be troublesome precisely because it presents a situation in which two principles collide.

If the Court must yield to legislative judgment in every area in which clear, consistent, neutral principles cannot be applied, then it may never be able to challenge the legislature. It is rather ominous that almost the only neutral principles Wechsler can think of are those connected with the post-1937 abdication of the Supreme Court to Congress in the commerce field.[79] The opponents of judicial passivity who cast a wary eye at neutral principles would profit, however, by remembering an old proverb that is constantly being attributed to one wise race or another: "My enemies' enemies are my friends." It has been the most judicially modest judges who have rejected standards and formulas as mechanistic, who have stressed balancing and case-by-case adjudication, and who have been most unwilling to translate the mandates of the Constitution into general standards for adjudication.

The reason is simple. Standards or principles have a certain "damn the torpedoes" quality. The court that views itself as champion and defender of a Constitutional principle is likely to go right out and strike down statutes that violate that principle. Or at least a court, having enunciated a standard that the legislature then proceeds to violate, will be under great pressure simply in terms of self-respect to put the legislature in its place. The unprincipled, unreasoned, *ad hoc* approach is convenient for judges who wish to talk their way out of conflicts with the legislature whenever they feel too weak for the battle. Standing on principle, in international, barroom, or legislative-judicial relations is likely to lead to a fight.

Standards, when they can be found, are weapons useful to the Court in preserving the judicial myth and urging the Justices to greater boldness. If Professor Wechsler means that the Court may act only when it can find standards, however, and if the standards for standards are placed so high that few or none can be found, then he has not discovered an alternative to Judge Hand's abdication. Instead he has simply found another road to judicial surrender.

The standards debate, then, cannot be reduced entirely to a clash between political and apolitical jurisprudence. It is true that those who attack the concept of neutral principles do so by stressing the political role of the Court. But they have been so fascinated by the Court as political actor that they have forgotten that it is also acted upon politically. The almost instinctive habit of viewing the Court as a thing apart reasserts itself in concern for what the Court can do to others but not for what others can do to it. Those who favor neutral principles have been worrying about what others can do to it. In many ways they have been more politically perceptive than their opponents. Unfortunately their method of protecting the Court, if carried to its logical extreme, would mean a return to an "apoliticism" that is intellectually indefensible in the light of present knowledge.[80] Furthermore, such a concept is so inappropirate to the demands of the real world that a court attempting to live by it strictly would be doomed to impotence.

The ghost of the original judicial realism, with its motto, "actions speak louder than words," hangs over the whole debate. Actions may speak louder than words, but words do speak, and in one sense the Supreme Court's only action is words. In so far as the search for standards is a search for politically effective words, it is a necessary one. Professor Wechsler fears what will happen if the Court is seen as a "naked power" group. Judge Arnold says that such legal theorists "design the clothes which conceal the person of the king and which give him his authority and public acceptance."[81] Surely here is the common ground between the proponents and opponents of neutral principles—and it is a political ground. If the Court is to be successful as a political actor, it must have the authority and public acceptance that the principled, reasoned opinion brings.[82]

Another potential common ground is in the area of valuation and interest balancing. The opponents of neutrality argue that the Court ought openly to pursue certain social values. If Americans want an impartial, nonpartisan Court, then that is one of the values the Court might well pursue. When the Court balances interests, the American interest in an impartial judiciary is one of the factors that must be weighed. In Professor Truman's terms, large numbers of, and perhaps most, Americans entertain certain expectations or values about the Court's neutrality—values that have been called the "judicial myth."[83] Political institutions survive and prosper to the extent that they satisfy widely held expectations about them. Here again the antineutralists have somehow abstracted the Court from the political process by imagining that it can sit back, choose long-range social goals or values, and pursue them. A political institution deals in values all right but not only the long-range goals of society; it must deal with society's immediate values and expectations about the institution itself. It is in this sense, not in the sense of some Platonc form of law, that Wechsler, *et al.,* are correct in arguing that the Court's standards must be drawn from inside—not outside—the law. In framing its opinions, the Court must satisfy popular expectations about the legal process. Satisfying such expectations, however, is not a political body's end but its means. It seeks to satisfy expectations in order to build the prestige necessary to pursue policy goals successfully. A court devoted only to creating the judicial myth and enhancing its own prestige would be simply strutting like a peacock. A court must use its prestige to further whatever long-range goals it has chosen. The standardists have concentrated too much on problems of expectations, institutional survival values perhaps, while the antistandardists have been too preoccupied with general social values. The two may be synthesized in that muddle of long- and short-term goals, values, and expectations called "politics."

The proponents of neutral principles have mounted a major and sustained attack on political jurisprudence. But if the doctrines they espouse as abstract truths and moral imperatives are treated as maxims of prudence—and too often in academic debate good practical advice is transmuted into bad philosophic universals—then they are more than nostalgic retrogressions. If the standardists mean that the Court may proceed only when it can find universally applicable standards drawn from the law itself, only when the Justices have purged themselves of policy preferences, and only when collective wisdom has reached a reasoned decision beyond the level of rationalization, then they strike not only for an apolitical court but also for a relic of ideas gone by. But if they mean that the Court should shape its opinions to recruit popular and professional support, compose its internal differences where possible, and make the preservation of the judicial myth an important determinant of when and where to act, then they offer cautions that the Court as a political body should heed.

The question then becomes one of political strategy. The

availablity of standards becomes one of the factors in the political equation. In those areas where standards are most readily available and reasonably defensible, the Court enjoys the greatest freedom to act. Where standards are more difficult to formulate or where the Court is badly split over what standards to apply, the potential damage to the Court's prestige must be weighed against the results. Where the creation or selection of standards would bring the Court into open collision with a politically powerful opponent or force it to do a patent injustice, then standards may not be the order of the day.

It would be presumptuous indeed to suggest that the debate over standards might well end at this point. But at least it might shift to a new level. Both sides have agreed that the word "neutral" is not sufficiently precise.[84] Both have acknowledged that, if principles do exist, they are few and difficult to find.[85] Both visualize the judge as a balancer of interests. Both would prefer carefully reasoned, fully articulated opinions to vague meanderings.[86] Both have declared that the Supreme Court is in some sense political.[87]

Both sides should now recognize that the nostalgic yearning of bench and bar for a prepolitical jurisprudence, for what one of the contestants has called "the return to doctrine,"[88] is an existential reality—a fact of American political life. The lawyers, both as practitioners and judges, are an important constituency of the Court and as opinion leaders, an important factor in the Court's relations with its broader constituency, the American public. Proponents of the new or political jurisprudence must listen to their opponents—not to counter their apolitical arguments—but to take account of the political facts that those arguments represent. To put it bluntly, the real problem is how the Supreme Court can pursue its policy goals without violating those popular and professional expectations of "neutrality," which are an important factor in our legal tradition and a principle source of the Supreme Court's prestige. It is in these terms, not in terms of the philosophic, jurisprudential, or historical correctness of the concept of neutral principles, that the debate should now proceed.[89] For the question, like most real questions about the Supreme Court, is not on the level of *the* Role of *the* Court or *the* nature of *the* law but involves the who, what, where, when, and why of particular areas of the Court's activity. At this level, both standardists and their opponents can contribute to political jurisprudence.

¶ Studies in Political Jurisprudence

I have argued that the main effort of the new jurisprudence is to put the Court back into the political context from which it has been torn by excessive preoccupation with Constitutional law. Nevertheless, even political jurisprudence has been written largely in terms of the Constitutional Court. Old habits are difficult to break. They must be broken, however, if either political jurisprudence or our understanding of the Court is to mature fully. For it is frequently those particular segments of the Court's jurisdiction involving nonconstitutional adjudication that most clearly illustrate and would be most illuminated by the concepts of political jurisprudence.

Although political jurisprudence has undertaken too little in largely confining itself to the Constitutional Court, it has also, in another sense, undertaken too much too quickly. Again borrowing from its predecessors, it began immediately to present hypotheses about *the* Supreme Court. In fact, *the* Court seems to have very different roles, powers, and patterns of behavior in different instances. The Supreme Court deciding the constitutionality of a Congressional investigation is very different from the Supreme Court deciding whether or not Congress intended a patent-holder's heirs or assignees to enjoy first renewal rights. The Court that forbids the President of the United States to seize the steel industry is not really the same Court that prevents a sick businessman sojourning in Florida from claiming his room and board as a tax deduction.

This diversity in the Court's functions is usually obscured. By concentrating on judicial review, we see a Court whose problems are similar from case to case. The "all Gaul" concept of American government, which is drummed into us from childhood, tells us that *the* Supreme Court is one of *the* three great branches of American government. So naturally we look for the Supreme Court. Finally, the fact that the Court is simply organized, consisting of nine men, all of whom sit on nearly every case, tempts us to the kind of quick generalization that is patently impossible for a large complex "branch" like the Executive. It may be possible to generalize about the Supreme Court as some brave souls do about Congress. The Court is after all more unified than many government bodies. But such generalizations should evolve as our understanding of the full range of the Court's business, in all its detail, develops.

Furthermore, lawyers and jurists are frequently familiar with the general political learning of their day and even use it occasionally when speaking of *the* Supreme Court. As soon as specific "legal" problems like patents or bankruptcy arise, however, all the political learning seems to be forgotten in favor of technical legal argument. A great gap exists between political and legal learning. If the student of law can be made to see the study of politics not as a rival but as an important tool in his own endeavors, then this gap may be closed. It does no good therefore to parade the general aspects of political jurisprudence, which the legal scholar and practitioner apparently finds too abstract to relate to his day to day work. He must be shown how political concepts can help him to understand the sources and implications of specific doctrines and Supreme Court decisions.

For these reasons and in the hope of making some contribution to the further development of political jurisprudence, I shall present here a series of studies of specific areas of the Supreme Court's jurisdiction. These studies are a part of the institutional, rather than the behavioral, wing of political jurisprudence, although neither of those terms is very satisfactory. More precisely, I am concerned with the actions of the Court as a whole and its relations to other segments of the polity rather than with the attitudes and actions of the individual justices. For readers most embroiled in current controversies, this explanation may seem simply an evasive way of saying that I am engaged in traditional rather than in behavioral analysis. I proceed by explication of and comment upon the legal doctrines the Court has enunciated. There is no attempt at quantification or formulation in terms of mathematical or other models. Indeed, so far as I can see, there is no methodological device involved that has not been traditionally available to legal analysis. If the course of political science lies from public law to judicial behavior,[90] at least in the rather special sense of "behavior" employed by some of its practitioners, this book does not move in the approved direction.

For those readers not embroiled in current controversies, all this discussion probably makes very little difference. Normally they might well be asked to skip the next few pages and get on with the business at hand. But the debate over methodologies and research directions is likely to be one of the key features of political jurisprudence for some years to come. Even the "outsider" therefore probably requires at least a brief look at the conflict to fill out the sketch of the field presented above.

At the outset of this brief excursion into the great debate, let me make clear that I face its problems as a student of courts and law, not as a political scientist *qua* political scientist. That is, I am primarily interested in shedding some light on the function of courts rather than in grappling with the problem of what kinds of work will best integrate public law into the mainstream of political science or contribute most toward the elevation of that discipline to the allegedly high levels of scientific prestige enjoyed by the other social sciences. Of course, courts are political institutions. Presumably, if we find out more about courts, we shall find out more about political science. In one sense, then, what is good for the courts is good for the discipline but perhaps only in the limited sense suggested by the apocryphal story of the famed automaker turned public servant. It is probably not in the best of taste to boast of one's parochialism, but it is the premise of this book that attitudinal-statistical approaches, whatever their contribution to a new science of politics, can at best provide only partial and supplementary methods for analyzing courts and law.

First, the new techniques themselves are heavily dependent upon traditional analysis. When scalogram analyses first appeared, the scales were constructed to show simple substantive attitudes based on the identities of the parties. It seemed unnecessary, therefore, to engage in any analysis of the opinions themselves except to label the parties as representatives of business, labor, government, and so forth. Legal analysis in the attitudinal-statistical area would then be reduced to noting that Justice Black voted for labor in case X and Justice Stewart voted against the individual and for the government in case Y. There was no need to pay any attention to the legal issues raised or the doctrinal positions taken. Much of the initial appeal of scalogram and bloc analysis was undoubtedly due to this apparent ability to unlock the mysteries of public law by simple counting, bypassing the traditional body of legal lore and methodology that seemed impenetrable esoterica to many political scientists.

Even those engaged in the new practices, however, soon began to insist the problem was not so simple. First, many cases obviously raise multiple issues and thus suggest multiple attitudes. When Justice X votes for the appellant in *A.F.L. v. Alaska,* a case involving state regulation of picketing, is he voting for freedom of speech, for labor, or for federal rather than state regulation of labor? While scaling techniques theoretically take care of this problem, multiple-issue cases complicate statistical analysis. It becomes necessary to spot and analyze them by traditional techniques, in order to fit them properly into the scales and to explain the apparent irrationality in the voting behavior of individual Justices that they frequently introduce into the statistical tables.

Second, and far more important, it soon became clear that if a complete picture of Supreme Court attitudes, judicial as well as economic, was to be presented, social and political attitudes would have to be described.[91] Certainly some Justices decided some cases on the basis of their attitudes toward the Supreme Court and the role of its Justices rather than on the nature of the parties. Since every case must be decided for one party and against the other, even those cases in which the role of Court attitudes was the key factor must at first glance have looked as if they might have been decided on the basis of attitudes toward the parties. Traditional analysis is required to distinguish those cases that are peculiarly likely to expose attitudes about the role of the Court and to discover what particular attitude is reflected in votes ostensibly cast for one party or another but actually cast for one role of the court or another. So far at least, experience has been that the more the attitudinalists deal with peculiarly judicial attitudes—like those toward *stare decisis,* deference to administrative agencies, judicial review, and judicial law making—the more traditional analysis is necessary to build their categories and explain their results.[92]

Furthermore, interest in the judicial or legal, as well as in the social and economic, attitudes of the Justices points up the most serious difficulty in attitudinal-statistical analysis. If judicial decision-making were completely unstructured, it would be clear that the attitudes of the Justices on political, economic, and social issues were always decisive. But where a great deal of structuring exists, it is difficult to determine whether the Justices' attitudes toward the structure or toward the economic and social values represened by the parties are decisive. For instance, let us suppose that we find Justice X consistenly voting for the unions when the parties are labor and management. This record may indicate either that he is prolabor or that decision in this field is heavily structured by a labor statute that was specifically designed by Congress to favor labor over management. It may then be discovered that, in another area not specifically covered by statute, Justice X also votes consistently for the union. This record may indicate either prolabor attitudes or perhaps that previous Court decisions have established strong prolabor precedents that curtail his freedom of choice. Finally, in yet a third area, Justice X may also vote for the union—this time against the government agency. This vote may indicate either a prolabor attitude or the Justice's objection to an agency's attempt to deviate from Congressional intent. In short, the Justice's performance may equally suggest either strong prolabor attitudes or strong attitudes toward what is or is not the proper role of the Court and the proper method of judicial decision-making.

The attitudinalist who remains convinced that prolabor attitudes are really at the heart of the matter then has two choices. He may either construct and reconstruct his scales and subscales in an attempt to control for all the other variables, hoping to show that labor attitudes are consistently decisive. Or he might simply show by traditional analysis that the law as written does not particularly favor unions, the precedents are not prolabor, and the administrative agency has not been engaging in bold ventures. The two approaches are equally useful and complementary.

Whenever the attitudinalist comes up with a consistent probusiness or procivil-liberties sentiment stretching across a single or several areas of law, it is usually possible to formulate one or another "strictly legal" reason for this consistency. The further the consistency runs and the more numerous the legalistic rationales necessary to explain it, the more suspicious we may become of a "coincidence" that so consistently leaves the legalities on the same socioeconomic side. But as far as social science propositions are ever amenable to proof, it may be more satisfactory to refute nonattitudinal analysis on its own grounds than simply to stick with the statistical inference. Furthermore, in an area that has always consciously striven for consistency and predictability, it would not be at all surprising if many consistencies that seem initially to stem from the value preferences of the judges turn out to be in fact the results of *rigorous* statutes and *rigorous* obedience to the etiquette of pleading and practice and the rules of legal reasoning, factors that must still be evaluated by traditional analysis.

Attitudinal analysis cannot thus achieve even its own rather narrow goals without the aid of traditional analysis in constructing its categories and proving, checking, correcting, and on occasion contradicting its results.

In addition, one of the peculiar features of both bloc and scale analysis is that they themselves offer evidence that attitudinal approaches, while they may be quite useful in explaining the decisions of certain individual Justices, are largely incapable of explaining the decisions of the Court. Group analyses have been most successful at determining attitudes when they have shown two relatively firm groups consistently opposing one another. But in such situations "swing Justices" typically determine the final decisions. Where attitudes are divined on the basis of membership in a group, the attitudes of the very Justices who decide the Court are least amenable to divination. Scalograms also typically show Justices with the most uniform votes ranged on opposite ends of the scale, with the decisive votes cast by those Justices in the middle. Even if the votes of the middle Justices are consistent in terms of the scale, their position in the middle indicates that they hold the attitude measured by the scale less strongly than do the other Justices. Those Justices who actually control the Court's decision are, by the terms of the scale itself, the least influenced by the attitude that the scaler is using to explain the behavior of the Justices.

Furthermore, because of preoccupation with the Constitutional Supreme Court, the new attitudinal techniques are first applied to Constitutional areas in which attitudinal differences tend to be sharply defined. In many areas of the Court's work, however, decisions are more often 7–2 or 8–1, so that group analysis is not very revealing.[93] For technical reasons, the reliability of scale analysis is also somewhat reduced the closer the Court approaches unanimity. But much more important is the consideration that near unanimity among the Justices strongly suggests the presence of some dominant structuring factor like a clearly worded statute, a commanding line of precedent, or a fixed relationship between the Court and another agency, which has sharply reduced the Justices' attitudinal freedom. In terms of explaining the behavior of the Court as a whole, attitudinal-statistical approaches thus encounter something of a paradox. Where attitudinal differences are most clearly operative and sharply defined, the attitude of those Justices who actually determine the position of the Court are the weakest and hardest to identify. On the other hand, where the attitudinally elusive "swing Justices" are not present, it is most likely that traditional "legal" considerations, rather than the socioeconomic attitudinal differences stressed by the new methods, are likely to be dominant or at least influential.

There has also been a general failure to emphasize that attitudinal-statistical studies are basically little more than the latest chapter in the history of judicial realism. We are currently faced with the same overenthusiasm for attitudinal-statistical studies that initially greeted realism. And, like that earlier extravagant response, this one is likely to fade when the incompleteness of realism as a jurisprudential system is fully appreciated. In a book that limits itself to the Supreme Court, I do not wish to venture into the broad debate about realism.[94] I am willing to content myself with Dean Pound's aphorism that a jurisprudence teaching only that law is a collection of judicial actions motivated by the values of the judges fails at the crucial point. It cannot tell the judge how to decide the case before him.

My concern is to indicate the incompleteness of the new attitudinal studies not for jurisprudence as a whole but for political jurisprudence. To analyze how the Supreme Court has reached a decision is not to assess the political impact or governmental function of the decision. Attitudinal studies concentrate on the internal workings of the Court. While they may show us something of the motivational components that go into various decisions, they can tell us little of the relationships between the Court and other government agencies.

This failure is all the more certain because the methodology of attitudinal studies implies excessive concentration on the question of who won. It is not who won, however, but the nature of the opinion in his favor that frequently carries the greater political significance. For instance, let us suppose two alternative solutions in a tax case against the taxpayer. In one, the Court reaches its decision by propounding the rule that the Court will not overturn long-standing administrative practices of the Internal Revenue Service. In the other, it decides on the merits that, in the particular instance, the I.R.S. has interpreted the statute correctly and the taxpayer is in error. Either alternative would be scored progovernment, antitaxpayer on the charts, but the two differ markedly in their significance for the policy-making process. One would vest the I.R.S. with sole policy-making responsibility so long as it remained consistent; the other would maintain the Court's policy role.

Another example brings out a different aspect of this phenomenon. Let us suppose again that the Court has two alternatives. First, it might find that a given payment from husband to wife was in fact alimony and therefore deductible for tax purposes. Or it might hold that, since the payment was labeled "child support" in the divorce settlement, it should be treated as nondeductible. In adopting the second alternative, it might establish the rule that tax treatment follows the labeling at the time of divorce. Alternative one would be classed on the charts as protaxpayer, while alternative two would be progovernment. In fact, of course, the reverse is true. Alternative two would open a giant loophole in the tax statutes. Child-support payments could simply be labeled "alimony" by the attorneys drawing the decree at the time of the divorce so that the husband's payments to the wife would be totally deductible.[95] Of course, these examples also illustrate the necessity for traditional correction to attitudinal-statistical analysis: Traditional analysis would show that the decision could not properly be labeled by the gross indicators customarily used by the attitudinalists.

My immediate point is a somewhat different one. If the Court adopts alternative one, it leaves itself and the I.R.S. as rival fact-finders in tax disputes. If it adopts alternative two, it freezes the I.R.S. out of policy-making in this area, for the Service would have no discretion. Furthermore, its adoption of such a rigid rule, with such high tax-avoidance potential and without much chance for I.R.S. intervention, would quite literally force Congress to amend the statute and drive Congress back into making policy in an area it might otherwise have left to the Service. Alternatives one and two thus have totally different political potentialities.

It is often in the doctrinal realm that the Justices shape the political role of the Supreme Court. Even assuming that the Court is always highly interested in which party wins, the flexibility of legal techniques is usually sufficient for the Justices to choose among several doctrinal alternatives. The doctrinal and therefore political content of most opinions is only tenuously related to which party won the case.

The doctrine of a case is, of course, that of the Court rather than of the individual Justices who compose it. And this proposition is not simply a fiction. Members of a circuit court may know in their hearts that Justice X became the fifth man in the majority enunciating a new rule only because he is blindly prolabor and not because he cares one iota for the rule. But the circuit court will nevertheless follow the rule. The majority that decides that the taxpayer may label his child-support payments "alimony" and take the deduction may consist of two judges who always vote for the taxpayer, one who always votes against administrative agencies, and one who modestly wishes to keep the Court from making decisions of fact. None may really care at all whether tax treatment follows divorce formality. But the rule enunciated will nonetheless shape the behavior of other participants in the tax policy-making process.

In the course of this book, I frequently engage in the anthropomorphism of saying that the Court intended to do X or made some decision because it wanted to attain position Y *vis-à-vis* another agency. Of course, the Court cannot intend anything. Only individuals have intentions. But it is what the Court intended in the sense of the operative effects of its decisions on subsequent patterns of litigation and prelitigation bargaining that is often the politically important factor—not what motivated the individual justices in voting the way they did. Since it is frequently *the* doctrine propounded by *the* Court that is politically significant, traditional doctrinal analysis is as important or more important to political jurisprudence than the analysis of individual attitudes.

It is not my intention here to proclaim an intellectual conflict where none exists. The attitudinalists do not claim to be the only true students of public law. Some of the new quantitative work is useful in the task of doctrinal explication.[96] The problem of moving from individual to institutional behavior is acknowledged throughout the social sciences and is particularly acute in political science. I can only conclude that traditional legal research is necessary in all phases of the study of courts, not to the exclusion of, but in conjunction with, other approaches. Whether that conjunction occurs through one student's attempting all the approaches in one place at one time or in each researcher using whatever technique seems most useful to his own problem and correlating the results through the normal interchange of the scholarly market place seems to me immaterial. I have simply chosen to concern myself with a different range of questions about the Supreme Court from that adopted by many who claim the title "judicial behaviorist."

Two more methodological notes are in order. Students of the Supreme Court generally proceed by the "leading case" method, the description and explication of peculiarly important cases. This method and the view of the Supreme Court as Constitutional Court are mutually supporting. Leading cases, those that individually have considerable impact on the nation, are almost invariably Constitutional cases, and the role of the Court in Constitutional litigation can be readily traced by spotting decisional landmarks. The absence of leading cases in non-Constitutional areas[97] is one of the factors contributing to such areas' exclusion from the mainstream of Supreme Court scholarship.

The Supreme Court's contributions to policy-making in such fields as labor and tax law are not made by sweeping judicial gestures but by the patterns and over-all effects of numerous decisions, none of which is individually very striking. In short, as with most administrators or decision-makers embedded in a highly bureaucratized governing structure, it is the day-to-day power over small decisions rather than the ability to change dramatically the whole course of government that often constitutes the key to judicial policy-making.

In my attempt to move toward study of the whole Court by showing the Court's policy-making role in certain non-Constitutional spheres, I have therefore tried to cover all the relevant cases, not simply the leading ones. Just as it remains impossible to reach final generalizations about *the* Supreme Court until one has considered all the facets of its work, it is impossible to make generalizations about the Court's work in any one area until all the decisions in that area have been reviewed. The Court's policy role must be finally exposed by cumulating the results of these supposedly minor decisions.

An attempt to describe and evaluate fully each and every tax or labor case would, however, degenerate into an unending catalogue from which it would be very difficult to extract useful hypotheses or generalizations. For purposes of economy, therefore, I have often dealt rather cavalierly with the cases, extracting from them only conclusions or doctrinal tactics and leaving aside much of their substance, both of fact and legal argument. This rather cryptic approach may leave those readers who are not otherwise familiar with the material at something of a loss as to the "legal" meanings of certain cases. They can, of course, go to the reports and find out. My purpose is not to provide a short course in tax or labor or antitrust law; it is to show something of the Supreme Court's functions *vis-à-vis* other segments of the polity, and I have gone to the substance of litigation only when it seemed necessary to an understanding of the Supreme Court's policy-making role.

This limited treatment of substance will also, I am afraid, prove annoying to those readers who insist that all decisions must be labeled "good" or "bad" and who demand alternatives to the latter. I am not generally concerned here with whether a given decision left the state of the law substantially better or worse than it found it—or with whether or not a given opinion was a masterwork of judicial craftsmanship. Nor do I wish to prescribe what the state of the law ought to be. I am concerned with the role of the Court, and, to the extent that my discussion is normative, it is about what the role of the Court, rather than the substance of the law, ought to be. Even in approving or disapproving a decision, my evaluation is usually based, not on whether I find the law that emerges from it desirable or undesirable, but on whether or not I find its implications for the role of the Court satisfactory.

More important, past experience indicates that, if one says of a case that it transferred decisional power from the courts to the I.R.S. or subordinated state interests to the Court's desire to avoid conflicts with the N.L.R.B., many readers will automatically interpret such statements as condemnatory of the decisions, particularly when there is no explicit statement of approval or disapproval. This reaction undoubtedly arises from the deeply ingrained notion that courts are discoverers of "right" law and should consider nothing but the "purely legal" questions. In reality, neither statement is in itself normative. The first is simply a statement of fact totally unrelated either to the motives of the Justices or the legal correctness of the decision. The second also says nothing of the substantive goodness or badness of the law arrived at in the decision, and its normative thrust depends on judgments about the proper relations between the N.L.R.B., the Court, and the states.

It is characteristic of political jurisprudence that it adopts much of the amorality of political science, describing rather than condemning or approving. But in an area as value-laden as public law, such an approach, while necessary to avoid obscuring descriptive findings, is likely to lead to the implication of values even when none is intended. Nevertheless, it seems to me desirable to proceed without continuous value statements on substantive legal questions, which would necessarily create a host of side issues to confuse and interrupt the basically descriptive purpose of these studies.

Also in the interest of economy I have chosen in several chapters to deal only with the Warren Court, which, for reasons stated in the individual studies, I have chosen to date from the 1956 term. Again, this approach is dictated by the rejection of the "leading case" method. In order to treat the whole pattern of cases adequately, a relatively short time span must be accepted. Some historical perspective is necessarily lost in order to develop fully a picture of the activities of approximately the present court.

Aside from the problems created by rejecting the "leading

case" in favor of an "all case" method, a major problem of emphasis and balance also arises in the chapters that follow. These studies have been chosen both to illustrate and to confirm the proposition that the Supreme Court is a political agency active in the various policy-making processes of government. The word "political" unfortunately has many meanings. To say that the Supreme Court is political and constantly to emphasize and re-emphasize its politicism is therefore likely to lead to misunderstandings. Obviously to say that the Court is political is not to say that it consciously serves as the tool of one political party or of certain political interests. Nor is it to say that the Court does and should think or talk or act exactly as do other political agencies. Surely the President is a political officer and the Congress a political agency, along with the Democratic Party, the Political Action Committee of the C.I.O., and the city council of Los Angeles. That does not mean that they all serve exactly the same functions in exactly the same ways. The challenge of institutional political analysis is to show what particular functions each political agency plays, describing both similarities and differences, overlaps and independencies.[98]

This book heavily emphasizes the similarity between the Supreme Court and other political agencies and the Court's integration into the whole structure of government. It is necessary to concentrate on similarities rather than on differences at this stage because of the extremely heavy freight of legal cliches that we carry as part of our intellectual heritage. The notion of a detached, law-discovering, objective, nonpolitical judge is so deeply embedded in the Anglo-American legal tradition that, even when consciously rejected, it tends to creep back to shape our thinking. For the moment, it is convenent to abandon our intellectual baggage in order to see what anyone unburdened by it would have seen long ago: courts that are an integral part of government and politics. Until this wide-eyed and historically innocent stance is adopted, the essentially political role of courts will be recognized only in occasional reluctant concessions to the dominant myth of judicial isolation and apoliticism, concessions that, once granted, tend immediately to disappear again when "serious" legal discussion begins.

All this argument may simply be quibbling. We may say that

the courts are essentially political and then, in describing the differences among various political agencies, show that the Supreme Court differs from Congress in being less directly political in some ways. Or we may begin with the proposition that courts are essentially nonpolitical and then note that the Supreme Court in some ways is somewhat political. But the latter approach inevitably treats policy or law-making by the Supreme Court and other courts as a deviant and disapproved function, and these normative concomitants seriously interfere with the discovery of what is actually going on.[99]

Intimately involved with these issues is the question of whether or not the courts, particularly the Supreme Court, are democratic and whether or not judicial policy-making is compatible with democracy.[100] If the Supreme Court is neutral and objective and simply applies The Law, then it is of course compatible with democracy. If the Court is a policy-maker, is it not then undemocratic, not being an elective body? Judicial policy-making thus becomes normatively deviant not only from the myth of judicial neutrality but from certain conceptions of democracy.

Here again normative judgment interferes with the process of finding out about what is actually going on. It seems to me preferable to take the Supreme Court as a given of the American governmental process, as we take the Pentagon and the House Rules Committee, rather than forever debating whether or not it ought to be there. Somewhere in the examination of every agency of American government, we may wish to ask to what extent the structure and function of this agency accords with whatever theory of democracy we have. And inevitably we shall find that some agencies are more democratic in some senses than others. But that is not the first question, nor is the agency's relative position on the democratic rank list likely to be the controlling factor in our evaluation of its performance.

I do not see why examinations of the Supreme Court must constantly labor under the whole burden of democratic theory. Again, for the moment, it seems better to begin with the simple nonideological proposition that the Supreme Court is here and is making policy in intimate connection with other parts of government. Later we shall add the finding that it is less democratic than some agencies and more democratic than others, as we analyze the differences among political agencies. This approach is all the more advisable when we have not yet settled the questions of whether or not we want totally democratic government or what exactly democracy is.

Too much study of the Supreme Court has been carried on by merely adding political epicycles to a traditionally conceived neutral center and by examining the real activity of the Court with the nagging suspicion that we are discovering feet of clay. It is the task of political jurisprudence to overcome the encumbrances of traditional approaches by beginning with the basic fact that courts are part of American government and politics. It should also note the differences between courts and other agencies as a variation on this theme and, in the real world at least, as differences of degree and not of kind. If the democratic critics of the Supreme Court wish to essay a total reconstruction of the whole of American government along lines that Dahl describes as "populistic democracy,"[101] I am certainly prepared to listen to their ideas about courts. But so long as the Supreme Court functions within a governmental matrix of mixed democratic and nondemocratic elements, whether or not to assign certain tasks to the Justices is no more and no less a question of democracy than whether or not to assign those tasks to any other government agency. In attempting to decide the desirablity of allocating decision-making power over labor matters to the Court or to N.L.R.B., for instance, the relative degree of direct popular control over each may be significant, but it is simply one factor among many. Certainly nothing can be solved by calling down a plague on both their houses because neither is selected by annual elections. It seems preferable to determine in each separate policy area whether judicial policy-making contributes to well rounded representation of interests or to popular control more or less than policy-making by some rival agency. This approach is surely more useful than issuing blanket condemnations of judicial action on the basis of an abstract model of democratic policy-making that does not reflect the realities of American government.

Underlying much of the continued attachment to the traditional vision of courts is the feeling that basically judges must, after all, follow existing law. They are not free to change the law whenever they please as "politicians" are. Again this difference is surely only in degree. For the executive branch must also follow existing law. Sometimes the administrator's discretion is considerably broader than the judge's. But in some areas, notably antitrust policy, the courts have a degree of discretion rarely enjoyed by bureaucrats. Even Congress, while theoretically free to change the law as it pleases, tends in practice to proceed by modification of existing statutes. Congress's bold new programs usually occur in areas where no law previously existed. The tenacity with which special interests cling to whatever existing legislation favors them and resist elimination of previously granted government largesse is well known and often leaves legislators almost as much enslaved to existing statutes as bureaucrats and judges.

I have sought, however, to acknowledge the Justices' relative subservience to law, even while concentrating on their policy-making functions. For the studies that follow are largely concerned with the doctrines enunciated by the Supreme Court. Doctrine is the half-way house between law, in the sense of statutes and precedents binding upon the Justices, and policy, in the sense of political choice unhampered by such bonds. In the formulation of legal doctrines, the Court seeks to harmonize existing law with its own policy choices. I do not mean that the doctrines that the Court enunciates are simply smoke screens designed to cover its political activities with a pall of legality. Doctrines like the "quantitative substantiality" rule in antitrust law or the "nether prohibited nor protected category" in labor law are at the same time acknowledgments by the courts that they are limited by statute and vehicles for effectuating one of the range of choices available within those legal limits. My concentration on doctrine will, I hope, serve as something of a counterbalance to my emphasis on judicial policy-making.

Nevertheless, the studies that follow were chosen basically because they show the Supreme Court at its most political. Everyone, for example, must admit that, in some way, the Supreme Court of *Baker v. Carr* was acting in the political sphere. But even the chapter on tax law is designed to indicate the political facets of what might at first glance seem an area of purely technical application of existing law. Indeed the principal thrust of the tax chapter is that it is impossible for the Supreme Court to remain neutral even by deliberate withdrawal from policy-making, since withdrawal itself aids some and injures others of the actors remaining in the political arena.

Each of the studies is also designed to support other hypotheses or methodological arguments put forward here. The discussions of Congressional investigation and reapportionment, for example, are presented along with studies on statutory interpretation to illustrate the mixture of Constitutional and non-Constitutional business done by the Court. Indeed the dominant theme of the chapter on labor law is the inseparability of statutory construction and judicial review in the work of the Court.

These studies also, I hope, illustrate the extent to which the justices must be not only political actors but students of politics in order to carry out their roles successfully. In reviewing Congressional investigations, the Court must act as political scientist, developing a description of how another agency of the government actually operates. In intervening in the reapportionment dispute, the Court willy-nilly becomes political philosopher forced to grapple with the problems of democratic theory. The antitrust laws establish the Justices as political economists who must somehow solve problems of economic organization within a *laissez-faire* framework dictated by the political ideology of the nation.

Along these lines, it is important to point out that political jurisprudence faces in two directions. So far, I have largely concentrated on the examination of legal materials to discover the political behavior of courts. But conversely, the political aspects of courts, once discovered, may be used to help explain and anticipate their doctrinal positions. Political jurisprudence may not only help students of politics to understand politics but also students of law to understand law—another reason why I have chosen the traditional path of doctrinal analysis. The chapter on investigation, for instance, focuses on a single doctrinal cluster, legislative purpose and its presumption. It attempts to show those basically concerned with questions of law that the unsatisfactory state of the Court's legal doctrine is the result of the Court's errors in political science. Similarly the chapter on taxation argues that the politics of the Supreme Court has become such an integral part of tax law itself that the legal practitioner must understand something of those politics in order to understand the law.

The tax study, along with those on labor and antitrust law was also chosen to indicate the Court's continuing and substantial role in the economy, a role that, as we noted earlier, tends to be obscured by concentration on the Constitutional Supreme Court. Antitrust decisions especially show that the Court retains areas of almost freewheeling economic power, which must be balanced against its reduced powers in the Constitutional sphere. These chapters suggest that those who have buried and reburied substantive due process in the economic sphere, and with it the role of the Court as protector of economic rights, have been too hasty in holding the wake because they have confined themselves to Constitutional provisions.[102] Statutory interpretation of the vast mass of complex but seldom automatically applicable federal economic regulation still leaves a wide scope for judicial assessment of reasonableness and fair play if the courts wish to make such assessments.

Finally, most of these materials illustrate the role of the Supreme Court within the policy-making process. The tax and labor chapters emphasize the interrelations between the Court and other agencies in policy-making processes that have no beginning or end—in which no agency has the final say and each contributes decisions that are then modified by the others. The antitrust chapter indicates that the contradictions and inadequacies of the general policy being pursued by the Court may be the real source of the apparent inadequacies of the Court's technical legal performance. An examination of *Baker v. Carr* shows that the Court may intervene when other agencies have proven themselves incapable of making policy and may act as catalyst in a stalled policy-making process.

In some of these areas, the Court is a major and highly active policymaker. In others, it can at best have only a minor role and is even more retiring than its potential would suggest. In still others, it chooses to retreat from major policy-making functions that it could exercise if it desired to do so. In this aspect of its behavior, as in most others, the chapters that follow will, I hope, prove that, while the Supreme Court is not all things to all men, it is many different things in many different situations.

2

The Supreme Court as Political Scientist: Judicial Review of Congressional Investigations

¶ Introduction

THE SUPREME COURT has long claimed the power to exercise judicial review over the investigatory activities of Congress. The most severe limitation the Court has imposed is the requirement of legislative purpose. Investigations must be conducted for the purpose of aiding Congress in making laws. But the Court has also introduced the doctrine of presumption of legislative purpose. The Justices will presume that the investigating committee and the Congress that authorized it had a legislative purpose in pursuing the inquiry.

It will be argued here that these two doctrines are completely interdependent, that once legislative purpose was required, presumption was bound to follow. It will also be argued that the two together so conflict with political reality that they cut the Court off from any effective supervision of actual investigative practice.

In short, because the Court has failed as a political scientist, that is, has failed to arrive at a realistic vision of the nature and function of a specific political institution, it has failed in its attempt to gain some control over that institution. A new approach is therefore suggested, which would abandon the purpose and presumption doctrines in favor of judicial acknowledgment of the real purposes and functions of Congressional inquiries. Such an approach would allow the Supreme Court to regain contact with the practical world of politics and thus permit it to impose more than theoretical Constitutional limitations on investigations, particularly on those that infringe upon First Amendment freedoms.

¶ The Presumption of Legislative Purpose

The notion of legislative purpose first became significant in *Kilbourn v. Thompson.*[1] The investigation in question was aimed at determining the causes for the failure of Jay Cooke's financial house. The Court's reasoning was simple, or rather simplistic, enough. The Constitution "has blocked out with singular precision, and in bold lines, in its three primary articles, the allotment of power to the executive, the legislative and judicial departments. . . ."[2] Inquiry into the propriety of private business transactions was clearly judicial, for it was designed to establish wrongdoing by individuals.[3] And such investigations "could result in no valid legislation on the subject to which the inquiry referred."[4] The investigation was characterized as judicial rather than legislative and was therefore judged to have exceeded the powers of the House of Representatives. By insisting that Congress did not have "the general power of making inquiry into the private affairs of the citizen,"[5] examining the committee's authorizing resolution for signs of Congressional intent, and disapproving an investigation that lacked legislative purpose, *Kilbourn* set the tone for the whole subsequent body of Constitutional litigation on Congressional inquiries.

But if we are to speak of legislative purpose with some hope of actual communication, it is vital to know whether "legislative" means "pertaining to lawmaking" or "pertaining to the legislature," that is, to Congress. In the first instance, "legislative purpose" means for the purpose of making law; in the other, it means for any purpose of Congress, lawmaking or other. But according to Justice Miller, all Washington is divided into three parts, a legislative part that makes laws, an executive that administers them, and a judiciary that decides individual cases under them. The three are clearly defined and mutually exclusive. If the *Kilbourn* investigation is judicial *ipso facto,* it is not legislative, and, if it is not legislatve, it is not for Congress. Or, to put it another way, if the investigation is not concerned with making laws, it is not legislative; if it is not legislative, it must be executive or judicial. It must then be the province of the President or the courts and not of Congress. Justice Miller's Constitutional theories made it unnecessary for him to define precisely the word "legislative" because for him the only legitimate purpose of Congress was to make law. *Kilbourn v. Thompson* thus tended to obscure the problem of legislative purpose at the same time that it introduced the doctrine.

The next important case was *McGrain v. Daugherty*.[6] While the investigation at issue concerned malfeasance in the Justice Department, Daugherty was a private citizen. The committee had evinced a desire to ask him about private banking transactions.[7] No mention of intended legislation appeared in the authorizing resolution, which was aimed at verifying the failure of the Attorney General to perform his sworn duties. Obviously, strict observance of the *Kilbourn* precedent might have put the investigation in danger. The Court did not want to do that. There had been a barrage of criticism directed against the restraints that *Kilbourn* had placed on Congressional inquiries.[8] The McGrain case involved Teapot Dome and had aroused tremendous public reaction. Its primary feature was not examination of private-citizen Daugherty by one part of the government but of one part of government by another.

The simplest course for the Court would have been to admit that Congress had always investigated not only for the purpose of making laws but also for many other purposes, among them the exposure of governmental wrongdoings. Unfortunately, the Court debarred itself from this politically realistic approach. For, in constructing an affirmative answer to the question of whether or not Congress had any investigatory power at all,[9] it adopted the simplistic Constitutional rhetoric of *Kilbourn*. Congress had the power to investigate because it "is an essential and appropriate auxiliary to the legislative function. . . . A legislative body cannot legislate wisely or effectively in the absence of information respecting the conditions which the legislation is intended to affect or change. . . ."[10] By relying on this notion of Congress as creator of law, the whole law, and nothing but the law, Justice

Van Devanter made it impossible to approve the investigation on the grounds that it was in support of a legitimate administrative, rather than lawmaking, function of Congress.

But Justice Van Devanter was unable to find any declaration of legislative purpose (lawmaking purpose) in the authorizing resolution, which is not surprising since none was intended. He was therefore driven to argue that, if the subject matter was appropriate for investigation, a presumption of legislative purpose was established, even though no such purpose was stated in the authorizing resolution. "An express avowal of the object would have been better; but in view of the particular subject matter was not indispensable."[11] In short, where no legislative purpose was evident, the Court would by presumption inject the purpose necessary to meet its self-invented requirement. Then the "particular subject matter," that is, the fact that Congress might have passed laws in this area if it had wanted to, is dragged in to support the presumption, although the presumption was necessary in the first place only because Congress obviously had not actually intended legislation. The presumption doctrine represents an admission by Van Devanter that, if he had really applied the requirement of legislative purpose suggested in *Kilbourn* and confirmed in his own opinion, he would have been forced to strike down an investigation that seemed legitimate to Congress, the public, and somehow to the Court itself.

Kilbourn and *McGrain* had only dealt with the question of whether or not Congress as a whole had a legislative purpose in authorizing given investigations. In *Sinclair v. United States,*[12] a contumacious witness challenged the legislative purpose, not of Congress in establishing an investigating committee, but of the committee in asking certain questions. As this investigation was also part of the Teapot Dome affair, like *McGrain* its most obvious features were oversight of administrative activity and public exposure of malfeasance. In order therefore to fit it neatly under the legislative purpose concept, the Court was forced to resort again to the presumption approach. Justice Butler picked up the hint in *McGrain* that an express avowal of purpose in the authorizing resolution was desirable. He held that if the subject matter was appropriate and if the resolution stated a legislative purpose, a presumption of purpose would be established.

Indeed it would, for Congress, which had met the *McGrain* test perfectly by picking a subject matter already declared appropriate by Justice Van Devanter and specifically stating a legislative purpose in its authorizing resolution. But why should these two factors establish a similar presumption for a committee of Congress? *Sinclair* really fails to distinguish between Congress and its committees and borrows for the latter a doctrine of presumption established for the former. We are now two steps removed from reality. And the second step, like the first, was taken because the Court, faced with investigatory activity it believed legitimate but excluded by the narrow lawmaking image of Congress, had somehow to drag lawmaking in by the back door.

In *United States v. Bryan,*[13] the Court took a third step by presuming the appropriateness of the subject matter and thus requiring only a declaration of purpose in the authorizing resolution. *Bryan* makes a nice "one-two" combination with *McGrain.* If the subject matter in any way suggests lawmaking but the resolution does not, play subject matter. If the subject matter does not but the resolution does, play resolution. The final step was taken in *United States v. Josephson,*[14] in which the presumption of committee purpose was made almost completely irrebuttable. A declaration of purpose in the authorizing resolution was held to establish conclusively such purpose "regardless of any statement by the Committee or its members intimating to the contrary." Here the combination is with *Sinclair*. Any distinction between Congress and committee is to be disregarded, so that the presumption worn by one will also clothe the other. And when the defendant bumptiously calls attention to the distinction, his rudeness is to be castigated by refusal to give any weight to evidence countering the presumption.

A weakening in the presumption doctrine was heralded by Judge Edgerton's dissenting opinion in *Barsky v. United States,*[15] which suggested that the courts should examine the actual purposes of Congress and its committees.[16] A further sign that the courts might be abandoning their uncritical acceptance of legislative purpose was Justice Frankfurter's refusal in *United States v. Rumely*[17] to accept the government's contention that an investigation of certain book sales had a valid legislative purpose because it was necessary to determine whether or not such sales constituted a device for avoiding the provisions of the Lobbying Act of 1946.[18] And *United States v. Icardi*[19] was the first case since *Kilbourn* in which a court explicitly held that an investigation lacked legislative purpose. It ruled that the presumption of innocence due the defendant outweighed the presumption of legislative purpose. The government had therefore to prove legislative purpose. Much dissatisfaction with the presumption of legislative purpose was also evinced in Justice Warren's opinion in *Watkins v. United States.*[20] Nevertheless, the cycle of cases from *Watkins* through *Barenblatt v. United States*[21] to *Wilkinson v. United States*[22] and *Braden v. United States,*[23] which will be discussed at some length below, not only continued to demand legislative purpose but returned to presumption of its existence—even in the face of an increasingly general conviction that the investigating committees are not primarily motivated by the desire to make law.

Although the presumption doctrine seems to have been somewhat weakened, the courts continue to cling to the requirement of legislative purpose. They are therefore driven willy-nilly back to the presumption doctrine in one form or another, in order to overcome the difficulties of investigations in living up to that requirement. Since these difficulties constantly arise, it seems obvious that there must be some disparity between the Supreme Court's Constitutional theory and the realities of American political practice. It is to those realities that we now turn.

¶ The Reality: The Division of Powers

We have seen that underlying the doctrine of legislative purpose is a vision of tripartite government in which each branch performs one function and one function only; the Congress makes law, the executive administers it, and the courts judge individual cases under it. That this vision is fundamentally incorrect is hardly a new or startling revelation. The judicial function is, for instance, certainly not the monopoly of the judicial branch. Even aside from the independent regulatory commissions and their mixed bag of quasi-powers, it has been recognized for many years that executive agencies constantly perform judicial tasks.[24] And it is

Congressional investigations themselves that show, when realistically examined, the judicial functions of Congress.[25]

Nor is the administrative process left entirely in the hands of the executive. In spite of a long train of self-limiting ordinances, the federal courts still exercise wide supervision over federal administration, if for no other reason than that judicial and administrative functions are so inextricably mixed in the executive branch that the courts cannot supervise one without supervising the other.[26] The Congress has always participated intimately in the administrative process through its power to specify the most minute details of administrative organization and expenditure.[27] The increasingly popular legislative veto has allowed Congress to reserve to itself the final say on such administrative questions as where a specific barracks will be built or to whom a given piece of surplus property will be sold.[28] And through the committee-bureau relationship, one of the most intimate in Washington, Congressional committees are constantly involved in the everyday business of the executive departments.[29] Here again, investigations themselves have been one of Congress's major administrative tools.[30]

Finally, the executive branch has for many years been the source of most legislation eventually passed by Congress. No modern President is without his legislative program, for whose passage the electorate increasingly holds him, rather than Congress, responsible. A recent commentator awarded the President the title of "Chief Legislator."[31] Writings on the Presidency continually stress the role of the executive in the lawmaking process.[32] And the debate over "judicial modesty" and the democratic propriety of judicial review rests on the realization that the Supreme Court's power to declare acts of Congress unconstitutional projects the judiciary, as well as the Presidency, into the lawmaking sphere.[33]

Indeed, the increasing tendency of legislative bodies to lose parts of their lawmaking functions, particularly to the executive, has led one of the most respected students of constitutional government to argue that

> The political function of representative assemblies today is not so much the initiation of legislation as the carrying on of popular education and propaganda and the integration and co-ordination of conflicting interests and viewpoints.[34]

But this emphasis on the propaganda and public-education functions of legislative chambers is not simply a reflection of the decline in the other powers of such bodies. Indeed, emphasis on direct Congressional contact with the public is part of Congress's struggle to maintain its other powers against executive encroachment. Perhaps the greatest source of a modern President's power is his position in the public eye. His capacity for making news, his access to the mass media, and his consequent opportunity to claim for himself the role of "voice of the people"[35] have constantly enhanced his power over Congress in both legislative and administrative matters. In this context, Congress's ability to exercise any of its traditional functions becomes increasingly dependent on its own ability to attract the public eye and build up a stock of public attention to counteract that of the President.

In a nation in which mass public support has increasingly become the coin of the political market place, the Constitutional balance of power among the three great divisions of government is more and more dependent on the ability of each to recruit general support. No matter how one visualizes the parceling-out of the lawmaking, administrative, and judicial functions, it is obvious that the Constitution intended each branch to have a self-preservation function, for the government of the founding fathers was predicated on the continued existence and at least semi-independence of the three component parts. Today, therefore, all three branches, whatever their other functions, have the Constitutionally legitimate function of attracting public attention and gaining public support.

The actual division of powers in Washington today, then, is not one in which each branch is solely concerned with the exercise of a monopoly in one governmental commodity. All three branches legislate, administer, and judge. And all three, as the price of continued effectiveness, must strive to sell themselves to the electorate.

¶ Congressional Investigations

The Supreme Court has argued that, as the sole purpose of the legislature is lawmaking, the function of legislative investigations must be to gather information for the purpose of making law. Once it has been shown that Congress has several purposes other than lawmaking, it should be evident, by the same reasoning, that investigations may also have several functions. In fact, investigation is a multipurpose Congressional tool. The aims of any given investigation are usually so intermingled that the examination of various distinct purposes is more analytically convenient than politically realistic.[36]

A catalogue of such purposes may begin with the widely recognized use of investigations as a means of Congressional participation in and supervision of the administrative process. Nearly all commentators on Congress have emphasized the importance of investigations for Congress's oversight of the executive branch and its enormous bureaucracy.[37] Indeed, the Supreme Court seemed to recognize the administrative purposes of investigations even as it established the doctrine of legislative purpose.[38] It specifically approved that administrative role in *Watkins v. United States.*[39]

It might therefore seem unnecessary to urge the Supreme Court to do something that it has already done, that is, to admit that investigations may legitimately have administrative as well as legislative (lawmaking) purposes. The difficulty is, as Marshall Dimock long ago pointed out,[40] that the Court did not recognize oversight of the executive branch as a distinct purpose of investigation but subsumed that activity under the lawmaking category.

It is perfectly true that investigations of the behavior of administrators may on occasion have for their purpose or result the revision of the statutes under which the administrators operate. But to concentrate on this aspect of administrative investigations is to miss their most important and, for our purposes, most significant functions. Bureaucracy is the core of modern government.[41] Both the President and Congress recognize this fact of political life and are constantly struggling for control of this key group. Since the bureaucratic chain of command at least theoretically runs up to the President, the Congress is at some disadvantage in the struggle. Investigations of administrative activity are one Congressional means of offsetting Presidential possession of the high ground. In short, Congressional investigations of administrators are not so much reflections of Congress's responsibility for passing laws as of its concern for keeping its share in the administrative, as opposed to the legislative, process.[42]

And Congress's principal source of influence over the bureaucrats is not in legislative correction of administrative wrongdoing subsequent to its exposure but in the exposure itself or more frequently in the threat of exposure. For the administrator, such exposure means punishment in the form of loss of prestige for both himself and his organization and, in extreme cases, even loss of his position and criminal prosecution. When congressmen attempt to impose their individual or collective wills on the bureaucrats, one of the principal factors aiding them is the administrator's knowledge that the activities of his organization may at some future time be subject to searching and public inquisition by the men seeking to influence him.[43]

By subsuming administrative investigations under the heading of investigations for legislative purposes, the Supreme Court has obscured two factors that lie at the heart of its own demands for a lawmaking and only a lawmaking purpose. First, a category of investigation that does not have as its sole or principal purpose the making of laws has from the very beginning of our government been recognized as legitimate.[44] Second, exposure of individual misconduct discovered in the pursuit of information, not necessarily for making laws but for its own sake, has always been an integral and essential part of this category of investigation.

Exposure is also a principal element in another type of investigation that has traditionally been undertaken by Congress. Whether or not Congress has a legitimate claim to the title "Grand Inquest of the Nation"[45] or possesses the "informing function" attributed to it by Woodrow Wilson,[46] it has in fact always sought to make the public aware of important national problems through investigations.[47] Congress has investigated every major area of the economy; a whole series of riots, scandals, and disasters; and all of our wars except the Spanish-American.[48] It has spotlighted the allegedly bloodthirsty practices of the merchants of death,[49] the concentration of economic power,[50] organized crime, juvenile delinquency,[51] and subversion.[52]

It is true that the gathering of information for the purpose of making law is often an element in the "problem" investigation, and indeed sometimes the problem is identified by the amount of proposed legislation on a given subject.[53] But only the most opaque pair of legalistic dark glasses can blot out the obvious exposing or general informing function of many such investigations.[54] Unfortunately, the public is not always interested in problems that affect the public interest. Congress seeks to arouse that interest through the publicity of investigation. The vast parade of repetitive witnesses before the various committees investigating subversion, like Kefauver's who's who of gangsterdom, was surely meant to expose "menaces" as well as to produce legislation. Otherwise, the Congressional mountain has labored to bring forth a legislative mouse. The very investigation that led to the introduction of the legislative-purpose doctrine was designed to educate the public about a new problem, the growth of an economic and financial structure in which the failure of a single firm could apparently precipitate a national depression. The "problem" investigation intimately combines lawmaking and educational or exposure purposes, and it is unrealistic to allow one to blind us to the other.

Indeed, exposure is not always directed at public education. Either administrative or problem investigations may become, at least in part, still a third kind of nonlawmaking investigation because of the exposure factor. We have already seen that exposure as punishment is an element in administrative investigations. Similarly, the exposure of wrongdoing in the course of problem investigations may lead to the punishment of individuals through public condemnation, the loss of employment, and various other social sanctions. In such instances, investigating committees seek to determine whether or not individuals, private citizens as well as public employees, have been guilty of misconduct, and the result of such determination is punishment of those judged guilty. Investigations of this kind certainly deserve the title of "judicial investigations."[55]

A second type of judicial investigation is that in which the committee's work serves as a preliminary to or integral part of actual criminal prosecution. We are not referring here to those instances in which witnesses are later tried for contempt or perjury, although such prosecutions may in fact be punishments for the wrongdoings that were being investigated rather than penalties for recalcitrance or lying. The series of investigations into the Teapot Dome scandal best illustrates this second kind of judicial phenomen. In that instance, investigations were used to uncover evidence that became the basis for criminal prosecution. The trials were followed by more investigations based in part on matters exposed in court. These investigations were followed in turn by more trials and finally by further investigations. The investigations were intended not only to provide the factual raw materials for prosecutions but also to supplement the sanctions of law. In several instances in which prosecutions failed, additional investigations were undertaken to obtain punishment by public condemnation where punishment by fine and imprisonment had been averted.[56] It is not only impossible to separate trials from investigations, in such cases; it is equally impossible to separate the various purposes of the investigations themselves. They provide a striking example of the combination of administrative, problem or public-education, and judicial purposes.

Finally, there is one purpose of investigations that may be called "legislative" in the broadest sense because it involves the legislature rather than legislation. We have already noted the President's ability to reach and to influence public opinion through such dramatic devices as the press conference and the nationally televised speech. Congress's lawmaking activities do not provide it with any similar advantages—but its investigative activities do. It can hardly be a coincidence that the tempo of investigation has quickened as Presidential activity and prestige have increased.[57] Nor, in this light, is it surprising that Congress has plunged so enthusiastically into investigating the menace of international communism at a time when the nation's preoccupation with Soviet threats has continually strengthened the prestige of that branch of government claiming primacy in the area of international relations. Investigations have served as an important means for bolstering Congress *vis-à-vis* the President in the continuous political struggle for public attention, which the President so often seems to be winning.

Congressional investigations are then multipurpose tools. Those purposes—lawmaking, administrative, educational, judicial, and self-preservative—closely parallel the general functions of Congress. This parallel suggests that in practice Congress has conceived of the investigation not simply as a scoop for gathering the raw materials of legislation but also as a flexible political device that can be utilized to implement any or all of its aims.

In this discussion of the realities of Congressional investigation, no distinction has so far been made between the purposes of Congress in employing investigations and the purposes of the investigators in pursuing them. Such a distinction is, however, essential. Since Woodrow Wilson warned that Congress was the prisoner of its committees,[58] it has become a truism that the standing committees are independent centers of power largely free of restraint by Congress as a whole and indeed largely in control of Congressional business.[59] Since the Legislative Reorganization Act of 1946[60] assigns the function of investigation to all the standing committees, the bulk of the investigative power is wielded by semisovereign entities whose purposes are their own and which have no necessary connection with the purposes of their parent bodies.

It is true that special investigating committees must seek authorizations from their houses of Congress and that all committees must go to Congress for funds to carry on investigations. But once begun, investigations tend to generate powerful popular support through their access to the communications media, and that support is used by committees as a weapon to force renewal of appropriations and authorization by Congress as a whole. Investigating committees stifle their opponents by identifying them with the evils being investigated. How many Congressmen can afford the risk of being branded procommunist or progangster for opposing the continuation of an investigation?

Furthermore, we have noted that investigations are multipurpose in nature and that the purposes are subtly and inextricably mixed. An investigation authorized by Congress for a given purpose may achieve not only that purpose but also two or three others. Or just enough of Congress's purpose may be mixed in with the actual purposes of the committee to mask deviation from the parent body's intent. Or the committee may begin by following the Congressional purpose, and then, after having recruited sufficient popular support to ensure its self-preservation, it may change its purpose entirely. In reality, therefore, the purpose of an investigating committee can never be assumed to be the same as that of Congress. Whether or not the two actually correspond is a matter that must be determined in each instance.

It appears that all the paraphernalia of legislative purpose and its presumption are in fact at odds with realities of Congressional inquiry. The problems resulting from the creation of such a judicial never-never land are reflected in the recent investigation cases.

¶ The Vicious Circle: *Watkins* to *Wilkinson*

At the height of the furor over communism and at a time when the dangers of investigations were being widely recognized, the Supreme Court issued an opinion in *Watkins v. United States*[61] that seemed to challenge many of the protections the Court had previously constructed for the investigators. The Chief Justice emphasized the potential danger of exposure by investigation to Bill of Rights freedoms[62] and stated that "the mere semblance of legislative purpose would not justify an inquiry in the face of the Bill of Rights."[63] The opinion noted the "possibility that the committee's specific actions are not in conformity with the will of the parent House of Congress"[64] and concluded that "the preliminary control of the [House Un-American Activities] Committee exercised by the House of Representatives is slight or non-existent."[65] Justice Warren spoke of the "wide gulf between the responsibility for the use of investigative power and the actual exercise of that power"[66] and of committee activity that "can lead to ruthless exposure of private lives in order to gather data that is neither desired by the Congress nor useful to it."[67]

Furthermore, in speaking of the necessary balance between public purpose and private right, Warren insisted that the Court cannot automatically assume every investigation fulfills a public need that overbalances any private right affected.[68] There is also a rejection, albeit a rather vague one, of the government's contention "that if there is any legislative purpose which might have been furthered by the kind of disclosure sought, the witness must be punished for withholding it."[69]

In short, the Chief Justice strikes at both the committee and at general presumption of legislative purpose. Nevertheless, much of the old approach remains. The investigatory power is traced to Congress's lawmaking function.[70] The "separation of powers" doctrine as it is usually stated, is invoked to forbid investigations seeking to "punish" those investigated.[71] No real challenge to the legislative purpose of Congress as a whole is made, however, as the Court can justify its decision simply by citing the committee as the villain. "The motives of committee members" are held not to vitiate the Congress's legislative purpose.[72] The result of this continued judicial conservatism can be seen in the last part of the *Watkins* opinion, which is quite distinct from the preceding part and contains the actual decision in the case. In this final section, the Court retreats from all the grand challenges issued earlier and simply requires that a witness be given some indication of why a given question is pertinent before he risks imprisonment by refusing to answer.[73] This reduces his protection and the Court's role of supervision to an insistence that the authorizing resolution or some facet of the hearing itself indicate the investigation's purpose with sufficient clarity to allow judgment of the pertinence of specific questions. *Watkins* was freed, not because the investigation threatened his basic Constitutional rights or lacked a legitimate purpose, but because certain procedural niceties had not been observed.[74]

If the latter part of *Watkins* ignores the several challenges to Congress offered in its introductory sections, *Barenblatt v. United States*[75] signals a step-by-step retreat to the Court's pre-*Watkins* position. Justice Harlan interjects the "gloss of legislative history"[76] to protect the House Un-American Activities Committee's authorizing resolution,[77] from the charges of vagueness that had been leveled against it in *Watkins*. For Warren's hints that the Court might look to what was really going on in security investigations, Harlan substitutes the standard patriotic condemnation of the dangers of communism.[78] A fairy story of St. Congress and the Red Dragon, coupled with the standard plea of judicial inability to examine legislative motives in the face of Congressional power,[79] puts the realities of investigations entirely beyond the reach of the Court. Then from the *Watkins* suggestion of a real balancing of interests we return to the usual semiautomatic balancing act of the judicially modest. The whole weight of Congress's general power to legislate on internal security is thrown into one side of the scale, the particular loss of personal rights to the individual being investigated is placed on the other, and the result is a foregone conclusion.[80]

The *Barenblatt* case was actually decided by reference to the latter portion of *Watkins.* Justice Harlan suddenly speaks as the political realist and goes over the committee sessions with a fine-tooth comb, finding sufficient statements, questions, and testimony to show that the witness must have known enough of the purpose of the investigation to make a reasonable judgment of the pertinence of the questions asked him.

The foundation of this decision is a further revitalization of pre-*Watkins* doctrines. *Barenblatt* reasserts the need for lawmaking purpose[81] and makes the required bow to the traditional version of the "separation of powers" doctrine.[82] Its major premises are precisely the same as those of *Watkins,* but Justice Harlan's principal task is to bolster the doctrine of presumption weakened in *Watkins.* The formal doctrine of presumption that frankly refused to look at reality is abandoned. *Barenblatt* introduces the doctrine of presumption in a new form. The foundation of this form is an elaborate play on words. The Court first requires Congress to have a legislative purpose for investigation. It then argues that investigations are a useful and often essential means to the end of lawmaking. Investigation thus falls within the scope of Congress's Constitutional powers.[83] Then, "so long as Congress acts in pursuance of its constitutional power, the judiciary lacks authority to intervene on the basis of the motives which spurred the exercise of that power." The Court will not look at the actual motives behind a given inquiry.[84]

Since it is Congress's motive, that is, whether or not it has a legislative purpose, that determines whether or not the investigation is actually within its Constitutional powers, how can judicial examination of its motives be barred by an assertion of its Constitutional powers? In fact, what the Court is doing is asserting as a general proposition that Congress investigates for legislative purposes and then refusing, on the basis of this assertion to examine whether or not such a purpose actually exists in specific investigations. As long as Congress might possibly have some legislative purpose for a given investigation—and it always might —the Court will presume that it does in fact have such a purpose in a particular investigation.

This approach takes care of the presumption for Congress as

a whole. It remained to repair the presumption for the committee, which was accomplished by refusing to examine the real purpose of the committee on the basis of the language in *Watkins*. "(M)otives alone would not vitiate an investigation which had been instituted by a House of Congress if that assembly's legislative purpose is being served."[85] Used in this way, without the repeated suggestions in *Watkins* that committees may go astray and Congress must guide them, such reasoning is *Sinclair* all over again. First, the Court presumes the "assembly's legislative purpose," and then it uses that presumption as a foundation on which to build a presumption of legislative purpose for the committee. If the witness pleads the motives of the committee, the Court can reply with the purpose of Congress; if he pleads the motives of Congress, the Court can reply with the "purpose, powers, motives don't count" gambit.

The most striking feature of *Barenblatt* is its combination of the old presumption game with the pretense of actual examination of the specific investigation. "Having scrutinized this record we cannot say that the unanimous panel of the court of appeals which first considered this case was wrong in concluding that the primary purposes of the inquiry were in aid of legislative processes." As this statement appears immediately after Justice Harlan's refusal to look at either Congress's or the committee's motives or purposes, it seems obvious that he "cannot say" because he cannot really "scrutinize." The record seen through the doubly darkened glasses of Congressional and committee presumption is hardly likely to yield anything but a legislative purpose. The presumption doctrine combined with the facts simply yields the presumption doctrine all over again.[86]

The cases of *Wilkinson v. United States*[87] and *Braden v. United States*[88] repeat and confirm all the *Barenblatt* retreats from the tentative advances of *Watkins*.[89] Again, the latter part of *Watkins* is employed to send the recalcitrant witness to jail. The Court finds that statements by the committee chairman and staff director and the Committee resolution authorizing the subcommittee are sufficient to have informed the witness of the pertinence of the questions asked.[90] In both cases, First Amendment claims are cavalierly rejected with a reference to the balancing arguments in *Barenblatt*.

Both look to the record only to the extent that it verifies legislative purpose. *Wilkinson* cites the committee resolution and statements by the chairman and staff director all of which refer to pending legislative proposals.[91] *Braden* rather vaguely suggests that *Barenblatt* established the proposition that Congress has a legislative purpose whenever it investigates "Communist infiltration and propaganda."[92]

Neither of these cases mentions the presumption doctrine itself, but both refuse to take any account of the defendants' attempts to prove lack of purpose. The defendants sought to show that, whatever the purpose of Congress as a whole or the general purpose of the House Un-American Activities Committee, the specific purpose in calling them as witnesses was not to gain information for pending legislation but to expose them to public censure for criticizing the activities of the committee. In *Wilkinson,* the Court replied that the circumstances described by the witness "do not necessarily lead to the conclusion that the subcommittee's intent was personal persecution of the petitioner."[93] Justice Stewart then went on to restate the *Watkins-Barenblatt* doctrine that the subcommittee's "motives alone would not vitiate an investigation which had been instituted by a House of Congress if the assembly's legislative purpose is being served."[94] *Braden* simply brushes aside the defendant's argument on specific purpose, on the grounds that investigation of the Communist Party, to which the defendant allegedly belonged, "was surely not constitutionally beyond the reach of the subcommittee's inquiry."[95]

These two opinions simply offer the presumption doctrine in new guise. There is no weighing of evidence for and against legislative purpose. Unless evidence "necessarily" leads to the conclusion of lack of committee purpose, it will not be given any weight at all. And even if it does necessarily lead to such a conclusion, it apparently still will be given no weight as long as Congress's purpose is legislative, for in such instances committee motives do not count. The *Braden* opinion wraps it all up by suggesting that, as long as the subject in general is one that might have been investigated for a legislative purpose, the Court does not care about the committee's actual purpose in the specific instance.[96]

¶ A New Approach: Abandoning Purpose and Presumption

The cycle of cases just discussed has left the House Un-American Activities Committee and its fellows substantially free from any outside control at the very time when public sympathy for its victims and distrust of its methods have begun to revive. Paradoxically, the Supreme Court has placed itself in the position of protecting investigating committees precisely because it seeks to maintain the theoretically very strict limitations on committees imposed by the "legislative purpose" requirement. As this requirement is absolutely out of harmony with political reality, however, the Court would have to strike down all investigations if it were to examine them realistically for legislative and no other purpose. Instead it must turn to the presumption doctrine, in order to inject the absent legislative purpose that it requires. Having asked too much, the Court receives nothing. It cannot use the purpose requirement to overturn investigations it does not approve, for to do so would be to launch a general assault on all investigations, including those it does approve. It cannot therefore really use the purpose requirement at all.

But the result is that, whenever the Court considers limiting investigations, it faces the prospect of having to limit the most important and wide ranging power of Congress, the power of legislation with which the Court itself has impregnated the investigating committees by strictly artificial insemination. It is, of course, not impossible to impose Constitutional limitations on lawmaking activity. But once law is injected into the matter for judicial consideration, whole hosts of the judicially modest arise to protest judicial interference with the sovereign will of the people embodied in the lawmaking of Congress.[97] The requirement of legislative purpose thus leads to the presumption of legislative purpose. And the presumption of legislative purpose leads to the presumption of Constitutionality with which the modest endow Congressional lawmaking.[98] As a result, Congressional investigations, wrapped in the double armor of these interdependent presumptions, rest safe from most lines of judicial attack.

By doing away with the requirement of legislative purpose,

the Court would place itself in a much stronger position. For instance, acknowledgment of the administrative purposes of many committee inquiries would allow the Court to avoid the appearance of acting in defiance of the lawmaking powers of Congress. Instead, the Court could act as referee between the Congress and the Executive in an area where their claims of Constitutional power conflict. This role is surely one that the modest could approve.[99] Similarly, by looking the judicial purposes of certain investigations straight in the face, the Court could claim the right to impose strict supervision over those matters in which judges are admitted to have special competence and a special grant of Constitutional power.

Most important, by acknowledging that exposure for exposure's sake has always been one of the purposes of investigation, the Court would be in a position to point out the perils of exposure investigations and to limit their invasion of Constitutional rights. The Justices could break out of the vicious circle of condemning exposure *per se,* which forces them to presume legislative purpose in order to avoid striking down all investigations in which exposure is an element and thus in the end completely bars them from protecting Constitutional rights against exposure precisely because they have so roundly condemned it in the first place. Having admitted exposure as one of the routine functions of investigation, the Court would be free actually to look at Congressional exposure and to determine whether or not, in specific instances, it has invaded the Constitutionally guaranteed freedoms of specific individuals.

The whole technique of balancing individual freedoms against society's interests in government activities interfering with those freedoms would greatly benefit from the abandonment of the demand for and presumption of legislative purpose. If balancing always begins by throwing the whole lawmaking power of Congress, particularly the power to legislate in the interest of national security, on one side of the scale, the individual rights invaded by investigation must almost always weigh lighter. The actual purposes of investigations frequently do not carry nearly so heavy a weight of social interest. Conversely, the exposure purpose of many inquiries presents a particularly grave danger to freedom of speech and association.[100] By recognizing exposure as a normal purpose of investigations, while at the same time stressing its potential danger to individual rights, the Court could begin to act as a real balancer of interests, striking down those inquiries that needlessly invade Constitutional liberties and upholding those in which exposure of some danger or misdeed is essential to our society.

Barenblatt, et al., shows how a presumption that the committee's purpose is the same as that of Congress as a whole peculiarly distorts judicial balancing. For this presumption poses a wholly unnecessary dilemma to the modest by confronting them with the whole weight of Congress, when in reality it is only the committee they face. The doctrine of judicial modesty is principally based on belief in democratic responsibility. The Congress is directly responsible to the voters, while the Court is not. The Court must thus yield to Congress as the sovereign voice of the people. But the committees are not identical with Congress, and they do not always yield to Congressional control. As we have already noted, the committees act as largely independent bodies. When the Court yields to a committee, it pays homage, not to the legitimate sovereign, but to one of his unruly barons. It is, I think, significant that one of the few instances in which Justice Frankfurter has been willing directly to challenge Congressional activity occurred when he departed from the presumption doctrine sufficiently to find a disparity between the purpose of Congress and that of one of its committees.[101]

Furthermore, judicial modesty is based on a calculation of the relative political power of Congress and the Supreme Court. Not only are the committees individually less powerful on the national scene than is Congress as a whole, but also the Court can often count on at least clandestine support from important elements of Congress when it takes on a committee. Many congressmen, who may not initially care actively to attack a given investigation would be glad passively to accept or even support a Court decision against the committee based on its failure to abide by the intentions of Congress. We do not argue that the Justices may attack any investigating committee at any time under any circumstances. But we do suggest that the Court may on occasion count on a favorable constellation of political forces for the protection of civil liberties against committee action. In short, abandoning the presumption of committee legislative purpose would mean that, in certain instances, the power of the Court could actually be used, not only to defend civil liberties, but to increase democratic responsibility by strengthening Congressional control over its own committees.

The very paradox built into the "legislative purpose" doctrine may prove particularly convenient for a Court trying to get rid of it. Because the requirement of legislative purpose imposes such a severe limitation on Congressional activity that it in fact imposes no limitation, the elimination of the requirement will, on its face, free the Congress from onerous judicial supervision while actually giving the Court more room to maneuver. For when the demand for legislative purpose goes, the need for presumption of such purpose goes with it. Congress is told that it may investigate for any purpose it sees fit—that it may have the Court's imprimatur for what it has been doing all along without it; the Court is free to begin real supervision of an area from which it has previously been barred by its own misreading of the political scene. The grant of additional powers to Congress nicely sugar-coats the extension of Supreme Court activity.[102]

A similar difficulty in the Court's initial approach to the purpose issue can aid the Court in escaping the doctrine without seeming to do so. Of course, nothing prevents the Court from flatly overruling both the purpose and presumption doctrines. It has recently provided us with a dramatic example of the reversal of two long-standing but unrealistic rules.[103] But if the Court prefers a more subtle approach, the very ambiguity of the word "legislative" introduced in *Kilbourn* may prove extremely useful. A gradual transition from "lawmaking" purpose to "Congress's purpose" can be accomplished simply by progressively approving more and more nonlawmaking Congressional activities under cover of the ambiguity of "legislative."

In fact, there is already sufficient careless wording[104] in earlier opinions to start the ball rolling.

> (T)he indispensable "informing function of Congress" is not to be minimized. . . .[105]

> The power of the Congress to conduct investigations is . . . broad. It encompasses inquiries concerning the administration of exist-

> ing laws as well as proposed or possibly needed statutes. It includes surveys of defects in our social, economic or political system. . . . It comprehends probes . . . of the Federal Government to expose corruption, inefficiency or waste.[106]

By continuing this process, the Court could eventually acknowledge all the real purposes of investigations while, at least in the transitional stage, holding fast to the comfort of the traditional verbal formula.

Since the Court is likely to continue to receive a fairly steady stream of contempt cases, this process of change could be begun at any time. Sentiment in favor of more active judicial supervision of at least some kinds of investigation has existed on the Court for some time.[107]

The most recent cases reaching the Court indicate the growing but still tentative nature of that sentiment. *Yellin v. United States*[108] and *Russell v. United States*[109] follow the tradition of *Watkins* and *Deutsch* in finding procedural loopholes through which the witness can escape, loopholes that can easily be plugged in the future, however. *Gibson v. Florida*[110] has much of the grand language of *Watkins* but may or may not be any more effective. It purports to do some real balancing between the state's need to know and the right of association of private groups instead of engaging in the false balancing of *Wilkinson.* Indeed it suggests something like the "preferred position" doctrine in holding that the state must demonstrate an "overriding and compelling state interest"[111] to justify invasion of First Amendment rights. But its basic rule is that "groups which themselves are neither engaged in subversive or other illegal or improper activities, nor demonstrated to have any substantial connections with such activities are to be protected in their rights of free and private association."[112] As the Court is unlikely to decide in advance and in opposition to legislative bodies, particularly Congress, the very question that most investigations are designed to decide—whether or not an organization is subversive or has been subverted—this principle is not likely to be a very great limitation on investigations. If libertarian sentiment flowers on the Court in the future, the broad language of *Gibson* may be much quoted, but for the moment it is probably nothing more than a special exemption for the N.A.A.C.P. from harassment by southern legislatures.

Hutcheson v. United States,[113] both in the majority opinion and the concurrence by Justice Brennan, continues to emphasize the "legislative purpose" doctrine and conducts what purports to be a realistic search of the record of the McClellan committee. This search results in the conclusion that the committee has not been engaging in exposure for exposure's sake. Fortunately for the Court, the McClellan committee has engaged in enough actual lawmaking activity to make the Court's supposedly realistic finding of legislative purpose seem fairly legitimate. Nevertheless, once the Court invokes the lawmaking-purpose requirement, as it did here, it inevitably must turn a blind eye to the less savory aspects of whatever investigation is in question, in this instance public exposure that came very close to the level of vigilantism. But, of course, this committee was not one of those about which libertarians are likely to be particularly sensitive, and *Hutcheson* offers no particular indication one way or the other about the Court's future attitude toward subversion investigations.

It may be argued that the extremely modest wing of the Court will block any further extension of judicial review. But I have tried to show that abandonment of the purpose-presumption rationale can be harmonized with their views.[114] Furthermore, abandonment of the traditional position need not come today or tomorrow, and changes in the Court's personnel have begun to create a more favorable market for the arguments offered here. Indeed, any current writing about the Court must be done against a background of great uncertainty and therefore expectation about its collective attitude in the next few years.

There are, of course, two assumptions underlying this discussion. The first is that Congressional investigations have invaded the rights of free speech and association protected by the Constitution. The second is that the Supreme Court should attempt to protect such rights against invasion. Neither proposition is self-evident. And it would take another discussion of similar length to offer sufficient evidence in support of either. It is enough, I think, simply to say that the arguments presented here are meant for those readers who share my assumptions. But it is possible to go one small step further. Most persons who have not been totally blinded by the "red menace" must surely admit that investigations have done some damage to civil rights, even though the question of whether or not they have done more harm than good must remain open. The abandonment of the purpose-presumption rationale is designed to allow the Court sufficient flexibility to continue its general approval of investigations, while occasionally and on a case-by-case basis, limiting some of their worst abuses.

As to the Court's responsibility for protecting the Bill of Rights, there is surely a hard core of opinion that staunchly demands complete judicial passivity. But the Supreme Court itself, even in the person of its most modest member, has never gone so far.[115] The position I have outlined does not involve the Court in any of those abstract formulas or rigid rules that are anathema to the modest.[116] Indeed it eliminates a couple. And it allows the Court to set its own pace and limits in protecting civil rights, so that the argument does not depend on acknowledgment of any specific level of judicial activity.

Finally, whatever one's assumptions about investigations and the civil-rights functions of the Supreme Court, it seems desirable that the Court do whatever it does clearly and realistically, instead of involving itself in the maze of fantasy and chop-logic that the demand for legislative purpose and the resulting presumption doctrine have created.

3

The Supreme Court as Labor Lawmaker: Whole Court or Constitutional Court?

THE LABOR-LAW BUSINESS of the Supreme Court is very large. It has demanded roughly a tenth of the Court's decisions in the past five years.[1] No attempt is made here to cover this body of material exhaustively. The theme of this chapter is the inseparability of Constitutional and non-Constitutional litigation. In labor law, the problems of Constitutional and statutory interpretation are so intertwined that hacking out the Constitutional decisions for consideration in courses or writings on Constitutional law or the Constitutional Supreme Court involves less dissection than mayhem. Understanding of either labor law as law or of the Supreme Court as labor policy-maker can only be impeded by such separation or indeed even by consideration of one Constitutional area to the exclusion of others. We do not mean that, in the monograph tradition of legal scholarship, one may not present a study in depth of some small area of the Court's labor jurisdiction but that the bits and pieces must somewhere be put back together again and not left scattered among artificially defined pigeonholes. The subject must be the Supreme Court and government regulation of labor—not something like the Supreme Court and the First Amendment, subhead picketing—if we are ever to understand what role the Supreme Court plays in the labor field.

I will begin with the one area of labor law that always seems to qualify for "Constitutional Supreme Court" treatment, the free-speech picketing cases, and show that the impact of these decisions depends upon the Court's federalism (pre-emption) decisions. These decisions will in turn be described as a function of the Court's attempts to construct a *modus vivendi* with the National Labor Relations Board (the primary-jurisdiction cases). That *modus vivendi* itself arises from the dual statutory interpretation of the Wagner and Taft-Hartley Acts by Court and Board. The observer cannot assess the grand Constitutional decisions unless he is also familiar with the whole pattern of "minor" statutory decisions on good-faith bargaining, secondary boycotts, and related matters to which much of the remainder of this chapter is devoted.

The very last portion of the chapter deals with the rights of employees *vis à vis* unions. This area in a sense symbolizes the whole field of labor law. Here Constitution and statutes are so interwoven that it is literally impossible to say whether or not present and potential employee rights are or will be considered Constitutional or statutory—or whether or not the Court is exercising powers of judicial review or of statutory interpretation.

My concern throughout the chapter has been with appproximately the contemporary Court, although it has sometimes been necessary to range back some years to show the roots of a doctrine. I have also dealt largely with the Court as Court and not with the Justices as individuals. It is, of course, clear by now that certain of the Justices have rather fixed attitudes toward labor, which may well be highly significant in explaining certain decisions.[2] Studies of the labor policies of some of the newer Justices are beginning to appear.[3] I have not gone into the views of individual Justices, partly from considerations of space and partly because, outside the free-speech picketing area in which I have discussed individual attitudes, the labor decisions have not exhibited the polarization evident in many of the civil-rights areas. When the decisions are more typically seven to two than five to four, individual differences are less significant than the sum represented in the Court's opinion. Those differences do, of course, merit extended treatment, but they seem less germane to my discussion of Constitutional and statutory indivisibility than do other matters that I find it necessary to present here.

¶ Picketing and Free Speech

The "state regulation of picketing" problem is a peculiarly complex one that illustrates exhaustively the Court's intermixture of Constitutional and non-Constitutional business. Considered independently, the state picketing cases present Constitutional issues of freedom of speech and federalism, in addition to the general policy issue of the place of unions in the American social and economic system. Furthermore, state-court injunction of picketing is intimately related to the problem of determining the boundary between Court and N.L.R.B. jurisdiction over union activity. The Court is thus confronted with a delicate task of policy co-ordination between state and federal agencies, a task often more difficult because the so-called political branches of the two sovereignties have themselves failed to make sufficient efforts at co-ordination.

Turning first to picketing itself, the story can be quickly told. Picketing was a tort at common law and, until the beginning of the twentieth century, had generally been considered unlawful in most American jurisdictions. In the period from the turn of the century until the 1920s, courts slowly modified their attitude. In a pair of 1921 decisions,[4] the Supreme Court seemed to indicate that the states might legalize some mild forms of picketing but not the more militant forms like mass or violent demonstrations. Then, in the *Senn* case,[5] the Court passed on the Constitutionality of a Wisconsin "little Norris-La Guardia Act" and thus, by inference, on the federal Act itself. The Court, speaking through Justice Brandeis, held that the state legislature might constitutionally forbid the enjoining of peaceful picketing and made a guarded and incomplete connection between picketing and freedom of speech.

In *Thornhill v. Alabama,*[6] the Court struck down a blanket antipicketing statute on the grounds of excessive interference with freedom of communication. Justice Murphy made a less guarded but still incomplete connection between speech and picketing. The opinion suggested to many, including apparently some members of the Court, that the states could no longer regulate peaceful picketing. The next year, the Court held in *Milk Wagon Drivers v. Meadowmoor Dairies*[7] that peaceful picketing might be enjoined when it occurred in a context of violence. But in *A.F.L.* v. *Swing*[8] it held that the states could not forbid peaceful "stranger" picketing, that is, picketing by persons not employed by the business being picketed. Justices Black, Douglas, and Reed dissented in the first of this pair, claiming that the *Thornhill* rule had collapsed at the first attack.

The next year the Court again decided a pair of related cases. Again one was decided "pro" and one "anti" picketing, leaving the Court's general attitude in doubt. In the *Ritter* case,[9] the Court upheld a state-court injunction that prohibited union picketing of a cafe a mile and a half from the building site where its owner was engaged in a labor dispute. In the *Bakery Drivers* case,[10] the Court struck down an injunction against the picketing of retail stores that bought goods from delivery-truck drivers involved in a labor dispute. Justice Jackson argued that, under the peculiarly mobile circumstances, the picketing was being done at the only place where it could be done effectively. Again the "liberal" bloc wrote separate opinions in both cases, claiming that *Thornhill* had been abandoned.

Then, in *Giboney v. Empire Storage and Ice Co.,*[11] an unusual set of facts led to a new "leading" case to set against *Thornhill.* The union had picketed in order to compel the employer to undertake a business practice that would violate a state criminal statute. The Court held that such picketing might be enjoined. The general rule of *Giboney* was, or was later stated to be, that the state might enjoin picketing whose end was the violation of a state policy. But *Giboney* was peculiar in that the picketing was aimed at compelling the employer to commit an illegal act; the state policy violated was one set down in a statute; and the statute concerned business practices not labor disputes, that is, the state had not outlawed picketing or matters relating to picketing. The state law was simply aimed at the enforcement of a state policy having nothing to do with labor.

Later cases, however, gave the *Giboney* precedent increasingly wide scope. In one case, the state policy had not been enunciated in a statute but was simply part of the general public policy of the state.[12] In another, the state policy was enunciated on the spot by the court doing the enjoining.[13] In a third, the employer would not have been committing a criminal act in yielding to union demands.[14] In yet another, the state statute was aimed directly at union activities, so that the injunction against picketing was not an incident but an integral part of a state program to limit and regulate union activities.[15]

Needless to say, Black, Douglas, *et al.*, had been opposed to this extreme extension of *Giboney,* which further undermined *Thornhill.* The last case in the series illustrates the conflict. In *International Brotherhood of Teamsters v. Vogt,*[16] the union sought unsuccessfully to organize the workers in a gravel pit. It then picketed the pit, and truck drivers refused to cross the picket line. Justice Frankfurter found that the picketing was an attempt to force the employer to coerce his employees into joining the union and that such coercion violated state policy and was therefore enjoinable. Justice Douglas, choosing to view the picketing as peaceful communication, spoke of the decision as coming "full circle" from *Thornhill* and representing "the formal surrender" of the principles enunciated there.

In all the cases decided against the unions subsequent to *Thornhill* with the exception of *Giboney,* a split occurred between the Frankfurter and Black-Douglas wings of the Court. This split, indeed the whole morphology of the "state control of picketing" cases, has commonly been explained as a dispute over whether picketing is or is not free speech. The argument seems deceptively simple. If picketing is an exercise of free speech, it cannot be infringed by the states. If it is an example of economic activity, it can be regulated.

This explanation is unfortunately exactly the sort of black and white "Constitutional" approach that obscures the intimate relations between Constitutional and policy judgments and between Constitutional and non-Constitutional areas of the Court's work. In the first place, it simply is not correct. Justice Murphy of the "propicketing" wing had been careful in *Thornhill* not to label picketing specifically as "free speech." It was Justice Frankfurter of the "antipicketing" group who first did so. And while Frankfurter stuck to this position, it was Douglas, concurring in *Bakery Drivers,* who first specifically argued that the picketing issue was not only one of free speech but combined elements of speech and economic coercion. Furthermore, it was Black in *Giboney* who established a permanent Constitutional place for the mixed "speech and economics" conception of picketing.

In fact, both wings of the Court continuously recognized that picketing was speech but more than speech. The actual dispute was not over whether or not picketing was to go in the free-speech pigeonhole but over how much protection the First Amendment offered speech, including picketing. Justices Black, Douglas, Murphy, and Rutledge, with later subtractions and additions, held the view that speech was immune from state regulation, except where the speech constituted a clear and present danger of a substantive evil. Justice Frankfurter and his followers believed that speech was subject to reasonable regulation in the interest of the state. Thus his votes and the controlling decisions in the two pairs of cases discussed above. State regulation of picketing where violence was involved, as in the *Milk Wagon Drivers* case, was, on balance, reasonable, in view of the state's paramount interest in maintaining good order and public safety. But the state could demonstrate no such interest in interfering with the speech of "stranger" pickets in *A.F.L. v. Swing*. The second pair concerned the location at which picketing might be allowed. Frankfurter had consistently argued that the state might regulate the time, place, and manner of speech, so long as such regulation was not used as an excuse for suppressing it. In the *Ritter's Cafe* case, the state had the right to exclude pickets from certain places. But in the *Bakery Drivers* case, where exclusion from the place in question would have actually quashed all effective speech, the state could not act.

The standard of reasonableness *within* the speech field, rather than the exclusion of picketing from speech, also accounts for the post-*Giboney* decisions. Where the end or aim of speech is the violation of various state policies in nonspeech areas, the regulation of speech becomes, in effect, a reasonable incident to the pursuit of those policies. Put another way, where the state's interest in a social policy like antitrust policy comes into conflict with the union's interest in freedom of speech, the two must be balanced. When the social interest outweighs the First Amendment interest, regulation of speech is reasonable.

When Justices Douglas and Black complain that the principles of *Thornhill* have collapsed or that the Court has surrendered and gone full circle, what they are really protesting is, not the exclusion of picketing from First Amendment guarantees, but the interpretation of those guarantees as forbidding only unreasonable regulation of speech. An inconsistency between the argument that picketing is speech and the position that picketing is subject to reasonable state regulation exists only for those who believe that the First Amendment forbids all state infringements on speech except under the kind of unusual circumstances envisioned by the "clear and present danger" rule.

This dispute over reasonableness *versus* clear and present danger also explains some seemingly gratuitous remarks in the picketing cases. Once Justice Frankfurter finds that a majority of the Court is going to approve state regulation of picketing, he is most anxious to label picketing "speech" so that the Court will have gone on record as espousing reasonable regulation of speech when it allows regulation of picketing. Reciprocally, once Justices Black and Douglas see that Court approval of some state interference even with peaceful picketing is inevitable, they are anxious to see more than speech in picketing, so that they may attribute the regulation to the nonspeech segments, while insisting that the Court has not actually approved regulation of speech.

It is important to understand that the dispute over picketing is in fact a dispute over how the First Amendment is to be interpreted, rather than over whether or not it is applicable to picketing. Such an understanding paves the way for an appreciation of the Supreme Court's intimate blending of general Constitutional judgment, statutory interpretation, and economic policy-making in the labor field. If reasonable regulation of speech does not violate the First Amendment, then the Supreme Court must determine the reasonableness of state actions in order to carry out its Constitutional responsibility. When the Supreme Court calls picketing "speech" and adopts the reasonableness test, it has then provided itself with an opportunity to supervise state labor policy.

One might then suspect that the First Amendment picketing cases do not form a separate entity but are in reality an integral part of the Court's general labor policy. A projection of the "state regulation of picketing" cases against the background of national labor legislation suggests that the First Amendment was initially used by the Court as a tool for co-ordinating federal and state labor policy. The Norris-LaGuardia Act of 1932 had legitimized and offered protection of picketing on the national level by forbidding the federal courts to enjoin picketing connected with labor disputes. *Thornhill* struck down a state blanket antipicketing statute. *Swing*[17] informed the states that "stranger"picketing, which was within the "labor dispute" category of Norris-LaGuardia could not Constitutionally be enjoined *per se* by state courts. *Ritter* indicated that "freedom of speech" guarantees still permitted reasonable regulation of time, place, and manner, regulation not excessively hostile toward the strike tactic. Instead of the customary supremacy clause, pre-emption doctrine, or broadly defined interstate commerce clause techniques of subordinating state to federal policy in the economic sphere, the Court here used the First Amendment. But, unlike the other techniques, the First Amendment does not subordinate the state directly and automatically to Congressional and N.L.R.B. commands. It subordinates them to federal policies through the medium of, and therefore only to the extent of, the Court's commands. In the late Thirties, *Senn* seems to have been a judicial message of encouragement to states that wished to catch up with federal labor policy. In the early Forties, the Court prodded the lagging states. By the end of the Forties, the Court seems to have felt that government regulation was lagging behind the growing power of labor, and, beginning with *Giboney,* it allowed the states to curb various coercive union practices.[18]

At its most extreme, the Court has even used its First Amendment powers to approve state bans on picketing that grow out of right-to-work laws.[19] But it would be simply incorrect to interpret the actions of the Court as stripping picketing of First Amendment protection. Picketing has not been returned to its common-law status of tort, illegal unless justified. Nor has it been returned to the realm of state police power subject only to interstate-commerce limitations. State regulation of picketing remains under Supreme Court supervision for reasonableness. It is the state that must justify the limitation, rather than the union that must justify the picketing.[20] This status exists precisely because the Court still operates in this area under the rubric of the First Amendment. But this use of the First Amendment has little to do with freedom of speech. It has instead become a constitutional hook upon which the Court hangs its reasonableness test. That test, wisely or unwisely, has been discarded in the economic area, so that it can be maintained in relation to picketing only as long as picketing is defined as speech. One can argue either that the Court is regulating an economic area because it is intimately related to free speech or that it is injecting free speech into an economic area in order to regulate it. Either way, the distinction between Constitutional-civil-rights areas and statutory-economic areas disappears.

¶ Pre-emption and Primary Jurisdiction

Until a few years ago, the discussion might have stopped here. But more recently a strong feeling has developed that what the Court gave to the states with one hand it has taken away with the other. This feeling stems from the 1953 decision in *Garner v. Teamsters Union,*[21] in which the Court seemed to give the broadest scope to the pre-emption doctrine, going so far as perhaps to hold that federal legislation under the interstate-commerce power had occupied the field of labor relations, particularly when an activity like picketing was involved. If the Court has indeed gone this far, then its post-*Giboney* evolution, as shown in the earlier picketing cases, seems futile and indeed abortive, giving the states broader and broader powers but only in the narrower and narrower and now almost nonexistent economic area in which no interstate commerce is involved.[22]

It is always dangerous, however, to assume that such internally inconsistent Court behavior is simply the result of one hand's not knowing what the other is doing. A survey of the pre-emption cases indicates, I think, that such contradictions as exist are due to a much more fundamental factor than judicial failure to think through the implications of one line of decisions for another. At the same time, it illustrates the inseparable tangle of Constitutional and non-Constitutional issues in the labor field. It might be added that this survey is oversimplified, in that it deals with the general tendency of the decisions rather than rendering close analysis of the precise language and findings. I have taken this tack for two reasons. First, there is so much loose and internally contradictory language in the opinions that nothing more than general tendencies can be extracted from most of them. Second, the Court itself has dealt so cavalierly with its precedents, distinguishing them sometimes on the facts, sometimes on the legal relationships brought to the case by the parties, but almost never on the actual language or doctrinal pronouncements, that systematic case-note analysis cannot increase our understanding of what the Court is doing.

The argument that follows is a bit complex, so that it might be best to provide a brief resume in advance. In an early case, the Supreme Court established three categories of labor-management actions: those protected by Secs. 7 and 8 of the Taft-Hartley Act; those prohibited by those sections; and those neither prohibited nor protected by the sections. The states might not regulate actions that fell in the first or second category because federal labor statutes are supreme over state statutes. The state might, however, regulate actions in the third category, for they are in no way covered by federal statute. This rule is the *Briggs-Stratton* rule.

In a later case, the Court tacitly abandoned the *Briggs-Stratton* rule and suggested that the state might not regulate any labor-management actions, not even those in the third category, unless they involved violence. This rule is the *Garner* rule. After some vacillation, in the cases following *Garner,* the Court has recently supported the *Garner* rule against the *Briggs-Stratton* rule in the case of *San Diego Building Trades Council v. Garmon.*

Under the *Briggs-Stratton* rule, the Court would have to decide whether or not the specific action in each case at issue fell within one of the three categories in order to determine whether or not the state had jurisdiction. The Court would have to determine whether the particular action was protected or condemned or neither by the National Labor Relations Acts. Under the *Garner* and *Garmon* rules, the Court would not have to make such a determination, for the states are never allowed to act except when violence is involved.

Using *Briggs-Stratton,* the Court risks conflict with the N.L.R.B., for that agency is also engaged in determining whether specific labor-management actions constitute violations of or are protected activities under the Act. Using *Garner-Garmon,* the Court risks no conflict because it does not determine questions of protection and prohibition. It is my contention that desire to avoid this conflict has been an important factor in the way the Supreme Court has drawn the boundary between federal and state regulation.

THE ANNOUNCEMENT AND REJECTION OF THE *Briggs-Stratton* RULE

Very generally then, the Wagner Act had been silent on the question of state powers, but in 1945 *Hill v. Florida*[23] indicated that activities protected by the Act were probably beyond state control. The *Briggs-Stratton* case of 1949[24] was the first major Court pronouncement on the issue after the passage of the Taft-Hartley Act. Justice Jackson attempted to establish the rule that union conduct neither protected nor prohibited by federal statute might be regulated by the states. Jackson also offered the first of many attempts at a formula for drawing boundaries between state and federal territory, when he suggested that the state might declare illegal certain methods but not the purposes of union activity. In two later cases, the Court indicated that peaceful strikes for higher wages were federally protected and therefore beyond the scope of state regulation.[25]

In 1953, *Garner v. Teamsters Union*[26] was decided. This case began a period of confusion, to put it mildly, for the Court. The main thrust of the opinion is that all union conduct, as long as it is peaceful, is completely outside the scope of state regulation because of the existence of federal labor statutes. This decision seems to be a repudiation of the *Briggs-Stratton* formula that allowed state regulation of at least that union conduct neither prohibited nor protected by the federal government. On the other hand, the Court, while distinguishing *Briggs-Stratton,* cites it with approval. The Justices could have simplified their work by holding that the conduct in question was prohibited by federal labor law. Then all they would have had to do to exclude state intervention was to follow the *Briggs-Stratton* rule. As the Court itself stressed that the state prohibitory statute under which the union had been enjoined was almost identical to federal prohibitory provision, such a finding was surely feasible. The Court refused to take this route because it would then have had to decide whether or not the union conduct actually violated (was prohibited by) the federal statute. Such a determination lay within the primary jurisdiction of the N.L.R.B. This early appearance of the N.L.R.B.

in the cast of characters is highly significant. We shall return to it again and again. It is also worth noting again that, if *Garner* is taken at face value as pre-empting the labor field for the federal government, it almost entirely destroys the wider state powers granted in *Giboney* and its descendant free speech-picketing cases.

LOOPHOLES AND CONFUSIONS IN THE *Garner* RULE

But the cases following *Garner* suggest that it is not to be taken at face value. In *United Construction Workers v. Laburnum Construction Corp.,*[27] the Court assumed that the violent employee conduct at issue was prohibited by the Taft-Hartley Act but nevertheless upheld a state damage award to the employer. This case might have had several different meanings *vis à vis Garner*. First, the remedy was civil damages rather than injunction. In *Garner,* both state and federal agencies offered the same remedy, an order prohibiting the union activity and subsequent criminal punishment. In *United Construction Workers,* the state award of damages was different from and supplementary to the potential federal remedy. Second, violence was involved in the later case, so that it might fall under the violence exception stated in the *Garner* pre-emption rule. Third, damages had been awarded under the state's common law of torts, so that pre-emption *à la Garner* might apply only to state labor legislation rather than to state laws of general application.

Even more suspicion was cast on *Garner* in the following year in a case involving a state injunction rather than damages.[28] The Court seemed to return to the *Briggs-Stratton* rule, at least to the extent that conduct that is not even arguably federally protected or prohibited fell under state jurisdiction. Much was also said about what the N.L.R.B. had or had not and could or could not do. And this very discussion seemed to undermine *Garner*. For if the state cannot regulate any peaceful union activity, federally regulated or not, what difference does it make whether the activity was or would be regulated by the N.L.R.B.?

Then violence again became the dominant issue. In a case in which violence actually occurred, the Court supported the state's right to act.[29] In another, *Youngdahl v. Rainfair, Inc.,*[30] the state enjoined acts likely to lead to violence and was upheld. This case may be read as simply applying the violence exception. But the Court also ruled that the conduct involved was not federally protected. In *Briggs-Stratton,* the Court had been willing to make such a decision. In *Garner,* it had declared that such decisions were to be made in the first instance by the N.L.R.B. Was *Youngdahl* then a return to the *Briggs-Stratton* approach? We shall return to this problem later. Then, in the *Farnsworth* case,[31] a *per curiam* citing *Weber* and *Garner,* a state injunction against picketing aimed at getting a union-shop agreement that would have violated the state's right-to-work law was struck down. Here again what the Court had seemed to give with *Graham,* which protected state right-to-work-law enforcement against First Amendment claims, it later largely took away.

International Union, U.A.W. v. Russell,[32] awarded damages to an employee in a suit against a union similar to that in which an employer had been awarded damages in *Laburnum.* Although the case involved violence, the Court did not specifically treat it under the violence exception of *Garner.* Instead the majority emphasized the problem of remedies, distinguished injunctive from damage remedies, and found the state damages supplementary to the federal remedies available. The dissenters attempted to apply the *Garner* reasoning to the problem of remedies. In *Garner* it had been argued that federal prohibition of an activity implied federal pre-emption of control over that activity. Anything that Congress had not prohibited, it had meant to leave free from any regulation. So the states were forbidden to regulate some activities because the federal government had regulated them, while also being forbidden to regulate the rest because Congress had not regulated them. Any activity that was not federally prohibited was *ipso facto* protected, so that there was no "neither prohibited nor protected" area for state action. The *Russell* dissenters argued that Congress, in providing some remedies for some conduct, had constructed a delicate balance of power between union and management that would be destroyed by the addition of state remedies. Anything that Congress had left unremediable had been intended by Congress to be unremediable, so that no state remedy could be viewed as supplementary.

International Association of Machinists v. Gonzales, a case we shall discuss in connection with the union-membership problem,[33] allowed damages to an improperly expelled union member, while stressing the supplementary-remedy argument and the fact that the damages were awarded under the general contract law of the state and not as part of a scheme of state labor regulation.

The increased state control over labor granted in the speech-picketing cases after *Giboney* thus seemed to be reduced to a meaningless gesture by *Garner,* which apparently excluded the states from everything but the extremely narrow area of intrastate commerce. The cases following *Garner* from 1954 to 1958 seemed to open loopholes allowing the states back into the labor field. But those loopholes were simply part of the confusion about pre-emption that the post-*Garner* cases had created.

THE RETURN TO THE *Garner* RULE

It was this confusion that the Court attempted to clear up in *San Diego Building Trades Council v. Garmon.*[34] First of all, Justice Frankfurter rejected all previous attempts to set up reserves of state power based on distinctions between public and private wrong, methods and purposes, injunctions and damages, or state laws of general application and state labor laws. He then disposed of *Russell* and *Gonzales* as falling under the violence exception to the pre-emption rule. No matter how rigid or flexible an interpretation has been given to the pre-emption doctrine, he argued, the Court has always held that the state might intervene to protect the peace. As *Garmon* did not involve violence, *Russell* and *Gonzales* did not apply, and the state might not intervene. In short, Justice Frankfurter solved the problem of overlapping federal and state interests with a meat ax. There is no delicate adjustment here but only the lopping-off of all state power except its universally acknowledged control over breaches of the peace.

Why did Justice Frankfurter, so often a defender of the "little laboratories," take this path? It is worth answering this question not only to learn more about a leading proponent of judicial modesty but also because the answer will shed a good deal of light on the basic political problems that underlie legal doctrines in the labor field.

The answer is a bit complicated, but let us begin at the beginning. In *Briggs-Stratton,* the Court had argued that the state might regulate whatever was neither federally prohibited nor protected. In *Garner,* it had adopted the opposite approach, suggesting that what Congress had not prohibited, it had intended to protect, so that nothing was left for the states. At the same time, it held that what was or was not prohibited or protected was a question that must be decided in the first instance by the N.L.R.B. rather than the courts. The conjunction of the "primary jurisdiction" and pre-emption doctrines was not a coincidence. If the state could regulate what was neither prohibited nor protected, then in appeals from state-court decisions, the Supreme Court would have to determine whether or not the specific behavior regulated by the state fell within any of the provisions of the Wagner and Taft-Hartley Acts. And it would have to do so without help from the N.L.R.B., as there is no place for the Board to enter cases that begin in the state courts and are brought on *certiorari* from the highest state court to the Supreme Court. If the Supreme Court does not want to risk clashes with the N.L.R.B. on whether or not specific employer or employee conduct falls under specific clauses of the federal labor acts and, if the Court must decide state regulation cases without the guidance of an initial "expert" decision by the Board itself, it must somehow prevent such cases from arising. It does so in *Garner* and *Garmon* by substituting nearly total federal pre-emption for the prohibited-protected doctrine. If the states cannot regulate even conduct that is neither protected nor prohibited, the Supreme Court need not invade N.L.R.B. territory by actually deciding what conduct is prohibited or protected. It need only flourish the Supremacy Clause. The proper relation between federal and state labor regulation is thus not determined solely by the relative weight or merit of federal and state claims but also by the relative power and self-confidence of two federal agencies, the Supreme Court and N.L.R.B. What purports to be an issue of federalism is in fact a problem of interagency relations on the national level.

COURT-BOARD RELATIONS AND THE DECISIONS BETWEEN *Garner* AND *Garmon*

That this interagency problem is the real issue for the Court is indicated by the cases subsequent to *Garner* that attempt to avoid its extreme solutions. There is an interesting clue in *Youngdahl v. Rainfair.*[35] The case involved the threat of violence and therefore, under the "violence exception," came under the powers of the states. But there is always at least the logical possibility that violent activity could also be federally protected activity. Indeed the union argued here that its activity was protected. In order to avoid such an impasse, the Court explicitly ruled that the conduct in question was not "protected." *Youngdahl* was the first case since *Briggs-Stratton* in which the Court had made its own judgment on the prohibited-protected categories prior to an N.L.R.B. ruling. The Court cites *Cox v. New Hampshire,*[36] a case defining what activity is or is not "protected" by the First Amendment, rather than by the labor statutes. Since the actual issue was preemption, the citation might be viewed as an error. It is not. The Court wished somehow to rule that violence, or at least the specific violence in question, was not protected, in order to avoid an insoluble conflict between state police and federal commerce power. At the same time it had to sidestep making an initial ruling on whether or not specific conduct is prohibited or protected by specific clauses of the labor acts, in order to avoid a clash between Supreme Court and N.L.R.B. Because the case involved picketing, the Court, for one instant and one instant only, treated it as a free-speech picketing case. The word "protected" is thus transposed from the context of the labor statutes, where the Court wishes to follow the "expert" lead of the N.L.R.B., to the context of the First Amendment, where the Court serves as its own expert.

It is this potential for shifting contexts away from the prohibited-protected clauses of the Wagner and Taft-Hartley Acts that also marks the other cases in which the Court allowed the states wider scope. *Laburnum* and *Russell* contain two factors, remedy and violence, which, as we have seen, can be used to differentiate them from *Garner,* the strict pre-emption case. In both, the Court argued that state injunctive remedies, remedies aimed at preventing or punishing the action, might clash with similar federal remedies. But damage awards designed to compensate the injured, rather than to stop the injurer, were found to be supplementary to and not in conflict with federal remedies. The response in terms of legal logic is easy or, rather, facile. The existence of damage remedies certainly does tend both to deter and to punish the injurer. Distinctions among injunction, criminal conviction, and damage award are largely artificial. All are legal sanctions designed to deter illegal actions.

Political logic is, however, another thing entirely. The very artificiality of the distinction is the important point. The Court wished to avoid a situation in which it would have to examine in detail the actual facts of a given labor dispute and decide whether or not one or a combination of those facts constituted activity protected or prohibited by the labor statutes. The tactics of labor-management warfare are infinitely subtle and varied. The task of putting each into the proper statutory pigeonhole—strike, secondary boycott, lockout, unauthorized work stoppage, and so forth—is one the Court apparently prefers to leave to an agency believed better equipped to deal with the "real" world, the N.L.R.B. If the Court were to use the prohibited-protected method of carving out state labor jurisdictions, it would have to undertake precisely this task itself. If the boundaries between state and federal power are to be drawn along the lines of remedies, however, the Court is out of the woods of labor relations and into the calm glade of legal convention where it is more at home. The distinctions between injunction and damages, criminal prosecution and civil liability, are distinctions that courts have always made, that they can and should make. On this matter, judges are the experts. In those cases in which the Court can shift the issues from the real world of events to the artificial world of legal categories, it can avoid conflict with the N.L.R.B. in precisely that area in which it feels weakest *vis à vis* the N.L.R.B., the actual day-to-day course of labor-management relations. When it can avoid such conflict, it is willing to give the states broader jurisdiction.

The presence of violence, the other factor in the *Laburnum* and *Russell* cases, is supportive of this Court position toward the Board and is intimately related to the temporary success of the "remedies" approach. The presence of violence allows the Court to invoke the long tradition of state police power. But violence plays another and more important part. It can be presumed that violent activity is not protected by federal labor law, for surely the national government does not condone or encourage force as a means of settling disputes.[37] In other words, violence releases the Supreme Court from having to make a real decision about the application of labor statutes to give activities. The decision is automatic. By process of elimination, the violent conduct is either prohibited or in the class of activities neither prohibited nor protected. In practical terms, there is almost no chance that the Board would ever actually find violent conduct protected and thus almost no chance of a clash between Board and Court. The Court would still theoretically be left with the problem of deciding whether the activity fell in the neither protected nor prohibited or in the federally prohibited category. For if the conduct were federally prohibited it would not, under the *Briggs-Stratton* rule, be subject to state regulation even though it were violent. But when damage remedy is added to violence, even this necessity for choice disappears, for even if the action is federally prohibited and thus not generally subject to state regulation, state damage awards are viewed as supplementary to federal sanction.

Where the elements of remedy and violence are combined, the Court need not decide what conduct falls into which of the three classes. There can be no clash between national protection and state regulation because violence is not federally protected. Nor does state intervention against violence clash with federal prohibitions, for state remedies are only supplemental to federal remedies. The Court is freed from the task of matching events to law, and therefore the state is free to act. To the judicially modest, the situation seems ideal. The Court does not have to compete in decision-making with expert administrators. The little laboratories of the states are not hindered by Supreme Court prohibitions.

COURT-BOARD RELATIONS AND THE *Garmon* CASE

We return then to the question, why *Garmon?* There was no violence in *Garmon*. Because there was no violence, there could be no automatic presumption that the activities was unprotected. Judge Traynor of the California Supreme Court had noted in his dissent that the absence of violence involved the risk of erroneous state-court decisions on the protected-prohibited categories. The risk was, of course, as great for the Supreme Court. Indeed *Garmon* seemed especially selected to illustrate this risk. The action involved was minority picketing for recognition. Whether minority picketing for recognition as a general category was or was not prohibited or protected by federal statute had not been finally decided at the time of *Garmon.* Subsequently, the Court ruled that picketing of this kind was not federally prohibited under Taft-Hartley.[38] *Garmon* in retrospect, and surely at the time for some of the Justices, became a matter of state damages for action neither protected nor prohibited.[39] Unlike the instances in which the Court can automatically assume prohibition, it raised precisely the spectre that the *Briggs-Stratton* rule had raised in the first place, the necessity of deciding whether or not a specific set of facts fell within the "neither prohibited nor protected" area. Directly faced with this problem in *Garmon,* as it had not been in the remedy-violence cases, the Court returned directly to the *Garner* escape hatch of nearly complete pre-emption with only the violence exception. Justice Frankfurter, who had been of the majorities in *Laburnum* and *Russell,* rejects the distinction between injunction and damage remedies and interprets the earlier cases as simply involving the violence exception. Furthermore, he suggests that the *Briggs-Stratton* rule is inapplicable because the Court is unwilling to make the necessary initial determination of the protected or prohibited status of the action at issue. On the other hand, he suggests that, if the Board could somehow make the initial determination of status, the states might be allowed jurisdiction. He denies that there has been any movement away from *Garner* and officially restates that doctrine.

Justice Frankfurter's vacillation between total pre-emption and the "loopholes" of *Laburnum* and *Russell* and even *Briggs-Stratton* signals the dilemma of the modest caught between their desire to give the states sufficient scope and their reluctance to risk clashes with the N.L.R.B. That this dilemma and not simply the problem of adjusting federal and state interests is the heart of the issue is shown by the concurrence in *Garmon* of that other defender of modesty, Justice Harlan.

Harlan seeks to reformulate the rules laid down in the earlier cases. First, the basic categories for pre-emption purposes are not violence-nonviolence but protected-unprotected. Conduct that is federally protected may not be touched by the states. Conduct that is unprotected in its turn falls into two categories: (1) neither prohibited nor protected and (2) prohibited. If the conduct falls in the "neither prohibited nor protected" category, it is subject to both state injunctive and state damage remedies. If the conduct is federally prohibited, it is subject only to those state remedies, like damages, that do not conflict with federal remedies. The crucial problem is who decides into which category a given action falls, how he decides, and when. For Harlan, violence is not significant as an exception to the pre-emption rule in deference to state police power but as a sure sign by which the Court can decide that conduct is federally unprotected. When violence is involved, the Court need only decide whether the action falls in the "neither protected nor prohibited" or in the "prohibited" category. When violence is not involved, the Court has the more difficult chore of deciding whether the conduct is protected or unprotected and, if unprotected, whether or not it is prohibited or neither prohibited nor protected. Justice Harlan, however, does not want to leave the Court a totally free hand to decide which category fits which action.[40] The Court may find an action unprotected only "if it is clear" that the conduct is unprotected but not if "it is fairly debatable whether the conduct . . . is federally protected . . .[41] Nor can the Court find that actions fall in the neither prohibited nor protected category "if the activities could have been considered prohibited."[42]

What then is the dispute between Harlan and Frankfurter? Formally Frankfurter casts doubt on and Harlan upholds the *Briggs-Stratton* "neither prohibited nor protected" reserve for state action. Frankfurter reads the past "violence" cases as having established violence as the only exemption to pre-emption, while Harlan sticks to the much broader categories of *Briggs-Stratton* and views violence only as an aid in the pigeonholing process. But the essential difference lies elsewhere. Frankfurter absolutely refuses to allow the Court to make initial decisions on the protected-prohibited status of any action and accordingly refuses to allow the states to take any steps that would require such decisions. Faced by the conflict between a relatively broad scope for state activity and possible clashes between the Court and the N.L.R.B. over interpretation of the labor statutes, he completely and abjectly surrenders state power in order to protect the Court completely. Justice Harlan, in order to leave some room for state activity, is willing to allow the Court to risk a few decisions when the actions seem clearly to fit into one or another of the categories, with the understanding that all doubts are to be resolved in favor of the

N.L.R.B.'s primary jurisdiction. Of course, even Harlan's position is narrowly circumscribed, showing that he is as aware as Frankfurter of the dilemmas involved.

POST-*Garmon* DECISIONS AND THE ARGUABILITY RULE

The debate between Frankfurter and Harlan has been described here at some length, not only because it illustrates the complex interactions that lie beneath such superficially distinct labels as freedom of speech, pre-emption, and primary jurisdiction, but because Justice Harlan was able to pick up the votes of Justices Clark, Whittaker, and Stewart. Harlan has sought to keep his views alive in subsequent opinions,[43] but *Garmon* has been cited as controlling in several later cases.[44] Where something more than a *per curiam* citation is given, however, the *Garmon* rule tends to be stated in terms of "arguably" prohibited or protected or "doubtful" cases falling under the primary jurisdiction of the N.L.R.B. Such wording makes it unclear whether Frankfurter's or Harlan's approach is being adopted.

The first major decision in this area since *Garmon, Marine Engineer's Beneficial Association v. Interlake Steamship Co.,*[45] continued the confusion. There the Harlan and Frankfurter factions (Frankfurter himself did not participate) joined in a single opinion using an "arguably prohibited or protected" formula to describe the *Garmon* rule. Indeed the formula was extended beyond *Garner,* for the question was, not whether or not a given action might fall under Secs. 7 or 8 of Taft-Hartley, but whether or not the Marine Engineers were a labor organization within the meaning of the National Labor Relations Act. The Court held that the status of the organization, as well as its activity, fell under the "arguable" rule. On the other hand, the Court chose to issue its first real interpretation of the rule in a case in which there was very substantial evidence to show N.L.R.B. jurisdiction, including previous Board findings that the Engineers were a labor organization, and Justice Stewart's opinion relied very heavily on that evidence. Does this decision mean that the Court requires something more than conjecture to meet the criterion of arguability?

In *Local 207 Bridge Workers,*[46] Justice Harlan himself showed that "arguably" could be stretched a very long way and emphasized that the reason it should be so stretched is the reluctance of the Supreme Court to decide independently whether or not complex fact situations fall within the ambit of Secs. 7 and 8. This case also extended the arguability test beyond the nature of the activity and the labor organization to the question of whether or not the individual concerned was an employee within the meaning of the N.L.R.A.

In fact, the Court seems to have been using the arguability test in the 1961 and 1962 terms to plug most of the loopholes of the *Garner*-to-*Garmon* period thus completing the protection of picketing from state regulation by using the primary jurisdiction doctrine to forbid the states to do what they had been allowed to do previously under a loose interpretation of the Fourteenth (First) Amendment.[47] For instance, as we shall see shortly, when Congress gave federal courts jurisdiction over labor-contract disputes, the Supreme Court held that the area had not been pre-empted, leaving the state courts their traditional power over labor contracts as a facet of the states' general jurisdiction over contracts. But in *In re Green,* the Court, using the arguability test, held that a state court was forbidden by the primary-jurisdiction doctrine from enjoining picketing under a no-strike clause.[48]

We saw that in the *Gonzales* case the state had been allowed jurisdiction over damage suits of improperly expelled members against their unions under the general contract law of the state. Following Frankfurter's suggestion in *Garmon* that state-federal boundaries were not to be determined by the type of remedy or by reference to whether the state statute was a labor regulation or a law of general application, the Court in *Local 100 of United Association of Journeymen and Apprentices v. Borden*[49] used the arguability doctrine to deny state-court jurisdiction over a damage suit by a union member against his union for refusal to refer him to an employer. In distinguishing *Gonzales,* the Court not only severely limited its application as a precedent but strongly suggested that it would be overruled in the future.

We have also seen that the Supreme Court had held in 1953 that the Fourteenth Amendment did not bar state injunctions of picketing designed to further purposes in violation of a state right-to-work law—but that in 1957, in a memorandum citing *Garner,* it had struck down a similar injunction. In 1963, the

Court in a full opinion, *Local 438 v. Curry*[50] used the arguability test again to strike down such an injunction on the grounds that the picketing might constitute a violation of Sec. 8 of the Taft-Hartley Act and thus would fall under the primary jurisdiction of the N.L.R.B.

Moreover, in the cases of the 1962 term upholding the agency shop against claims that the anticlosed-shop provisions of Taft-Hartley forbade it, the Court held that states might find agency-shop contracts in violation of their right-to-work laws under the Taft-Hartley provisions maintaining state authority in this area. But the Court held over for reargument the question of whether or not state courts could grant injunctions against agency-shop practices.[51] The language of Justice White strongly suggests that the states will not be allowed this power because it would interfere with the N.L.R.B. It will surely be the final triumph of the primary-jurisdiction doctrine if the Court holds that the state does not have the power to enforce a valid state law in a sphere specifically reserved to the state by Congress because the offense might arguably fall within the jurisdiction of the N.L.R.B. Should Supreme Court deference to an administrative agency go so far as to strip the state of the power to enforce a law that everyone—Congress, Court, and Board—acknowledges the state has the constitutional and federal statutory authorization to make?

COURT-BOARD AND FEDERAL-STATE RELATIONS AND THE PRE-EMPTION CASES

Special attention should also be paid to a long footnote in *N.L.R.B. v. Insurance Agents International Union,*[52] which reiterates the *Garmon* stand on *Briggs-Stratton* and refers to the "neither prohibited nor protected" doctrine as a "now discarded approach to pre-emption." This case, which does not itself deal with pre-emption, demonstrates that one of the essential concerns of the Court in this area is not state-federal but Court-Board relations. A central issue was whether or not the activity complained of was prohibited by the National Labor Relations Acts. It had been precisely this same form of activity that had been involved in *Briggs-Stratton.* As the Court had introduced the prohibited-protected doctrine in that case, it had had to decide whether or not the activity was prohibited. It decided that the activity was not prohibited and thus fell under state control. At that time, no N.L.R.B. position had been established. Subsequently the N.L.R.B. had developed a long line of rulings holding this particular type of activity to be prohibited under the Acts. In the *Insurance Agents Case,* the Court was asked to enforce its *Briggs-Stratton* interpretation of the statute against the more recent N.L.R.B. practice. It refused because to do so "could amount to saying that the Board would be foreclosed in its adjudicative development of interpretation of the Act by a decision rendered long ago, not arising in review of one of its own orders, at a time when its own views had not come to what they now are. . . ." The Court cited this very problem as the defect that had led to the abandonment of the *Briggs-Stratton* approach to pre-emption. *Insurance Agents* provided the Court with a vivid example of the clashes that might arise with the N.L.R.B. out of determinations of protection and prohibition incidental to pre-emption decisions. It, therefore, served as a new occasion to renounce the *Briggs-Stratton* pre-emption doctrine, even though that doctrine had no direct bearing on the case.

One other pre-emption problem should be briefly noted. Sec. 301 of the Taft-Hartley Act[53] provides that, where interstate commerce is involved, suits between employers and unions for violation of contract may be tried in federal courts. The Court, in the *Lincoln Mills* case, then declared that such cases were to be determined by federal substantive law. This decision created the possibility of conflict between federal courts applying federal law and states trying such cases under normal domestic contract law. Federal pre-emption was a possible way to avoid this conflict. In this instance, the N.L.R.B. was not directly involved, and the Court took the compromise step of continuing to allow state jurisdiction while requiring that the states use federal substantive law.[54]

Generally speaking then, the opposite of federal pre-emption is not state action but Supreme Court action. What determines whether the state may or may not act is, to a great extent, the Court's assessment not of the relative positions of state and national governments but of the relative positions of Supreme Court and National Labor Relations Board. The Court's First Amendment position on state regulation of picketing is, as we have noted, finally determined by its position on pre-emption, since what it gives the states with one hand, under a permissive reading of the First Amendment limitations, it takes away with the other, under a nearly total doctrine of federal pre-emption. Then we find that the Court's views on pre-emption actually rest less on calculations of federalism than on considerations of its own relations with the N.L.R.B.[55] Those relations are in turn obviously shaped primarily by the "mine run" of N.L.R.B. cases that reach the Court, and those cases will almost always involve, not the "Constitutional" questions of free speech and federalism, but the "non-Constitutional" routine statutory interpretation of the various labor-relations acts of Congress. Any attempt therefore to separate the "Constitutional" labor cases from the Supreme Court's general labor jurisdiction is bound to be both futile and misleading. Similarly, any attempt to view the "non-Constitutional" cases through the blinders of orthodox canons of statutory interpretation, without consideration of their Constitutional impact and their foundation in the relations between two rival central decision-making bodies, would obscure the Court's real labor problems. Accordingly, we now turn to the Court's direct dealings with the N.L.R.B.

¶ Activities Protected and Prohibited by Sections 7 and 8 of the National Labor Relations Acts

It is not possible to describe the Supreme Court's pattern of decisions in the cases under the Secs. 7 and 8 as either entirely modest or extremely activist. The Court does decide a fair number of cases in which interpretation of one or both sections is a major issue—about twenty with opinions in the last five years. This figure is not so large as to indicate hyperactivity in this field, nor so small as to indicate total withdrawal. Most of the cases are the result of circuit conflict and in a sense are thrust upon the Supreme Court. Nevertheless, several of its rather important decisions have not involved such conflict. Even when showing every outward sign of vigor and decisiveness, however, the opinions have sometimes evaded the real issues and evinced reluctance to make real commitments on policy questions.

For instance, in *N.L.R.B. v. Local 1229, Int. Brotherhood of*

Electrical Workers,[56] union members in the midst of a labor dispute with a television station had distributed handbills condemning the quality of station programing and management, without mentioning that the union was involved in such a dispute. The Board upheld the discharge of the union members on the ground that their actions were "indefensible" and therefore not protected by Sec. 7. A circuit court reversed the Board on the ground that conduct had to be "unlawful" and not merely "indefensible" to fall outside Sec 7. The issue here is obviously an important one. "Indefensible" would leave the Board with a wide discretion; "unlawful" would require the Board to find a violation of Sec. 8 or of some unpre-empted state statute before upholding dismissals. Curiously enough then, the case involves an element similar to that of the pre-emption cases—the "neither protected nor prohibited" category. Under one standard, the Board and the courts might find that some actions within this area constituted sufficient justification for dismissal. Under the other standard (unlawfulness), no action within the category could warrant dismissal. Of course, no issue of primary jurisdiction arises. Under either standard, the Board would first decide whether or not a violation of Sec. 8 had occurred. Under the "unlawful" test, the Board would stop there. Under the "indefensible" test, it would then decide whether or not conduct not prescribed by Sec. 8 was nevertheless intolerable.

The Supreme Court decided this clash over applicable standards by refusing to deal with Secs. 7 and 8 at all. It upheld the discharges under Sec. 10c, which permits discharge for cause, a section that had not even been discussed by the Board and circuit court. The Court de-emphasized the fact that the handbill distribution had in reality been part of a labor dispute and emphasized that the handbills did not purport to be part of a labor dispute. Having thus separated the activity from the labor dispute and therefore from Sec. 7, the majority apparently interprets the 10c "cause" provision as being independent of Sec. 7 protections. The opinion is so worded that it may be read as saying two quite different things simultaneously. It may be that this particular activity does not qualify for Sec. 7 protection because it is separable from a labor dispute and therefore that the Court is reading 10c independently of the Sec. 7 protection against discharge only *in this particular case*. On the other hand, it may be that, as a general proposition,

10c sets up an employer right of discharge regardless of Sec. 7 protection.

In other words, in order to avoid interpreting Sec. 7, the Court goes to Sec. 10c. It is then confronted by the argument that Sec. 10c must be read in connection with Sec. 7 if Sec. 7 is to have any meaning.[57] Having just escaped, it is in danger of holding firmly that Secs. 10c and 7 are separable. To avoid these dangers, the Court takes refuge in the particular facts before it to treat Sec. 10c as independently decisive in this particular case, no matter what its general relation to Sec. 7. The Court thus begins with one uncertainty, "indefensible" *v.* "unlawful," and, while preserving it, adds another, Sec. 10c read independently *v.* Secs. 10c and 7 read together.

The Court does not always take the easy and unsatisfactory way out, however. Indeed, the Secs. 7 and 8 area is marked by strong judicial attempts at policy-making. One of the most startling examples of judicial intervention is the *Borg-Warner* decision.[58] The labor acts impose the duty to bargain on "wages, hours, and other terms and conditions of employment." Refusal to bargain is a violation of Sec. 8. In this case, the employer had insisted upon the inclusion of an advisory strike-ballot provision in future contracts, and its insistence had led to the breakdown of bargaining talks. Did this insistence constitute refusal to bargain? The Supreme Court framed the rule that "It is lawful to insist upon matters within the scope of mandatory bargaining and unlawful to insist upon matters without . . ." and then held that the strike-vote provision was "without," so that insistence constituted refusal to bargain. The Court seemed to assume that the rule it enunciated was already the accepted one. It was not. The problem was before the Court for the first time. In the case itself, the circuit court opposed the Board. The rule had been used by several lower courts, but the circuits were in conflict. Some members of the Board itself had opposed the rule.

The Supreme Court's adoption of the rule has considerable potential impact. Prior to *Borg-Warner,* the language of the Act seemed to indicate that there were only two categories of subjects for bargaining—mandatory and illegal. Good-faith bargaining seemed to be required on any matter about which the Act did not forbid employer-union agreement. Now there seems to be a third category, matters neither mandatory nor illegal. In this area, employer or union can ask for concessions but cannot continue to ask for them in the face of opposition, for such insistence would constitute refusal to bargain. The Court thus puts itself in the position of ultimately having to decide what subjects fall in which category and therefore of having itself to set the boundaries and tempo of mandatory collective bargaining. Furthermore, in holding the strike-vote controversy outside the scope of mandatory bargaining, the Court indicates that it will not draw the lines of mandatory bargaining so broadly as to make its own distinctions purely formal. Indeed, the strike-vote finding seems to run counter to the general expansion of the mandatory-bargaining category and to echo unsuccessful attempts at the time of Taft-Hartley specifically to exclude certain matters from the mandatory-bargaining area. Here the Court has made a rule for the guidance of the fact-finders, indicated that it is a rule with teeth, and has surely recognized that the rule both embodies a major policy decision and paves the way for subsequent judicial policy-making.

There is always the suspicion, of course, that bold Court enunciations of standards may simply be judicial rubber-stamping of Board policies. The Court refused to apply the "unfair labor practices" label to lockouts by members of multi-employer bargaining groups when the circumstances suggested that the union might be whipsawing (striking against one member and then another but never against all at the same time).[59] Such a decision obviously has important consequences for the balance of power between management and labor. It reduces the union's chances of "picking off" one firm at a time while financing its strike from the wages of workers at the unstruck locations, thus successively subjecting each struck employer to the pressure of the competitive advantages of his unstruck colleagues. But for all the Court's apparent boldness, it was merely backing an already existent Board policy.

Similarly in *International Ladies Garment Workers v. N.L.R.B.,*[60] the Court held that a union that has signed an exclusive-representation contract when it in fact represents only a minority of the employees can be deprived even of its right to represent that minority. Here again the Court's policy is important in restraining union conduct but was initially the policy of the Board.

COURT OVER BOARD

It is more correct, however, to describe these cases as ones in which the Board's and Court's policies coincide, for there is no pattern of total subservience of Court to Board. In *Office Employees v. N.L.R.B.*,[61] the Board interpreted the National Labor Relations Act in such a way as to exclude unions acting as employers from the Sec. 8 restrictions on employers and refused, under its discretionary powers, to assert jurisdiction over unions as a class when acting as employers. The Supreme Court held that the Board was incorrect in exempting such unions from Sec. 8 restrictions and had exceeded its discretionary powers in treating unions as a distinct class of employer and withdrawing its jurisdiction over that class. With ever-growing union bureaucracies themselves struggling for unionization, this decision is hardly an insignificant one and runs totally contrary to the policy line the Board wished to pursue.

The reserved-gate picketing cases illustrate this Court leadership but also show the more typical give-and-take between Court, Board, and Congress. When two or more employers use the same premises, and the employees of one strike, does their picketing of the premises constitute a secondary boycott of the other employers? The wording of the Taft-Hartley Act is so sweeping that, if read literally, it would forbid all union attempts to prevent others from dealing with the struck firm. "It shall be an unfair labor practice for a labor organization to engage in a strike or a concerted refusal in the course of their employment to use, manufacture, process, transport, or otherwise handle or work on any goods, articles, materials, or commodities or to perform any services where the object thereof is: (A) forcing or requiring . . . any employer or other person to cease using, selling, handling, transporting, or otherwise dealing in the products of any other producer, processor, or manufacturer, or to cease doing business with any other person. . . ."[62] The Court and Board, however, both read the Act to prohibit secondary but not primary boycotts. Strikers might seek to persuade others to stop dealing with the struck firm, but they might not seek to persuade others to stop dealing with firms dealing with the struck firm. Congress approved this stand in 1959. But the Court was then left in the position of having to make final decisions about the line between primary and secondary boycotts.

Obviously, when two employers occupy the same premises and work in co-operation, picketing designed to dissuade employees from working for one is likely to look suspiciously like picketing against the second as well. Who might establish picket lines where became a crucial secondary-boycott question. The Board had first used the test of ownership of premises, the so-called *Ryan Construction* test. Picketing directed against the owner of the premises might be carried on at the premises. Where the union struck a firm carrying out activities on another's premises, it had to seek out the struck firm's own home grounds for its picketing. This test seemed adequate for permanent sites but faltered when picketing of a ship in dry dock arose. For such ambulatory sites, the Board then evolved the *Moore Dry Dock* test as an exception to the *Ryan Construction* rule. Under the *Moore* test, the union might picket the secondary location if the picketing was limited to times when the situs of the dispute was the secondary employer's premises; picketing occurred only when the primary employer was engaged in his normal business at the situs; picketing was limited to places reasonably close to the location of the dispute; the pickets were clearly in dispute only with the primary employer. Then in the *International Rice Milling Company* case,[63] the Court undercut the *Ryan Construction* test. The *Moore Dry Dock* test was then the only one left, even though it had not been designed as a general rule but as an exception to the rejected general rule.

Then a new fact situation appeared. At some large plants, a certain gate or gates are reserved for the employees of independent contractors performing services within the plant. The contractors do not own the premises, but they work in conjunction with the owner. For picketing purposes, the sites are in a sense separate. And of course the site is not really ambulatory. Faced with this problem, the Court ruled in *Local 761, International Union of Electrical Workers v. National Labor Relations Board*[64] that the *Moore Dry Dock* test was the proper one for "reserve gate" picketing and then established criteria by which the Board was to determine when the reserve-gate situation actually did or did not exist. Essentially the Court held that, where outside contractors were performing conventional maintenance or other routine chores, they could not claim reserve-gate status. The Court returned the case to the Board for reassessment of the facts in the light of the rule. There may be something essentially illogical and perhaps unworkable in applying a test designed for ambulatory sites to a stationary one. One may argue that the Court preferred to take an existing Board-approved test rather than to invent one of its own and thus showed considerable hesitancy in the policy-making realm. On the other hand, it may be that the reserved-gate situation is itself an exception that the *Moore* test happens to fit as well as it fits the exception for which it was designed. Whatever the argument, the Court has been interpreting the statute, picking and choosing among the Board-constructed tests, tinkering with the application of tests it approves, and instructing the Board on how to determine whether or not fact situations fall within the Court-defined scopes of the Court-selected tests.

Furthermore, several typical features of Court policy-making in the Secs. 7 and 8 area occurred in this case and should be emphasized. One is the Court's tendency to seek moderate interpretations of Congressional language that may be too sweeping. The Court forbids secondary boycotts rather than all boycotts. Second, the Court is likely to seek a compromise position between the demands of labor and management. The *Moore Dry Dock* test and the whole concept of reserve gates strike a middle ground between unrestricted picketing and excessive management interference with the strike weapon under cover of the secondary-boycott provisions. Finally, the Court's instructions to the Board on how to determine whether or not a legitimate reserved-gate situation exists exhibit a common-sense approach. A consideration of the whole situation, not mechanical application of formulas to certain isolated facts, is to be the basis for determination.

Many of these characteristics are also apparent in another secondary-boycott case, *Local 1976 v. N.L.R.B.*[65] The so-called "hot cargo" clause has proliferated in labor contracts, probably because it represents a nonmonetary union demand that does not immediately affect the employer and therefore tends to be yielded in the give and take of bargaining, in return for some immediate union concessions. Such clauses provide that union members will not be required by their employers to handle goods produced by struck firms. The National Labor Relations Act does not specifically reach "hot cargo" clauses but only forbids a striking union from inducing the employees of an unstruck (secondary) employer to a "strike or concerted refusal" to work for the purpose of "forcing or requiring" an employer to cease doing business with the initially struck (primary) employer.[66] Nevertheless, the "hot cargo" clause seems to achieve by advance agreement what the Act prohibits the unions from achieving on the spot. For a widespread interlocking system of such clauses would apparently allow any large union to deny effectively all or most business to a struck employer. On the other hand, before the case was decided, Congress had twice refused to ban "hot cargo" provisions.[67]

What then if a union had induced employees of a secondary firm to refuse to work on materials from a struck firm and then pleaded a "hot cargo" clause as a defense against its claimed violation of Sec. 8(b)(4)(A). One solution, adopted by the Second Circuit, had been to uphold such contract provisions as a valid defense and thus to allow a private contract to undermine the enforcement of a public statute. Another, adopted in some dissenting and concurring opinions by members of court and Board, would have been to hold "hot cargo" clauses inherently invalid. Such clauses would be considered not as defenses but as *per se* violations.

The Supreme Court took a compromise position, one that left it room for further policy-making in the future. It noted that the statute prohibited unions from inducing employees, but not employers, to boycott. It found that "hot cargo" clauses were directed at inducing employers and not employees to boycott and thus were not prohibited by the Act *per se*. On the other hand, since the contracts were strictly in the realm of union relations with employers, their existence could not be used by the union as protection against a Board finding of such improper conduct of unions *vis à vis* employees as inducing them to secondary boycotts.

The end result seems to be that "hot cargo" provisions are valid but that, if the employer does not voluntarily observe them, the union cannot strike to enforce them since such a strike would itself constitute inducing employees to engage in a secondary boycott. There has been some criticism of this decision for creating a valid obligation without means of enforcement. But there is some indication that the Court, by holding the provisions valid, was leaving the way open to enforcement by suit or arbitration, as such means would be strictly in the sphere of union-employer rather than union-employee relations. The Court seems to have been deliberately providing itself with a means for making further adjustments in the "hot cargo" area as the situation developed.[68]

In a case involving the distribution of leaflets in a company parking lot, *N.L.R.B. v. Babcock,*[69] the Court also indicated that it would choose the rules or standards under which the Board operates. The Board had held that no distinction was to be made between employee and stranger (nonemployee) activity on the employer's property. As the Board had found that no location adjoining the plant was suitable, it had held that the employer must allow nonemployees on his property for purposes of union activity. The Supreme Court said that it was indeed the Board's task to balance the interests of labor and management but that it must do so under the rules of law established by the Court.

Justice Reed proceeded to read the Board a lesson on what the rules were and how to apply them. The Board had been incorrect in refusing to distinguish between employees and strangers. When employees were involved, the employer might make no restriction on union activity on his property unless he could demonstrate that the limitation was necessary to maintain production and discipline. When strangers were involved, the employer might make such restrictions as he liked unless the union could show that no other alternative means of communication was available.

In the given fact situation, there was no practical point of distribution between the plant and the town where most of the employees lived. The Board had seized upon this fact and declared that it satisfied the "no other means" standard. The circuit court had found the proximity of the town and the concentration of workers' residences there sufficient to provide an opportunity to communicate with the workers outside the plant. The Supreme Court was apparently telling the Board that, if it would only understand what it was balancing in each instance, it would not make the mistakes for which the circuit court correctly chastised it. When employees, who are after all invited on to plant property, are involved, the balance is between workers' freedom of speech and management's interests in labor discipline and efficient production. Protection of union activity will therefore be the rule and its restriction the exception possible only when production is disrupted. Where strangers are involved, the balance is between workers' freedom of speech and private property rights. Here the property owner's normal right to exclude uninvited persons is the rule and invasion the exception justified only when freedom of speech can be preserved in no other way. The Board by muddling workers and strangers together had failed to give proper weight to the rights of private property *vis à vis* noninvitees and had thus incorrectly weighed the facts.

The *Mastro Plastics*[70] case also underlines several key features of Court behavior in this field. The Court backs the Board but provides its own interpretation of the statute at issue. The statutory language is construed broadly where, if taken literally and independently of the general policies of the Act, it would have given a different result, one probably in conflict with the general intentions of Congress. A union had asked for modification of its contract and then had struck before the sixty-day cooling-off period required by the Act had expired. The Court held that Congress had intended the sixty-day period as a restraint on economic strikes—strikes designed to achieve better contract terms—with the intention of encouraging peaceful bargaining for contract changes. As the Board had found as a matter of fact that the union had struck not to press its demands for contract modification but in reprisal for unfair labor practices by the employer, the Court found that the strike did not fall within the scope of the sixty-day rule. In short, "offensive" economic strikes are limited by the sixty-day rule; "defensive" strikes are not. The Court chooses neither to enforce the statute rigorously across the boards nor to interpret it out of existence but to enforce it selectively. And it requires the N.L.R.B. to determine the facts that will in turn determine in each instance whether the statute does or does not apply.

N.L.R.B. v. Lion Oil Co.[71] brought a more general problem of interpretion of the sixty-day rule before the Court for the first time. The language of the statute, if read literally, seems to declare a very strict no-strike policy during the life of a contract, for it apparently allows a strike only sixty days after the contract termination date. This instance seems to be another in which the Congress was more sweeping in its wording of a special provision than its general intentions justified. The Board had originally dealt with this problem by ignoring the literal interpretation. The Eighth Circuit had responded by following the literal meaning and allowing no strikes during the contract period.[72]

The facts of the particular case provided materials for a compromise. The long-term contract provided for renegotiation and modification at an intermediate date. If either party wished to enter into renegotiation, it was to give notice sixty days before the intermediate date and, if renegotiation were unsuccessful, it could terminate the contract after another sixty days' notice. The union struck sixty days after the intermediate date. It had given notice of its desire to modify the contract but had not given a second notice of its desire to terminate. The Board held that no second notice was necessary when a renegotiation date had been contractually set and the strike did not occur until sixty days later. The Eighth Circuit Court countered with the literal no-strike interpretation of the statute. The Supreme Court backed the Board but did so by, in effect, treating the long-term contract with annual renegotiation provisions as if it reopened the whole question of continuation, modification, or termination annually. In other words, the Court suggests that it will not allow the union to strike whenever it wishes within the term of a contract—although it does not finally commit itself on this point—nor will it lightly deprive a union of the strike weapon for the whole period of a long-term contract. Instead it creates a legal framework in which unions and management can set the intervals between potential strikes *within* the period of a long-term contract by setting the intervals between renegotiation dates. This decision neither prohibits strikes during contracts nor allows strikes anytime during contracts. It does allow potential strikes at intervals during contracts, the intervals themselves to be determined in advance by collective bargaining. The Court has at least partially filled the vacuum created by the ambiguity of Congressional intentions.

Of course, this relative boldness of the Supreme Court in establishing legal rules or standards must be seen against the background of the Court's deference to the Board when fact-finding is involved. The Justices had originally believed that their review of Board fact-finding was limited to determining whether or not there was any factual support in the record for the Board's findings. Only when there was none would they intervene. The Court was later informed by statute that it was Congress's intention that the courts enforce only those Board orders backed by "substantial" evidence, considering the record as a whole.[73] But the Supreme Court has left the task of determining the substantiality of evidence largely to the circuit courts, to which the Board must apply for enforcement of its orders.

On the whole, the Court's position seems to be that it will leave the facts to the Board but will retain for itself ultimate responsibility for framing the standards, criteria, and rules for determining whether or not a given set of facts constitutes a violation of the labor statutes. As we have seen, in the enunciation of these standards, the Court more often than not ends by backing the Board. It cannot therefore be said with absolute certainty that the Court is exercising an independent function. It may simply be rationalizing Board positions. Yet the Court has opposed the Board often enough to suggest that it has reached some independent conclusions even when agreeing with the Board.

Indeed it seems highly probable that the Court visualizes its task as holding the activities of an expert administrative agency in line with the intentions of Congress. This probability is one reason why the problem of interpreting a given statutory provision in the light of over-all Congressional labor policy is so crucial in many of these cases. The labor statutes are long and complex. Because of the endless proliferation of labor-management tactics, any given provision is likely to be too narrow or too broad to meet certain maneuvers. In attempting to meet all the twists and turns, the language of a given provision may be so broadly or harshly worded as to be destructive of other provisions unless adjustments are made among them. Furthermore, the Congress often follows two contradictory policies at once. It is impossible to have maximum protection of the strike weapon and maximum labor stability at the same time. In its legislation, Congress seeks to express some balance between such competing goals, but the balance is likely to be expressed only in the Act *in toto.* Each individual provision tends to favor one interest or another.

As the administrative agency constantly in the field, the Board is therefore in an excellent position to shape the real labor policy of the government. Excessive emphasis on certain provisions, strict reading of some clauses even when such reading tends to undermine others, and "technical" decisions that affect policy goals all may have considerable impact on the actual balance of power between labor and management. The Board can play upon the interrelated complexities and contradictions of literally hundreds of clauses of labor legislation to do a considerable amount of policy-making on its own.

As it is charged with the ultimate responsibility for statutory interpretation, the Court can and does make sure that the Board's choices of individual notes do not stray too far from the Congressional chords. The Court's effort to enunciate standards or rules in the Secs. 7 and 8 cases is one facet of its more general task of maintaining some sort of balanced view of the whole system of labor legislation. Aside from the cases already discussed, several others illustrate this judicial approach. In *N.L.R.B. v. Drivers,*[74] the Board held that picketing by a union that did not represent a majority of the employees—when designed to compel immediate recognition as exclusive bargaining agent—was an unfair labor practice. In other words, it distinguished between permissible organizational picketing and coercive representational picketing—picketing to force the union on the employees as their representative. At this point, the whole problem of distinguishing organizational from representational picketing was being much discussed. When taken literally, Sec. 8 provisions seemed to justify the Board's position. Yet that position would have allowed the Board to develop out of this single Sec. 8 clause a powerful antistrike weapon. More specifically, it would have allowed the Board to deal with the minority-union and exclusive-representation problems by means of a technique that might have substantially limited picketing as a means of fostering union growth.

The Supreme Court reversed the Board and found for the union's right to picket under the circumstances in question. Yet in the next term, the Court held that a minority union could not become an exclusive bargaining agent.[75] The Court has thus held that the union may legally picket for something it cannot legally have, a somewhat paradoxical position! But the key to the paradox seems to be the Court's understanding that the Sec. 8 clause on which the Board rested was ambiguous, that the "representation *versus* organization" distinction was itself ambiguous when applied to the real world of labor relations, and that wide use of the distinction by the Board might result in a much more serious limitation on strikes than the Taft-Hartley Act as a whole intended. The Court refused to allow the Board to embark on a policy substantially limiting the strike weapon without a clearer indication from Congress that it had intended to deal with the minority-union problem in this way. In fact, the Congress shortly thereafter did reply with new legislation that attempted to state its position more clearly and did away with the distinction between organizational and recognitional picketing.[76]

Another case decided in the same term,[77] which dealt not directly with Secs. 7 and 8 but with the six-months statute of limitations on complaints of violation, shows the Court again opposing the Board. The details are not important here. What is important is that the majority engaged in an extremely elaborate statutory construction in order to contradict the much more natural interpretation of the Board. The Board's interpretation would have satisfied the phrasing of the clause in question, but the Court obviously felt that it would not satisfy the general labor policies of Congress, which seemed to be undermined by the specific wording the legislators had adopted for this particular clause.

In *Radio Officers' Union of Commercial Telegraphers Union v. National Labor Relations Board,*[78] on the other hand, the Board had avoided a mechanical interpretation in favor of one based on legislative intent and was upheld by the Court. The Taft-Hartley Act defines as an "unfair labor practice" "discrimination in regard to hire or tenure of employment or any term or condition of employment to encourage or discourage membership in any labor organization. . . ."[79] In this case, or rather these three cases, the union induced the employer to discriminate in wages, seniority, and other matters that could not actually have encouraged or been intended to encourage union membership as the union was not admitting new members. Similarly, the employer's actions against members delinquent in their dues could not literally have been intended to encourage membership as the delinquents were already members.

Nevertheless, the Court found that the employer actions did violate Sec. 8. The Court in effect held that Congress meant to reach not only those particular discriminations that, in the specific instances, actually encourage particular employees to join the union initially but also the kinds of employer discrimination that generally foster the growth and health of unions. The Court does not technically go this far. Nevertheless, it broadly defines "membership" as including good standing. And it examines the inherent nature of the discriminatory acts, while dismissing as inconclusive the fact that the unions were not actually recruiting at the time. Both approaches indicate its intention, shared by the Board, of following the spirit rather than the letter of the Congressional pronouncement.

A COMPROMISE BETWEEN COURT AND BOARD: *Per Se* RULES

Radio Officers also introduces the problem of *per se* rules, which has been a battleground for the Board and the courts. The employers in this case had argued that their actual intentions and the actual effects of their actions were crucial to application of the statute. As they had not personally intended to encourage union membership by their discrimination and as the discrimination in this particular instance had not brought more members into the union, the statute had not been violated. The Court replied by borrowing the common-law presumption that a man intends the natural consequences of his acts and by arguing that, whatever the immediate results, the long-range consequences would surely be to encourage membership. In short, the Court came very close to holding that the types of employer conduct involved were *per se* violations of the statute, no matter what the immediate circumstances surrounding the conduct. These cases furnish, in a sense, one episode in a rather long and somewhat contradictory attempt by the Court to deal with the *per se* approach to economic regulation.

Per se rules have been widely used in government regulation, particularly in antitrust activities. In the labor field, they usually appear in the enforcement of the Sec. 8 clause that brands refusal to bargain "in good faith" an unfair labor practice. The statute itself seems to define "good faith" in terms of the states of mind of the bargainers, a subjective test. Prior to 1958, the circuits had interpreted the statute in this way, insisting on a determination of the actual states of mind of the bargainers based on all the facts surrounding the bargaining. The Board, on the other hand, had evolved *per se* rules for what constituted good faith. It had held that certain actions themselves constituted bad faith or conclusive evidence of bad faith, regardless of the subjective intent of the bargainer and the other circumstances involved.

The dispute between the circuits and the Board reached the Supreme Court in *National Labor Relations Board v. Truitt Manufacturing Co.*[80] Before discussing that case, however, it seems worth while to pause for a moment in order to examine why the Board favored the *per se* approach. First, there is the general problem of proof. The burden of proof is extremely difficult when subjective tests are involved. It is comparatively simple to establish the fact that a company or union did something; it is extremely difficult to prove what its thoughts and intentions were while it was doing it. Under the subjective test, the Board might even have to prove what the putative offender was thinking by proving all the things he was not thinking, a Herculean task indeed. For instance, after claiming that it could not increase wages, a firm might refuse to supply the union with the company records necessary to support its claim. This refusal might seem obviously to indicate bad faith on the part of management. On the other hand, it is always possible to dream up other reasons. The company's refusal may have been motivated by a desire to preserve its credit rating or a fear that a competitor's analysis of its cost data would betray trade secrets. It might be incumbent on the Board to show that none of the other suggested motives was actually present, in order to maintain a finding of bad faith. It is of course even more difficult to prove what is not in the mind of a bargainer than to prove what is.

There is, moreover, another powerful force related to the proof problem, which leads the Board toward *per se* rules. The Board is under terrific case-load pressure. *Per se* rules reduce that pressure in two ways. They simplify the handling of particular cases. If a certain event occurs, the statute has been violated. No need to examine all the "ifs, ands, and buts." Second, a clear listing by the Board of absolutely prohibited bargaining tactics tends to prevent many violations by providing advance warning to the bargainers. More generally, *per se* rules may be viewed as an example of the normal tendency of bureaucracies to simplify and routinize their work. The *per se* approach relieves the Board of the duty to consider all the facts of very complex situations by allowing it to pick out one fact as decisive and to announce that it will be decisive in all future cases as well.

It was with these factors in mind that the Court dealt with *Truitt*. The Board had used the *per se* approach to find bad faith in a company refusal to surrender records to the union in support of its claims of financial inability to pay higher wages. The Circuit Court denied enforcement of the Board order on the grounds that the Board had not considered all the facts to establish the actual, subjective good or bad faith of the company.

The Supreme Court upheld the Board by conceding that a refusal to hand over records by itself "may support" a finding of bad faith. At the same time, it noted that the particular facts were determinative in each situation. As Professor Cox has pointed out,[81] this was not a decision but a refusal to make one. The Court is asked whether or not the *per se* approach is valid. It upholds the Board, which used a *per se* approach. But it pretends—and it is sheer pretense as Justice Frankfurter points out in his dissent—that the Board did not use a *per se* approach. Rather, it pictures the Board as having found one fact, the refusal of records, independently conclusive, among all the facts it considered, of the bargainers' actual states of mind. This picture is simply more pretense, for that one fact could not by itself be enough to prove the employer's state of mind. Having been flatly confronted with the conflict between the Board's *per se* and the circuit's subjective tests, the Court refused to commit itself.

The decision is not a modest one, however, in the sense of judicial abandonment of the field or refusal to make policy. There is a judicial policy enunciated in *Truitt,* although it is a compromise policy. The Court actually held that *one* fact may be conclusive of bad faith in those instances when *all* the facts of the cases justify the conclusive use of one fact. This standard coincides with neither the *per se* nor the subjective test but is somewhere in between. When the entire situation suggests that a certain action on the part of one of the bargainers itself constituted bad faith, the Board may focus on that action and need not show that the action could not possibly have been motivated by anything else but bad faith.

Furthermore, the Court itself maintains ultimate control over when the *per se* or quasi-*per se* approach may be used. It will ultimately decide whether or not the "particular facts" justify relying on a single fact in a particular case. By pretending not to see the Board's *per se* approach in *Truitt,* it also reserves the option of discovering and condemning the *per se* approach in subsequent Board actions in which it finds the approach unacceptable.

Two terms later, the Court showed again that it was not particularly receptive to *per se* rules.[82] Again a balance between two Congressional policies was necessary. An employer is permitted to prohibit outside union solicitation of workers on his property in the interest of production discipline. At the same time, under the so-called "employer free speech provisions" of Taft-Hartley, he may seek to persuade his employees not to join a union. But when the employer's two rights are put together, they seem to permit the employer to propagandize his employees against the union without providing any opportunity for countervailing union communication with the employees. The District of Columbia circuit, therefore, held that, in and of itself, an employer combination of antiunion speeches with refusal to allow union speakers constituted antiunion coercion of his employees (an unfair labor practice) even when his speeches were not threatening and there was no proof of actual coercion.[83] The Supreme Court reversed this decision, stressing the duty of the Board to consider all the facts and to determine whether or not real coercion had actually occurred.

In *National Labor Relations Board v. Insurance Agents International Union,*[84] the Court returned to the good-faith problem. The insurance agents' union had carried on a "work without contract" program involving slow-downs, insubordination, and absenteeism during contract negotiations. The Board explicitly rejected the subjective good-faith test and held that the union activity constituted a refusal to bargain even while acknowledging that the union had sincerely wished to reach agreement and had acted properly at the bargaining table. Where the Board had held in *Truitt* that an isolated act was sufficient to establish bad faith without regard to all the other facts, in *Insurance Agents* it found an isolated act sufficient to establish bad faith *in spite of* all the other facts. The Board, under the "bargaining in good faith" clause, assumed the authority to prohibit certain specific actions no matter what the subjective good or bad faith of the bargainers. The Supreme Court, in an opinion that was widely read as a blow against the spread of *per se* rules, reversed the decision, holding that the Board had no authority to treat the use of economic coercion during bargaining as conclusive evidence of bad faith.

N.L.R.B. v. Katz[85] is one of the latest episodes in the saga of *per se* rules. During the course of contract negotiations, the employer raised wages, increased sick leave, and granted merit raises. The Board rejected the examiner's general finding of bad faith and found these specific unilateral acts to be in themselves violations of the good-faith bargaining requirement. The Second Circuit refused to enforce the Board order, insisting that the totality of conduct must be considered and subjective bad faith established. The Circuit relied heavily on *Insurance Agents*. The Supreme Court reversed, distinguishing *Insurance Agents* on the grounds that the use of economic pressure while bargaining was one thing, refusal to bargain another. It interpreted the unilateral actions on issues that were the subject of bargaining as an actual refusal to bargain. Note that the Court found a refusal to bargain in fact—not a *per se* but an actual violation. On the other hand, it also said that the unilateral actions "conclusively manifested bad faith . . . even . . . though no additional evidence of bad faith appeared."[86] The Court does not specifically approve or reject either the *per se* or the subjective test. There is therefore no way of knowing precisely what the case means. It seems to me, however, that the Court reverted to *Truitt*. In certain instances to be determined by the Court on the basis of a common-sense assessment of the whole record, a certain action may of itself be deemed conclusive evidence of subjective bad faith. Considering the whole situation in each instance, the Court found the particular actions in *Truitt* and *Katz* sufficient to establish bad faith and found the action in *Insurance Agents* insufficient to do so.

Another case outside the good-faith area provides a summary of the Court's attitude toward *per se* rules. In *Local 357, International Brotherhood of Teamsters v N.L.R.B.,*[87] the Board declared hiring-hall agreements illegal *per se* as violations of the Sec. 8 provision forbidding employers to discriminate against nonunion employees. The Court specifically rejected the Board's *per se* approach. It then established the test that the Board must use—whether or not the "true purpose" or "real motive" of the hiring hall was discrimination. The Board was ordered to look at the facts surrounding the agreement. It is not within the Board's power to find hiring-hall agreements illegal on their faces. The Court emphasized its role of overseeing the Board's fullfilment of Congressional intent. It found that Congress had not meant to eliminate the hiring hall as such. The Board therefore might not do so by administrative decision.[88]

On the other hand, the Court said that "The existence of discrimination may at times be inferred by the Board . . . But surely discrimination cannot be inferred from the face of the instrument when the instrument specifically provides that there will be no discrimination . . . because of the presence or absence of union membership." (There had been such a clause in the agreement at issue.) In other words, the existence of a hiring hall might be taken as conclusive evidence of discrimination where there is no antidiscrimination clause and when all the circumstances surrounding the case suggest that the agreement be taken as conclusive. Here again then the Court rejects *per se* rules as such, provides the statutory test, requires the Board to look at the facts, but still allows reduction of the Board's burden of proof when common sense seems to warrant such a reduction.

One other case, which seems at least superficially to fall into the *per se* category should be mentioned. In *N.L.R.B. v. Erie Register Corporation,*[89] the company had given twenty years' seniority to workers hired to replaced strikers and to strikers who returned to their jobs during the strike. The Board found this action to be a discriminatory practice in violation of Sec. 8. The company responded that *National Labor Relations Board v. Mackay Radio and Television Co.*[90] had acknowledged management's right to hire nonunion help during a strike in order to maintain operations, that the grant of seniority was necessary to attract such help as the grant served to guarantee that new workers would not be laid off when the strike was over, and that the intent of the company had not been to discriminate against union members but simply to attract necessary new workers. The Board had refused to hear evidence of subjective intent.

The Supreme Court held that the Board might find the institution of the superseniority plan sufficient of itself to establish discrimination without hearing evidence on the actual intent of the company. It can be said that the Court had upheld a Board *per se* approach in which intent is automatically inferred from a single action. There is some language in the opinion to support this interpretation, but actually this case is not a *per se* case at all. In effect, the Court is arguing that, while the subjective intent of a firm introducing superseniority may be to preserve its business rather than to discriminate against strikers, the actual effect of such plans is inevitably to discriminate against strikers. Even if only the best of intentions on the part of management are assumed, the situation involves an inevitable clash between the interests of labor and those of management. The intent of management is, therefore, irrelevant. A Board finding that superseniority is discrimination not permitted by the N.L.R.A. is quite literally not a *per se* finding of discriminatory intent but a resolution of this objective clash of interests in favor of labor. The Court holds that the Board is not only authorized by Congress to strike down actions motivated by discriminatory intent but to strike a balance between the legitimate interests of business and labor when they are in conflict. Here the balance is struck in favor of labor. Unlike the true *per se* cases, in which an evil intent is a necessary element in the offense and is inferred from the action, the Court here holds that no evidence need be taken on intent, not because evil intent may be inferred from the action, but because the best of subjective intentions may be assumed and the practice may still be condemned.

A holding that in effect permits the Board to find an action illegally discriminatory no matter what the intentions of management may seem to open the flood gates to a stream of N.L.R.B. decisions that are in fact *per se* findings of intent disguised as "balancing of interest" cases. When the Board is tempted, as it often is, to brush aside evidence on intent while actually deciding on the basis of intent, it might in future disguise its high-handedness by borrowing the "balancing of interests" language of *Erie,* at least in the "discriminatory practice" as opposed to "refusal to bargain" cases. But for the moment at least *Erie* seems to be *sui generis.* The Court carefully emphasizes that, due to *Mackay,* there are two independent, legally sanctioned rights in conflict. One is the right of business to hire new employees to maintain operations during a strike. The other is the right of union employees not to be discriminated against. The Court held that the Board in this instance must balance these two legitimate rights rather than performing its typical function under Sec. 8, that is, declaring some actions illegitimate as such.

Aside from its ambiguous *per se* aspects, several other points should be made concerning *Erie.* First, while the Court specifically says that it does not wish to cast any doubts on *Mackay, Erie* is totally illogical unless it does. *Mackay* had held not only that a company might take on nonunion help to maintain operations during a strike but that it might retain the nonunion workers after the strike even if it meant that strikers would not be rehired. In *Erie* the seniority granted was only for the purpose of determining retention preference in case of future layoffs and not for any of the other benefits that are normally dependent on seniority. According to *Mackay,* 400 men can go on strike, the company can hire 400 new men, and after the strike is over—having jobs for only 400—it may retain the nonstrikers and dismiss the strikers. Under superseniority, the company rehires the 400, bringing its staff to 800 and, if it is later forced to cut back to 400, dismisses the 400 strikers. Either way the strikers lose their jobs to the "scabs" because there is not enough room for both. The Court and Board are probably condemning superseniority because, under *Mackay,* whether or not the strikers are rehired is an obvious and immediate question over which the management and the strikers will necessarily bargain. Under superseniority, management may lull the strikers by promises of rehiring them all after the strike is ended and then later dismiss them. But this reasoning implies a naivete on the part of unions that *Erie,* in which the union fought superseniority tooth and nail, itself belies.[91]

Second, as Justice Harlan pointed out in his concurrence, the

Court does not make clear whether it is backing a Board order that it takes to reflect a balance against superseniority in this particular case on the basis of its particular circumstances or is approving a general Board policy condemning superseniority. There is language in the opinion suggesting that superseniority might be acceptable under peculiarly compelling business circumstances. The Court's whole treatment is sufficiently ambiguous to allow both it and the Board considerable room for future maneuver.

The *per se* cases have been described in order to shed further light on the relations of the Court to the Board. In most of the earlier cases, many of which show Board-Court agreement, the two, coincidently so to speak, might have settled on the same policy, or agreement might indicate Court subordination to Board. In these cases, however, the Board has a strong institutional interest less in the substance of the decisions than in the method, *per se* rules. The negative reaction of the circuits shows that courts do not share this institutional interest and further that a large body of judges find the *per se* approach detrimental to the policies of Congress. If the Supreme Court should support the Board on this issue, it would seem to be subordinating the interests of both courts and Congress to that of the administrative body. The *per se* problem therefore seems to provide a perfect test case for discovering the political relationship between Court and Board.

Unfortunately, the Court does not provide us with perfect test results. Most evident is the technique of compromise found throughout the Secs. 7 and 8 cases—here between *per se* and subjective approaches. Compromise may be read as Court reluctance to challenge the Board openly. But the nature of the compromises, including the one over *per se* rules, seems to me rather to indicate a desire by the Court to choose a viable labor policy of its own through middle-ground positions that avoid the pitfalls of either extreme. The unimpeded growth of *per se* rules would allow the Board to regulate the specifics of bargaining behavior far beyond the desires of either labor or management and the intentions of Congress as expressed in the "good-faith bargaining" clause. On the other hand, the burden of proof imposed by the subjective test is so difficult to meet that strict enforcement would emasculate the bargaining clause. The Court chooses to allow a reduction in this burden when the result in terms of labor policy seems desirable to the judges, while still holding the check-rein on *per se* rulings by the Board.

Furthermore, the Court has sometimes backed and sometimes opposed the Board and, by the language and pattern of its *per se* decisions, has been successful in preserving the options, to use the modern jargon. Its record may be viewed as vacillation and evasion of the real issues. But again it seems to me that the result is to leave some policy initiative with the Court. It is now in the position of approving those Board uses of *per se* rules that it finds satisfactory by labeling given actions "conclusive" evidence of bad faith. At the same time, it can strike down those rulings it does not approve by calling the actions inconclusive and admonishing the Board to look to the entire record.

THE SUPREME COURT AS GENERAL SUPERVISOR OF SECS. 7 AND 8

The Court's performance in the area of *per se* rules does not, then, totally clarify the Court's record in the interpretation of Secs. 7 and 8. We do not find the Court boldly challenging the Board or meekly agreeing to whatever it demands. It has no daring or unique labor policy of its own. Nor does it leave all policy-making to others. Taken all in all, however, the Court has not adopted a modest stand in the Secs. 7 and 8 area. It keeps its hand in the field. It announces standards and rules of interpretation and insists upon its right to supervise the application of these rules by the Board. It has carved out for itself the role of mediator among the conflicting demands of a complex body of legislation and of rein on any tendencies of the Board to favor some provisions at the expense of others. It seeks to adopt common-sense, middle-ground positions that embody the practicalities of labor-management relations.

What accounts for this position, which is so much bolder than that taken in so many other areas? Statutory authorization might be placed first. The legislation establishing the N.L.R.B. provides that its orders may be enforced only through application to the circuit courts, which are to exercise independent judgment on questions of law and substantiality of evidence. Congress has thus specifically invited, indeed commanded, continued judicial intervention. Not that the Supreme Court necessarily acts as an ally of the circuits against the Board. It frequently finds for the Board rather than the circuits. As many of the cases reaching the Court do so because of conflicts on the circuits, it often decides, not between Board and circuit, but between circuit and circuit. Indeed, because the circuits speak with many voices against the Board's single command, they are not in a very strong position. But by one of the natural paradoxes of politics, the circuits, no matter how weak, strengthen the Supreme Court's position *vis à vis* the Board. For the circuit subordinates of the Supreme Court are commanded by Congress to supervise the Board, and therefore, through the channel of the circuits, the Court receives a special authorization from Congress to oversee the Board.

The second factor in the Court's relative activism is the simplicity of the subject matter. The Secs. 7 and 8 cases do not involve highly technical or mathematically expressed subject matter like that in rate-making or the almost indecipherable complexities of modern corporate transactions and accounting methods that becloud tax law. At which gate a picket may stand and whether or not an employer need allow union organizers on his property are questions that involve situations we can all visualize and deal with in terms of the cruder forms of Aristotelian logic. To be sure, the facts of any given situation may not be crystal-clear, and the impact of a particular decision on later management-labor relations may not be extremely easy to anticipate. That is why considerable deference is shown to the Board's administrative expertise. But the Board itself must deal with its problems not in terms of a special vocabulary or "scientific" technique but in the rough categories of sit-down and bad faith, rights to strike and private property, which are not likely to intimidate a layman, let alone a judge. The Court can formulate standards like those in the reserved-gate picketing cases precisely because it can visualize the relatively simple physical arrangements of gates and employee flow at an industrial plant in a way it can never visualize the interrelations of the rate structure for hauling coal from Wheeling to Cleveland with the comparative advantage per ton of steel produced in Pittsburgh and Gary, Indiana. In the labor cases, both the situation type and the situation sense, to use Llewelyn's terms, emerge fairly clearly, tempting the judge to make decisions himself rather than to leave them to the experts. For all the talk of agency expertise, most labor problems still must be solved, by whoever solves them, through a kind of crude, common-sense compromise between the interests of labor and management.

Finally, the nature of the legislation governing labor relations may inspire some of the Court's activism. Congress has not given the administrative agency a clear, consistent, and unified command that requires only administrative elaboration. It has issued a multitude of commands, typically in omnibus legislation, that must be sorted out and adjusted to one another. Furthermore, probably because of the political excitement surrounding labor legislation, the wording of each specific command tends to be more extreme than the intentions of Congress as a whole. The N.L.R.B. is not faced simply with the task of administrative enforcement but with one of basic statutory interpretation on a large scale. It is not surprising then that the Supreme Court, which has never given up its claim to paramountcy in this field, should feel ready, willing, and able to step in here.

FREE SPEECH AND FEDERALISM UNDER SECS. 7 AND 8

We began this discussion of Secs. 7 and 8 hoping to discover something about the Court's behavior in the free-speech and federalism cases. If we had discovered that the Court was simply yielding to the Board in the whole Sec. 7 and 8 area, the conclusion would have been simple. The federalism, primary-jurisdiction cases could have been viewed as one unit of the Court's total retreat and the Justices as surrendering states' rights along with their own.

The Court's actual behavior, however, suggests another and somewhat different explanation of its primary-jurisdiction approach to state labor regulation. The Court is willing to announce standards or rules of interpretation. It tells the N.L.R.B. under what circumstances it may protect a "reserved gate" from picketing, whether or not it may treat employed and "stranger" union recruiters alike, whether a renegotiation provision of itself satisfies the "sixty-day notice" rule, whether or not "lockout" is justified by "whipsaw," whether or not unions must be treated as employers *vis à vis* their own staffs. It is even willing to tell the Board how much of the facts to consider[92] and when one fact may be considered to the exclusion of all others. What it is not willing to do apparently is actually to apply its general rules to the facts of particular cases. It is up to the Board, using the rules of interpretation approved by the Court, to determine whether or not a particular set of facts constitutes violation of the statute. Cases must go to the Board first so that this task may be done. And if the Board uses the wrong rule, then the case must be returned to the Board so that it may apply the right rule.

The Court does not therefore seem to be limiting state jurisdiction solely because of fears that it will itself become entangled with labor-law interpretation *via* appeals from state tribunals. It is willing enough to get entangled to the extent of general statutory interpretation. Apparently then, the reason why the states may not be more active in the field of labor regulation is primarily that the Justices want the Board to act as fact-finder and interpreter in labor disputes. Is this choice good or bad? At least, the states' power does not seem to have been simply one of the garrisons captured by the Board in a general Court surrender inspired by overweening judicial modesty. On the other hand, it is unclear why the states should lose their power simply because the Court prefers that the Board rather than itself should deal with the facts of labor disputes. If the Court had claimed that the Board, because of its expertise, was the only body capable of interpreting the statutes, it would be another, although perhaps no more palatable, story. Then the Board would have to have first crack at all cases because it alone could establish what the statute governing the cases meant. But why should not a state court be equally as competent as the Board to establish the facts of a labor dispute and decide under general rules reviewable by the Supreme Court whether or not those facts constitute an activity protected or prohibited by federal statute? In fact, so long as the ultimate power of statutory interpretation remains with the Supreme Court, why should not both the state courts and the Board act as triers of fact?

The principal difficulty seems to be that a state court might decide that a particular set of facts did not, for instance, constitute a violation of Sec. 8, while the Board in the same or another case might find that it did. Since the tactics of labor-management warfare are by now fairly routinized, substantially the same facts are likely to appear several times, sometimes in state and sometimes in federal actions. The party that unavailingly asserted Sec. 7 or 8 coverage in a state court might well be tempted to go to the N.L.R.B. for vindication, so that court and Board would be confronted with exactly the same facts. When such a conflict arose and when both the state court and the Board had used the same general rules for applying the statute, the Supreme Court would be compelled to choose between the two findings of fact, that is, to make a factual analysis of its own. The Secs. 7 and 8 cases show that the primary-jurisdiction doctrine allows the Court to avoid precisely this chore. For under this doctrine, the Board's finding on whether a given set of facts falls under the protection of Sec. 7 or the prohibition of Sec. 8 occurs first and finally determines the issue so that a conflict over facts between Board and state court cannot arise. The limitation of state power over labor relations can therefore be traced, through the Sec. 7 and 8 cases, to the Supreme Court's reluctance to get involved in the minutiae of fact-finding and interpretation in labor cases.

¶ Section 301

Additional evidence that the primary-jurisdiction doctrine is neither a function of Supreme Court reluctance to participate in labor lawmaking nor of a desire on its part to exclude the states entirely from labor law in order to tidy up the federal structure is to be found in the *Lincoln Mills Case* and its successors. Sec. 301 of the Taft-Hartley Act provides for federal-court jurisdiction in suits concerning labor contracts, an area that had previously fallen entirely to the states as part of the general law of contracts. The statute does not, however, indicate whether the federal courts are to use the substantive law of the states in which the contract disputes arise or federal substantive law. The Court might have entirely avoided a decision on this issue either by declaring Sec. 301 unconstitutional, as Justice Frankfurter claimed in dissent, or by "remanding" the question to Congress by means of the kind of opinion suggested by Professor Bickel in a much commented-upon article.[93] Instead, the Court sailed boldly ahead and held for the application of federal substantive law—a federal common law of labor contracts that the federal courts would now create. The Supreme Court not only settled a ticklish issue of federalism but established itself as the overseer and ultimate creator of a whole new body of federal law.

The Court tidied up the federalism package in the *Dowd Box*[94] and *Lucas Flour*[95] cases by holding that the states might continue their traditional jurisdiction over labor contracts but would have to apply federal substantive law. *Lincoln Mills, Dowd,* and *Lucas,* taken together, again illustrate the "policy-making by compromise" approach to labor law taken by the Court. The Justices had been faced with four alternatives. They could deny all federal jurisdiction by declaring the statute unconstitutional or by "remanding." They could allow concurrent federal jurisdiction but under state substantive law by analogy with *Erie v. Tompkins.*[96] They could allow concurrent federal jurisdiction complete with federal substantive law. Or they could end state jurisdiction entirely through the pre-emption doctrine. A fifth alternative, allowing concurrent jurisdiction with each jurisdiction using its own substantive law, was not actually available because of the sheer chaos it would have engendered particularly in the large industrial states. The Court took one of the two middle-ground alternatives and it apparently chose the one less favorable to states' rights because of the need for uniformity in the administration of national labor policy. Put another way, the *Erie v. Tompkins* solution is built to handle problems that are basically state and only incidentally federal problems. *Lincoln Mills* and ensuing cases deal with a problem that is basically federal in that it concerns labor legislation and only incidentally state in that it concerns contracts. In one, the federal court uses state law; in the other, the state court uses federal law in concurrence with federal courts using federal law. The compromise also goes a level deeper. The federal substantive law to be used is a federal common law that did not exist at the time of *Lincoln Mills* and will have to be developed case by case. In many instances, if a state court is to administer federal common law, it will have to create that law itself. Furthermore, the federal courts, instructed to use their common-law talents, will undoubtedly look to precedent in many instances, and about the only precedents they will find are the decisions of the state courts, which have been active in this field for many years. While the federal courts will probably play the leading role in the creation of a federal common law of labor contracts, the state courts will surely wield considerable influence.

The Supreme Court has already taken some steps to nurture the new common law to which it gave birth. In the *Warrior and Gulf Navigation Cases*[97] and *Drake Bakeries, Inc. v. Local 50, Bakery Workers,*[98] it enunciated two interrelated rules of interpretation for labor contracts that contain general arbitration clauses. Exceptions to such clauses contained in the contract will be narrowly interpreted. The general intent of both parties to arbitrate expressed in a general arbitration clause will be presumed to extend to the dispute at issue before the Court until very substantial evidence to the contrary is presented.[99]

Then, in three cases in the 1961 term, the Court ruled that only the union and not its agents may be sued under Section 301,[100] that management must go to arbitration under a contract with both arbitration and no-strike clauses even when the union has struck,[101] and that an employer may not seek an injunction to enforce a no-strike clause.[102] The last decision seems to run counter to the Court's general tendency to favor arbitration. For the Court held that the Norris-LaGuardia Act ban on federal injunction of unions in labor disputes had not been displaced by Sec. 301's grant to the federal courts of jurisdiction over labor contracts. In effect, then, when an arbitration clause exists, employers are bound by it, but unions may not be enjoined from striking during arbitration or in defiance of the arbitrator's decisions. There seems thus to be little incentive for employers to accept the general arbitration clauses whose scope the Court has seemed so anxious to extend.[103] The decision also largely undercuts the use of no-strike clauses to ensure industrial peace, for they can now only be enforced by damage actions after war has broken out.

Actually, however, the Court has not been following contradictory lines of policy. When the cases are taken all together, what emerges is the Justices' desire that Sec. 301 not develop into a strong management weapon against the unions. The Court does not wish to be used as a strike-breaker through Sec. 301 suits on no-strike clauses or as a channel for management evasion of arbitration through suits over exceptions clauses. The common law that emerges seems to rest on the principe that contract provisions and remedies are to be harmonized whenever possible with the by now traditional rights of labor to carry on economic warfare of the kind not normally countenanced in a commercial-contractual setting. Labor-contract problems are not to be treated as normal contract disputes between two parties of equal legal significance and identical qualities but in the light of the unique position of unions defined by Congress in the Norris-LaGuardia and Wagner Acts. To put it bluntly, the evolution of a common law of labor contract, as directed by the Supreme Court, seems, at the moment at least, to be aimed at resolving all doubts and ambiguities in favor of labor. Curiously enough, this phenomenon bears out the old saw about the conservatism of common-law courts. For what the Supreme Court, with its reverence for Norris-La Guardia and its worried references to *Danbury Hatters,* is doing is to bring the now hoary outlook and sentiments of the '30s into the labor law of the '60's.[104]

In two cases in the 1961 and 1962 terms, the Court dealt with state court activities under Sec. 301 and incidentally revealed some of the tangled considerations that underlie its doctrines. *In re Green*[105] purported to be a pre-emption case, and the Court found that a state court may not enjoin picketing when an unfair labor practice might arguably be involved, even though it is acting under Sec. 301 to enforce a no-strike clause. In *Smith v. Evening News,*[106] the Court held that a state court may entertain a suit for damages under Sec. 301, even when an unfair labor practice is involved. It thus becomes clear that, while *Green* deals in a sense with federal pre-emption, it is not essentially a case of the relations between state and central government but simply an extension of the Court's *Atkinson-Sinclair* policy that, under Sec. 301, courts shall not act as strike-breakers through injunctions to enforce no-strike clauses. The Court actually invokes the arguability version of the pre-emption doctrine not because it wishes to avoid conflict with the N.L.R.B. or because it wishes to exclude the state from labor relations but because it wishes to suppress the court injunction at all levels as an antistrike weapon. In *Smith,* in which damages rather than injunctions are involved, the Court is content to allow the state courts to proceed with judgment of actions that fall squarely within Sec. 7 or 8.

Is *Smith* then finally an assertion of states' rights running counter to *Garmon* and its progeny? I think not. *Smith* is simply an extension of *Lincoln Mills* to the states. The state courts are not granted concurrent power with the Board because they are *state* courts but because they are courts. The Supreme Court had already decided that it was willing under Sec. 301 to make its own independent decisions, rather than bowing to the primary jurisdiction of the Board, because it makes those decisions under a separate body of self-created law rather than under Secs. 7 and 8. It therefore does not have to come into conflict with N.L.R.B. on the interpretation of Secs. 7 and 8. Because state courts in Sec. 301 cases use that same body of independent law, the Supreme Court can review their decisions again without having to make commitments about whether specific fact situations do or do not fall within Secs. 7 or 8. The state courts are therefore allowed to act in Sec. 301 cases because the Supreme Court has discovered that this section allows courts, and more particularly the Supreme Court, to intervene in labor affairs without risking direct clashes with the Board over the specifics of Secs. 7 and 8.

Viewed within the framework of federal pre-emption, these two cases are contradictory. *Green* is among the several recent cases that progressively narrow the scope of state activity by invoking the jurisdiction of the Board. *Smith* strikes in just the opposite direction by creating a reserve of state power in spite of Board jurisdiction. But, viewed as Sec. 301 cases, *Green* and *Smith* are quite complementary, the former imposing the Supreme Court's "no injunction" policy on state courts as well, the latter allowing the state courts the same latitude as the federal courts whenever it is possible to avoid direct conflict with the Board.

In any event, the Court's decisions in the area of labor contracts have not been marked by a complete or even general reluctance to make law and policy. They confirm the pattern indicated by the pre-emption and Secs. 7 and 8 cases. There is judicial activism to the extent of formulating compromise labor policies and enforcing the intent of Congress, even when such enforcement requires considerable judicial activity. Coupled with this activism is the desire to thrust factual analysis of individual cases under rules established by the Court onto others, whether N.L.R.B. or arbitrators.

¶ The Rights of Union Members

Another area of Supreme Court activity in the labor field so entangles Constitutional and statutory interpretation that it alone might serve as a sufficient illustration of the unsatisfactory nature of the traditional, Constitutional-law approach to the Court. The cases concern employee's rights *vis à vis* unions. The Supreme Court has upheld state bans on closed and union shops against a whole barrage of Constitutional claims centering on the First and Fourteenth Amendments. The arguments of the unions have been ingenious, but the Court's decisions boil down to the simple position that the Constitution nowhere guarantees the right of a union to contract with an employer to exclude everyone but its own members from employment. This statement puts the matter negatively. Positively there seems to remain on the Court a glimmer of that by now old-fashioned view that a man should be able to earn his living without having to pay tribute to another man or set of men to whom he does not wish to submit himself. The glimmer is fairly faint, however. For if the Court finds no Constitutional objection to anti closed- or union-shop laws, neither does it seem to find any such objection to pro-union-shop laws. The Court upheld the union-shop provisions of the 1951 Amendment to the Railway Labor Act and has questioned neither the ban on closed shops nor the authorization and regulation of union shops contained in the Taft-Hartley Act. It has recently found that the "agency shop" is authorized under the federal labor statutes.[107]

Aside from Bill of Rights problems some issues of federalism are involved. The Court has upheld state right-to-work laws that go beyond federal law. The Constitionality of such laws, so long as they did not "run afoul of some . . . valid federal law,"[108] was confirmed before the passage of Taft-Hartley. After passage, the Court said "provisions of the Taft-Hartley Act made it even clearer than the National Labor Relations Act that the states are left free to pursue their own more restrictive policies in the matter of union-security agreements. Because Par. 8(3) of the new Act forbids the closed shop and strictly regulates the conditions under which a union-shop agreement may be entered, Par. 14(b) was included to forestall the inference that federal policy was to be exclusive."[109] But where, in the Railway Labor Act, Congress has specifically authorized a closed shop, although confined to one industry, the closed-shop agreements in that industry are valid because of federal supremacy, even in those states with right-to-work laws.

THE UNIONS AND NEGRO RIGHTS

Having sketched the legal background, we turn to a crucial problem of employee rights, union discrimination against Negroes, a problem inextricably entwined with closed-shop and right-to-work legislation.

Professor Wellington has dealt with the problem in an admirably concise article built around the cases of *Oliphant v. Brotherhood* and *Railway Employees' v. Hanson*.[110] Hanson was a Negro employed in the offices of the Union Pacific Railroad in Nebraska. The constitution of the Railway Employee's Department (A.F.L.) forbade Negro membership. The union had a union-shop contract with the railroad pursuant to the 1951 Amendments to the Railroad Labor Act.[111] Hanson was therefore threatened with loss of employment. Hanson, and later Oliphant, resorted to the courts, arguing that the union's refusal to admit him and the company's consequent refusal to employ him violated the Fifth and Fourteenth Amendments. Normally, of course, these Constitutional provisions apply only to government and not private action. Oliphant's task was to show that the union and railroad action was somehow government action. It has been argued at times that labor unions and corporations have grown so large and wield so much power over the lives of so many citizens that they are in effect private governments to which the Constitutional limitations on "public" government should be extended. Such an extension would, however, imply Constitutional supervision by the Supreme Court over much of the economic life of the nation. The Court seems unwilling to embark on such a career.

On a lesser scale, two arguments from *Shelley v. Kraemer*[112] are open to Oliphant. In *Shelley*, restrictive covenants in real-estate deeds were held valid by the Supreme Court, but court action to enforce the covenants was held to be state action in aid of discrimination in violation of the equal-protection clause of the Fourteenth Amendment. Oliphant could then argue that, if the court refused to order his admission to the union, that refusal would be governmental action in aid of a discriminatory agreement. The difficulty is that *Shelley* had held private discriminatory agreements valid when followed voluntarily and only condemned positive action by the state to enforce such agreements when they were not being kept voluntarily. In Oliphant's case, the court, in refusing him remedy would not be positively aiding segregation but merely maintaining a hands-off policy toward a voluntary agreement among the union members and between the union and management.

A second variant of *Shelley* is available, however, because Nebraska has a right-to-work law. If it were not for the Railway Labor Act, which pre-empts the field, the Nebraska right-to-work law would guarantee Oliphant his job. The union's action is so intertwined with positive federal intervention in Nebraska affairs that it therefore becomes a government action. Several difficulties arise from this line of argument. First, refusal to admit Negroes to railroad unions would be unconstitutional in the "right to work" states but not in others. It would be politically impossible for the Court to defend union discrimination in New York and condemn it in Nebraska.

More important, the federal statute does not require union shops. It takes a hands-off position toward voluntary agreements of that sort between the railroads and the brotherhoods. Following the logic of *Shelley* then, there is no positive state action in aid of segregation so that the existence of the federal statute does not seem to infect union action with a "governmental" quality. Or, as Professor Wellington argues, a finding of unconstitutionality would mean that whenever a pre-emptive statute was involved, the federal government would be barred from taking a hands-off position and would be required to impose positive Constitutional duties on the private parties making agreements regulated and authorized by its legislation.

These arguments are not absolutely irrefutable. First, the Court could argue that, where the federal government pre-empts such an area as labor contracts, which have traditionally been under state control, it actively intervenes even when there is no contrary state law, that is, even in the states without right-to-work laws, because it interrupts the states' normal capacity to pass such a law. The federal government would thus have been considered to have acted in both Nebraska and New York, and discrimination would be unconstitutional in both. Professor Wellington outlines this argument but feels that it has been contravened by the argument based on the logic of the *Shelley* case already described. But the latter approach can also be questioned. Professor Wellington manages to dispose of the white-primary cases[113] but, I think, unsatisfactorily in light of the peculiar circumstances surrounding the union-shop provisions of the Railway Labor Act. In *Smith v. Allwright,* the State of Texas attempted to divest itself of all connection with the state Democratic primary after the Supreme Court had ruled that state-administered all-white primaries for "private" political parties constituted state action in violation of the Fourteenth Amendment. The Supreme Court refused to see an end of state action in the formal transfer to a "private" organization of power that had, for many years, been wielded by the state. Admittedly, *Smith* is not completely clear. It can be distinguished in many ways from Oliphant's case. Nevertheless, its aura at least remains.

As we have already noted, the Railway Labor Act of 1932 had prohibited union shops on the railroads. The Taft-Hartley Act of 1947, while generally permitting union shops, allowed enforcement of state right-to-work laws. The railroad brotherhoods had fought bitterly for the union shop once their controlling position was established, and the Congress gave them the 1951 amendments permitting union-shop contracts. In view of Congress's knowledge that union shops would be the inevitable and immediate result of changing its long-enforced earlier rule and considering that the changes are, in effect, a special exception to its permissive state right-to-work-law policy, the amendments constitute a hands-off policy only in the most formalistic sense. It is rejection of such formalism that permeates *Smith v. Allwright.* It would surely not be impossible for the Court to find that, where federal legislation carves out a special union-shop area to be protected from state intervention, unions exploiting that special protection are the beneficiaries of positive government action and that their discrimination, protected and enforced by federal labor law, is in effect governmental discrimination.

Professor Wellington himself would prefer a variation of this argument that would entirely avoid the *Shelley v. Kraemer* problems of "positive" and "hands off" governmental attitudes toward voluntary agreements. He finds it feasible for the Court to hold that, in view of the long-standing, extensive, and detailed regulation of labor relations by the federal government, union membership policies and security agreements are not voluntary agreements but operative parts of a fully articulated federal labor policy. This policy, like most governmental policies, falls under Constitutional limitations. Union discrimination therefore falls under Constitutional ban, not because there has been positive governmental action in aid of a voluntary private discrimination *à la Shelley,* but because the discrimination has become part of the government's scheme of labor regulation itself.

Having said so much, Wellington's modesty gets the best of him. To bring union action directly under the Constitution rather than simply under federal statutes might result in passing labor policy-making initiative from Congress to the Supreme Court and bringing many heavily regulated private groups under judicial supervision. Furthermore, aside from the general question of who should make broad policy, once the unions were under Constitutional control, the Court would have to supervise the day-to-day internal affairs of the unions. It would then either have to check the unions at every turn, a chore for which it is institutionally unfit, or adopt a rule of reasonableness. Judging by the use of the reasonableness rule as a Constitutional limitation on Congressional policy, such a rule applied to unions would only add a coat of Constitutional whitewash to nearly anything the unions did. True, the objection to Supreme Court rather than Congressional action might not be great in the *Oliphant* case itself, as Oliphant is a member of one minority group that is not properly represented in Congress and so might well be entitled to Supreme Court protection. And even the rule of reasonableness would forbid racial discrimination in union affairs. But extending the doctrine of state action for Oliphant might lead to its general extension with consequences that would cause the modest to blush.

Fortunately, Professor Wellington has another, strictly statutory remedy for Oliphant. The Railway Labor Act and the Taft-Hartley Act both grant to majority unions the right of exclusive representation under certain circumstances. In *Steel v. Louis-*

ville Railroad,[114] the Supreme Court implied from these provisions a duty on the part of the union to represent fairly all the workers for whom it was the exclusive bargaining agent, union members or not. In the *Steele* case, the Court found that the union had discriminated against nonmembers solely because they were Negroes. (The contract obtained by the union gave whites seniority advantages over Negroes.) The Supreme Court can now hold that experience has shown that any union that does not admit Negroes will not fairly represent them. Union discrimination could then be struck down as a violation of the labor statutes rather than of the Constitution.

The only objection to Wellington's solution is that it looks rather like the *per se* rules that the Court has tended to avoid. The question would not be, Had the union in fact represented nonmember Negro employees fairly? Membership discrimination would be a *per se* violation of the duty to represent fairly. Nevertheless, in view of the Court's vigorous pursuit of segregation in all its forms, scruples about *per se* rules might easily be overcome, particularly as in these instances it can often be shown that all the circumstances surrounding the case indicate that exclusion from membership should be taken as conclusive.

Even if this statutory approach were adopted, however, it would be naive indeed to argue that the Court had subjected the unions to statutory but not Constitutional limitations. A decision favorable to Oliphant would surely be as much a consequence of the school-segregation cases as were the *per curiam*s that directly refer to it. The letter of the finding might be statutory, but the spirit would be that of the "equal protection" clause.

In any event, Oliphant lost his case. The Supreme Court refused *certiorari* but with a clear invitation to try again. "In view of the abstract context in which the questions sought to be raised are presented by this record the petition for writ of *certiorari* is denied."[115] The N.A.A.C.P. announced that it would then try again against all forms of union discrimination.

THE UNIONS AND POLITICAL ACTIVITY

The Court has also avoided formal Constitutional commitment on another type of employee right, the union-shop question. In *Railway Employees v. Hansen,*[116] Hansen had protested paying dues to the union under a union-shop contract protected from a state right-to-work law by the Railway Labor Act amendments. There the Court seemed to accept the argument that the federal pre-emption constituted a sufficient nexus between government and union action to raise Constitutional issues. It did not have to face up to the problem of declaring a union action unconstitutional, however, for it found that the First and the Fifth Amendments had not been violated by requiring employees to support financially their bargaining representative. The Court expressly reserved Constitutional judgment on "the exaction of dues . . . as a cover for forcing ideological conformity"[117] or "for purposes not germane to collective bargaining. . . ."[118]

Precisely these issues arose in *International Association of Machinists v. Street*.[119] Street, who was also a railroad employee covered by the Railway Labor Act, did not want any portion of his dues used by the union to support political candidates or legislative programs that he did not favor. The Supreme Court found for him but not on Constitutional grounds. By heroic striving, it managed to construe the Railway Labor Act as forbidding the use of Street's dues for purposes that displeased him. There was thus no need to touch on Constitutional questions. The Court's exposition has left so many problems in its wake that no one knows what it means. All it gives is some hints.

The majority opinion, that is, the four-man opinion written by Justice Brennan and concurred in by Justice Douglas, professes to use statutory interpretation to avoid Constitutional issues. Two sorts of Constitutional issue were involved. First, was the union action governmental action? If not, then no Constitutional issues arise, for the relevant Constitutional prohibitions apply only to government actions. Second, if the union action was government action, did it violate the First Amendment? *Hansen* had suggested that expenditures to further collective bargaining did not violate the First Amendment but that "political expenditures" might. The majority opinion may thus mean that the Court did not wish to decide whether or not the Constitution is applicable to union action (whether or not union action is state action) or, having decided that the Constitution was applicable, did not wish to enunciate a Constitutional rule delimiting which expenditures violate the First Amendment and which do not.

Furthermore, only one Justice wanted to declare unconstitutional the statute providing railroad union shops protection from state laws. And only two of the Justices suggested that the union might have to choose between a union shop and political expenditure. Apparently all that is required is that those people who specifically object shall be relieved from paying the part of their dues that would normally go to union "political" expenditures. Only prolonged administration of the decision will tell whether or not it will have even the slightest effect on union finances. Furthermore, even in terms of the individual protester, the union need only raise its general dues slightly to maintain the level of both the net dues of the protester and its own political expenditures. Finally, although Georgia, the state in which the case arose, does not have a right-to-work statute, the Georgia Supreme Court declared the right to work to be part of the public policy of the state. Was the Court's concern about Constitutional problems limited to states with right-to-work statutes or policies? We do not know.

Apart from all this uncertainty, the intriguing element in the decision is its wonderful mixture of Constitutional and statutory elements. In order to avoid a Constitutional decision, the Court has read the statute to command that the Justices prevent the expenditure of union dues of protesting members for political, as opposed to collective-bargaining, purposes. The Court thus imposes the same standard it would have imposed had it answered all the Constitutional questions against the union. The Court is in effect requiring the union to obey the First Amendment by requiring it to obey the statute. Surely the statute would not have been interpreted in the way it has been were it not for the First Amendment. *Street* may then be a trial run before a return to the *Oliphant* problem. There too the aura of the Constitution can tinge statutory interpretation in order to impose Constitutional burdens on the union without labeling union action as "government action."

Of course, the advantage, in the eyes of the modest, of Constitutional limitation by statutory interpretation is evident. Congress, so it is argued, can always correct the Court by amending the statute. This possibility arose in the *Street* situation, for Congress might conceivably amend the labor statutes to provide specifically for union political expenditure or define collective-bargaining expenditure very broadly to include all union spending that would improve its bargaining position. Such a broad definition might include spending to promote certain forms of labor legislation or even to support candidates favorable to such legislation and thus to legitimize expenditures that would seem to be "political" under the Court's present interpretation. If the Court should go on to aid *Oliphant's* successors as it has aided *Street,* however, the Congress would hardly be free to correct a Court misapprehension of its meaning. Civil-rights legislation may indeed pass Congress with difficulty, but the day seems past when Congress will pass a statute specifically authorizing discrimination in union membership.

Street has been a much criticized decision and rightly so. First, the remedies problem seems overwhelming. Unions are organized federally with taxes on locals levied by nationals in varying amounts for varying purposes. Tracing the proportion of an individual protester's dues spent for "political" purposes through this maze is very difficult.[120] Second, the Railway Labor Act has both a union-shop clause and a pre-emption clause barring state jurisdiction over union security agreements. It is the union-shop clause that the Court has interpreted to mean "no political expenditure." But it is the pre-emptive clause that presumably creates many of the Constitutional problems. It should be remembered that the nexus between government action and union action that creates a Constitutional problem seems to be the federal government's protection of union-shop agreements from actual or potential state right-to-work laws. In other words it is the pre-emption clause that gives rise to this particular interpretation of the union-shop clause. The Taft-Hartley Act contains almost exactly the same union-shop clause as the Railway Labor Act, but it does not contain a pre-emption clause—indeed it contains exactly the reverse. *Street* paves the way for similar cases under Taft-Hartley. Does the Court interpret the union-shop clause of Taft-Hartley in the same way as that of the Railway Act? If so, it will have adopted an extremely strained interpretation unjustified in this instance by the need to avoid Constitutional issues presented in *Street.* If not, it will have held that Congress meant two entirely different things on the two occasions when it used almost exactly the same words.

Professor Wellington, back in the fray in the *Supreme Court Review,*[121] also objects that the decision leads the Court into supervision of internal union affairs, a task for which history shows the courts are unsuited. I am not sure whether history shows that courts *per se* are institutionally incapable of handling unions or only that the specific courts we have had in American history, courts whose judges were inimical to the labor movement, were incapable of dealing with unions fairly. We are too often prone to say that someone or some institution is incapable of solving a problem when what we really mean is that we do not like its solution.

Nevertheless, it is surely true that we cannot predict much success for a Court that attempts to draw the line between political expenditures and expenditures designed to improve the bargaining position of the union. This prediction is not based on the institutional weakness of courts but on the political weakness of the distinction with which the Justices would have to work. The whole basis of labor's collective-bargaining position is a series of federal and state statutes arising from labor's success in the political arena. Furthermore, with increasing executive intervention in major labor disputes, the unions' interests as collective bargainers include the persons holding office as well as particular legislative programs. The political realities simply do not match the judicial doctrines.

Nevertheless, *Street* is symptomatic. Some members of the Court at least have moved beyond the attitude that concern for the rights of individual employees forced into mass unions is simply a rationalized form of union-busting. Without accepting *in toto* the doctrine that unions and corporations are "governments" themselves and so subject to Constitutional limitations, the Court is moving toward either an expanded concept of governmental action or a closely related technique of reading Constitutional limitations into the protective statutes. Of course it was these statutes that suggested in the first place that the supported organizations might fall in the governmental sphere. *Street* shows that union action toward employees is now within the aura of the Constitution, and no one should be surprised at further Constitutional limitation by statutory interpretation.

Indeed, the Court has not been alone in adopting this combination of Constitutional and statutory methods. In the Labor Management and Reporting Act of 1959, Congress enacted a "bill of rights" for union members that includes free-speech and due-process guarantees. The statute provides for suit in the federal courts to redress violations of these rights. The statute also grants members a parallel to the equal-protection clause—"equal rights and privileges" within the union. All that the Court imputed, probably incorrectly, to Congress in *Street* thus actually occurs here. Congress has brought Constitutional limitations to the unions and provided for corresponding judicial review of actions in violation of those limitations, even though this review takes the courts deep into internal union affairs. It has done so by statute and has thus formally given the Supreme Court statutory rather than Constitutional duties, but it will be hard indeed to distinguish the statutory Court from the Constitutional Court in this area.

¶ Conclusion

To recapitulate briefly, the Supreme Court's increasingly permissive interpretation of free-speech limitations on state regulation of picketing has been counteracted by its vacillating but recently severely federalist stand on the permissible scope of state *vis à vis* federal labor regulation. The restriction on state activity has come about largely through the primary-jurisdiction and preemption doctrines. These doctrines seem to be based less on considerations of state *versus* national power, that is, on Constitutional questions, than on the Supreme Court's desire to harmonize its relations with the N.L.R.B., that is, on questions of the balance of political power *within* the central government. Just as the First Amendment cases depend on the federalism cases, the federalism cases depend on those in which Court and Board meet to work out their differences. The federalism cases, which deal after all with protection and prohibition under Secs. 7 and 8, are a subcategory of the general area of statutory interpretation of Secs. 7 and 8. An examination of the more general category indicates that the Court has sacrificed state power not as part of a general surrender to the Board but as an element in a *modus vivendi* in which the Board is left almost entirely free to determine whether or not particular fact situations fall under the provisions of Secs. 7 and 8, so long as it uses the general standards formulated by the Court.

The Court, in formulating these standards, visualizes itself as a compromiser of rival extremes of policy and a watchdog for Congress, keeping the Board from trespassing beyond the limits set by Congressional intention. The Court's willingness to take an active part in labor law making when it has Congressional support is further indicated by its acceptance of the Congressional invitation or quasi-invitation to create a whole new body of labor-contract law. The contract cases themselves offer a neat tangle of Constitutional and statutory issues. It is therefore necessary to examine a whole range of cases that seem to involve rather routine statutory interpretation, in order to explain the Court's Constitutional judgments on federalism and thus on First Amendment issues.

Finally, in the relatively new area of employees' rights *vis à vis* unions, a technique of Constitutional limitation by statutory interpretation seems to be evolving, a technique that defies dissection into Constitutional and non-Constitutional elements. Some of the suggestions about Negro rights in the last part of this chapter may have already been rendered partially obsolete by the passage of the Civil Rights Act of 1964, which contains provisions aimed at union discrimination. This very fact, however, strongly supports the proposition that, in the area of union-member rights, statutory and Constitutional elements are inextricably mixed.

4

The Supreme Court as Policy-Maker: The Warren Court and Federal Tax Policy

THE SUBJECTS of this chapter are taxes and the Supreme Court —hardly an unnatural combination but nevertheless one rarely made.[1] Yet tax policy-making involves the interaction of the Congress, an administrative agency (the Internal Revenue Service), and the courts. It offers just the type of intergovernmental problem with which those who analyze judicial review have been struggling on a broader scale. The I.R.S. has high access to the Court, in terms of both volume of litigation and of gaining relatively sympathetic hearings. The Service is also a pressure group, at least insofar as it has certain institutional interests and policy preferences that it seeks to persuade the judiciary to support by appropriate decisions. An examination of the Justices' tax decisions therefore provides a kind of case study in the politics of the Supreme Court.

The politics of the Supreme Court in the tax field largely revolves around the question of who shall decide—the I.R.S. or the Court? As we shall presently see, Supreme Court treatment of any given piece of tax litigation is largely dependent on certain general patterns of reaction that the Court has established. And these patterns are related less to the legal aspects of the cases before it than to the Court's vision of its own position in the tax policy-making process *vis à vis* Congress and the I.R.S. The politics of the Court thus becomes an integral part of tax law.

The two most striking features of the Warren Court's[2] record on substantive tax issues are its desire to avoid overinvolvement in complex economic matters and its general, but not complete, submission to the guidance of the Internal Revenue Service. The first is, of course, not peculiar to the field of taxation. It has been much commented upon in such other economic areas as bankruptcy and copyright litigation.[3] And, in many instances, submission to I.R.S. is simply the reciprocal of judicial noninvolvement. For, if the Court will not take the lead in interpreting the Revenue Code, then the Service is left alone or at least dominant in the field. In any event, judicial retreat from economic complexity and judicial deference to the agency that administers that complexity are so intimately related that their separation in the discussion below is largely for analytical convenience.

¶ Judicial Abstention

The Warren Court's gingerly approach to taxation is not reflected in an absence of tax decisions from the reports. The Court takes a fair number of cases involving both substantive and administrative or procedural problems.[4] These cases typically, however, reach the Court because of conflicts on the circuits or between the circuits and the Tax Court,[5] conflicts that the Supreme Court feels unable to ignore because of its special responsibility for maintaining uniformity in federal law. On the whole, the Court has kept a very tight rein on its exercise of review.[6]

The Warren Court's modesty in the tax field has been maintained not only by its limited *certiorari* policy but also by the very techniques it has adopted for deciding those cases that it has accepted. Foremost among these techniques is the Court's predilection for reducing the case materials to the simplest possible forms. Since the legal devices at issue are often exceedingly complex, the Court frequently ignores legal form and focuses on economic substance. In *Knetsch v. United States,*[7] for example, a case involving a complex borrowing and insurance transaction that in effect enabled the taxpayer borrowing at 3.5% to earn at 2.5% while claiming his interest payments as a deduction, the Court found the transaction a sham. It held that, in spite of the formal loan arrangement, no borrowing and therefore no interest payments had actually occurred. Symptomatically, Justice Black, speaking for the dissenters, objects, not to the reducing of technical and complex legal devices to the simplicity of what "really" happened, but to the possibility that the majority decision will result in a flood of cases in which the Court will be asked to distinguish between transactions of commercial substance and tax avoidance devices. The dissenters modestly assign such a chore to the Congress rather than to the courts.

Libsom Shop v. Koehler[8] also illustrates the Court's desire to stay out of the complexities of law. The taxpayer, a corporation formed by the merger of sixteen former corporations, attempted to take advantage of the member firms' loss carry-overs, which are available only to "the same taxable entity."[9] The Court exhibited little desire to examine the corporation laws under which the merger took place in order to establish whether or not the new corporation was technically a continuation of the old ones. Instead it relied almost entirely on the fact that there had previously been sixteen firms where there was now only one and found that the new corporation was not entitled to the carry-overs.

Similarly, in *Putnam v. C.I.R.*,[10] in which a guarantor who discharged a loan claimed a bad-debt deduction, the Court, while purporting to decide the case by reference to the common law of subrogation, seems to have looked to the substance of the transaction rather than to the technical distinctions among lender, borrower and guarantor.[11] Recently, in *Turnbow v. C.I.R.*,[12] the taxpayer rested his case on a complicated set of assumptions derived from the complex Code provisions for stock transfer and reorganization. The Court, repeatedly stressing the actual nature of the transaction, refused to clothe a factually simple matter in an elaborate set of legal hypotheses and found, while breathing an almost audible sigh of relief, that the factual situation made it unnecessary to venture into the legal questions raised by the parties.

Where the reality might lead the Court deeper into the complexities of taxation, however, and where consideration of the formal aspects of the situation will allow the Court to avoid those complexities, the formal aspect may well triumph. In *Fi-*

delity-Philadelphia Trust Co. v. Smith,[13] where an annuity plan and an insurance policy were so combined as to constitute in fact one parcel, the Court insisted upon maintaing the separate formal identities of the two, even while admitting that their purchase constituted a single transaction.[14] The advantage to the Court of this approach is that it seems to lead to uniform tax treatment of the proceeds of all assigned life-insurance policies, whether purchased in annuity combinations or not. Such treatment would presumably reduce the Court's need to handle this type of case. Here the Court is willing to go along with and thus to be responsible for interpreting legal technicalities in a given case—if the end result is to reduce the Court's future tax workload.

In *Meyer v. United States,*[15] the Court seized upon the fact that a single insurance policy had been issued in order to avoid dividing the proceeds into two properties for estate-tax purposes, although in common-sense terms two properties had come into existence. In *C.I.R. v. Lester,*[16] the Court held the periodic payments of a husband to his divorced wife to be entirely deductible alimony, although the payments were to be reduced by one-sixth when any of the three children in the wife's custody married, gained majority, or died. (Child-support payments, unlike alimony, are not deductible.) In *United States v. Davis,*[17] a husband's property settlement in connection with his divorce was treated as an arms-length transaction involving only the marital rights of the wife. The Court refused to recognize the fact that, while a settlement might formally be such a transaction, in fact husbands often pay partly in compensation for marital rights and partly simply to obtain release from unwanted partners. The Court recognized the legalistic but not the emotional elements of divorce. In all three cases, the Court tended to ignore the economic and social realities, and the result was to allow the Court to avoid examining the complex details of financial arrangements by treating them as simple wholes.

In *Maximov v. United States,*[18] the Court was asked to deal with the problem of a trust established in the United States, all of its beneficiaries, however, being British. The trust had enjoyed capital gains. Under the income-tax convention between the United States and the United Kingdom, "A resident of the United Kingdom not engaged in trade or business in the United States shall be exempt from United States tax on gains from the sale or exchange of capital assets. . . ."[19] The trustee argued that to subject the trust to capital-gains taxation would in effect subject the British beneficiaries to this tax. The Court disposed of the matter by focusing on the formal proposition that a trust is "a separate 'person' and distinct tax entity, apart from its beneficiaries." The trust, being a resident of the United States, was subject to the tax. Although the actual effect is to submit British citizens to a capital-gains tax to which they would not be subject if they held the stocks involved directly rather than through a trust, the Court is quite willing to stick to the formal legal principle involved here because to do otherwise might commit it in the future to tracing actual international financial relationships, relationships that are frequently complex.[20]

In *Whipple v. C.I.R.*,[21] the taxpayer had organized a corporation, of which he retained 80% of the stock, and had made loans to the corporation. When the corporation was unable to repay these loans, the taxpayer claimed them as bad debts for tax-deduction purposes. Bad debts are only deductible when incurred in connection with trade or business. It has become a common practice in the United States for an individual to incorporate himself for purposes of operating a business. Nevertheless, the Court seized upon the formality that legally it was the corporation rather than the taxpayer that did business, the taxpayer being technically only an investor. Investing is not a trade or business, and thus the debt incurred by the taxpayer *qua* investor was not a deductible business-connected debt. The decision in *Whipple* blocked the efforts of several lower courts[22] to move toward a more realistic view of the incorporated small businessman. The formal approach appears to be attractive to the Supreme Court because it, for the moment at least, allows the Court to make a decision without getting involved in the extremely complex legal and financial relationships typically created when an individual uses closely held corporations in connection with his personal business ventures.[23]

A companion technique to that of reducing complex situations to simple ones has been the Court's policy of refusing to construct or enforce general rules. Instead of establishing legal standards, an approach that would push it head and shoulders into the policy-making realm, the Warren Court has typically decided cases only on the particular facts involved.

For instance, in *Automobile Club of Michigan v. C.I.R.*,[24] the Club received one annual dues payment in any month of the calendar year in return for road service in the succeeding twelve months. Its net income was thus the annual dues minus the cost of providing the road service in each of those succeeding months. Under the actual method of accounting, it therefore showed one-twelfth of the dues as gross income in each of those twelve months, even though some of the months fell in the next tax year. The Court, however, found the entire lump sum to be income within the tax year in which it was received.

Since the auto club's position seemed to be in line with the general principle that taxable income should correspond to business income as determined by normal accounting practices,[25] the Court had the opportunity to make a major pronouncement on the accrual method. Such a pronouncement seems to have been sorely needed. But the Court rested its decision on a determination that the auto club's accounting method was "purely artificial" because there was in fact "no relation" between dues and services rendered.[26] The Court thus avoided making any rule on the treatment of prepayments by taxpayers who keep books on the accrual method by finding that, in this particular case, the payments involved were not actually prepayments.

In *Auto Club v. Michigan,* the Court had reasoned that, when a lump-sum payment for twelve months of future service had been made, there was no way of telling how much service would be provided in which month. It was this factor that apparently led to the condemnation of a bookkeeping system by which the lump sum was divided into twelve equal parts, each part to be treated as income in one of the twelve succeeding months. The American automobile Association responded by preparing statistical analyses of past service demands to show how much service had actually been provided in what months and preparing its accrual books on the basis of predictions of the distribution of future service demands from past experience. The Court, again deciding on the facts, still found this arrangement to be artificial, an inaccurate reflection of the actual relation of payments to demands for service.[27]

Then, in *Schulde v. C.I.R.*,[28] the problem arose in connection with dance contracts providing for a certain number of lessons each year and thus far more predictable than the emergency road-service contracts in the auto-club cases. The Court again backed the Commissioner's discretionary decision that accrual did not accurately reflect business realities. Without offering any real rules or guidelines, it provided a long list of reasons why accrual was artificial in this particular instance, including that the times of the lessons had not been specified and that the customers might never show up to take the lessons for which they had paid in advance.

In three cases, the Court has consistently struck down, on the particular facts, accrual-bookkeeping arrangements that seem to follow normal accounting practices. The Court has thrown the whole accrual method into doubt without having provided any specific rules for determining when accrual techniques are or are not legitimate.[29]

C.I.R. v. Duberstein,[30] *United States v. Kaiser,*[31] and *Stanton v. United States*[32] dealt respectively with a Cadillac given to a man who had supplied business leads, a gratuity to a retiring church administrative official, and strike benefits. The Court was asked in effect to restate its rule distinguishing gifts from income. By judiciously citing both the majority and dissenting opinions in the formerly governing case, *Bogardus v. C.I.R.,*[33] the Court avoided constructing any rule at all.[34] More important, by stressing questions of fact rather than of law[35] and by refusing to establish a new rule while muddying the old, the Justices have turned the trial court into the court of last resort for most cases and sought to stem the stream of appeals that used to arise under the *Bogardus* rule.

Even in *Knetsch,* where the Court was willing to decide the instant case, it decided solely on the basis that no indebtedness and therefore no deductible interest within the intent of the statute had in fact been created. It refused to confirm or deny a circuit-court rule that, when tax avoidance was the sole motive of a transaction, no interest deduction might be had.[36]

In *Parsons v. Smith,*[37] the Court had the opportunity to review a whole catalogue of tax-court and circuit rules for determining when strip miners, who did not own the mineral lands they mined, had sufficient "economic interest" in them to claim depletion allowances. But Justice Whittaker contented himself with mentioning each test in turn without committing himself to any one or combination of several as decisive.[38] The Court was also asked for a rule, this time on what constituted "away from home" business expenses, in *Peurifoy v. C.I.R.*[39] It refused to propound a rule and treated the problem as strictly one of fact-finding,[40] even though there was a long-standing legal conflict on the circuits that had not been resolved by a previous Supreme Court opinion.[41]

In avoiding rigorous rules, the Warren Court is frequently aided by the vagueness of both the statutory language and its predecessors' opinions. When *Tank Truck Rentals v. C.I.R.*,[42] *Hoover Motor Express Co. v. United States,*[43] and *C.I.R. v. Sullivan,*[44] all cases involving tax deductions for rather atypical (criminal) "business" expenses, were decided, the Court easily avoided making a general rule. The statute speaks of "ordinary and necessary" expenditures, and earlier courts had insisted that these words were intended not as terms of art but as reflections of business practice.[45] The Court can therefore content itself with examining the realities of business practice on a case-by-case basis without formulating any general explanation of its apparently contradictory decisions in these three cases.

Just as the Court will look away from reality toward form, however, if such a glance simplifies its business, it will also on occasion make a rule. In the Lester case,[46] it holds that, unless child-support portions are specifically defined in alimony payments, the whole sum may be treated as deductible alimony. The Court had ducked the problem as long as it could.[47] It finally decided the question only in the face of a massive conflict that involved the Tax Court and the First, Second, Sixth, Seventh, and Ninth Circuits.[48] Under this pressure, it chose a rule sufficiently simple to solve the circuits' problems and sufficiently simple-minded to insure that, if policy is to be made in the future on this question, it will be made by Congress and not the Court.[49]

In *United States v. Gilmore,*[50] the Court also formulated a rule. In that case, the taxpayer was the majority shareholder in three corporations. His income largely consisted of salary drawn as an employee of these corporations. His wife sued him for divorce on grounds that, if proven, would have led to a division of community property in which the taxpayer would have lost his majority stockholdings in the three corporations. Furthermore, he argued, without that majority position and with large blocks of stock in the hostile hands of his former wife, he would have lost his salaried positions. The taxpayer therefore claimed that the cost of litigating the divorce, or at least that portion attributable to preventing his wife from claiming half or more of the community property, was an ordinary and necessary business expense. The revenue code provides for the deduction of ". . . ordinary and necessary expenses . . . incurred . . . for the conservation of property held for the production of income."[51] Without the expenditure, the taxpayer could not have maintained his salaried position.

The circuit courts had taken differing positions on the I.R.S.'s view that such costs of divorce litigation were not deductible. The Supreme Court itself had available two precedents. In *Lykes v. C.I.R.,*[52] the Court had rejected the contention that legal expenses incurred in contesting the assessment of a gift-tax liability were deductible. The taxpayer claimed that, if the gift tax were assessed, he would have to liquidate his stockholdings to pay the tax and therefore that legal expenditures to fight the assessment were necessary for the "conservation" of income-producing property and thus deductible. The Court rejected his claim, saying, "deductibility turns wholly upon the nature of the activities to which they relate. . . . Legal expenses do not become deductible merely because they are paid for services which relieve a taxpayer of liability. That argument would carry us too far. It would mean that the expenses of defending almost any claim would be deductible by a taxpayer on the ground that such defense was made to help him keep clear of liens on whatever income-producing property he might have."[53] In *Kornhauser v. United States,* however, the Court did allow the deduction of certain litigation expenses on grounds that, "where a suit or action against a taxpayer is directly connected with . . . his business, the expense incurred is a business expense. . . ."[54]

Any realistic examination of divorce litigation today indicates that it is not simply a personal matter but involves in many instances important business and financial considerations. Indeed, quite often business considerations are the crucial ones, shaping the whole course and tactics of the litigation. *Gilmore* is a case in point, with both parties fighting on grounds that were unnecessary to obtain a divorce but crucial to the issue of who would receive how much of the community property.

Bearing in mind the real nature of modern divorce, it seems that the rule to be derived from the precedents is that expenses attributable to that part of divorce litigation directly connected with maintaining the taxpayer's business position are deductible, while those concerned with his general liability to his spouse are not. *United States v. Patrick,*[55] decided the same day and in the same way as *Gilmore,* illustrates this point. The taxpayer, having been assigned liability for alimony and the payment of all legal fees in a divorce proceeding, made arrangements with his former wife through their attorneys to meet his liabilities by transfer of stocks in such a way as to disturb his business position least. He sought to deduct his legal fees for this arrangement. Those of his legal fees incurred in the divorce proceedings themselves are attributable to the personal aspects of the divorce and his general liability to his wife. Those incurred in the later arrangements to meet that liability in such a way as to best maintain his position of control over the newspaper that he published can be considered business expenditures.

The difficulty with such a rule, of course, is that it would require the courts to look at the complex reality of divorce litigation, untangling in each instance the personal and general liability from the specifically business aspects. The Court, therefore, formulated a different rule in *Gilmore.* ". . . The origin and character of the claim with respect to which an expense was incurred, rather than its potential consequences upon the fortunes of the taxpayer, is the controlling basic test of whether the expense was 'business' or 'personal' and hence whether it is deductible or not under Sec. 23(a) (2)."[56] It will be some time yet before we know precisely what this rule means in other areas of litigation, but, in connection with divorce, it simply means that no litigation costs are deductible. Divorce litigation is treated by the Court as a personal not a business matter for tax purposes. Indeed the rule is something of a sham, for quite obviously what the Court is actually deciding is that no divorce-litigation expenses are deductible and then creating a rule from which it can derive this conclusion.

In one of those rare instances in which we find the Court making a rule, we thus find that it does so simply to avoid the reality and complexity of the actual world and its tax problems. The rule is nothing more than a statement by the Justices that, in order to keep the courts out of making real decisions on real tax problems, they choose to treat every divorce suit as an indivisible entity, which it quite patently is not, and then to say that every such entity is a personal not a business matter. The rule in *Gilmore* is not really a rule but a refusal to make rules in the divorce area.

There is also a sort of quasi-rule in *Whipple v. C.I.R.*[57] The Court found that, when the taxpayer's only relation to his closely held corporation was his majority stockholdership, loans that the corporation failed to repay the taxpayer were not business-connected bad debts because personal investing is not a business within the "trade or business" category of the Internal Revenue Code. This finding offers a rule in the sense of a generalizable statement that will cover all such cases in the future. But it covers only the narrowest range of the possible relations between an individual businessman and his corporate alter egos. The Court noted, for instance, that, if the individual were employed by the corporation and could be deemed to have made it a loan in order to preserve his job, then the debt might be business-connected. Indeed, in *Whipple,* the Court remanded the case for a determination by the lower courts of whether or not the loan might be deemed connected with the taxpayer's business of being a landlord, as he rented a privately owned building to his corporation and presumably might have made the loan in order to keep a tenant. Even while suggesting the range of problems, however, the Court resolutely refused to make any general rules or set any standards to guide the lower courts in determining at precisely what point the taxpayer's relations to his company become sufficiently intimate to bridge the formal gap between majority stockholder and closely held corporation.

Penetration from legal form to economic reality and refusal to formulate general legal rules may be the weapons of a politically active Court that refuses to limit its discretion either by legal mumbo jumbo or its own previously announced formulas. But they are only weapons for an active Court that chooses to use them as such. The Court that adopts a case-by-case approach may establish for itself a roving commission to supervise decisively the policy-making of the lower courts and other governmental agencies. The Court that consistently looks to economic reality may, by sufficient judicial activity, markedly influence the tone and trend of governmental supervision of business.[58]

When the Court makes only an occasional decision and that under duress, however, the case-by-case approach becomes in reality a few isolated decisions limited to their particular facts. The emphasis on facts shifts the burden of supervision to the trial courts. The refusal to make rules in a highly codified and rule-laden area of public policy becomes a refusal to participate in policy-making. The avoidance of technicalities in a technical field allows a Court only to shout occasionally that what the Revenue Service or the taxpayer is doing in a particular instance is too damned silly to tolerate. A not very dignified, but I think accurate, picture is that of an adult court that seeks to ignore the little circuits—stepping in only when it must stop a fight and then merely to quiet the children without taking sides or committing itself to the game because, as an adult, it would have to take the lead if it decided to play.

But if the Court will not lead or even play, there are others eager to do so.

¶ The Court and the I.R.S.

The Warren Court's general reluctance to commit itself in the tax area is, of course, partly a cause and partly a result of its relationship with the I.R.S. The connection between general judicial passivity and particular deference to a specific fellow agency can best be seen in cases that involve long-standing Treasury Regulations and Service Rulings.[59] For instance, in *Cammarano v. United States,*[60] the Court was confronted with the question of whether or not lobbying expenditures were deductible as "ordinary and necessary" business expenses. We have already noted the Court's reluctance to establish any rules for interpreting this phrase. In *Cammarano,* it seized upon two interrelated devices to escape responsibility for rule-making. First, it emphasized the long-standing administrative practice of the I.R.S. Then the opinion notes that Congress had re-enacted the code provision without alteration subsequent to the establishment of this practice. Congress must therefore have approved the practice. Justice Harlan concludes that the Treasury Regulations had "acquired the force of law" and "themselves constitute an expression of a sharply defined national policy."[61]

The re-enactment doctrine is, of course, of itself somewhat dubious, for it seeks to establish what the legislature meant from what it has not said.[62] The doctrine also assumes that Congress was aware of a clear and consistent line of administrative and judicial interpretation at the time it chose to keep silent. Aside from the general problem of imputing to Congress a clear awareness of anything, particularly in the complex tax field, neither the administrative nor judicial treatment of lobbying expenditures seems to have been sufficiently consistent to warrant application of the re-enactment doctrine in this case.[63]

More important than whether or not re-enactment actually applies in this particular case or in *Massey Motors, Inc. v. United States,*[64] another important case combining re-enactment with long-standing practice, is the whole set of tactics applied by the Court. The I.R.S., like any bureaucracy, seeks to develop whenever possible a consistent line of practice. Because of the periodic Code revisions, tax law may be viewed as in a state of nearly constant re-enactment. When the Court invokes long-standing administrative practice and the re-enactment doctrine, it therefore tends to contract out of the tax-law field entirely. The administrative agency by action and the Congress by inaction have made all the legal decisions. None is left for the Court to make. And when the Court withdraws, it leaves the field largely in the hands of the agency that makes the long-standing practice. Court retreat implies I.R.S. advance.

Of course, when the Service vacillates, it may tempt the Court into a more active role and lose its case as it did in *Haynes v. United States,*[65] in which the Court stressed Service inconsistency. Or, when the Service itself wishes to abandon long-standing practice, the Court may be unwilling to give up its crutch to please the Commissioner.[66] The Service, however, is not always debarred from changing its mind[67] and can hope to be upheld particularly when it has followed a new interpretation consistently after abandoning the old one and when the new interpretation has been followed for some time before it is tested by the Court.[68]

The Court generally uses long-standing practice and re-enactment to keep itself out of policy-making in the tax field. In those cases in which the Service also uses these doctrines, the situation is ideal because the Court avoids both rule-making and conflicts with the Service. When the Service wishes to break with long-standing practice, the doctrines are of less use to the Court because they would involve the Justices in conflict with another tax agency, would involve them in the policy-making process—precisely what the doctrines were designed to avoid. As long as the Service can provide some facade of consistency, the Court is therefore unlikely to emphasize the "long" in "long-standing." The Court's limited *certiorari* policy means that the Service is likely to have a fairly extended period in which to make a new "long-standing" practice before the taxpayer finally manages to bring it before the Court. The inevitable result is that the Court, in attempting to avoid involvement in tax policy, acts willy-nilly in support of the I.R.S.[69]

Nor should the I.R.S. be considered a "neutral" agency that simply does what the courts have left to it. The Service has a strong and persistent sense of its own institutional interests. Quite naturally, its view of the public interest—largely in terms of maximizing the flow of tax dollars—becomes inextricably mixed with institutional interests in its own success and prestige. What is good for the Service seems good for the country and *vice versa*. What is good for both is to get the maximum yield from the taxpayer, perhaps even when the Congress does not desire such an end.

Several of the key cases with which the Warren Court has dealt illustrate the Service's skill and persistence in fulfilling its vision of proper tax policy.

Hertz v. United States[70] involved the concepts of useful life and salvage value. Useful life had for forty-five years been taken by businessmen, the I.R.S., and the courts as a measure of how long an item would perform an economic function, no matter how many successive owners used it. Depreciation was calculated as the difference between initial cost and salvage value distributed over the useful life of the item.[71] Until 1939, when an item was sold for more than it cost less depreciation, the proceeds were treated as income. But Sec. 117(j) of the 1939 Revenue Code shifted these receipts to the capital gains category. Sec. 167 of the 1954 Code allowed accelerated depreciation for items with useful lives longer than three years. The capital-gains combined with the acceleration provisions may permit substantial tax advantages to businesses that sell some of their capital goods, particularly if they "overdepreciate."

The Service tried to get Congress to repeal Sec. 117(j). When that move failed, it attempted to narrow the application of both Secs. 117(j) and 167 through a series of rulings, most of which proved abortive.[72] In 1956, after both approaches had failed, the Service simply redefined "useful life" as the period in which the item was used by one company. Salvage value then became the sale price of the item to a second company. The new definitions considerably narrowed the difference between initial cost and salvage value, particularly in periods of inflation, and thus reduced total depreciation. At the same time, they deprived firms that kept items less than three years of the benefit of the accelerated-depreciation provisions.

If these definitions became law, the Service would succeed in avoiding what it considered the unfortunate results of the two Congressional enactments. On to the Courts. The Fifth and Ninth Circuits disagreed on whether the new or the traditional definitions were valid.[73] The Supreme Court granted *certiorari*. The Service's new definitions were upheld. The taxpayer paid more taxes. There is more than one way to skin a cat.

In *C.I.R. v. Hansen*,[74] the Court dealt with a complex problem of accrual bookkeeping, bad debts, and the relation of retailers who guaranted loans to the finance companies who make them. The details are unimportant here. The point is that, under the interpretation of the problem adopted by the I.R.S., some retailers would actually be paying taxes on gross rather than on net income.[75] At the behest of the American Institute of C.P.A.s, Congress passed legislation to solve the problem.[76] The section was repealed shortly after enactment because the I.R.S. failed (refused?) to adopt regulations necessary to restrict the scope of the statute sufficiently to make it workable.[77]

Defeating Congress was not enough. Since the 1930s, the circuits had consistently opposed the Commissioner's interpretation. In 1958, the Commissioner finally succeeded in getting the Sixth and Seventh Circuits to back him against earlier decisions by the Third, Fourth, Fifth, Eighth and Ninth Circuits.[78] The Supreme Court affirmed the supporters of the Commissioner. The taxpayer left six men on base but was unable to score the crucial run. The Service won.[79]

Automobile Club of Michigan v. C.I.R., which we have already discussed, involved another I.R.S. fight. As in *Hansen,* the Service's position ran counter to normal accounting practices, and Congress legislated to bring the Commissioner into line.[80] The Treasury, this time by direct appeal to Congress rather than by inaction, had the statute repealed.[81] This Congressional action did not settle the legal question but simply returned it to its original state of uncertainty. The Service still needed and sought Supreme Court confirmation of its view, particularly as the Tenth Circuit had taken the opposite position.[82] But, in this instance, the Court would not go all the way. It made the taxpayer pay but, deciding on the facts, refused to make a firm rule on the Commissioner's behalf.

Then, in *American Automobile Association v. United States*[83] and *Schulde v. C.I.R.,*[84] the Court read into the Congressional repeal a deliberate affirmation on the part of Congress of the Commissioner's long-standing practice. This reading was a willful distortion of Congressional intent. It concentrated entirely on the corrective statute and its repeal, ignoring the fact that the basic statutes, which have always been read as requiring the I.R.S. to approve normal accounting practices, were still in effect.[85] What is more, the majority refused to recognize that the principal motive for repeal had not been to condemn accrual practices but to avoid the massive revenue losses that would have occurred if large numbers of taxpayers had suddenly switched over to the accrual method.[86]

Why has the Court adopted this approach? The basic provisions of the Code involved in these cases serve two functions. First, they generally direct the Service to approve normal accounting practices and specifically mention accrual as such a practice. Second, they give the Service discretion to disapprove methods that do "not clearly reflect income." The Service had in effect been using this second statutory provision to contravene the first in certain commercial areas by finding that in each instance the accrual method used did not clearly reflect income. The amendment that was passed and then repealed was designed to prevent these Service tactics.

If the Court were to admit that passage and subsequent repeal of the amendments simply brought the problem back to where it had started, it might also have to admit its own responsibility for stopping the Service from exercising its discretion in such a way as to undercut the basic intent of the statute. Presumably the Court would have to make rules in order to bring the Service into line. By interpreting repeal of the amendment as approval of the way in which the C.I.R. had used his discretion, the Justices relieved themselves of responsibility for disciplining the Service and allowed the Court to continue purportedly deciding each case on its facts without making any rules.[87]

The Service may on rare occasions lose, however. In 1951, Senator Kefauver introduced legislation to abolish income-tax deductions for "business" expenses incurred by professional gamblers. The legislation did not pass.[88] In spite of an American Law Institute recommendation,[89] no such provision appeared in the 1954 Code. The Attorney General then announced that the executive branch would do administratively what Congress had failed to do.[90] In *C.I.R. v. Sullivan,*[91] however, the Supreme Court refused to interpret the business-expense provisions to exclude a bookie's rent and salary payments.

We have already seen that the Supreme Court takes tax cases largely because of conflicts on the circuits. The cases just discussed indicate that such conflicts are not merely the results of coincidence. Once the Service has made up its mind, it fights hard and continuously. If it loses in one court in one year, it goes to another in the next.

Peurifoy v. C.I.R.[92] provides a sort of digest of the whole struggle. Congress used very broad language concerning travel deductions: "[w]hile away from home in the pursuit of a trade or business."[93] The Service immediately set about narrowing the provision by interpretation. "Home" was taken to mean place of business rather than residence, so that a person with long-term business dealings at a distance from his residence could not claim extended rent and food expenses as travel-connected. Without disclosing whether it intended to support or rebuff the Service, the

Congress re-enacted the old language in the 1954 Code.[94] The Service thus met with a draw in Congress.

Meanwhile, the Commissioner had obtained mixed judgments from the circuits on the "domicile *vs.* business" issue.[95] Because of the conflict, the Supreme Court took *Flowers v. C.I.R.*[96] but avoided reaching a decision on the real issue. Under the new Code, a squabble between the Tax Court and the Fourth Circuit[97] brought *Peurifoy* to the Court. Again the Court avoided the issue by holding that the Tax Court decision hinged on a finding of fact that the Circuit found "clearly erroneous" on a "fair assessment of the record" so that there was no reason for the Supreme Court to intervene.

The Service achieved a little better than a draw in the courts. It generally won its cases but not its rule. As long as the Service has a draw from Congress and the courts, however, it can and does, as the everyday working agency in the field, make its policy views the prevailing ones on this issue.[98] Furthermore, it always has the long-term hope of winning from the Court, as a reward for its persistence, an affirmation of its views under the "long-standing practice" and re-enactment doctrines.

This kind of situation points up one of the principal difficulties of "long-standing practice" doctrine. Underlying that doctrine is a rough analogy to *stare decisis*—a long line of consistent decisions supposedly indicating a common kernel of truth. But in the body of law shaped by *stare decisis,* the decision-makers are, at least theoretically, impartial judges who have independently arrived at that kernel. Service consistency is not then evidence of the "truth," even in the rather mythical and idealized sense that judicial consistency is. It is simply an indication of the Service's well developed policy position.

Braustein v. C.I.R.[99] presents a curious twist on the Service's usual campaigns to close loopholes. The collapsible corporation device had at one time allowed certain taxpayers to shift receipts that would normally have been considered income into the capital-gains category. In the 1939 revision of the Internal Revenue Code, Congress closed this loophole.[100] In doing so, however, it also worded the revision to require certain taxpayers to shift receipts that would normally have been considered capital gains into the income category, thus providing a loophole, so to speak, for the

I.R.S. The I.R.S. quite naturally has not tried to close this loophole. A taxpayer managed to get help from one of the circuits. The Service persisted in its view, and a conflict on the circuits resulted. The Supreme Court, resorting to the plain-meaning rule, backed the Service.

This case illustrates how the Court's fear of complex problems and its deference to the I.R.S. are mutually supporting. For the Court makes quite clear that the basic reason it will not act to aid the taxpayer is that it is unwilling to get involved in the complicated factual and financial analyses that would be necessary in order to determine whether in each instance the taxpayer has used the collapsible-corporation form as a tax avoidance device or was legitimately entitled to capital-gains treatment. By treating the legislative provisions, which are too inflexible really to meet the problem, as commands against flexibility, the Court specifically sanctions the Service's inflexibility, largely because that inflexibility protects the Court from involvement in difficult tax problems.

One more episode is worth outlining as a panorama of the battlefield. There is no need here to concern ourselves with what the battle was about. On a question of tax treatment of carved out oil payments, the Service had until 1946, with one exception,[101] taken a position favorable to the taxpayer. As a result, various tax avoidance devices had flourished.[102] Beginning in 1946, the Service reversed its position in a series of rulings that sought to close the "loopholes."[103] The new Service position was consistently opposed by the Tax Court[104] backed by the Fifth Circuit.[105] The Service managed to achieve a favorable decision from the Fifth once,[106] but then it suffered more reversals.[107] In the same year, however, it convinced the Seventh Circuit to reverse a Tax Court decision and thus to put itself in conflict with the Fifth Circuit.[108] Meanwhile, the opponents of the Service had tried and failed to get favorable legislation,[109] and the Service had also failed to get Congressional confirmation for its position.[110]

The Supreme Court took *C.I.R. v. P. G. Lake, Inc.*[111] as a result of the circuit conflicts. By the familiar device of hinging its decision on the fact situation, it avoided any real lawmaking. By affirming the Commissioner against this one particular taxpayer, however, it gave a boost to the Service position, particularly *vis à vis* the Fifth Circuit. The Service will undoubtedly continue to push its program.

In most of these cases, there may be some dispute over what Congress "really" intended either in terms of what it meant when it wrote the statute or what it would have wanted when it saw the practical consequences of the statute it wrote. As tax legislation is usually written in the vortex of conflicting policies—particularly between Congress's desire to maximize revenue and to encourage business investment and at the same time to have every man pay his fair share—it is often difficult to decide which policy should receive the most weight in any particular situation. The point is that the Service has a policy that it persistently tries to implement. If Congress will not respond, it tries the courts, and if the courts will not respond, it tries Congress. If one court will not help, it tries another. If no one else will help, it helps itself. If it does not make headway on one tack, it tries another.

The Supreme Court thus cannot avoid being one of the factors that the Service manipulates to achieve its ends. It is not that the Court must always yield to the Service—*Sullivan* is an example —but that it cannot escape from the realm of tax policy because the Service will never let a potential source of support escape entirely. Even its refusal to decide issues is not a "neutral" act but a tactical factor of which the Service can take advantage. For, as the day-to-day decision-maker in the tax field, the Commissioner, unless positively stopped, can continue to establish long-standing practices that are effective in collecting today's tax money and eventually may become so entrenched as to win tomorrow's Congressional or judicial ratification.

Complexities must be faced, and rules must be made. If the Court refuses to do the hard work, the Service gladly takes on the job abdicated by a potentially powerful competitor.[112] One of the curious paradoxes of this situation is that, in those cases in which the Service does invite the Court to take a more active role in the formulation of tax policy, either by dealing with complexities or formulating rules, it is likely to lose. In the three tax-exempt-gift cases, *Duberstein, Kaiser,* and *Stanton,* the Court refused to adopt the rules pressed by the I.R.S. or any others for that matter.[113] The Service also asked for a general rule and lost its case in *Hanover Bank v. C.I.R.*[114] In *C.I.R. v. Lester*[115] and *Fidelity-*

Philadelphia Trust Co. v. Smith,[116] in which the Service asked the Court to look at the complex realities behind relatively simple legal forms, the Court refused to back the Commissioner.

Nevertheless, the whole pattern of cases discussed here indicates a very high level of success for the Service. It would be incorrect, however, to interpret this success entirely as the I.R.S.'s victory over a retreating Court. For the Court's deference to the Service is based not only on misgivings about its own competence but also, to a certain extent, on parallel policy views in the Service and the Court. The factors of judicial modesty and policy preference so interact that it is impossible accurately to weigh the relative importance of each. The Court might be less willing to defer to the Service on grounds of competence if it were less satisfied with the policies the Service is pursuing.

It is suggestive that the one piece of active policy-making the Court has done in the tax field has found the Court and I.R.S. completely in accord on the question of depletion allowances. Depletion allowances have in many ways become the latter-day equivalent of the tariff. The executive branch struggles constantly to reduce what is in effect a set of special privileges. Yet every time the President goes to Congress for a revision of the statutes, logrolling sets in, and Congress extends the special privileges still further. The Executive responds by using whatever descretion is available to it to reduce the scope and impact of the statutes as much as it dares.

The mining industry has not only succeeded in gaining extremely high levels of subsidy and in gradually extending the subsidies to cover a very wide range of minerals, but it has also attempted to squeeze every last drop of profit out of its legislative victories. Depletion is calculated as a percentage of the value of the mineral product. As each stage of processing adds value to such a product, the further along the processing chain the depletion allowance is claimed, the greater the advantage to the taxpayer. For instance, if a company mines clay, which it then processes into clay pipe, it will obviously get a much higher allowance if it can calculate depletion on the basis of the value of the pipe rather than on the value of the clay as it comes out of the ground.

In the real world, it is extremely difficult to draw the line between the last stage of processing necessary to prepare an ore for its eventual manufacturing use and the first stage of manufacture itself, particularly when integrated firms that perform all stages are involved. Congress has sought to draw that line by declaring that depletion may be claimed at the point that the ore becomes "a commercially marketable mineral product."[117] Integrated miners have tended to interpret these words as referring to the point at which they can actually sell their products. The Internal Revenue Service has sought to calculate the allowance at the first point at which a market exists.[118] The clay miner *cum* clay pipe-maker thus seeks depletion allowances based on the value of his pipe, arguing that pipe is the first stage in the process at which it is feasible to, and at which he actually does, sell his mineral product. The Service insists that, as a market for clay exists in the United States, it is the clay and not the pipe that is the commercially marketable mineral product.

In view of the constant tension between the Executive and Congress over depletion allowances, it is not surprising that a conflict on the interpretation of "commercially marketable mineral product" arose between the I.R.S. and the circuits, which envisioned themselves as the guardians of legislative intent.[119] This conflict first reached the Supreme Court in *United States v. Cannelton Sewer Pipe Co.*[120] There was a sufficiently unusual fact situation in *Cannelton* to allow the Court, using its common tactic of deciding on the peculiar facts, to render a decision of no general applicability at all. Instead, the Court enunciated the general rule that ". . . integrated mining-manufacturing operations [are] to be treated as if the operator were selling the mineral mined to himself for fabrication. . . . It would, of course, be permissible for such an operator to calculate his 'gross income from mining' at the point where 'ordinary' miners—not integrated—disposed of their product."[121] Such a point comes after the application of processes that can be considered "the 'ordinary' normal ones applied by the non-integrated miner."[122] Thus the Court backed the I.R.S. across the boards against the circuits.

Furthermore, the Court said, "The question in depletion is what allowance is necessary to permit tax-free recovery of the capital value of the minerals."[123] Now, in terms of Congressional intent, this statement is patently untrue. The depletion provisions have been set in a totally arbitrary way by Congress with no apparent attention to any but the "you scratch my back, I'll scratch yours" principle. What the Court has done is announce that it will impose its vision of the public interest on the statute—a vision that seems to correspond exactly with that of the Executive.

The cement industry was particularly interested in the *Cannelton* decision. Cement-makers mine limestone and process it into cement. Nearly all cement-makers are integrated, so that there is almost no open market for the crushed limestone that goes into the finished product. For this reason, the cement industry has always insisted that it is entitled to depletion allowances based on the value of the cement itself, which is rather as if U.S. Steel were to claim depletion allowances based on the value of the steel rather than on that of the iron ore. The industry had been backed by the circuits and opposed by the I.R.S. in this position. After *Cannelton,* it went to Congress for more help. But even Congress was unwilling openly and specifically to approve an interpretation of depletion for the cement industry that, in many instances, including the one that finally reached the Supreme Court, allowed healthy, going concerns to report no income at all for tax purposes. Instead, Congress approved a compromise that allowed the cement-makers to settle with the Service on a point in the processing chain roughly halfway between raw limestone and finished cement.[124]

At least one member of the industry was unwilling to make this compromise and fought the battle on the old lines. The circuits, in the person of Judge Barnes of the Ninth, made a last-ditch defense of Congress and its industrial friends, throwing up every possible argument in the face of what even Judge Barnes obviously expected would be Supreme Court hostility.[125] He was right, and the Supreme Court cavalierly reversed his decision in the *Monolith Cement* case, handing down a *per curiam* opinion that reiterated the pronouncements of *Cannelton* without even bothering to deal with the very real issues of fact and law that Judge Barnes had raised. In fact, it broadened the rule, declaring that the allowance "should be cut off at the point where the mineral first became suitable for industrial use or consumption."[126]

The Court, which frequently invokes the "clearly erroneous" rule in tax cases,[127] in this instance directly overturned the basic findings of fact made by the trial court on the strength of a single piece of evidence judiciously plucked from the record.

It is worth reporting the depletion controversy at some length, for *Cannelton* and *Monolith* show that the Court is capable of making decisive contributions to the tax policy-making process when it chooses. Given its usual deference to the I.R.S., the Court may find it easier to intervene, as it did here, on the side of the tax collector than on that of the taxpayer, but I for one would like to think that *Cannelton* and *Monolith* show the Court's ability to intervene against a patent inequity in the interpretation of tax law, quite apart from its support of the I.R.S.

The Warren Court has actually been somewhat ambivalent on tax policy. On one hand, it has inherited the position of its predecessors that "The legal right of a taxpayer to decrease the amount of what otherwise would be his taxes, or altogether avoid them, by means which the law permits, cannot be doubted. . . ."[128] On the other, it seems to have ruled that transactions whose sole purposes are tax benefits will not be countenanced.[129] In a fairly consistent line of opinions, it also casts a wary eye on capital gains, depletion, depreciation, accrual, interest, gift, medical-deduction, business-expense, and loss-carry-over devices that seem to it to shortchange the Treasury.[130] The best advice that two prominent practitioners seem able to offer their clients is that the courts will approve clever tax-saving arrangements unless they are *too* clever and *too* successful.[131]

As a court of law, the Supreme Court cannot condemn the citizen for taking maximum advantage of the rights and privileges reserved to him or conferred upon him by the statutes. Yet the Justices find something immoral and therefore not permissible in devious maneuvers through the complexities of the tax structure to avoid a burden that every citizen should and must bear. The Court is thus caught between morals and law, with the usual confusion and ambiguity that result from such a position.[132] What seems to emerge is a judicial distaste for tax-avoidance devices, perhaps not so strong a distaste as that of the Service but one running along parallel lines. Judicial preference and judicial modesty thus become mutually reinforcing factors in support of deference to the Commissioner.

An interesting example of this mutual reinforcement is the

Court's general reluctance to make rules. As we have noted, one reason the Court avoids rule-making is that the formulation of rules would thrust it into the very center of tax policy-making. Another is that rule-making would mean potential conflict with the Service. But a third is that precise rules are more easily circumvented than imprecise ones, so that the Court remains purposely vague in order to put a damper on tax-evasion maneuvers. The refusal to make rules is clearly motivated by desire for judicial retreat from policy-making. At the same time, the Court implements as many of its policy preferences as it can without cost to the Justices' modesty.

¶ Policy-Making and the Supreme Court

Professor Lowndes notes in a recent article[133] that the case for a court of tax appeals has been convincingly argued[134] and that the continuation of Supreme Court jurisdiction in this area is justified only if the Court is making a unique contribution to tax law. After an historical survey of the cases, he concludes that it has contributed little more than random, confusing, and intermittent intervention and that there is therefore no reason for it to continue in the field.

I argue neither for nor against a court of tax appeals. But it does not necessarily follow from the Supreme Court's inactivity that a new tax court is desirable. In terms of political reality, there are three governmental agencies making tax policy: the I.R.S., the Congress, and the courts. The Supreme Court is currently reluctant to make policy decisions. Indeed it is this reluctance, rather than any inherent disability, that seems to lead to the randomness and confusion of which Lowndes so rightly complains. The available alternatives are, therefore, to maintain the *status quo;* to establish a Court of Tax Appeals; or to bring the Supreme Court back into tax policy-making.

The first alternative is, it seems to me, most appealing to the friends of the I.R.S., for the Court's supposed neutrality and passivity are likely to be of considerable advantage to the Service. For those who wish the courts to be active, either of the latter two alternatives seems equally worth considering. As the Court's past unsatisfactory record rests on relative inactivity, it follows as logically from the record that the Court should now become more active as that it should go out of business altogether. The difficulty is that arguments over the projected court of tax appeal and the more general problem of what and how much the Supreme Court ought to do in the tax area have been conducted in terms of procedure, clarity, consistency, and other "legal" niceties. It is time the problem is viewed in terms of the politics of policy-making.

The I.R.S. is constantly in the field and can claim technical skill in a highly technical area. The technician has a marked advantage in our increasingly complex government because he can put on the armor of his expertise to shield his policy preferences against attacks by the nonexpert. "It just can't be done" or "It's fine in theory, but it just won't work" is the ultimate weapon in the specialized bureaucrat's war with the politician or other generalist.

The Congress has begun to fight back by turning its revenue committees[135] into increasingly technical agencies that develop their own expertise by staying constantly in the business and handling more and more technical details on their own.[136] Congress has realized that constant commitment is the only way to stay in the game.

The courts must realize the same thing. The Supreme Court's refusal to plunge into the day-to-day complexities and technicalities of tax law means that it largely abdicates any real policy-making role. And, as deference to the I.R.S. is one of the principal techniques by which this abdication is carried out, the Court's retreat is not even a neutral act *vis à vis* the Service and the Congress but tends to increase the power of the contestant whose vast technical skill already gives it a great advantage over its opponent.

Conversely, the establishment of a court of tax appeals would introduce an agency that would be a significant rival to the I.R.S. because its sources of strength would be the same as those of the Service: technical knowledge and its corollary, day-to-day contact with the problem. In effect, the judiciary would do exactly what the legislature has been attempting to do, establishing its own technicians as a counterweight to the administrative bureaucracy's expertise.

There is, however, a self-defeating feature in such attempts. The political generalists called congressmen establish specialized and expert Congressional committees to help them control the technicians called administrators. But the congressmen are likely, in the long run, to find themselves dominated by the specialized committee precisely because it knows more about the subject than does the Congress at large. There may be some advantage to being dominated by the technician called "Congressional committee-man" rather than by the technician called "administrator," but, either way, the role of the generalist, the reasonable man who is uncommitted in advance to any specialized program or orthodoxy, is lost. The creation of the technician called "judge of the court of tax appeals" raises the same difficulty. We are likely to lose what we want most from judges involved in the policy-making process—a relatively balanced and uncommitted outlook.

It is for this reason that the third alternative, a Supreme Court active in the tax field, seems most attractive. The Court has shied away from tax matters presumably because it feels a lack of competence. But it is precisely that lack of expertise that may allow the Court to introduce the touch of general influence so desirable in an increasingly specialized field. The Court seems to be in an excellent tactical position to perform this task.

First, the generalist who enters a technical field often becomes more and more engrossed in technical problems. As we have already noted, this gradual specialization is one of the principal problems of Congress, which keeps assigning groups of its generalists to watch the bureaucrats through the committee system only to have the committees evolve special policy views of their own, which they then press on Congress. The Court is not only inexpert, but the Justices have so much work to do in other fields that they never can become expert. They will always perforce bring a wide range of political and legal concerns to their tax decisions.

Second, the adversary system provides a unique advantage for generalists attempting to see through the expert's tactic of disguising his policy preferences as statements of technical fact. Here again the problem in Congress is that, having been assigned a technical field, the committee tends to become the larger body's sole source of advice in that field.[137] The Court, because it has the opportunity of hearing argument by two opposing technicians, is not the prisoner of either.

In this connection too must be viewed the frequent objection that the Court cannot venture ambitious supervision of the executive or independent regulatory agencies because it cannot and should not attempt to match their staff and research resources. Surely the very basis of the adversary system is that it forces the parties to provide the Court with the research results necessary for informed decisions. In a very meaningful sense, the Court always has at its disposal in a given case more and better staff resources than does the I.R.S. For it has the Service staff plus the taxpayer's staff to provide it with the raw materials for decision. That the two provide only partial and conflicting views is so much the better for the generalist attempting to avoid technical domination. In this sense, the Court gets a better staff product than does the Commissioner, who hears only his career subordinates.

Third, the Court has its own armor of expertise. Frequently the layman must accept expert advice not so much because he believes it but because, in terms of practical politics, he cannot afford to risk acting against the advice of "the man who knows." "On advice of counsel," "my doctor warns," and more recently "but the engineers told me" or "the lab boys said" are powerful weapons for both offense and defense in the political and social arena. The layman, needing these weapons, must often obey the expert.

But tax law is tax *law*. The Supreme Court has a perhaps diminished, but still considerable, reputation as an authoritative interpreter of law. The I.R.S. may be the expert on taxes, but the Court is the expert on law. The Court has its own prestige as a "man who knows" to balance that of the technicians with whom it deals.

Here again the Court seems to be in a somewhat better position than its fellow generalist, Congress. When the I.R.S. says, "we know taxes," the Court says, "we know law," and law is surely more respected than taxes in this country. When the I.R.S. says "we know taxes," the Congress can reply only "we know politics," and this reply puts Congress at a disadvantage, for Americans apparently believe that taxes should have nothing to do with politics.[138]

To suggest a more active role for the Supreme Court in the tax policy-making process may be somewhat startling to some people, for it calls up a vision of Court *versus* Congress as rival lawmakers. Such a vision is startling, however, only because it is oversimple. The lawmaking process is complex. Surely the reply to the question, "Who makes law?" is not, "Congress and Congress only." Any elementary study of American government begins with the proposition that the executive branch is the source of most legislation. The bureaucracy drafts the bills that compose the President's legislative program, and Presidential support or opposition is a key factor in determining whether or not any program becomes law. For that matter, pressure-group influences shape and may even determine the inclusion or exclusion of many provisions of many laws. Furthermore, it has become a commonplace that those who are responsible for administering a statute after its passage have much influence over its final meaning and impact. And surely we need not here go through that whole ancient and tedious battle about whether judges make law or simply discover it. I know of no school of jurisprudence or student of law who does not concede that judges do and inevitably must make law.

To say that any governmental or indeed private group does or ought to make law simply means that it makes law *with* Congress and not necessarily *against* it. Congress never makes law by itself. It acts under the influence of many outsiders. The suggestion that other agencies enter the lawmaking process does not imply that such agencies dictate solutions to legislative problems but means only that they add their preferences for certain policy goals to those of others in the internal-revenue field. Each naturally develops an institutional interest in a particular goal. As long as Congress and the Service are alone in the field, therefore, the sum total of the tax policy-making process may yield a greater emphasis on revenue than on such other goals of Congress as encouragement of investment. The Supreme Court might well act in this area, as it is urged to do in so many others, as balancer of competing interests. It need not and probably should not develop a rigid tax philosophy of its own, but it should instead seek to intervene by righting the balance of the various interests to which Congress is generally responsive whenever some of these interests become obscured in the process of administering and altering tax policy.

Finally, it would be the height of absurdity to counsel Supreme

Court withdrawal from policy-making because of some naive theory that only Congress should make law, when the result of such withdrawal would be more policy-making by an agency that, according to the same theory, has even less right to make law than have the courts—the I.R.S. If any conflict emerges from introducing the Supreme Court into tax policy-making, it is likely to be that of the Supreme Court *versus* I.R.S. as rival interpreters of Congressional statutes. I cannot see how this conflict would be incompatible with even the most naive and uninformed view of Congressional supremacy in the legislative process.

There is, then, a great deal to be said for greater Supreme Court activity in the tax field. By its withdrawal from that field, the Court has created a political vacuum. Perhaps if the Supreme Court will not fill it, a court of tax appeals should. At the moment, it is the I.R.S. that seems to have expanded into the empty territory.

¶ Conclusion

In any event, the Court must come to understand that its hands-off policy does not simply keep the Justices out of the tax policy-making process. There is no neutrality in politics. Retreat by one party inevitably helps some and hurts others of the remaining contestants. Of course it may be that the Court's present policy preferences are so in harmony with those of the I.R.S. that its retreat makes some political sense. But because the Court cannot, as the legal system is presently constituted, entirely escape tax chores, its present hesitant attitude imparts a confusion and vagueness to the corpus of tax law that appear undesirable in terms of the Court's general institutional interest in the quality of the legal system. Even if the Court's retreat is a calculated move to help the Service, and I think it is stretching the imagination to say so, it would still therefore seem more desirable to help the Service by mild but steady action than by inaction broken by sporadic activity under pressure from conflicts on the Circuits.

More practically, the lawyer preparing tax cases with a view toward appellate-court decision might do well occasionally to look above and beyond the technicalities of the matter before him to the general pattern of Court activity. At the moment, he seems most likely to win those cases in which decision for his clients would allow the Court to avoid legal and factual complexities or rule-making or in which decisions for the Service would deeply involve the Court in tax policy-making. Such, for better or worse, is the present position of the Warren Court.

5

The Supreme Court as Lawyer, Political Theorist, and Political Scientist: *Baker v. Carr* and After

IT IS DIFFICULT to see how a book about the politics of the Supreme Court could be written today without a discussion of *Baker v. Carr,*[1] which has made the phrase "political question" a common term in Constitutional discussions and has projected the Court into a problem—the apportionment of state legislative districts—that is eminently political in the best, worst, and indeed every sense of that word.

Was the Court bound by its past experience to avoid intervention in the apportionment problem? Was its decision to intervene an improper exercise of judicial power? Having decided to act, did it choose actions compatible in form and content with the exigencies of American politics in general and the Court's position in particular? We shall deal with these problems in this chapter.

In *Baker v. Carr,* the Supreme Court held that federal courts might properly hear and decide cases in which it was alleged that the right to vote was being abridged because some legislative districts were considerably larger than others. The case arose in Tennessee, which had not been redistricted since 1901 and where districts varied so much in population that a vote in one county was equal to nineteen in another. Justice Frankfurter protested that, no matter what the abstract rights and wrongs, the whole issue presented a "political question," that is a kind of question that the Court had traditionally and rightly refused to decide.

One might begin by dismissing the whole problem as based on a false distinction between "political" and "judicial." Indeed, this verbal formulation is derived from an incorrect or at least rhetorical notion of separation between politics and law. All Constitutional questions, indeed nearly all questions handled by the Supreme Court, are political. But it would be fruitless to stop at facile criticism of an unfortunate choice of adjective. The formula should probably read "question not properly soluble by courts," but "political question" has been hallowed by long usage and signifies a real problem, which cannot therefore be disposed of by semantics.

Justice Frankfurter argued that, if the Court were to grapple with the issue of malapportionment, it would be dragged into a mass of partisan politics and conflicting political theories that courts would do better to avoid. There is no naive distinction, no empty formalism here but rather a real warning to a real court about a real problem. *Baker v. Carr* does present a "political question." Does it, however, present a political question that the Court cannot answer, or, is it like so many other questions, one for which the Court should supply a politically prudent answer?

¶ The "Political Questions" Doctrine

It seems best to begin at the beginning, with the origin and nature of the "political questions" doctrine and the treatment of previous election cases by the Supreme Court, in order to discover precisely how far the Court was bound by precedent and past experience at the time it chose to decide *Baker*. Not only may experience be an intrinsically useful guide, but also a Court confronted with the necessity of openly breaking with a fixed and previously controlling doctrine is in a far different position, and I speak of political position, than one that writes on a clean or ambiguous slate. This difference is particularly evident when the decision is likely to stir the winds of controversy. Doctrine and precedent may be too dear to lawyers and lawyer-instructed public, but, as long as they are cherished, they are potent political weapons as well. Indeed it may be the nicely hallowed ring of "political questions," rather than the substance of the doctrine itself that makes it politically significant.

The history of the "political questions" doctrine is familiar to every student of Constitutional law. It merits at least a brief discussion in all the texts and casebooks. Yet there has been little serious independent study of the doctrine: a single monograph and a handful of articles prior to the *Baker* decision.[2] Perhaps this paucity is owing to the fact that there has been only a handful of cases in which the doctrine has been invoked. One thing the cases and commentary do reveal clearly, however, is that the doctrine lacks clarity. Definition is certainly possible. For instance, Hart and Wechsler say, "every question about official action which is not a judicial question is a political question in the sense that it is a question to be decided by one or the other of the political departments of government, or by the electorate."[3] But the definitions tend to circularity. Political questions are those that the Court refuses to decide, and whatever the Court refuses to decide is a political question. This circularity could be broken if some discernible pattern were to emerge from the cases, that is, if the definition were not constructed *a priori* but built up, in the traditional way, by analysis of the decisions in wihch the phrase appears. It must be said in advance that such analysis yields only a crazy-quilt structure, but it is the only structure we have or are likely to get.

SUBJECT MATTER

The simplest classification of the "political questions" cases is by subject matter. As long as we look only to the gross subject categories and not to the particular issues or internal rationales of the cases, an almost satisfactorily distinct boundary between political and other cases seems to emerge. The broadest of these subject categories is that of relations between nation and nation. The Court refuses to decide on questions of recognition of foreign governments.[4] Nor will it decide on the diplomatic status of foreign envoys or whether or not foreign governments have been empowered to make the agreements they have made with the United States.[5] The Court will not determine international boundaries.[6] It will not independently determine when a state of war was commenced or terminated.[7] It will not, in general, interpret treaties.

Trouble begins to appear in these last two categories, however. In setting the beginning or ending date of a war, the Court relies on Congressional or Presidential pronouncement. When such pronouncements are not clear, the Court must perforce take some initiative. For instance, in 1861, President Lincoln issued a blockade proclamation. When Congress convened three months later, it passed legislation approving the President's acts and taking various other steps to put down the rebellion. In *The Protector,*[8] the Court had to determine whether or not a state of war had existed in the months between proclamation and statute. Although Congress, rather than the President, has the power to declare war, and although Congress had never specifically defined the proclamation date as the beginning of hostilities, the proclamation was interpreted by the Court as announcing the commencement of the war. The Court thus does in some instances exercise discretion on this question.

Similarly, the Justices do not exclude themselves entirely from the interpretation of treaties. The Court will not interpret or seek to enforce treaties in which such public rights as sovereignty over territory are involved. It will interpret treaties in order to enforce private rights arising from them. Whether public or private rights are involved, however, it will not determine the validity of a treaty or seek to enforce it against alleged abrogations or violations by the United States government.[9]

By a process of rough analogy, the Supreme Court has taken the same hands-off attitude toward certain other subjects as it has taken toward the relations between nations. One of the "political questions" areas has always been Indian affairs. The first important "political questions" case was *The Cherokee Nation v. Georgia.*[10] The Indians sought to enjoin the Georgia legislature from enforcing Georgia law in tribal territory. Although the decision technically rests on another ground, Justice Marshall viewed the dispute as one between the sovereign State of Georgia and a neighboring power—the tribe—both seking to exercise sovereignty over the same territory. He refused to intervene in this clash of sovereignties. In a separate opinion, Justice Johnson cited this doctrine as the principal ground of decision.

Subsequently, the Court has also refused to intervene in disputes between the tribes and the federal government. The actual doctrinal situation is a bit obscure, but this obscurity reflects the oddity of the facts. The tribes are not actually sovereign nations enjoying traditional treaty relations with the United States. The Court has been careful not to say that they were. Nor, on the other hand, are they simply collections of regular citizens like Lions Clubs. While there has been much talk of wardship, the Court has in effect treated the tribes as quasi-nations in quasi-treaty relations with the United States. Disputes between tribes and national government are thus disputes between nations rather than between citizens and *their* government and are thus defined as "political" rather than "legal." As the Court will not interfere with the political branches' alleged violations of a treaty with China, so it will not interfere with their alleged violations of tribal rights. Indeed this attitude was evident as early as the *Cherokee* case, in which Justice Johnson suggested that it was up to the political branches of the government to decide whether or not they wished to allow violations of the treaties they had entered into with the Indians.

The analogy of "inter-national" relations, in the root meaning of that term, has also been carried over into the area of relations between state and state and between state and nation. In *Luther v. Borden,*[11] the primary "political questions" case, the Court refused either to recognize or to withhold recognition of a given government of Rhode Island—precisely as it would have refused to decide for itself whether or not to recognize a given government of Peru. In *Pacific Telephone v. Oregon,*[12] the plaintiff urged that Oregon's constitutional provisions for initiative and referendum were in violation of the federal Constitution. The Court argued that such a finding would in effect destroy the legal status of the existing government of Oregon. The Justices would not allow themselves to be put in the position of giving or withdrawing recognition from state governments. Both these cases arose under the Constitutional clause guaranteeing a republican form of government. It might be clearer simply to say that republican form is an independent subject heading within the "political questions" category. But it seems to me that *Luther* and *Pacific Telephone* are also to be viewed as parts of a series of "state as quasi-sovereign nation" cases. For the Court is being asked to decide whether or not a specific government is the *de facto* or *de jure* government of the state in question. The Court was asked to perform the same task in *Georgia v. Staunton,*[13] in which the government of Georgia sued for an injunction against enforcement of the Reconstruction Acts, which would have destroyed the existing government and replaced it with another. The Court refused. When the question was whether or not to "totally abolish the existing state government," the Court would not act.

A year later, in *Texas v. White,*[14] the Court had to determine whether or not the provisional government of Texas was capable of suing in a federal court, that is, whether Texas was a state or not. The Court found that it could not make an independent judgment on such a question. Unfortunately, this case is another one of those instances in which the "political questions" doctrine becomes blurred at the edges. The Court professed to follow Congress's judgment on the existence or absence of "stateness" in Texas. It seized upon some legislative ambiguities to decide that Congress had decided that Texas was a state when, as Justice Greer pointed out in his dissent, Congress had decided exactly to the contrary. Here the letter of the "political questions" doctrine is present, but the spirit falters.

To round out our picture of the relation of political questions to the notion of states as sovereigns, a few more cases should be mentioned. The Court will not deal with retrocession of federal territory to a state.[15] In *Rhode Island v. Massachusetts,*[16] Justice Taney dissented from a decision adjusting the boundaries between the two states on the grounds that the Court might not enter into disputes about the reach of sovereignty. And, in *Georgia v. Staunton,* the Court was particularly careful to hold that Taney would have been correct if boundary questions were actually questions of sovereignty. The majority had been correct in *Rhode Island,* Justice Nelson argued, because such questions concerned property not sovereignty.

Two final areas must be mentioned. In *Field v. Clark,*[17] the Court refused to decide whether or not the wording of the statute in question, as it appeared in the statute books, corresponded with the version passed by the Congress. And, in *Coleman v. Miller,*[18] the Court would not indicate whether a time limit on state ratification of Constitutional amendments was necessary or not. Here again, however, the subject matter is not completely immune from court jurisdiction. The Court has decided on the merits that the two-thirds-vote requirement for proposal of amendments means two-thirds of those present,[19] that Congress can impose a time limit if it chooses,[20] and that Congress can choose between the state-legislature or the convention mode of ratification.[21] But, in all these cases, the Court's decisions are permissive toward Congress. The Justices seem to be saying that, while they will interpret a law or a Constitutional provision and will even declare an existing law unconstitutional, they will not question or refuse to recognize the existence of a law or amendment acknowledged by the other branches, and they will not refuse to recognize a foreign government similarly acknowledged.

With the possible exception of this last subject category, the Court had, before *Colegrove v. Green,* employed the "political questions" doctrine only when dealing with the relations of sovereign or quasi-sovereign bodies to one another. As a court of domestic jurisdiction, the Supreme Court will interpret and review laws, but it takes the laws as given. Even when it declares a law unconstitutional, there is no question that it was a law. That is, because its job is to interpret and to adjust laws *within* an established legal system, it will not decide which of the two legal systems is the established one. Nor will it decide which of two sovereigns should prevail, for their relationship to each other is outside any one given legal system.[22] This theme is present even in the enactment cases. The Court will decide how to administer a given statute or Constitutional provision, but it will not question the "givenness" of laws and amendments. An analysis of the subject matter of "political questions" cases therefore suggests that "political" for the Court means basically not the interpretation and Constitutional review of laws but the very existence of laws or legal systems.

POLITICAL RIGHTS, POLITICAL POWERS, AND POLITICAL QUESTIONS

Robert Hale, in his book *Freedom Through Law,*[23] provides another analysis that sheds considerable light on the "political questions" doctrine. He finds three separate categories: political rights, political powers, and political questions. The Court sometimes refuses decisions not because the questions must be decided by others but because the rights alleged are political. In the *Cherokee* case, for example, both Justices Thompson and Johnson argued that the rights alleged by the Cherokees were not personal or property rights but rights of sovereignty. Indeed, all the issues raised in the *Cherokee* cases were decided shortly thereafter in *Worcester v. Georgia,*[24] in which the question was presented in the more conventional guise of conflict between federal and state jurisdiction. Similarly, the Court, in *Georgia v. Staunton,* stressed that Georgia claimed rights "not of persons or property, but of a political character . . ." In *Rhode Island v. Massachusetts,* Taney argued that, if the question of boundary had arisen in the context of a suit over ownership of land, the Court could have decided it. And the majority did decide the question in that case because it interpreted the problem as one of rival property claims.

Sometimes, according to Hale, the problem is that the Court is asked to exercise what it considers to be political rather than legal power. Justice Marshall in the *Cherokee* case was reluctant to enjoin the whole operation of Georgia government because "It savors too much of the exercise of political power to be within the proper power of the judicial department."[25] In *Pacific Telephone,* Justice White argued that a ruling against Oregon would require the Court to construct a new government for the state—an action manifestly beyond its powers.

Finally, Hale argues that some cases involve true political questions, in the sense of questions that branches of government other than the Court are Constitutionally assigned to answer. The best example is *Luther v. Borden.*[26] As that case was a trespass-damage suit, the right claimed was private and the remedy requested well within the normal jurisdiction of courts. It was the question of which government was the real government that could not be decided by the Court because such questions are Constitutionally within the scopes of Congress and the Executive.

Political questions, as opposed to political rights or powers, seem closely allied to the "separation of powers" concept. Most of the political questions that the Court has refused to decide have concerned foreign policy, which has always been considered peculiarly an Executive and Congressional, rather than a judicial, matter. And the Court early decided that the founders had intended enforcement of the "republican form of government" clause to be left exclusively to Congress and the President.

AN ARMORY OF ARGUMENTS

Indeed, separation of powers has been one of the principal weapons in the armory of rationales that the Court has employed in defending the "political questions" doctrine. It is necessary to sketch these rationales briefly because they keep popping up in the reapportionment cases. We are not now dealing with subject areas or Professor Hale's categories but with certain lines of argument showing why the Court cannot decide certain cases. This distinction may seem somewhat artificial. It is a convenient one, however, because it helps to explain *Colegrove v. Green,*[27] in which Justice Frankfurter tried to extend the "political questions" doctrine into a new subject area by using the old rationales.

The same set of arguments keeps reappearing. Nearly all these arguments are used in the leading case, *Luther v. Borden.* They can most easily be illustrated by the Court's argument there. As *Luther* involves private property rights, however, one argument frequently used to excuse Court inactivity could not be employed —the notion that the Court will deal only with personal rights and not with sovereign prerogatives. It must be added, of course, that this argument is not well founded. The Court has constantly dealt with a whole range of states' rights under the supremacy, interstate-commerce, and taxing clauses, not to mention the Fourteenth Amendment.

Turning to *Luther* itself, we find Justice Taney ringing most of the available changes.[28] The first is that, where there is no existing rule of decision, the question is political because "It is the province of a court to expound the law, not to make it."[29] Simply to expound this position is to refute it. Surely, the Court fashions many of its own rules and makes some of its own law. Under the canons of judicial modesty, the absence of rules or standards may be grounds for avoiding a decision, but such absence does not define an area as absolutely beyond judicial authority.

Taney then uses the "separation of powers" approach. He finds in the "republican form of government" clause a Constitutional assignment of the question before him to Congress and, by its delegation, to the President, whose decision is binding on the Court.

One of Taney's most telling points rests on expedience. "The ordinary course of proceedings in courts of justice would be utterly unfit for the crisis" of armed clash between two rivals for state power.[30] Many expediential arguments have been made in connection with the "political questions" cases. Most have concerned what Professor Hale calls the "political power" segment of the doctrine. The Justices have sometimes given expression to their fears that the President or state legislatures simply would not obey the Court, that in practice the Court could find no remedy. There would therefore be little use in deciding the question. This line of argument can hardly define the boundaries of political questions. A great many judicial decisions are not self-enforcing. If the Court labeled every question "political" in which it depended upon the Executive or the states to carry out or not actively to oppose its mandate, it would have almost no judicial business left to do. And the question of whether or not a suitable, as opposed to an enforceable, remedy can be found is a routine one for courts of equity jurisdiction and is therefore not of much use in setting the boundaries of the "political questions" doctrine.

There is, in addition, an argument (touched upon by Taney) that combines separation of powers, expedience, and the notion that the Supreme Court is a court of last resort. The Court, so it is argued, will decide only cases in which its decisions are final. In cases concerning foreign affairs or the republican form of government, the "political" branches would feel themselves entitled to independent judgments even subsequent to Supreme Court opinions. The Congress might choose not to seat representatives from states that the Court had ruled met the "republican form" requirement. The President might recognize governments to which the Court had refused recognition. The Court will not decide cases in which its decisions are subject to review by Congress or the President. The difficulty with this position is that it rests on an assumption of decisional finality that is simply not applicable to American experience. The Congressional and Presidential reversals of the Court usually offered as illustrations differ only slightly in degree and certainly not at all in kind from a whole range of powers Congress and the President have and constantly exercise to reverse, thwart, modify, and evade Supreme Court decisions. Ultimately, of course, under our Constitutional system of checks and balances, each branch has the power to frustrate the others totally by carrying its prerogatives to their logical extremes. More important, American politics is an endless process and not a series of discreet *tableaux*. Only the most barren Constitutional formalism could evade the discovery that Supreme Court decisions are simply thrown into the hopper with myriad other decisions by other agencies of government, all of which interact mutually to modify one another. If the Court were to decide only those cases in which its decisions would be final, it would decide few cases indeed.

I have perhaps taken too broad a view of finality. It may be that "final" means only the last and binding decision on a given set of facts and between specific parties. But under this definition, even the most "political" of the Court's decisions would often be final. Certainly *Luther v. Borden* would have been. The finality argument refers, it seems to me, not to the specific disposition of the case at issue but to the finality of the broader findings involved. Once beyond immediate disposition, we are simply in a world of degrees where court decisions are only more or less final—and usually less.

The element of expedience is often generalized by outside commentators, although not by the Justices, into a definition of "political questions" as those that are simply "too hot to handle." It is difficult to see how this quality can be viewed as either necessary or sufficient for a definition of "political questions." The Court labels "political" a decision on who owns the Falkland Islands for purposes of settling a marine insurance claim or on whether or not Nebraska has ratified the Child Labor Amendment, but it does decide cases like *Dred Scott,* the income tax case, the school segregation cases, and *Dennis v. United States*. It may well be true that the Court has occasionally used the "political questions" doctrine as one of its many devices for avoiding "hot ones," but it is impossible to predict whether questions are or are not going to be labeled "political" by comparing their fever charts.

The one point at which expediency does seem to serve a definitive function for the doctrine is in the foreign-affairs area. While bows are made to the separation of powers, almost the entire area of foreign relations has been assigned exclusively to the political branches by the Court because of the inexpedience of speaking to other nations with two potentially conflicting voices.

Running through the whole catalogue of arguments or rationales connected with the "political questions" doctrine, one finds several that are logical. But no one or combination provides the necessary or sufficient qualities of a political question, with the possible exception of the "separation of powers" principle. It is possible to show that several of these arguments occur frequently in "political questions" cases. It is not possible to say that, whenever one or two or all of these arguments apply, the Court has consistently labeled the question "political."

THE "POLITICAL QUESTIONS" DOCTRINE IN *Colegrove v. Green*

It is against this background that Justice Frankfurter's opinion in *Colegrove v. Green*[31] must be considered. His problem was a difficult one. The subject matter of the case did not fall within the traditional categories for political questions. It was not a question of foreign relations or of the existence of a statute or Constitutional amendment. Unless one were to argue that declaring a state apportionment arrangement unconstitutional would destroy the legitimacy of the last elected legislature, there is no question of recognition of or mediation between quasi-sovereigns. No Justice has seriously suggested that a finding against a given apportionment would have such repercussions for the sitting legislature. Indeed, *Colegrove* seems to fall completely outside the kind of sovereignty, "inter-national" relations, and recognition subject areas that are traditionally associated with the doctrine. It is simply a request that a single domestic law of a single state be found unconstitutional as applied to the citizens of that state. The case arises *within* a legal system that includes the Fourteenth Amendment and its power to control state law, a system taken as given by all parties. Justice Frankfurter cannot therefore simply rely on precedent. He must manage to bring the "political questions" doctrine into a subject area distinct and quite different from those to which it had previously been applied.

Professor Hale's categories also indicate Justice Frankfurter's difficulties. Colegrove was not seeking vindication of political rights. To be sure, he asked for the right to vote. But the "political" in "political questions" refers not to the political process but to political, as opposed to private or individual, rights. Public, sovereign, or governmental rights are "political" if any are. Colegrove's rights are his personal rights; they are not comparable to the right of Georgia to control the Indians or of Spain to cede Florida. Nor is the question one of political power. The Court was not asked to enjoin the state as a state or its entire legal system or to demand that the United States government live up to its treaty obligations. The injunction is to be directed at a few state officials in conjunction with their duties under a single state law—surely a routine exercise of judical power.

Frankfurter's one source of comfort is in Hale's third category—pure political questions. The Court might argue that the question of what constitutes proper apportionment is not one that it can decide. But when the Court has invoked the "pure questions" doctrine, it has usually done so under the "separation of powers" rubric. It cannot decide because the Constitution has specifically given the power of decision to one or both of the other independent and coequal branches of the national government. *Colegrove* involves Congressional districts, and the Constitution grants Congress control of its own membership and elections:

> "The Time, Places and Manner of holding elections for . . . Representatives, shall be prescribed in each state by the legislature thereof; but the Congress may at any time by law make or alter such regulations, . . ." (Art. I, Sec. 4.) "Each House shall be the judge of the elections, returns and qualifications of its members, . . ." (Art. I, Sec. 5.)

A simple grant of power to Congress, however—even a most explicit one like "The Congress shall have power . . . to regulate commerce . . . among the several states, . . ." (Art. I, Sec. 8)—does not put the exercise of that power beyond Court supervision. The argument used in *Luther* and elsewhere is that, in certain instances, the Constitution has vested the decision of Constitutional questions in Congress *rather than in the Court*. The Constitutional provisions do not specifically assign election questions to Congress as opposed to the Court. More important, the Fifteenth Amendment has always been read to authorize Supreme

Court intervention in both federal and state elections, so that, whatever the founding fathers may have meant, the power of decision on the Constitutionality of Congressional elections is not now vested exclusively in Congress. If the "equal protection" clause of the Fourteenth Amendment is read to include voting rights, it too presumably allows the Court the same powers of decision over Congressional elections as the Fifteenth Amendment does. When Article I provisions are read in conjunction with the Fourteenth and Fifteenth Amendments, Congress's power over its own elections does not seem to include exclusive authority to decide all election questions. Like most of its other powers, it is only the power to legislate subject to judicial review. It might as well be said now that the "separation of powers" argument cannot be brought to the support of the "pure political questions" category in *Baker v. Carr,* which involves only state legislative districts. Without that support, Hale's third category is an even weaker reed for Frankfurter, *et al.*

Frankfurter's basic tactic in *Colegrove* was to offer as many as possible of the traditional rationales linked with the "political questions" doctrine, in order to support an extension of the doctrine to an entirely new area, that of apportionment. First, the Justice seeks to convince us that the right involved is political not private. "The basis for the suit is not a private wrong, but a wrong suffered by Illinois as a polity."[32] The difficulty is, of course, that the Court had long since ruled that the right to vote and to have one's vote counted is a personal right guaranteed by the Constitution.[33] It may be true that the "real" motive of Colegrove is to insure that urban interests are "adequately represented in the councils of the nation."[34] But what he is specifically asking is that he personally be "adequately represented." While there may be some eventual impact on Illinois's rights, as a polity, the case itself involves only Colegrove's rights as an individual voter.

To be sure, this argument is more formal than substantial. There are undoubtedly far broader issues here than one man's right to have his vote counted equally with other votes. The rights are those of urban and suburban elements in Illinois. The rights of political groups or classes of citizens are often adjudicated in courts when they can be represented by one member of a given class—as they can be here. The only state right involved is that of Illinois to discriminate among various classes of its citizens. That right is not related to the basic existence of the state as a quasi-sovereign or to its relations to other quasi-sovereigns. It is therefore not a political right within the scope of the "political questions" doctrine. The issue is one of routine adjudication; has the state used its powers to deprive individuals of rights guaranteed them by the Constitution?

Justice Frankfurter goes on to an argument of expedience. The Court cannot reapportion Illinois. All it can do is to declare the existing apportionment invalid and, in the absence of action by the Illinois legislature, to force the state into elections at large.

> The upshot of judicial action may defeat the vital principle which led Congress, more than a hundred years ago, to require districting. This requirement, in the language of Chancellor Kent, "was recommended by the wisdom and justice of giving, as far as possible, to the local subdivisions of the people of each state, a due influence in the choice of representatives, so as not to leave the aggregate minority of the people in a state, though approaching perhaps to a majority, to be wholly overpowered by the combined action of the numerical majority, without any voice whatever in the national councils."[35]

But this argument proves too much. Distaste for elections at large is so great that it seems certain that legislative action would not be absent. The inexpedience anticipated is so inexpedient that it is unlikely to occur.

There follows a hint of the "courts-only-make-final-decisions" rationale. The House might refuse to seat members elected at large. We have already seen that this rationale is not very sound in itself. It is doubly unsound when linked to the twin improbabilities that the state would elect at large and that the House would refuse to seat an entire state delegation to Congress. Even if all these improbabilities came to pass, there would still be no situation in which the Court and one of the political branches had taken opposite positions on the same question. The House would simply have decided that election at large was invalid—not that the old apportionment was valid. This situation would be quite different from one in which the Court might say that the Falkland Islands belonged to Argentina while the President claimed they belonged to Britain.

Then comes the attempt to mix the "political" of "political questions" with the "political" of "party politics," which Justice Black's dissent labels as "mere play upon words."[36]

> "Nothing is clearer than that this controversy concerns matters that bring courts into immediate and active relations with party contests. . . . The one stark fact that emerges from a study of the history of Congressional apportionment is its embroilment in politics, in the sense of party contests and party interests. . . . Courts ought not to enter this political thicket."[37]

Of course, the one clear fact that emerges from a study of the history of the "political questions" doctrine is that "political" refers to public bodies and their relations to one another and not to party politics. We shall note presently that the Court had begun to interfere in party politics long before *Colegrove.*

I have left for last Justice Frankfurter's strongest argument, that of separation of powers:

> Authority for dealing with such problems resides elsewhere. Article I, Sec. 4 of the Constitution provides that "The Times, Places and Manner of holding Elections for . . . Representatives, shall be prescribed at any time by Law make or alter such Regulations, . . ." The short of it is that the Constitution has conferred upon Congress exclusive authority to secure representation by the States in the popular House and left to that House determination whether States have fulfilled their responsibility.[38]

That may be the short of it. The long is somewhat different. If the House were to refuse to seat members, for any reason or for no reason, the Court might well call the question "political" in the sense of being assigned entirely to the political branches. Congress's power to regulate the time, place, and manner of elections is not, however, a "sovereign" power of the House to determine its own membership but simply one of its powers of legislation. Like its other legislative functions, this one is subject to judicial review. Congress's power to pass election laws no more displaces judicial review in this area than its power to pass laws prohibiting subversion displaces judicial review in that area. Surely if Congress were to pass a law requiring a different literacy test for whites than for Negroes, the Supreme Court would invoke the

Fifth Amendment and would not simply dismiss the question as "political." If the Court can exercise Constitutional supervision over Congressional election laws, it surely can do the same for the states. There is no specific grant of exclusive supervision over state election practice to Congress in Art. I, Sec. 4, nor is there anything to suggest that the Court is debarred from normal Constitutional supervision of state laws.

Having run through Justice Frankfurter's arguments in *Colegrove,* we must surely conclude that his case is "not proved." He has given us many reasons why the Court might wish to avoid decision in this case. In fact, he has given us one of his famous essays in judicial modesty, complete with democratic appeal from the autocratic courts direct to the people.

> "It is hostile to a democratic system to involve the judiciary in the politics of the people . . . The Constitution has left the performance of many duties in our governmental scheme to depend on the fidelity of the executive and legislative action and, ultimately, on the vigilance of the people in exercising their political rights."[39]

But an appeal, even a very convincing appeal, to judicial modesty does not constitute a successful invocation of the "political questions" doctrine. For the "political questions" doctrine goes far beyond mere judicial modesty. A Court may presume the Constitutionality of a statute, may go to great lengths of statutory interpretation to avoid a Constitutional issue, may rest its findings on procedural rather than substantive grounds, and so forth. But all these tactics are discretionary, and the Court's option to go to the Constitutional heart of the matter the next time around without contradicting its own previous position, is not diminished. Such modesty appears in many Constitutional areas in which the Court nevertheless recognizes justiciable issues and questions as ones that it must decide. Modesty has been most in evidence in connection with the First Amendment, which the Court has never treated as political. In any kind of case, a Justice may be justified in urging caution or even avoidance of decision after he has looked into the issues. Invocation of the "political questions" doctrine, however, is an attempt to erect judicial caution into an abstract dogma. Justice Frankfurter did not plead that, in this particular case, considering all the circumstances and the Court's power and institutional capabilities, it would be best not to act. He declared that then and from then on the Court should not ever be able even to look at, let alone to decide, this whole category of cases.

In invoking the "political questions" doctrine, Frankfurter, having decided that it was unwise for the Court to decide *Colegrove,* sought to elevate his decision into a binding principle to prevent all later Courts from deciding whether or not they wished to decide such cases. That is why it is not enough to say that the definition of "political questions" is circular. What the Court will not decide is a political question, and a political question is one that the Court will not decide. This statement may embody all that the doctrine really means. But it is not all the doctrine pretends to mean, and it may be the pretense that counts. If Justice Frankfurter could have fastened the pretense of the "political questions" doctrine on the apportionment question, he would have done much more to bind the Court to his particular modest outlook than he could have done by simply convincing the Court to adopt one of the more routine rationales of judicial modesty. He would have committed the Court to the same modesty in all future cases as it adopted in *Colegrove.*

If there is any content at all to the concept of political question, *Colegrove* does not seem to fall within it. Districting is not within the traditional subject areas of political questions. The arguments that Frankfurter proffers in order to raise the problem of *Colegrove* into a new political question may provide good reasons for judicial caution. But he cannot distinguish electoral matters sufficiently from the normal run of Court business to qualify them for the special and rarely used category of political questions. At the very best, there can only be a draw on logical grounds. One side may argue that, when the Court tampers with the mode by which the lawmakers are chosen, it does not take the law or the legal system as given but questions the very foundations of the legal system and the legitimacy of government. The other replies that the electoral laws are laws like any other laws, that voting rights are Constitutional rights like other rights, and that the general powers or sovereignty of the existing government are not at issue. It seems to me that the burden of proof lies with those who wish to extend a questionable and ill defined Constitutional doctrine into a new area. The challenge has not been met.

¶ The Elections Cases

That it has not been met becomes even clearer after viewing *Colegrove* in the context of the series of cases before *Baker v. Carr* in which the Supreme Court concerned itself with elections. An examination of these decisions indicates that the Court has never treated election cases as political within the meaning of the "political questions" doctrine.

THE WHITE-PRIMARY CASES

The white-primary decisions provide the clearest example of judicial supervision of the franchise. In a series of opinions,[40] the Court met and overthrew one device after another for excluding Negroes from effective voting rights in the southern states. Not only did the Court find that primary-voting rights are entitled to the same protection as voting in general elections, but it also refused to exempt the Democratic Party itself from regulation, no matter how carefully the Party had been separated from the state government. The Court ruled that exclusion of Negro voters from either primary or regular elections by either state government or party action is unconstitutional. These decisions, which began long before *Colegrove* and continued after it, never invoked the "political questions" doctrine, even though the Court was concerning itself with both state electoral laws and the internal workings of state political parties. The fact that it had to involve itself in party politics did not lead the Court to sacrifice Negro voting rights to the "political questions" doctrine.

The Supreme Court has also ruled in connection with Congressional elections that Art. I, Secs. 2 and 4 secure the "right of qualified voters to vote . . . and to have their ballots counted. . . ."[41] Furthermore, the Court has held that the dilution of the vote resulting from ballot-box-stuffing violates that Constitutional right.[42] Generally then, there is no question that the Court treats the right to vote as a Constitutionally protected right and, more important, one that will be protected by the courts.

EARLY APPORTIONMENT CASES

Apportionment or districting, however, represents a special category within the subject category of elections and voting. It is therefore necessary to describe the Court's treatment of such cases both before *Colegrove* and in the period between *Colegrove* and *Baker v. Carr*.

The first case is *Smiley v. Holm.*[43] The Minnesota legislature had passed a Congressional redistricting bill. The governor vetoed the bill, and the legislature ordered the Secretary of State to enforce it despite the veto. A voter petitioned the federal courts for an injunction directing the Secretary of State not to hold elections under the vetoed bill. He alleged that the bill was a nullity and that the proposed districts violated the Congressional Apportionment Act of 1911, which required such districts to be compact and to "contain an equal number of inhabitants as nearly as practicable." The Secretary of State demurred on three grounds: first, that Art. I, Sec. 4 of the Constitution was intended to place responsibility for districting in the legislature alone; second, that the Act of 1911 was no longer in force; and third, that "the asserted inequalities in redistricting presented a political and not a judicial question."

The Court decided the case solely on the veto issue. It held that Art. I, Sec. 4 intended that the legislature fix time, place, and manner by law. As long as the state constitution provided that a legislative act did not become a valid law without the Governor's signature, the redistricting bill was not valid. As the districting act was thus held to be a nullity, the Court specifically refused to examine issues of the size or shape of the districts established under the act. Questions of the applicability of the Act of 1911 were held to be abstract, for no districts, equal or otherwise, legally existed. The "political questions" doctrine was not mentioned at all. The district court, which had refused the injunction, was reversed and the case remanded to it for further action.

This case is of more than historical interest because, at a later date, it convinced one Justice in *Colegrove v. Green* that the "political questions" doctrine was not applicable to apportionment cases. In fact, the decision is ambiguous. The case did involve apportionment. The voter was held to be entitled to injunctive remedy. In this sense, *Smiley* does stand for the proposition that the Court may enforce individual voter rights by making decisions on the merits in apportionment cases. The Court did not, however, indeed it carefully refused to, decide the questions of whether or not the voter's right to an equal vote had been violated, whether or not the substantive districting met Constitutional standards, or whether or not it could decide such questions if they arose. It did not declare that there was fair or unfair districting but only that there had been no districting. It did not validate the voter's right to have his vote counted equally. It merely validated his right to have his vote counted under an electoral law rather than under no electoral law. It did not therefore commit itself on whether or not it would or could intervene if an electoral law did exist. In a sense, it achieved the ultimate in modesty by refusing to decide whether or not there was a question that it must refuse to decide.

Wood v. Broom[44] presents a curious repetition of the same pattern. We have already seen that the Act of 1911 required compact, contiguous, and equal districts. The Act of 1929 omitted this provision without specifically eliminating it. There was sufficient statutory ambiguity to support argument both for and against the continued validity of the provision after 1929. *Wood v. Broom* revolved about this issue and the issue of whether or not the Court could or should take jurisdiction in apportionment cases. The latter issue was phrased in the language of equity, a problem to which we shall return later. The majority decided that the Act of 1911, which the petitioners alleged had been violated, was no longer applicable and that there was therefore no need to touch the jurisdictional issue. Justices Brandeis, Stone, Roberts, and Cardozo argued that the Court should not take jurisdiction and that there was therefore no need to decide on the continued applicability of the Act of 1911. It is impossible to tell whether or not some members of the majority would have gone along with these four if they had allowed themselves to consider the jurisdiction question. As it stood, however, there was no majority either for or against the proposition that the Court could not decide apportionment questions. As in *Smiley,* the crucial issue was not whether actual apportionments are Constitutional or unconstitutional but whether a certain statute was or was not currently valid. In both instances, the holding that the statute was not valid decided an apportionment case, but the Court did not pass judgment on the substance of apportionment.

In the same term as *Wood v. Broom,* the Court dismissed a lower-court injunction on grounds of mootness. No other apportionment case was decided until *Colegrove,* in which three Justices introduced the "political questions" doctrine and three wished to decide the case on its merits. Two Justices did not participate. Justice Rutledge thus cast the deciding vote. He made perfectly clear that, but for precedent, he would have invoked the "political questions" doctrine. It is important to note, however, because of our interest in *Baker v. Carr,* that his version of the "political questions" doctrine applied solely to Congressional districting.

> But for the ruling in *Smiley* v. *Holm,* I should have supposed that the provisions of the Constitution, Art. I, Sec. 4, that 'The Times, Places and Manner of holding Elections for Representatives, shall be prescribed in each State by the Legislature thereof; but the Congress may at any time by Law make or alter such Regulations . . .'; Art. I, Sec. 2 vesting in Congress the duty of apportionment of representatives among the several states 'according to their respective Numbers'; and Art. I, Sec. 5, making each House the sole judge of the qualifications of its own members, would remove the issues in this case from justiciable cognizance. But, in my judgment, the *Smiley* case rules squarely to the contrary, save only in the matter of degree.[45]

For Rutledge, *Colegrove* presented a political question, not because political rights were involved, a problem of remedy existed, or the prerogatives of a sovereign were at issue, but only because the Constitution assigns to Congress, for its exclusive decision, questions of its own membership.

Actually, however, Justice Rutledge did not invoke the "political questions" doctrine. He did not do so because he felt bound by the decision in *Smiley v. Holm,* which he read as holding squarely that the issues in *Colegrove* were justiciable. We have seen that *Smiley* is not completely clear. What seems to have happened is that Rutledge refused to make the crucial distinction that Frankfurter made *sub silentio* and that would have enabled Rutledge to join in his opinion. For Frankfurter it is not apportionment as a whole subject that falls under the "political questions" doctrine but the question of whether or not a given scheme of districting is fair or equitable. It is precisely this question that *Smiley* and *Wood* avoided. But Justice Rutledge was apparently unwilling to subdivide the apportionment area. The question he poses—May courts handle Congressional apportionment cases?—meets with a clear affirmative answer in *Smiley*. Frankfurter's question—May Courts examine the substance of districting arrangements?—is not answered in *Smiley* at all, and, therefore, each justice is free to formulate his own answer.

It must be added that Justice Rutledge, having found the issues justiciable, also found another way of avoiding decision in this particular case. He concurred with Frankfurter that no action should be taken, even while refusing to endorse Frankfurter's "political questions" argument. *Colegrove* therefore presents us with a 4–3 majority for doing nothing and a different 4–3 majority against application of the "political questions" doctrine.

APPORTIONMENT AND THE LORE OF EQUITY

Between 1946, the year of *Colegrove,* and 1960, the Supreme Court refused, in *per curiams* and memoranda, to decide a number of apportionment cases.[46] Such opinions are usually refusals of writs of *certiorari.* Since the Court's exercise of its *certiorari* powers is discretionary, a refusal of *certiorari* implies nothing about jurisdiction or merits. It is simply a statement that the Court for reasons known only to itself does not wish to consider or to decide a given case. If the cases in this period had been dismissals of *certiorari,* nothing more could have been said here than that they yielded no information and left the situation precisely as it had previously been. The apportionment cases, however, typically come to the Supreme Court on appeal rather than on *certiorari* for reasons that it is not necessary to explain here. Theoretically the Justices must decide appeals. The Court is not, however, obligated to write a full opinion or to take any positive action. It may simply offer a one-line memorandum with or without supportive citations of precedents. It may resort to a whole series of formulas, from refusal to note probable jurisdiction to dismissal of appeals, any of which offers only a hint of explanation. For instance, a dismissal of appeal with citation of a decision that dismissed a similar case for mootness is supposed to mean that the Court did not consider the merits of this appeal but only decided that the case was moot. A refusal to note probable jurisdiction means that the Court, having examined the case, finds that the would-be appellant did not meet the jurisdictional criteria that allow for appeal rather than for *certiorari.* There are almost endless variations. They are necessary because, under the statutes that allow in certain matters a right of appeal as opposed to the privilege of requesting *certiorari,* the Court cannot simply say, "We do not feel like handling this one." Each variation theoretically means something because the Court is forbidden by statute to mean nothing, as it does when it refuses *certiorari.*

As a result, elaborate arguments can be constructed concerning precisely how these appeal memoranda are to be treated as precedents. All such arguments rest, however, on the assumption that the memoranda actually do mean something. In fact, in a large but indeterminate number of instances, the Court today is treating appeals as discretionary, exactly as it treats requests for writs of *certiorari.* Many of its appeal memoranda mean nothing other than that the Court does not wish to decide this kind of case at the moment. Furthermore, even if we play the game of assuming meaning, no clear message usually emerges. The cases cited may contain several holdings, and the citation may not indicate which is decisive in the case at hand. The citations may be to peripheral decisions that can only be related to the instant case by a long chain of logic that the one- or two-line memorandum does not provide. Or the citation may be to an ambiguous holding in an earlier case. In spite of tortured efforts by various protagonists involved in the *Baker v. Carr* litigation to derive precedents binding on the Court from these staccato opinions, no clear meaning or line of precedents emerges to aid either side. About all that can be said is that the Court has usually refused to help malapportioned voters when they asked for help. At the most, these decisions support Frankfurter's "political questions" position negatively by embodying refusals to act on apportionment cases. There is no specific affirmation of Frankfurter's doctrine, an affirmation that would have been vital in view of his failure to recruit majority support in *Colegrove.*

The one extended opinion in this period was *McDougall v.*

Green.[47] At issue was an Illinois statute that required nomination petitions for certification in state primaries to contain at least 200 signatures from each of fifty of the state's 102 counties. The Progressive Party had collected far more than the required total number of signatures but had not fulfilled the distribution requirement. It challenged the requirement in the Courts. The Supreme Court, *per curiam,* held that:

> . . . the State is entitled to deem this power not disproportionate. . . . It is allowable state policy to require candidates for state-wide office should have support not limited to a concentrated locality. [The Constitution does not] deny a state the power to assure a proper diffusion of political intiative as between its thinly populated counties and those having concentrated masses, in view of the fact that the latter have practical opportunities for exerting their political weight at the polls not available to the former.[48]

Now this opinion surely appears to be a decision on the merits and not a refusal to take jurisdiction. On the other hand, the Court did not act to upset the state scheme, and its citation is to *Colegrove v. Green* and to *Colegrove v. Barrett,*[49] a case in which it refused to take jurisdiction. The one case in this whole period in which the Court uttered more than a cryptic phrase is therefore as ambiguous as the rest.

In order to complete an analysis of the legal picture confronting the Court at the time of *Baker v. Carr,* it is necessary to look at one more body of legal lore, that of equity. Unlike white-primary litigation, the apportionment cases usually involved injunctions rather than damages. Injunction is not a legal but an equitable remedy. The language of equity has therefore appeared in apportionment cases since the beginning, and, more particularly, most of the arguments against Court intervention have been clothed in the rhetoric of equity rather than in that of political questions. Typical of these arguments are the plea by the four concurrers in *Wood v. Broom* that "the decree should be reversed and the bill dismissed for want of equity. . . ."[50] and the *per curiam* statement in *South v. Peters* that "federal courts consistently refuse to exercise their equity powers in cases . . . arising from a state's geographical distribution of electoral strength. . . ."[51] Justice Rutledge based his crucial vote for nonintervention in *Colegrove* on equity grounds.

The difficulty is that the language of equity is highly ambiguous. In the days when equity and common-law courts were rivals, there was considerable fencing over jurisdiction. A body of rules arose that placed certain kinds of case outside the jurisdiction of equity courts, those in which an adequate and timely remedy existed at common law, for instance. Put another way, certain "subject matter is not of equitable cognizance." Of course, a petitioner might also be refused equitable relief because the equity of the case was not with him, that is, because he had not actually been wronged. In effect, he would simply lose his case on the merits rather than because it was outside the jurisdiction of the court.

Finally, for various historical reasons, equitable, unlike common-law, remedies are said to be discretionary. This characterization does not mean that a judge can arbitrarily grant or refuse injunctions. It does mean that a body of rules has grown up that, in certain circumstances, allows a judge to withhold relief even though he feels that he has proper jurisdiction and that the petitioner has or is about to suffer an injury. For instance, if the remedy would not be timely, that is, if the potential injury that the injunction was designed to prevent were to occur before the Court could successfully intervene, no injunction would be issued. More generally, equity courts employ a "balancing of equities" doctrine. If more harm than good were likely to occur from equitable intervention, the Court would not act.[52] A classic example is that of the small chicken farmer who seeks an injunction against the operation of the neighboring vast industrial complex whose smoke sickens his chickens. The Court has jurisdiction, the man is being injured through no fault of his own, but the Court will not close down the huge factory to save the tiny chicken farm.

All these ways of refusing equitable relief can be easily intermingled with "political questions" considerations. Equitable discretion is based on concern for the adequacy of the remedy similar to that often found in the "political questions" cases. When a proponent of "political questions" doctrine claims that the polity's right to democracy and not the individual's right to vote is at issue, he may conclude that, since no individual right has been violated, the individual has not been wronged and therefore that equity does not lie with him. If the Court does not have jurisdiction over political questions, it does not have equitable jurisdiction over cases involving political questions. If it does not have equitable jurisdiction over a particular kind of case under the rules of equity, that kind of case may be labeled "political" by those who use that label for whatever cases the Court will not decide. Equity and "political questions" doctrines thus get all mixed up in the apportionment cases.

More important, the various refusals of equity get all mixed up with one another. When the Court declares that it has consistently refused to exercise its equity powers,[53] what does it mean? It might mean that the Court does not have jurisdiction to try these cases (1). Alternatively, the Justices might be saying that they have examined the facts and found that the individuals in these cases are not really being wronged (2). This finding in turn might mean that the rights claimed are political not personal, so that the individual has been wronged but not personally wronged (2a); or that in this particular case the facts are not as alleged and that therefore no wrong has been done because no malapportionment has occurred (2b); or that it is not substantively inequitable to distribute electoral power unevenly in the manner in which it has been distributed in these cases (2c). On the other hand, the Court might mean that in each of these cases there was either no time to impose a suitable remedy or that in these instances any feasible remedy would have done more harm than good (3). It makes a considerable difference which alternative is correct. If (1) or (2a) is correct, then the Court would be on record as opposed in principle to intervention in apportionment cases. If one of the other variants of (2) or (3) is correct, the Court's record would indicate merely that the particular cases that have actually come before it have not merited relief, each case having been decided on its own particulars. But aside from Justice Rutledge's specific choice of (3), we do not know what the Justices meant. None of their decisions has translated the cryptics of equity into English.

THE "POLITICAL QUESTIONS" DOCTRINE AND REAPPORTIONMENT BEFORE 1960

To sum up, the "political questions" doctrine is not itself very precise. The only relatively clear way of delimiting it is to list certain general subject categories that have traditionally been treated as political, largely those having to do with the relations between sovereigns or quasi-sovereigns. Elections have not traditionally been one of those subject areas. In addition, Professor Hale has described three political categories: political power, political rights, and issues Constitutionally assigned to the political branches for decision. Apportionment does not satisfactorily fit any of these three categories. Injunction of individual state election officials is well within the power of the courts. The rights infringed are the voting rights of individuals rather than the political rights of sovereigns. The question of fair and equitable Congressional elections might arguably fall entirely to Congress, which has been Constitutionally authorized to supervise its own elections and to determine its own membership, but these Constitutional authorizations do not apply to state legislatures.

In addition, a whole assortment of arguments has developed for use in labeling any given case political. Some of these arguments can be applied with some success to reapportionment, but Justice Frankfurter's opinion in *Colegrove v. Green* shows that not enough can be mustered with enough success to justify completely the extension of the "political questions" doctrine into areas where it had not previously been applied. Frankfurter makes a better case for a sort of working, day-to-day judicial modesty than for erecting that modesty into the iron-clad and permanent limitation on Court power implied by the "political questions" doctrine.

Indeed, the decisions indicate that the Court has traditionally handled election cases even when they seemed intimately related to party politics. A majority of the Justices or at least of those voting has apparently held apportionment cases to be within their jurisdiction in all the cases that the Court has decided with extended opinions. On the other hand, prior to 1960, the Court had never decided against the state on the substantive merits of the districting scheme actually employed and had used a great deal of language suggesting it would or could not. But most of the language consisted of unexplicated formulas from the lore of equity, which did not explain what the Court actually meant. On the basis then of historical and logical examination of the "political questions" doctrine; presentation of the precedents in the election and, more particularly, the apportionment areas; and analysis of the language of equity, in which many crucial points were couched, it is impossible to make a totally convincing case either for or against use of the "political questions" doctrine in malapportionment cases. The Court in 1960 found itself in a totally ambiguous situation of law, logic, and precedent. It is such ambiguity that allows judicial choice and thus paves the way for judicial policy-making.

Gomillion v. Lightfoot

So far, we have used the year 1960 to mark the nearer limit of the apportionment cases before *Baker*. In that year, *Gomillion v. Lightfoot*,[54] which in retrospect seems a forerunner to *Baker*, was decided. The Alabama legislature redrew the municipal boundaries of Tuskegee to exclude all Negro residents from municipal elections. The Negroes went to the federal courts, requesting an injunction against enforcement of the act as violative of the Fourteenth and Fifteenth Amendments. Among other defenses, Alabama raised the "political questions" doctrine and cited *Colegrove v. Green*.

Justice Frankfurter wrote the opinion of the Court granting the injunction. He distinguished *Colegrove* by a series of arguments. His principal point was that the legislation was not an ordinary geographic redistricting but was "solely concerned with segregating white and colored voters by fencing Negro citizens out of town. . . . This Court must judge, and uniformly has judged, statutes that however speciously defined, obviously discriminate against colored citizens [invalid]. The [Fifteenth] Amendment nullifies sophisticated as well as simple minded modes of discrimination."[55]

Frankfurter's basic strategy then is to claim that this case is not a districting case at all but one involving the deprivation of Negro voting rights. He rests his entire opinion on the Fifteenth Amendment, which deals exclusively with minority-group voting rights, carefully avoiding the Fourteenth Amendment, whose "equal protection" clause is relevant to all kinds of malapportionment.

Two supplementary arguments are also provided to distinguish this case from *Colegrove.* In *Colegrove,* the alleged evil resulted from legislative inaction. Here the legislature had acted positively. In *Colegrove,* the citizen's vote was diluted. Here the citizen had lost his vote entirely. Both of these arguments are a bit shaky. The distinction between legislative action and inaction is politically unsatisfactory. Every student of legislatures will testify that the stifling of proposed legislation—or indeed the refusal to propose it—is often the most deliberate and effective mode of legislative activity. The Negro voters of Tuskegee did not lose their rights to vote in local elections. The rights had simply been transferred from one local political unit to another—from city to county. This transfer represented a very considerable diminution of the political effectiveness of the voter as voter. But was it really, in any but the most sophistic sense, a greater diminution than that suffered by the urban voters in Illinois? In Alabama, voters lost voting impact by being districted out of the city. In Illinois, they lost it by being districted into the city.

Gomillion, then, adds a final ambiguity to all the ambiguities that have gone before. The Court enforces a citizen's Constitutional claim to vote by interfering with electoral boundaries drawn by the state legislature and rejects application of the "political questions" doctrine to the case. On the other hand, the Court defines the case as falling not in the malapportionment but in the racial-discrimination category and goes out of its way to rest its opinion on the Fifteenth Amendment, which is not applicable to normal malapportionments, rather than on the Fourteenth, which is.

¶ *Baker v. Carr*

It is against this background of legal indeterminacy that Justice Brennan wrote the majority opinion in *Baker v. Carr.* First, to clear up some of the confusion, the opinion distinguishes questions of jurisdiction from those of justiciability. Jurisdiction involves determination of whether or not the case "comes within that language of Art. III . . . and of the jurisdictional statutes which define those matters concerning which United States District Courts are empowered to act."[56] "Justiciability" refers to whether or not "the matter is considered unsuited to judicial inquiry or adjustment."[57] Justice Brennan quickly finds that the Court does have jurisdiction, for appellant alleges a violation of the Fourteenth Amendment and thus brings a case "arising under the Constitution." Since even Justice Frankfurter's dissent seems to concede that the Court has jurisdiction in this sense, there is no need to belabor the point. The real issue is "justiciability," which signals the whole "political questions" controversy.

Justice Brennan struggles long and hard with the "political questions" doctrine. His basic approach is to argue that what is or is not a "political questions" case must be determined on a case-by-case basis, as there are no closed categories of "political questions" cases. To prove his point, he surveys such traditional subject categories as foreign relations, dates of duration of hostilities, and status of Indian tribes, which show that in each area the Court actually has decided some cases but not others. But if Justice Brennan wishes the court to decide whether or not to invoke the "political questions" doctrine on the basis of the particular factual and legal situations presented in each case,[58] has he not come very close to admitting the circularity of definition that has always lurked behind the doctrine? When determined on a case-by-case basis, is not the political question any question the Court will not answer, and is not any question the Court will not answer a political question?

In this sense "political question" is simply a fiction behind which to hide whatever judicial impotence the Court is unwilling to confess. If, as Professor Wechsler insists, the Court has a Constitutionally imposed duty of judicial review, then it cannot decide the Constitutionality of some laws or actions while refusing to decide that of others. It cannot say, "This law is unconstitutional, but we refuse to find it so." The "political questions" doctrine, at least in its case-by-case version, is a make-believe that relieves the Court of embarrassment concerning its Constitutional duties. Instead of "In this case the law is unconstitutional, but, in spite of our duty, we refuse to find it so," the Court can self-righteously say, "This is a political question, and we do not decide political questions." Undoubtedly Justice Brennan's intention was to counter Justice Frankfurter's attempt in *Colegrove* to freeze permanently his own considerations of judicial modesty into the Constitutional law of apportionment. But his case-by-case approach goes very far toward undermining the whole "political questions" doctrine.

Nevertheless, Justice Brennan wishes to save the doctrine. He seeks to do so by arguing that, while there are no closed categories of "political questions" cases, "analytical threads that make up the political questions doctrine"[59] can be traced through the otherwise chaotic collection of cases. The threads or "isolable reasons"[60] that he discovers are (1) a textually demonstrable Constitutional commitment of the issue to a co-ordinate political department; (2) a lack of judicially discoverable and manageable standards for resolving it; (3) the impossibility of deciding without an initial policy determination of a kind clearly for nonjudicial discretion; (4) the impossibility of a court's undertaking independent resolution without expressing a lack of the respect due co-ordinate branches of government; (5) an unusual need for unquestioning adherence to a political decisions already made; and (6) the potentiality of embarrassment from multifarious pronouncements by various departments on one question.

After the rather lengthy survey of the "political questions" cases we have already undertaken, it seems unnecessary to prove at great length that these threads have very little definitional value. Clearly Justice Brennan does not mean that a case is political only if all these factors are present.[61] Would the presence of any one be sufficient to label a case political? Factor 4 is surely not a litmus for political questions. It has been present in many cases that the Court has decided on their merits—most recently and dramatically *Youngstown Sheet and Tube v. Sawyer,*[62] in which the Court roundly chastised the President for illegal and unconstitutional conduct. Factor 5, with its adjective "unusual," is hardly definite enough to be a useful criterion for anything. Factor 3 is not a criterion at all but a restatement of the problem. The whole "political questions" controversy is a dispute about whether or not "clearly . . . nonjudicial" policy determinations exist and where to draw the line between judicial and nonjudicial. Factor 6 looks suspiciously like the old "foreign relations" subject heading reintroduced as a thread. In fact, the threads break down into the arguments or rationales we have already examined and found wanting. Justice Brennan cannot mend the "political questions" doctrine with these broken or nonexistent threads, and we are left with a doctrine without fixed content to be applied case by case.

Actually, Justice Brennan makes separation of powers (expressed in the first thread) the dominant element in his analysis of political questions, subordinating the other threads to it.

> . . . It is the relationship between the judiciary and the coordinate branches of the Federal Government, and not the federal judiciary's relationship to the States, which gives rise to the "political question". . . It is apparent that several formulations which vary slightly according to the settings in which the questions arise may describe a political question, although each has one or more elements which identify it as essentially a function of the separation of powers.[63]

We have already noted that the "separation of powers" argument is one of the few relatively successful rationales for political questions. It may well be that its emphasis by Justice Brennan is tactical. The majority of the Justices wishes to hold *Baker* justiciable but does not wish to do so by a frontal assault on the "political question" doctrine itself. The problem is, therefore, how to show that *Baker* does not fall under the doctrine without, by the same arguments, totally destroying the doctrine *qua* doctrine. Emphasis on separation of powers is ideal for this purpose. The "political questions" doctrine is allowed a solid base, and that base just happens to be one that is not applicable to the case at hand. Apparently Justice Brennan is saying that, while not all "separation of powers" cases are "political questions" cases—the threads apparently identify those that are—all "political questions" cases are "separation of powers" cases.

Two difficulties arise for anyone trying to subsume all political questions under separation of powers. The first is the guarantee clause. Even Justice Brennan's survey of subject areas, which is designed to show that no subject area is always treated as political, indicates that the Court has consistently treated "guarantee clause" questions as political. But Justice Brennan argues that guarantee cases are political, not because they concern the organization of state government, but because they all involve the threads and more particularly the problem of separation of powers. His analysis of *Luther v. Borden* and its successors is designed to show that the Court found these elements decisive, and further case analysis is devoted to proving that, when questions of state government organization have arisen independently of the guarantee clause, the Court has treated the issues as justiciable.

Actually, the "guarantee clause" cases present an insoluble tangle. When viewed in the over-all pattern of political questions, they seem to be informed basically by the Court's desire to stay out of issues of basic sovereignty, rather than by its concern with separation of powers. It is true, as Justice Brennan notes, that "separation of powers" arguments are used in these cases, but, as he admits, so are other arguments that are concerned not with the Court's ties to President and Congress but with the impropriety of judicial determinations of basic issues involving state sovereignty. It can be argued that the Court has treated questions of state government organization under the guarantee clause as nonjusticiable and other such questions as justiciable because guarantee cases contain the "separation of powers" threads. It can be equally well argued that the questions of government organization that typically arise under the guarantee clause involve basic issues of state sovereignty, while those that arise under other clauses involve simply the Constitutionality of particular actions of state governments rather than their very existence. It might be for this reason, rather than because of separation of powers, that the "political questions" doctrine is invoked under the guarantee clause and not under other clauses.

The other great problem that Justice Brennan encounters in attempting to subsume all political questions under the "separation of powers" heading is the "standards" question. Brennan repeatedly links the absence of "satisfactory criteria for a judicial determination,"[64] "standards that defy judicial application,"[65] clearly definable criteria for decision,"[66] and "judicially discoverable standards"[67] to the "political questions" doctrine. He attempts to show that the "absence of standards whereby the choice between governments could be made by a court . . ."[68] or the "lack of criteria by which a court could determine which form of government was republican"[69] is at the root of judicial withdrawal from the guarantee clause. We have already seen that "a lack of judicially discoverable and manageable standards"[70] is the second of his threads for identifying political questions.

The problem is, of course, that, if absence of standards may define political questions, why must all "political questions" cases be "separation of powers" cases? These two threads have no necessary connection with each other. Certainly, it is possible to visualize cases in which no direct issue of separation of powers was involved but in which clear standards were nevertheless missing. Indeed, the dissenters insist that *Baker* is precisely such a case. Justice Brennan keeps stuffing the standards rubric into the "separation of powers" category, but it keeps popping out at the edges. His usual technique is to link standards verbally with the relations of the Court to other branches.

> Not only does resolution of such issues frequently turn on standards that defy judicial application, or involve the exercise of a discretion demonstrably committed to the executive or legislature; but many such questions uniquely demand single-voiced statement of the Government's views.[71]

> Having already noted the absence of standards whereby the choice between governments could be made by a court acting independently, Chief Justice Taney now found further textual and practical reasons for concluding that, if any department of the United States was empowered by the Guaranty Clause to resolve the issue, it was not the judiciary; . . .[72]

All this line amounts to is the old argument that, if there are no legal standards, then the matter is political, and that a political matter falls to the political branches. It is simply a play on words to say that all cases in which standards are lacking must be decided not by the Court but by other branches and that, therefore, all standards cases are "separation of powers" cases. If issues for which standards cannot be found are political questions, they are political questions because standards cannot be found and not because Congress or the President may eventually deal with them without standards.

If the absence of standards emerges as a "political questions" criterion independant of separation of powers, Justice Brennan is running into troubled waters. For then, it could be argued that *Baker* admittedly does not involve separation of powers; that there is no question of Constitutional assignment of the decision to Congress or the President; but that *Baker* does involve a lack of standards—and therefore, that *Baker* is a "political questions" case. Justice Brennan seeks to avoid this problem by asserting first, that no case that does not involve separation of powers has been considered a "political questions" case and, second, that *Baker* does not involve lack of standards. "Judicial standards under the Equal Protection Clause are well developed and familiar . . ."[73] His own repetitious insistence on standards as an alternative to separation of powers in defining political questions undermines his first assertion. His second, as the dissenters delight in pointing out, does not rise above the level of fiat, as he proposes no standards for apportionment cases.

Justice Brennan's real error is in the persistent invocation of standards itself, in which he becomes involved in a kind of anachronism. We have already examined the current preoccupation with standards or neutral principles. The Justice reads this preoccupation into the earlier "political questions" cases in which it did not exist. The Courts that wrote the several "political questions" decisions had not had the benefit of analyses by Professor Wechsler, *et al.* While some suggestions of the issue can be found here and there, consideration of the standards problem does not play a prominent part in the history of the "political questions" doctrine. Not that the problem of formulating standards did not exist in many of these cases, even if it was only half-thought-out and half-articulated. It simply had not been an important or necessary element in developing the doctrine.

Furthermore, the problem of formulating standards has never been considered peculiar to political questions. Professor Wechsler himself used *Brown v. Board of Education,*[74] a case to which no one has applied the "political questions" category, as the principal vehicle for his analysis. He also quite correctly noted that the standards problem had first become acute in the "economic rights-substantive due process" cases. The imprecision of the "reasonableness" criterion was one of the more important elements in the Court's withdrawal from this area, but surely the "political questions" doctrine was not invoked to cover that retreat. In short, the problem of standards is one of those general considerations of judicial modesty with which the Court has been struggling for some time. It is not and need not be peculiarly associated with the "political questions" doctrine. Many of the categories of cases that especially involve standards problems have never been labeled "political," and many cases labeled "political" do not especially involve standards problems.

Justice Brennan's basic tactic is to define the content of the "political questions" doctrine by case analysis, in order to show that *Baker* does not fall within the definition. If he were to convince us that his definition in terms of separation of powers was correct, he would automatically make his case. Unfortunately, he is both unconvincing and self-contradictory. Moreover, his "thread" analysis only succeeds in perpetuating the amorphousness of the doctrine rather than in establishing a closed category of political questions. Without such a closed category, he cannot demonstrate conclusively that *Baker v. Carr* does not fall within the doctrine. But can his opponents demonstrate conclusively that it does?

Justice Frankfurter's opinion is surely the most powerful of those delivered in *Baker v. Carr.* In large part, it is an extension and recapitulation of his position in *Colegrove v. Green,* and it labors under the same difficulties. If the "political questions" doctrine has any content at all, that content has not historically included reapportionment, so that the burden of proof is with those who wish to extend the doctrine.

We have already noted that *Colegrove* and its successors did not specifically subsume reapportionment under the "political questions" doctrine but did refuse judicial intervention. We also noted that the formula used in the *per curiam*s following *Colegrove* are theoretically explicit legal commitments with precedential value but, in current Court usage, may often be nothing more than discretionary refusals to deal with specific problems at specific moments. In analyzing *Colegrove* and ensuing cases, Justice Brennan naturally claims that there is no precedent for labeling reapportionment a "political question." In reply, Justice Frankfurter gives us the other side, emphasizing that the Court has refused to intervene in the previous reapportionment cases. So far Justice Frankfurter could easily go, but he could achieve no more than a draw with Justice Brennan. He therefore attempted to go one step further, claiming that "the political question principle as applied in *Colegrove* has found wide application" in the string of cases from *Cook v. Fortson* to *Mathews v. Handley.* As the "political questions" principle was not applied by a majority in *Colegrove* and as only the most tortured legalism could find the application of any principle in the cryptic *per curiam*s following that case, this additional step was a false one.

It might be added that *MacDougall v. Green,* from which Justice Frankfurter quotes, largely undermines his post-*Colegrove* analysis, as it was decided on the merits. In fact, what we find here and throughout the rest of Justice Frankfurter's opinion is the same tactic he adopted in *Colegrove,* a confusion of categories and a vague extension of the "political questions" doctrine. Any given decision that refused judicial intervention in apportionment issues or any argument in any case supporting such refusal is subsumed under the "political questions" heading. As long as they resulted in decisions against the voters involved, decisions and arguments based on jurisdiction, justiciability, standing, mootness, equitable discretion, and the merits are all tossed in the same "political" pot. As a result, Justice Frankfurter can say to his own satisfaction that all the reapportionment cases "applied . . . the political questions principle,"[75] but in reality he has said nothing more than that before *Baker* the voter never won.

Justice Frankfurter follows his draw with the majority on the issue of immediate precedents with an analysis of the history of the "political questions" doctrine to counter that of Justice Brennan. He too proposes some key elements as linking all the "political questions" cases. "From its earliest opinions this Court has consistently recognized a class of controversies which do not lend themselves to judicial standards and judicial remedies. To classify the various instances 'political questions' is rather a form of stating this conclusion than revealing of analysis."[76] Justice Frankfurter's preoccupation with standards is subject to the same objections as Justice Brennan's. His choice of remedies as the element to complete the "political questions" concept is not sufficient because it covers only one category of political question, which Professor Hale has referred to as "questions of political power."

In fact, Justice Frankfurter soon stops trying to put the whole weight of the doctrine on the inadequate foundations of standards and remedies and shifts to what seems to be our previously discussed "too hot to handle" rationale.

> The crux of the matter is that courts are not fit instruments of decision where what is essentially at stake is the competition of those large contests of policy traditionally fought out in non-judicial forums, by which governments and the actions of governments are made and unmade.[77]

Here we have standards, remedies, quasi-sovereignty, and separation of powers all mixed together. In this mixture, the outlines of the doctrine blur and fade into the historical and analytical mist that always seems to engulf them. Justice Frankfurter gives us an assortment of arguments, elements, and definitions, none of which alone or in combination is sufficient to define a separate and distict category of political questions. None seems the necessary condition for all "political questions" cases. None is found exclusively in "political questions" cases. With varying degrees of persuasiveness in various situations, all may be used to convince a court to avoid decisions in particular cases. They are all part of the general armory of judicial modesty, and none is capable of defining a special, historically sanctioned, comfortingly automatic and absolute category.

Justices Brennan and Frankfurter both begin in the same way. Each attempts to construct a legal pigeonhole labeled "political questions," the one to prove that the reapportionment cases do not fit it, the other to prove that they do. Justice Frankfurter is no more successful in his construction than is his colleague. He is, therefore, equally unable to make a conclusive showing that *Baker* fits into the "political questions" category as Justice Brennan is to show that it does not.

There is one element in the doctrine, however, that is relatively definite. The Court has always refused to decide cases under the guarantee clause. It will be remembered that Justice Brennan sought to overcome this objection in two ways. First, he showed that the guarantee cases were political because they contained the same "threads" as the other political questions cases and not because they concerned the organization of state government. Second, he noted that *Baker* was not a guarantee but a Fourteenth

Amendment case and that, even when guarantee and other Constitutional claims had been intermingled in previous cases, the Court had dealt with the other Constitutional provisions on their merits.

Justice Frankfurter again tries to meet his opponent head on. He too finds in the guarantee cases the same elements that mark all political questions. But his elements amount to a whole catalog, including the Justices' reluctance to interfere in the organization of state government. He then attempts to link the guarantee clause so closely to the "equal protection" clause that they cannot be separated.

> The present case involves all of the elements that have made the Guarantee Clause cases non-justiciable. It is, in effect, a Guarantee Clause claim masquerading under a different label. Here appellants attack "the State as a State,". . . a court could not determine the equal-protection issue without in fact first determining the Republican-Form issue, simply because what is reasonable for equal-protection purposes will depend upon what frame of government, basically, is allowed. To divorce "equal protection" from "Republican Form" is to talk about half a question.[78]

Here again is a whole medley of arguments. The most prominent is the whole unsatisfactory analogical approach. First, he tries to distill the "elements" that occur in a category of "political questions" cases. Then he shows that the same elements exist in the case at hand, thus showing it to be a "political questions" case. In this sense, when Justice Frankfurter claims a "masquerade," he is simply summarizing his whole previous inconclusive argument. And he attempts to do so without admitting that he is extending the "political questions" doctrine into the "equal protection" area, where it had not previously been used.

The second argument is that the appellant is not suing for protection of his own vote (a private right) but for judicial correction of the inadequacies of a state government *qua* government, that is, for the righting of a public wrong. This argument is simply a repetition of the debate in *Colegrove*. One side keeps saying that an attack on a state's apportionment scheme is an attack on the legitimacy of the whole state government. And indeed it is, in the sense that the electoral scheme is the matrix and foundation of an elected government. The other side replies that the Court is only being asked to declare a single state statute unconstitutional and to enjoin a handful of state officers from carrying out one statute—a routine Supreme Court chore that does not challenge the sovereignty of the state. The classic "guarantee clause" cases involved the issue of whether a given government was the real government or whether there was any government in the state at all. Neither in *Colegrove* nor in *Baker* was the Court asked to declare that the sitting government in the state had no power to govern, as it was asked to do in *Luther* and *Pacific Telephone*. *Colegrove* and *Baker* involve more than the Constitutionality of *a* law, for the law in question is not an ordinary one, but less than an assault on the sovereign power of the existing government. As usual, Justice Frankfurter does not lose his point. Neither does he gain it.

Frankfurter's final argument is a kind of logical *ad horrendum*. The Supreme Court must establish a sort of basic model of what a republican form of government is and must make sure that each state conforms to that model before it can decide whether or not the voting scheme of that state is equitable. This whole argument calls up a vision of the United States as similar to the Holy Roman Empire or the Balkans, with the Supreme Court picking its way through myriad dissociated and fundamentally antagonistic governmental forms. In the United States, the "republican form" issue has not been fundamentally raised and need not be fundamentally solved because it does not fundamentally exist. The few cases in point have a comic-opera quality when compared with the great struggles over governmental forms that have raged in other portions of the world. No matter what the abstract logic—a tool that Justice Frankfurter, as a loyal Holmesian, so often eschews—the Supreme Court in practice need not question nor uphold the republicanism of any state in order to deal with apportionment questions.

This final link of republican form to equal protection is really a first stage in Justice Frankfurter's general discussion of standards. Nevertheless, his examination of the "political questions" doctrine ends with this attempt to link guarantee and equal protection. The discussion of standards is really part of Justice Frankfurter's over-all judicial modesty and not part of the "political questions" doctrine *per se*. For we have already noted that the absence of standards for decision is neither a necessary nor a sufficient quality of political questions. Even had Justice Frankfurter proved beyond a shadow of a doubt that there were no standards available for deciding *Baker v. Carr,* he would still not have shown that reapportionment fits into the historically defined "political questions" category. At best, having demonstrated the absence of standards, Justice Frankfurter would have shown that the political questions category *ought to be* extended into the reapportionment area.

At the end of the whole debate over political questions, therefore, we find no compelling legal certainties or precedents. The doctrine cannot be precisely defined. Nor can the subject areas in which it is applied be exactly outlined. Every commentator can extract various threads, arguments, or elements that are associated with the doctrine. None of these factors, individually or in combination, satisfactorily delimits the doctrine. Depending on what defining factors are chosen, reapportionment does or does not fall under the doctrine. Depending on what precedents are chosen and how they are interpreted, reapportionment has or has not been held by previous Courts to fall under the doctrine.

At best then, the whole debate over political questions and reapportionment is inconclusive, leaving the Court perfectly free to choose whatever course it wishes. Actually, however, the proponents of the doctrine seem, to me at least, to lose. Granted that there are certain cases at certain times that a particular court would be well advised, for a variety of reasons, not to decide. Then let them not decide those particular cases at those particular times. The evil of the "political questions" doctrine is that it elevates a single expediential act into a matter of binding Constitutional principle. Once the Court has labeled a certain matter a "political question," is will be confronted forever after with its own declaration that courts should never decide that kind of question. He who wishes to immortalize judicial modesty in a certain sphere by invoking the "political questions" doctrine must then show that the Court should not decide not only this case at this time but any such case at any time. Having failed to gain more than a draw on doctrinal and precedential arguments, Justice Frankfurter fails to carry the burden of proof with which he himself so often saddles the exponents of rigid and static doctrinal positions.

¶ The Supreme Court as Political Theorist

It now remains to take up the immediate question of whether or not the Court should have intervened in *Baker v. Carr* and to take it up without the freight of vagaries implied by the "political questions" doctrine. It is at this point that Justice Frankfurter's examination of standards is relevant. First, are precise standards available for the decision of apportionment cases? Second, if not, does the absence or vagueness of such standards militate against judicial intervention?

Justice Frankfurter's treatment of the first question is one of the few pieces of recent Supreme Court writing that is both politically informed and politically informative. It represents fully and frankly the Justice as political scientist.

> Appellants appear as representatives of a class that is prejudiced as a class, in contradistinction to the polity in its entirety. However, the discrimination relied on is the deprivation of what appellants conceive to be their proportionate share of political influence. This, of course, is the practical effect of any allocation of power within the institutions of government. . . . It would be ingenuous not to see, or consciously blind to deny, that the real battle over the intiative and referendum, or over a delegation of power to local rather than state-wide authority, is the battle between forces whose influence is disparate among the various organs of government to whom power may be given. No shift of power but works a corresponding shift in political influence among the groups composing a society.
>
> What, then, is this question of legislative apportionment? Their complaint is simply that the representatives are not sufficiently numerous or powerful—in short, that Tennessee has adopted a basis of representation with which they are dissatisfied. Talk of "debasement" or "dilution" is circular talk. One cannot speak of "debasement" or "dilution" of the value of a vote until there is first defined a standard of reference as to what a vote should be worth. What is actually asked of the Court in this case is to choose among competing bases of representation—ultimately, really among competing theories of political philos-

ophy—in order to establish an appropriate frame of government for the State of Tennessee and thereby for all the States of the Union . . .

The notion that representation proportioned to the geographic spread of population is so universally accepted as a necessary element of equality between man and man that it must be taken to be the standard of a political equality preserved by the Fourteenth Amendment—that it is, in appellants' words "the basic principle of representative government"—is, to put it bluntly, not true. However desirable and however desired by some among the great political thinkers and framers of our government, it has never been generally practiced, today or in the past. It was not the English system, it was not the colonial system, it was not the system chosen for the national government by the Constitution, it was not the system exclusively or even predominantly practiced by the States at the time of adoption of the Fourteenth Amendment, it is not predominantly practiced by the States today. . . .

The stark fact is that if among the numerous widely varying principles and practices that control state legislative apportionment today there is any generally prevailing feature, that feature is geographic inequality in relation to the population standard. Examples could be endlessly multiplied. . . . These figures show more than individual variations from a generally accepted standard of electoral equality. They show that there is not—as there has never been—a standard by which the place of equality as a factor in apportionment can be measured. . . .

Apportionment, by its character, is a subject of extraordinary complexity, involving—even after the fundamental theoretical issues concerning what is to be represented in a representative legislature have been fought out or compromised—considerations of geography, demography, electoral convenience, economic and social cohesions or divergencies among particular local groups, communications, the practical effects of political institutions like the lobby and the city machine, ancient traditions and ties of settled usage, respect for proven incumbents of long experience and senior status, mathematical mechanics, censuses, compiling relevant data, and a host of others . . . in every strand of this complicated, intricate web of values meet the contending forces of partisan politics. The practical significance of apportionment is that the next election results may differ because of it. Apportionment battles are overwhelmingly party or intra-party contests.[79]

Justice Frankfurter is certainly correct in speaking of a "complicated and intricate web of values." For, ultimately, issues of apportionment rest on fundamental conceptions of democracy, and very little has been settled about the basic nature of democracy. To begin with, there is no unified theory of democracy, no historically central school of democratic thought, no single democratic philosopher *par excellence*. It is, therefore, impossible to construct a single *a priori* theory, model, or definition of democracy that will command universal support.

This difficulty in *a priori* construction has led to a considerable number of attempts at constructing an empirical theory or description of democracy by extrapolating and systematizing those observed features of government and politics common to countries generally labeled "democratic." Aside from a kind of inherent circularity, several seemingly insurmountable problems block this approach. The "democratic" countries exhibit a very wide range of often fundamentally differing political and social institutions. Each in turn contains certain internal arrangements that appear logically and operationally contradictory to one another but equally fundamental to the political system. Examples could be given, but simply to mention the French Fifth Republic should be enough. The Fifth Republic also reminds us that some of the "democratic" countries are considered more democratic than others, so that, when factor X is found to be common to democratic nations A and B but not to C, it may be concluded either that X is not a basic democratic factor or that C is not so democratic as A and B. Finally, it was much easier to employ the empirical approach when some nations openly proclaimed themselves democratic and others antidemocratic. Today, only a handful of countries would admit to being anything other than democracies. Some working *a priori* definition of democracy must be employed, in order to select the nations to be empirically studied—and we are back to the unsolved definitional problems again. Perhaps if this book were being written ten years from now, the rapidly developing methodology of comparative political analysis[80] would have begun to provide us with some concrete answers in place of this never-ending barrage of questions and problems—but it would still be too late, alas, to inform *Baker v. Carr*.

The absence of a unified democratic theory, which is so often bemoaned, is not actually very surprising or generally very distressing. There is, after all, no unified theory of monarchy or aristocracy or indeed of any form of government. Much of the concern is not really for a cohesive philosophy, which seems patently impossible at the moment, but for a unified ideology to use as a weapon against that other supposedly unified ideology, communism.

The absence of a coherent democratic philosophy is, nevertheless, instructive for our purposes. In tracing the factors that account for this disunity, we shall have outlined the basic problems of political theory and philosophy that confront the Supreme Court in the reapportionment sphere. The one area of universal agreement is at the etymological level. "Democracy" means the power of the people or, in the most conventional terms, government by the people. Except in some philosophies not generally considered part of the democratic tradition, the people is looked upon as a collection of individuals rather than as an organic whole. Government by the people therefore becomes, for nearly all democratic theorists, equal opportunity for every individual to participate in governing. The difficulty lies in translating this notion of individual political equality, common to all democrats, into a mode of government. As long as the people remains the people, it is simple enough to say that the people may have whatever it wants. But what if some of the equal individuals want something different from what others of the equal individuals want? How can the political equality of all be maintained and decisions still be reached on decisive questions? The central institution common to nearly all democratic thinkers has been elections on a "one man, one vote," majority-rule basis. But this approach has been almost universally admitted to be an expediential compromise rather than an ideally democratic solution. For, behind all the Rousseauesque sophism, democracy has been preoccupied not with the act of governing but with the acts of government. It is not enough that all citizens participate equally in governing. All must also receive some of the benefits they seek through participation in government. Each man is the best judge of his own interests and should be allowed to choose those policies of government that further his own interests. If the choice before the people is policy X or non-X and is decided by majority vote, each individual may participate equally, but the 60% who want X get what they want, while the 40% who want non-X do not. The latter are then in a very real sense not receiving equal political treatment.

It is precisely this problem that has led to the unending dialogue over majority rule and minority rights. Some scholars have insisted that talk of minority rights is a deviation from the logic of democracy.[81] They are incorrect, and they are incorrect because they have confused a working and imperfect expedient with a fundamental principle. The principle is political equality. Majority rule is the only expedient available to turn this principle into practice, but it is a democratically faulty device because it deprives the minority of political equality. That is why the tension between majority rule and minority rights is an inherent feature of democratic thought itself.

Two supplementary problems of majority voting as a democratic instrument should be mentioned. First, voting does not measure intensities. What if 40% of the voters wants X very intensely, while 60% do not want X but are only mildly opposed to it? Second, voting procedures often do not and perhaps cannot order multiple issues transitively. That is, it may be impossible for an individual or a majority to express by the normal mode of "yes-no" voting that it prefers A to B but will take B rather than endure C. If B is the first issue proposed, does it vote "yes" or "no."[82]

It must constantly be remembered, therefore, that majority-rule elections are not democratic goals or even essential elements *per se* of democracy. They are simply expediential and rather rough means of achieving the real goals of democracy: government by the people and political equality among the individuals composing the people.

Even the emphasis on political equality in the abstract, that is, devoid of institutional problems, is not entirely satisfactory. For it has frequently been argued that political equality without individual freedom is not democracy but a cruel hoax. This point can be made in various ways. Political equality is meaningless without the freedoms of speech and assembly and the security of person against reprisals that are essential to political participation. Political equality is undesirable if it allows the majority to tyrannize, in the form of majority rule, the minority. Without individual freedom, the individual democrat falls into the grip of the numerical fallacy that Ernest Barker has noted.[83] The individual gives up full control of himself in return for control of one thousandth or millionth part of the master who commands the whole of him as a slave.

It may be possible to argue that the introduction of minority freedom or indeed of any freedom is a direct deviation from the logic of democracy, for each minority freedom implies a corresponding limit on the power of the people to govern as they please. Nevertheless, the addition of the element of freedom to the element of equality has been so universal that we never really hear of democracy but only of Constitutional democracy or liberal democracy. Currently, of course, there is also people's or socialist democracy, but it is precisely because there is so much agreement on the need for freedom in a democracy that we deny that people's democracies are democratic. Whatever the *a priori* logic of "democracy," the historical experience and institutional arrangements of "democracies" provide for sufficient limitations of the majority will to protect certain minimums of individual liberty.

Next it must be noted that not only political equality but even government by the people is not a simple element of democracy. Quite obviously, the people *qua* people cannot govern themselves *à la* the direct democracy of the New England town meeting. Emphasis on the inability of the mass to govern itself has been reintroduced into Wsetern political thought by the "elitists," Mosca, Pareto, Michels, and others. Elitism is often presented as the philosophical opponent of democracy. It is not necessarily so. Mosca, who is surely the fountainhead of modern elitist thought, managed personally to combine his philosophy with a variety of liberal democratic sentiments. Indeed his definition of the "political class" (he did not use the term "elite" nor the title "ruling class") is so broad as to include all of the politically active elements of a democracy. Two groups of elitists have subsequently arisen. While one group seems to propose the elite as a contradiction to democracy,[84] the other fashions a synthesis of elitism and democracy in which the people choose among governing elites that succeed one another and are subject to popular influence *via* elections.[85]

At this point, elitism merges into more traditional views of representative and party democracy. The people cannot govern themselves, and they therefore choose representatives to govern for them and hold those representatives responsible through a system of elections. The people cannot initiate policies, but they can choose among alternative policies championed by alternative parties. As soon as these elements are introduced, real confusion ensues. Democracy has never worked out a coherent theory of representation.[86] Should the representative body be a microcosm of the body politic? If so, should not proportional representation, rather than single-member-district plurality elections, be introduced? If not, in what sense do the representatives represent? Are we speaking of virtual representation—the kind of representation Burke meant when he said that each M.P. represented all Englishmen no matter which ones elected him. Is geographic representation satisfactory in an advanced industrial society in which crucial interests tend to be functional? In either event, is a representative to serve as an instructed delegate or as a free agent held in check only by the prospect of the next election? Is a representative's loyalty to his particular constituents or to the public interest as a whole?

Except for stress on equality of voting and majority decisions, there is no accepted "model" of a democratic electoral system. The British and American single-member-district system is defended on a wide range of practical rather than theoretical or normative grounds. Nevertheless, it is subject to the basic anomoly that, given equal party distribution, a party winning 51% of the votes in each district would capture 100% of the legislative seats. If, in fact, party distribution has not been equal, that is a matter of historic and geographic accident. And the actual inequality has sometimes led to overrepresentation for the majority party and sometimes to exactly the opposite. Two-member districts have also been proposed in recent years.

The addition of parties further complicates matters. Americans have long been subject to devoted accolades to the disciplined British two-party system and to condemnation of both our own loosely structured parties and French multipartyism.[87] There have also been spirited defenses of the American way.[88] Countries that have generally been labeled "democracies" have certainly shown every possible variation from strictly disciplined two-party systems to highly proliferated multipartyism. As with single-member districts and for much the same reasons, two-partyism has been defended less as an essential feature of democracy than as a historically sanctioned system that works.

Moreover, when the people choose, are they to choose men or policies? Under the impact of the elitists and the public-opinion surveys that frequently show both public apathy and ignorance, the answer in recent times has generally been "men." But the defense of British-style two-partyism has often been presented in terms of two ideologically oriented parties presenting distinct alternative programs for the voter's choice, contrasted with the absence of programmatic articulation and unity in American parties. On the other hand, the French parties are conventionally criticized for being too doctrinaire, and the British parties in recent years have become less and less programmatically distinct. In fact, we have arrived at an odd mixture of men and policies. In the face of public ignorance, we generally invoke a sort of democratic mysticism and plead that the public, or at least the American and British public, is capable of choosing good men for office. At the same time, there is a lingering feeling that voters should vote on some more rational basis than the candidates' smiles.

There is one final complication in the policy realm. If indeed voters are to some degree privileged to vote for their policy choices rather than simply for candidates, how do they articulate those choices effectively in party-oriented elections? If party A and its candidates favor policies X and Y and if party B favors anti-X and anti-Y, how does the voter whose preferences are X and anti-Y vote?

The democratic theories of party and representation become a shambles. Although elections play a crucial role in democratic politics as traditionally conceived, it remains difficult to determine exactly what relationship is supposed to exist between the elected and the electors and in precisely what format the candidates should be presented to the voters.

Finally, a new approach to democratic politics makes many of the traditional problems of democracy seem irrelevant while raising problems of its own. In the simplest view of democracy, the people are divided into two segments, majority and minority, and their representatives are similarly divided into the ins, who have received the mandate of the majority, and the outs, who have not. The newer view replaces this simple dichotomy with a fragmented view of both the representatives (leaders, elites, governors) and the people (electorate, mass, governed). The leadership of a modern democracy is frequently referred to as a "polyarchy."[89] There are, not one or two bodies of leaders, but a great many different elites, each with different levels of power depending upon the issues at hand. The emphasis is on competition among the elites[90] and upon decision-making as a form of bargaining among the various power-holders.[91] This vision is, of course, constructed not by *a priori* reasoning from basic premises about democracy but from examinations of the actual power structures in nations alleged to be democratic. It seems undeniably true that, if we ask who governs in any of the modern democratic states, the answer will not be a single name or a single party but a long list of individuals and associations that have varying degrees of control over various governmental affairs.

Similarly, the electorate seems to be less an amorphous whole, ready at every moment to be split into majority and minority, than a conglomeration of groups that vie with one another, forming and reforming various coalitions. Each group is formed around some interest or value that is not shared equally by all members of the polity and that the particular group seeks to further *vis à vis* the values of other groups.[92] The terms "pressure group" and "pressure-group politics" have thus become staples of modern political discussion.[93]

The concepts of majority and minority are not, of course, totally displaced. Groups come together to form majority and minority coalitions on given issues.[94] Furthermore, groups may wage their campaigns against one another by appealing to progressively larger and larger circles of the electorate until finally one group wins over the other because it is able to enlist majority support or at least the backing of such a large segment of public opinion as to suggest majority support.[95] Finally, the phenomenon of overlapping is much in evidence. Individuals do not belong to one group but to many—as, for example, the veteran, employed by U.S. Steel, union member, home owner, fisherman, Boy Scout leader, and booster of Gary, Indiana. Such overlapping memberships mean that the groups are not hard and discrete entities, like billiard balls clicking off one another on the table of politics—or if they are, at least the billiard balls have some very marshmallow-like qualities. Group appeals, to be satisfactory even to their own membership, must have sufficient universality to enlist adherents of more than one value or, at the minimum, not to affront too many adherents of other values.

The fragmentation of the populace and that of their representatives are, of course, closely interrelated. In fact, much of democratic politics consists of groups and their leaders vying and bargaining with one another for policies and governing positions necessary to effect those policies. The representatives of various groups hold various public offices, and public officers are the targets of various group activities.

The whole approach tends to displace majority-vote elections from a central place in democratic politics. If bargaining among groups is a key feature of politics, then we are not faced with simple "majority-minority," "yes-no" questions but with adjustments, with compromises between minority and minority rather than with majority domination of minority. The most immediate restraint on representatives is not the Damocles's sword of the next election but the web of bargains that have been, or hopefully will be, struck with other representatives. Furthermore, the bargaining process impinges heavily on the electoral process itself. This impingement is most obvious in the Presidential nominating conventions. But it is also visible in a host of negotiations undertaken outside the electoral process. An agreement to allow Senator X from Wyoming his amendment to the Federal Grazing Act, in return for his support on the Foreign Service Retirement Act, may be more crucial to Senator X's re-election than his stump appearances before the electorate.

Elections thus remain crucial to democracy in the sense of providing the matrix in which politics operates. But electoral strength and the power of constituents to punish representatives by withholding votes are only one among many interacting factors determining the relative political strengths of various individuals and collections of individuals.

About all we can be sure of, then, in speaking of democracy, is that we mean government by the people and political equality for each of the persons who collectively compose the people. We also know that elections decided by majority votes are customarily associated with democracy but as an expediential means rather than an absolute value. Furthermore, the problem of minority rights seems always to be closely associated with democracy. Beyond this point are a bewildering assortment of institutional arrangements and political processes, which seem more or less compatible with democracy but which form no logical pattern and seem subject to no regular criteria of compatibility. Once we go beyond the grammatical singular of *the people* to the political plural of the individuals and groups that compose the people, we are sure of nothing except that each change in rules or institutions, like election laws that translate the abstraction of "government by the people" into actual governing activity, bolsters the political positions of some individuals and interests and undercuts those of others.

American experience has recognized, indeed it embodies and exemplifies, these tensions and uncertainties of democratic thought. Robert Dahl,[96] borrowing some of his terminology from other sources, has identified two main strands in American democratic thought and practice, the Madisonian and the populistic. The former emphasizes the group nature of politics and the rights of minorities. It attempts to devise a framework of government that will avoid majority tyranny and restrain and purify the ultimate power of the people. The Madisonian aspects of our government include separation of powers with checks and balances in our national government, the federal division of powers, an independent judiciary, and representative institutions to screen the passions of the people through the greater wisdom of the outstanding men chosen by the people as their governors. Populism, on the other hand, seeks to reintroduce direct popular control by such devices as the initiative and referendum, an elective judiciary, direct election of senators, and so forth. It emphasizes majority rule while seeking to reduce the malevolent influence of "special" interests. The "Madisonian" and "populistic" labels may be somewhat misleading because they tend to identify the two ideological currents with specific periods and political movements in American history, the one with the era of the founders or Federalists, the other with the 1880s and after and the Populist and Progressive movements. In fact, both strains of thought coexisted from the first days of the republic, and both continue to coexist, sometimes with curious intermixtures and crossovers. For instance, the strong Presidency, which was established as a check on the excessively "popular" legislature, has become the most "popular" branch of government, while the legislature is now often defended as the spokesman for various interest groups whose voices may be ignored by a President pursuing his version of the general public interest. Dahl correctly concludes that what we have today is neither Madisonian nor populistic democracy but an American hybrid. We have solved the problems, or rather reduced the tensions of democratic theory, by crude pragmatic selection of governmental institutions. Of course, Americans often say "pragmatic" when they really mean "confused," "contradictory," or "undecided." We have simply been content to carry the two conflicting strains of democratic thought, or rather the whole freight of puzzles and contradictions implicit in democratic theory, without sorting them out, labeling them, and arriving at a logically ordered set of ideas and institutions. We have no scholasticism of democracy. It is probably not so much the individual and temporary solutions we evolve that are pragmatic. One set may be no more useful than another. It is the basic refusal to deal with the problems of government in rigid logical or ideological terms that has been useful in maintaining the stability and continuity of American political experience. Our pragmatism lies in refusing to engage in divisive philosophical discourse and not in the particular institutions that mark that refusal. Of course, it must be added that, whenever any given institution is so unsatisfactory to so many that it promises to reintroduce divisive philosophies, then it ought to be and usually has been altered sufficiently to reduce tensions. In this sense, institutional changes are pragmatic changes.

Apportionment is one of the institutional foci around which the tensions of democratic theory crystallize. It is directly related to that central theme of democracy—political equality—but, as we shall presently see, it involves nearly all the theoretical issues. Apportionment must be viewed in the framework of democratic theory before a final evaluation of Justice Frankfurter's desire that the Court withdraw from the area can be made.

From the populistic point of view, the argument is comparatively simple. Political equality can readily be translated into "one man, one vote." Because elections are the central institution of democracy, inequality in elections creates basic political inequality.

Moreover, majority rule is the basis of democracy, and malapportionment may allow a minority of the voters to elect a majority of the representatives. As the legislative bodies decide policy by majority vote and as the legislators represent their constituents, the minority instead of the majority would be making policy. Apportionment must therefore be arranged so that the vote of each individual is equal to the vote of every other.

Most of the simple persuasiveness of this argument breaks down however, when the real problems of democratic theory are introduced. For the populistic position rests on an excessive and mistaken preoccupation with majority rule in elections. The democratic test of institutions is whether or not they contribute to effective democracy, however it may be defined in democratic theory. Majority elections are themselves means to this end and subject to this test, rather than being independant components of democracy. Viewed in this light, the acceptance of a purely majoritarian and equalitarian electoral arrangement is undercut by several factors.

First, because the problem of minority rights and tyrannous majorities is still very much with us, it may well be that the electoral process itself should contain protections for minorities. As long as we continue to maintain minority-protection features in our political structure as a whole, there is no *a priori* reason for not maintaining them in any given part of that structure. One possible protection for some minorities may be to allow additional weight to their votes.

Second, because of the problems of transitiveness and intensity, any electoral process is an imperfect reflection of "the people." The question is not one of a democratically "pure" electoral process *versus* a democratically "impure" one. The process is always impure. This fact suggests that impurities are to be approved or disapproved on the basis of their total effects on the governmental system and not simply rejected because they are impure.

Third, modern democracies, or at least those that we should admit as democratic comrades, insist not only on equality but on freedom as well. "Freedom" is a tricky word. We shall not plunge here into distinctions between negative and positive freedom, freedom from and freedom to, freedom to participate and freedom to be left alone. One man's freedom may well be another man's slavery in several senses. It may well be that the ability of some to take advantage of electoral bottlenecks to protect certain of their freedoms from government interference is in effect a restriction on the freedom of others to make government serve their ends. But we are then left with a clash of freedoms that cannot be resolved by a simple definition of "freedom" as the right of equal participation in governing. In California, for instance, how free in any sense would the voters of sparsely settled Modoc and Alpine Counties be in a state government totally dominated by the "equal" votes of the citizenry clustered around San Francisco and Los Angeles?

Next we come to the problem of parties and representatives in general. For better or for worse, we do not presently have programmatic parties or representatives who serve as instructed delegates. The people elect representatives to positions of trust in which those representatives must exercise discretion in choosing policies. An element of virtual representation creeps in here, willy-nilly. While the legislator will, to a certain extent, seek to anticipate his own constituents' policy preferences, he also feels some obligation to employ the discretion granted him in the public interest. "Public interest" is difficult to define,[97] but it surely refers to the legislator's conscious obligation to govern in the interests of all, and not simply in the interests of his own constituents. Legislative bodies and individual legislators are always caught in the dual grip of public interest and constituency pressure. The element of virtual representation reduces the "excessive" influence of overrepresented groups by recruiting their representatives to broader views. At the same time, such overrepresentation may succeed in bringing otherwise neglected interests before the eyes of the legislature.

Finally, the view of politics as intergroup bargaining substantially alters the traditional concept of elections. In fact, much of the political process is carried on by negotiation among various interest groups on the basis of their own strengths and their access to various strong points in government. The degree of any citizen's political effectiveness is therefore determined by the degrees of organization and skill of the groups to which he belongs, the number of groups to which he belongs, and the powers of the agencies of government to which those groups have access. For instance, a resident of Senator McCarthy's constituency who is a veteran, a member of the U.A.W., an employee of the General Motors tank factory, and an ardent fisherman has more political influence than an elderly lady from Green Forks, Idaho, whose sole interest is weaving and selling straw tea caddies. In general, the urban and industrial sectors of society spawn groups and group action. Members of these sectors find themselves amid unions, corporations, city councils, chambers of commerce, ethnic and racial minority associations, and a wide range of government agencies especially attuned to their problems. The President and the bureaucracy, which have become increasingly powerful in American government, have also become increasingly oriented to these sectors, so that the many groups representing urban interests enjoy more and more access to more and more powerful governmental agencies. When political power is determined on the spot by one's ability to trade influence in one government agency or support by one pressure group for the favors of another, when the passage of a given piece of legislation depends not only on what the voters will eventually prefer but on a maze of deals among Executive and Congressional agencies, then immediate group strength, influence, and access may be far more important than eventual ballot strength. Indeed, as we noted earlier, tactical strength in the arena may even to some extent determine electoral strength. The group or alliance of groups that can materially influence legislation particularly favorable to a given representative's constituents may exert considerable leverage on him, not only because it can vote or not vote for him, but because it can help to bestow or withhold the plums that will determine the votes of those who do vote.

All this discussion simply means that the electoral process is not the only political process. Indeed, a major share of our politics consists of negotiations, both public and private, among various interest groups and segments of government. In this sphere of negotiation, political equality is difficult to attain. In fact, it is extremely difficult to assess what degrees of inequality actually exist. The difficulty of both diagnosis and cure is due to the informal basis of political power in this sphere. Such power rests not on a relatively simple thing like votes but on complex interrelations of social and economic power, prestige, occupation of key positions on the governmental terrain, organization, personal charm, skill at manipulation, and many other factors. No false dichotomy should be drawn between elections and politics by negotiation. Electoral strength is one of the factors in determining strength in the political arena, and the total of strength achieved in that arena may help to determine electoral strength. More than one senator has returned to Washington on the strength of his claim that he could "do more" for Massachusetts or Oregon or Alabama.

Considering political equality in the electoral process *in vacuo* is therefore a mistake. If the keystone of democracy is political equality, then achieving equality in the electoral process at the cost of heightening inequality in politics generally would be a hollow victory indeed. This result might well be what equalitarian reapportionment would produce at a time when political power is shifting rapidly away from the rural and agricultural sectors of society and when government is being increasingly dominated by urban and industrial interests. Nevertheless, no firm generalization can be made on this point, especially when, as in *Baker,* we are dealing with state apportionments subject to the differing political evolutions of the various states. It may be true that in some states so much political power has shifted to urban-industrial interests that the rural populace is being seriously underrepresented in the total process of government. In others, quite the reverse may be true.

Nor is it feasible to calculate the total inequalities in the political process and precisely to assign countervailing inequalities in the electoral process. The relative power positions of political participants vary greatly from issue to issue and shift rapidly. They are subtle, partially hidden, and extremely difficult to measure. In the absence of really reliable past-performance records, electoral handicapping is impossible.

We do know that changes in electoral arrangements change the general balance of political power, just as any change in the rules of the political game helps some participants at the expense of others. Undoubtedly, a shift toward greater formal equality of votes will aid urban and suburban citizens at the expense of rural areas, at least in the state legislatures. But such a shift is not commanded by democratic theory. In the absence of absolute philosophical commands and precise modes for carrying out such commands, the real question may be one of political prudence rather than of political morality. "Democracy" does not require reapportionment. Nor is it clear precisely how reapportionment would affect the ultimate problems of democratic theory. It is clear that reapportionment will have certain immediate effects on certain political contestants. The politically significant issue is, therefore, all things considered, whether or not we want to increase urban and suburban power in the political process.[98]

To repeat, then, Justice Frankfurter is correct. There are no standards for proper apportionment available either from political philosophy (what democracy ought to be like) or political theory (what democracies have in common). Frankfurter goes on to show that apportionment schemes have, in fact, varied widely. Furthermore, in place of the "one man, one vote" standard fallaciously derived from oversimplified principles of democracy, what possible standard or principled argument can be made for any particular outer limit to inequality? If a proportion of ten to one is unacceptable, is nine to one acceptable? If so, what about eight to one? There is no rational place to draw the line at the bottom end of the spectrum short of one to one. The Justice as political theorist discovers that democratic theory does not provide clear or objective standards in the apportionment field.

¶ Political Decision—Without Standards

Is Justice Frankfurter correct, then, in arguing that, because of the absence of standards, the Court should not decide *Baker v. Carr?* Stripped of the smoke screen of the "political questions" doctrine, which does not bind and cannot really help the Court in this case, what is the ultimate question in *Baker v. Carr?*

Necessarily many of the issues involved are those that I have indicated earlier in discussing neutral principles. Curiously enough, in *Baker* a potential neutral principle is actually available. I say "curiously" because in many areas no such principle, not even an unacceptable one, is framable. "One man, one vote" is a clear enough principle that can be applied consistently in all future cases—or at least could be declared the universal standard for lower houses of the legislatures. This principle was not specifically enunciated in *Baker* apparently because the Justices themselves did not feel that it was entirely in accord with American political experience. A moral lurks here somewhere. Neutral principles are almost impossible to frame in most areas of Constitutional law—try constructing one for free speech, for instance. And in the rare instances in which they are framable, they seem unacceptable. In fact, American politics does not proceed by the logical unfolding of neutral principles. A political agency that could only act when neutral principles completely consonant with American experience were available could therefore never act at all. *Baker* nicely illustrates the point that serious commitment to the philosophical-legal aspects of Wechsler's doctrine, as opposed to its rhetorical-political elements, would doom the Court to impotence or imprudence. The absence of a satisfactory neutral principle in *Baker* does not thus of itself justify Court withdrawal unless one favors total judicial abstinence in the Constitutional field.

The absence of standards does, however, present problems of which the neutralists are acutely and properly aware and that it would be politically prudent for the Court to consider. If *Baker* had triggered a situation in which the Court had subsequently been required to say that a proportion of five to one was all right but that six to one is not, it would have exposed the Justices in a most arbitrary position. The problem of finding stopping points short of one to one was therefore a significant minus in the political equation presented to the Court. It is significant and might, indeed I think has, led the Court to caution. However it was not decisive. After all, the ultimate question is one of Court prestige. In any given area of law, exposure of arbitrariness damaging to judicial prestige is not the single deciding factor. This loss must be balanced against the gains in prestige that may flow from the same opinions that expose the arbitrariness.

The greatest damage to Justice Frankfurter's standards argument flows, however, from the general philosophy of judicial modesty of which it is a part. Justice Frankfurter has never argued that the absence of standards precludes political decisions. Political decisions by the Supreme Court are what he seeks to preclude. Where standards are not available, the Court must pass problems to those governmental agencies that are vested by the people with political discretion, particularly the legislatures. Judicial withdrawal in nonstandards areas is inextricably linked with the presence of other agencies to do the jobs. Justice Frankfurter has never faced the problem of what the Court should do when faced with a wrong for which no principled correction is possible and for which no other governmental body will take responsibility. Congress and state legislatures, like Big Brother, are always watching. In his *Baker* opinion, he thus echoes what he has said many times before: "Appeal must be to an informed, civically militant electorate. In a democratic society like ours, relief must come through an aroused popular conscience that sears the conscience of the people's representative."[99] But in *Baker* the echo is hollow. The judicially modest have always worshiped a democratically organized, majority ruled, voice-of-the-people legislature that never was. To invoke that vision in *Baker* is patently ridiculous both because the very malapportionment at issue exposes the fiction and because the case finally reached the Court precisely because legislatures had so resolutely refused to act.

The analogy to one phase of the "preferred position" doctrine is fairly clear.[100] It may be argued, albeit unrealistically, that the Court should step aside to allow the political process outside the Court to right wrongs as long as the political process itself remains operative. But where the wrong affects the channels of political action themselves, the evil becomes self-enforcing, and the Court has the right to intervene to restore the political flow. Just as it is silly to tell a man who complains that a statute prevents him from speaking freely to go out and get the statute changed by speaking against it, it is silly to tell a man who complains that the legislature has stolen his vote to go out and vote the legislature out of office.

The absence of standards then does not in this case absolutely preclude judicial intervention. Indeed, in a rather strange way, it is the absence of precise standards and the ambivalence of American feeling toward the one principle available—"one man, one vote"—that provide the foundation for successful Court intervention. We can play the game of "If five to one is all right, why isn't six to one all right?" as long as we please, but no matter how long we play it we shall never persuade anyone that eighteen to one is all right. This statement is not logical. It is simply practically and politically true. That eighteen to one is "just too damned much" may be difficult to express in judicial and judicious language, but it is nevertheless the consensus of the nation. Furthermore, it may often be true that, without the shield of neutral principles or fixed standards, the Court puts itself at the mercy of attackers screaming "arbitrary," "injudicious," and so forth. The attacks are likely to come in the shape of more or less convincing slogans—"states' rights," "pure white southern womanhood," "communist conspiracy," and the like. Once the opponent of *Baker v. Carr* has shouted "arbitrary," what can he shout next—"hurrah for inequality, up the gerrymander"? He cannot and has not been able to shout "states' rights" successfully because the people of the states in question have by and large welcomed the Court's pronouncement and hurried toward reapportionment. Nor can he successfully wave the flag of rural virtue when the public opinion he is seeking to enlist is overwhelmingly nonrural.

The Court's opponent had no compelling slogan, but the Court had an excellent one. Even before the Court proclaimed "one man, one vote," that slogan was constantly used to defend its actions. And while the "populistic" vision of democracy is not our exclusive vision, it was sufficiently powerful to ensure overwhelmingly favorable popular response to the *Baker* opinion.

We found in our initial examination of standards or neutral principles that, unless one is enchanted with some absolute philosophy of law, their presence or absence is simply one factor in the political equation that determines whether or not courts can and should act. They are basically a defense device to screen the Court's necessarily political functions and to contribute to the Justices' prestige. The absence of standards or neutral principles in *Baker* is thus not crucial because the opinion strikes such basic chords in the American political mind that it establishes its own defense and gathers its own prestige.

Standards or neutral principles may be considered *a priori* truths. More realistically, they are loci of consensus. A neutral principle is neutral because everyone can agree upon it. One basic principle is available in the reapportionment area. There is obviously a strong consensus in this country, and, in fairness to Justice Frankfurter, we must admit that we know it because of *Baker v. Carr* and did not know it at the time the case was decided, a consensus on the point that eighteen to one is too much.

The American tension between Madisonian and populistic democracy, our acknowledgment of the problems of political theory and philosophy involved in the concept "democracy," has led us to the principle of moderation. No one facet of the complex and contradictory body of democratic thought may be carried to its logical extreme. Our neutral principle is "too much is too much," and it is precisely this principle that the Court enunciated in *Baker*.

To sum up, excessive preoccupation with logically precise and consistent standards would have doomed the Court to inaction in a field where no logically precise standards can be found, where no other agency of government is free to right the alleged wrong, and where a nonprincipled, moderate, common-sense decision would enlist the public support necessary to make the decision effective and to preserve the Court's prestige. As there is nothing in the history and usage of the "political questions" doctrine that requires the Court to stay out of the reapportionment area, there is nothing in the standards or "neutral principles" approach that persuasively restrains judicial activism there.

Indeed *Baker* may well illustrate one of the basic inadequacies of the "neutral principles" approach. What we frequently want out of courts is a common-sense statement rather than a resounding principle. You may administer the third degree to the suspected murderer for a little while—but not too hard and not too long. You may favor rural voters a little, but they must not be given overwhelming power over an urban majority. *You must* act as a reasonably prudent man, but *you* need not have anticipated that wearing a red necktie would cause a dog to bite him. Very often, we see courts grappling to put what "anyone can plainly see" into the language of the robe, but our satisfaction with courts is less a function of their linguistic success than of their ability to make the practical adjustments that the situation requires. This statement is all the more true in an area of law like that raised in *Baker,* in which black and white principles seem neither desirable nor available.

We must now turn to a final set of legal handcuffs that seem to Justice Frankfurter to constrain the Court—absence of remedies. Just as Justice Brennan had dismissed the standards problem, he had said of remedies only, "we have no cause at this stage to doubt the District Court will be able to fashion relief if violations of constitutional rights are found . . ."[101] We have already noted that the remedies problem is not so extreme as to throw *Baker v. Carr* into the "political questions" category. Justice Frankfurter is, however, less concerned with the shibboleth of state rebellion than with certain practical problems. If the Supreme Court declares a given apportionment unconstitutional, what happens next? The Court cannot take positive action in prescribing a new apportionment, nor can it force the legislature to enact a new one. Even if the legislature does act, the Court cannot force it to do a better job than it did the last time. If it does not act, elections will presumably have to be held at large in violation of the long-established American principle of single-member districts.

These problems are serious, but they constitute at most only a minor obstacle to court action. First, any finding of unconstitutionality is followed by a hiatus, for in no area can the Supreme Court write a new statute to replace the one found unconstitutional or force a legislature to do so. Presumably, and this presumption is supported by experience, where the voided law played an essential role in the state's legal system, the legislature will pass a new one rather than sulking while the citizens of the state suffer. It is also likely to pass a better one, one not likely to be voided again, for exactly the same reason. In fact, the Supreme Court has often gone through the process of striking down a given statute while setting criteria of Constitutionality, sometimes quite vague criteria, and then reviewing new legislation to determine whether or not it meets those criteria. Indeed, it has on occasion struck down the second effort and asked for a third. The Court's lack of positive statute-drafting powers has not in practice led to important gaps in state law.

Moreover, it is the very American distaste for at-large elections, particularly among legislators themselves, that pushes apportionment into precisely that essential category in which the legislature cannot afford to remain inactive.[102] Finally, if the Court is responding to widely felt public sentiments, it can depend upon the catalytic effect of its decisions to create sufficient political pressure to provide positive remedies for the evils it has condemned.

¶ The Court as Political Actor

Neither the historically defined "political questions" doctrine nor the problems of standards and remedies therefore precludes Supreme Court intervention in the apportionment area. On the other hand, neither is the Court's Constitutional mandate so clear nor considerations of judicial modesty so lacking that such intervention is absolutely required. We are thus permitted to decide *de novo,* so to speak, whether or not the Court should intervene.

It is necessary to emphasize this *de novo* aspect because such questions usually are accompanied by a whole load of intellectual baggage packed with neatly pressed cautions about the role of the judiciary, the undemocratic nature of judicial review, the special place of the Supreme Court, and so on. We have seen that none of these considerations is decisive or indeed very helpful in this case. Let us begin again then with the simple position that the Supreme Court is a government agency, one among many, and not a special, unique, Olympian, extra-governmental phenomenon. Let us begin with the same attitude that we would take toward the I.C.C. or the Bureau of Land Management. Maybe it should do the job and maybe it should not, depending on the problem, the political forces at play, and the other agencies available for the same task.

First, let us look at the problem. There is a substantial malapportionment problem in the state legislatures.[103] Urban and suburban residents are severely underrepresented. With increasing shifts in population, this underrepresentation has increased steadily since 1900. There is no need to go into the figures here. They have been presented exhaustively elsewhere.[104]

Second, there are the political forces. Malapportionment as it exists today is a reflection of and a vehicle for urban-rural conflict. It also involves party conflict, for in many states, at least in the minds of the voters, "urban" is identified with "Democratic" and "rural" with "Republican." As the suburbs are the most underrepresented, however, and as they present varying mixtures of Republicans and Democrats, party considerations are often not clear-cut. Finally, "rural" is often equated with "conservative" and urban with "liberal," so that malapportionment involves liberal-conservative ideological conflicts. Urban conservatives are frequently found voting to maintain rural (read "conservative") domination of state legislatures. On the whole, however, apportionment seems basically to involve the distribution of governmental goods and services among urban core, suburban, and rural areas.

The political strength of metropolitan areas, in terms of both total voters and interest-group activity, has increased very substantially at the same time that their relative positions in the state legislatures have declined. This discrepancy has put an increasing strain on state-city relations. The strain is exhibited in movements toward metropolitan autonomy; an increasing number of direct contacts between city and federal governments that bypass the state; demands for creation of a federal Department of Urban Affairs; and increasing interest in reapportionment itself. Not that malapportionment is the sole cause of city-state conflict or of new city ties with the federal government, but it is one of the causes. More important, malapportionment has become an important issue in that conflict.

We noted earlier that there might on occasion be good reason for granting certain minorities excessive strengths in the electoral process to compensate for their weaknesses elsewhere in the political process. Rural minorities like those in California or Michigan, for instance, certainly seem to fit into this category. Overrepresentation of the politically weak is, however, limited by the reciprocal consideration that a representational system strongly at odds with the distribution of real political strength in the community is a danger to the community itself. We may seek to aid the politically weak but not at the cost of alienating the politically strong. The breaking of state-city ties and indeed the tremendous wave of antimalapportionment activity subsequent to *Baker* itself are signs of increasing alienation and distaste for the electoral system among extremely powerful elements in the states. It seems perfectly clear that urban demands for electoral reform cannot be completely ignored.

Indeed, the Court's very decision in *Baker v. Carr* and the flurry of subsequent litigation indicate that urban political demands had become so powerful that they could no longer be resisted without danger to the entire political system. I am aware of the potential circularity in the argument. It would be all too easy to excuse Supreme Court intervention in behalf of any group demand by arguing after the fact that intervention itself proved that the demand was a politically significant one not being satisfied elsewhere. Each intervention would then be its own justification. Whether or not the Court acts as the safety valve of government, opening under dangerous political pressure to which other segments will not yield, is in every instance a question of fact. Some Court intervention may, after all, be gratuitous. But this observation hardly seems to apply to *Baker,* for the Court had for years repeatedly shown its reluctance to intervene and, nevertheless, had been constantly bombarded with reapportionment cases. The consistent, long-term pressure on the Court before *Baker* and the extremely favorable public reception of that decision, at a time when throwing darts at the Court had become a national sport, indicate that the political sentiment involved was not a minor or aberrant political claim that would have dissipated itself if ignored.

What agencies of government are available to satisfy that claim? The state legislatures are the agencies basically charged by custom and Constitution with electoral reform. They have failed to do the job properly for obvious reasons. Every discussion of malapportionment must return again and again to this basic short circuit in the American political process. We have always provided an institutional answer to the question of who guards the guardians. Elections do. But who then can guard the elections? Surely not the elected guardians who have a vested interest in maintaining the system that gave them office.

Generally speaking, we look to legislatures to adjust intergroup conflicts and to ensure that the demands of politically powerful groups are not so thwarted as to create dangerous tensions in the political system. In this particular instance, the legislatures have failed us, and we must look to some other government agency. State governors offer some hope, for in most states malapportionment plays only a peripheral role in their elections. In fact, however, neither gubernatorial influence nor veto has proven an effective weapon against legislative intransigence, probably because governors, concerned for their legislative programs and budgets, do not wish to antagonize the legislative bodies whose support they need. State courts are potentially very useful agencies, particularly in those states that have specific constitutional provisions that are being violated. But the state courts, following the lead of the Supreme Court, had, with but a few exceptions, refused to intervene.[105] If the state courts are the proper agencies to act, the Supreme Court must get them started. State legislatures, governors, and courts have thus not dealt successfully with urban restlessness. Nor has Congress or the President. The "political branches" have so long shirked their duties even in the area of Negro voting rights in the states, for which they are given specific responsibility by the Fourteenth and Fifteenth Amendments, that there is no reason to believe that they would intervene on behalf of urban voters. Indeed, except for the amorphous and unused "republican form of government" clause, there seems to be no Constitutional mandate for them to do so. Certainly, they have not done so. We are therefore, left with the Supreme Court as apparently the only agency available to do the job. As part of a governmental system designed to accommodate conflicting interests by allowing each access to and representation by some segment of the structure, the Supreme Court is therefore functioning properly when it acts as spokesman for an increasingly pressing political interest that can find no satisfaction elsewhere.

¶ The Court as Political Scientist

On balance then, there were no compelling reasons for judicial inaction either in the Court's own doctrines or in the nature of the question presented, while there was one very compelling reason to act: The Court was the one government agency available to do a job that a very large segment of the population wanted done. The Court was right to act. But did it act rightly? That is, did it choose a course of action that met the demands and operated within the limits of its own and its "clients'" positions within the American governmental structure and political culture. To answer this question, we must first answer the question, What exactly did the Court do? And that is not an easy question to answer from the opinions in *Baker* itself.

Technically, of course, all the Court did was to instruct lower courts that they might in the future hear and decide apportionment cases. The decision was in this sense jurisdictional rather than substantive. The Court does not provide any specific rules for what constitutes a Constitutional or unconstitutional apportionment. It does, however, supply some clues. The difficulty is that there are several sets of clues that do not necessarily all point in the same direction.

First, the Court finds that the case arises under the "equal protection" clause. With the benefit of hindsight, we can now be sure that many members of the Court felt that "equal" protection meant real equality in voting. But such an interpretation can only be drawn from the words of the Fourteenth Amendment itself and its invocation by the Court. There is not a single statement anywhere in the majority or concurring opinions to suggest that the Court was requiring absolute equality among voters.[106]

On the contrary, we find numerous suggestions that complete equality is not the rule.

> . . . arbitrary and capriciously apportioned representatives . . . without reference . . . to any logical or reasonable formula whatever.[107]

> wholly arbitrary . . . based upon no lawfully pertinent factor whatever.[108]

> . . . offensive to the Fourteenth Amendment in its irrational disregard of the standard of apportionment prescribed by the State's Constitution or of any standard, effecting a gross disproportion of representation . . . , placing them in a position of constitutionally unjustifiable inequality vis-a-vis voters in irrationally favored counties.[109]

> A citizen's right to a vote free of arbitrary impairment by state action has been judicially recognized . . .[110]

> . . . it has been open to courts since the enactment of the Fourteenth Amendment to determine, if on the particular facts they must, that a discrimination reflects no policy, but simply arbitrary and capricious action.[111]

> The traditional test under the Equal Protection Clause has been . . . invidious discrimination. . . . Universal equality is not the test; there is room for weighting. . . . The prohibition of the Equal Protection Clause goes no further than the invidious discrimination.[112]

> I take the law of the case from *MacDougall v. Green* . . . It is clear that the Court based its decision upon the determination that the statute represented a rational state policy. . . . The frequency and magnitude of the inequalities in the present districting admit of no policy whatever . . . the apportionment picture in Tennessee is a topsy-turvical of gigantic proportions. . . . Tennessee's apportionment is a crazy quilt without rational basis.[113]

> . . . the Court does not say or imply that state legislatures must be so structured as to reflect with approximate equality the voice of every voter. The Court does ont say or imply that there is anything in the Federal Constitution to prevent a State, acting not irrationally, from choosing any electoral legislative structure it thinks best suited to the interests, temper, and customs of its people. . . . The Fourteenth Amendment permits the States a wide scope of discretion in enacting laws which affect some groups of citizens differently than others.[114]

What the Court seemed mainly to be saying was that arbitrary and invidious inequalities were unconstitutional.

In short, it was impossible to say exactly what the Supreme Court accomplished in *Baker v. Carr,* or rather the Court did not accomplish anything very exact. There has been considerable criticism of this vagueness, particularly by Justice Frankfurter and others of the judicially modest. It must be said first that the modest are hoist by their own petard in this case. It was their long insistence on dealing with reapportionment in jurisdictional rather than in substantive terms that prevented substantive standards from emerging. *Baker* is perforce preoccupied with removing the jurisdictional roadblocks on the path to substantive decision because the modest have been manning those blocks so long and so bitterly. Moreover, case-by-case adjudication rather than the premature enunciation of abstract formulas has always been a hallmark of modesty. Yet the jurisdictional maneuvering of Justice Frankfurter, *et al.,* has prevented such case-by-case adjudication in the area of apportionment. With the exception of *MacDougall v. Green,*[115] *Baker* was, in a sense, the first reapportionment case. The Court managed to avoid decision on the merits in all the others. Was not *Baker v. Carr,* then, an example of wisdom in inviting, rather than anticipating the results of, case-by-case adjudication? Finally, the modest and indeed most students of higher courts insist on the desirability of a firm record from below as a prerequisite for sound appellate decision. In *Baker,* there was no such record on the merits and therefore could be no sound appellate decision precisely because the lower court had adopted the modest tack of finding the question nonjusticiable and refusing to reach the merits.

More important, Justice Brennan's majority opinion left open to the Court a wide range of alternatives ranging from "one man, one vote" to the acceptance of any reapportionment scheme whose rationality a state legislature is prepared to defend, allowing it to choose a particular alternative to fit each future case. One can either praise such an approach for its flexibility or condemn it for leaving the gate open to judicial arbitrariness. But the choice depends on suppressed major premises about the role of the Supreme Court. Once one accepts an active role for the Court in the reapportionment area, the wide range of alternatives is desirable. To use T. D. Weldon's grammatical construct,[116] if the Supreme Court is to contribute to the settlement of the reapportionment problem, then it should construct its opinions so as to leave itself considerable room for maneuver.

There are several reasons why, the most important of which derive from the discussion of democratic political theory presented earlier. The calculated ambiguity of *Baker v. Carr* might have earned the Court high marks as both instinctive and conscious American political theorist. As we have seen, democratic theory lives in the tension between majoritarianism and individualism. Its goals are political equality and freedom. Majoritarian elections and representative government are not ends or values in themselves but are at best instrumental values, "good" only to the extent that they contribute to the goals of liberal democracy. Democratic theorists cannot simply say—and American democratic theory has never consistently held—that "one man, one vote" majority rule is "good." They can say only that "one man, one vote" majority rule is good so far and only so far as it contributes to maximum individual political equality and freedom. No democratic theorist can state flatly and finally just how much of the "one man, one vote" principle should be introduced into American politics. He can only make rough adjustments based on estimates of the political consequences.

It is exactly this approach that the Court took in *Baker* when it, in effect, said that Americans have reached a consensus that a proportion of eighteen to one is a hindrance to democracy. Neither they nor we, however, can say that a one-to-one proportion always maximizes democracy. In *Baker,* the Court stated the American balance between "Madisonian" and "populistic" democracy and avoided binding itself to precise standards of representation, any one of which would be theoretically incorrect because democratic theory does not contain any such precise standards.

It is at this point that the Court as political theorist might have become Court as political scientist, analyzing the actual operation of the political forces around it. For once the democratic theorist recognizes that electoral equality is not equivalent to political equality or freedom but is simply a means that sometimes contributes to and sometimes conflicts with these ends, he must decide when, where, and how much electoral equality should be added to or subtracted from the political system in which he operates, in order to make it more democratic. Given the complexity of contemporary American politics, such assessments are always difficult, but one thing is fairly certain. Whatever the assessments, they are likely to suggest delicate adjustments rather than sledge-hammer blows. It seems highly unlikely that either a continuation of the present crazy quilt of malapportionment or introduction of total and immediate equalization of votes will yield a democratically ideal result. The *Baker* decision allowed the Supreme Court to make its own case-by-case assessment of the political balance in any given state and to fit its remedies to the situations it found. When it is recalled that the processes of group politics may give to members of certain groups far greater political influence than to others and that the relative strength of various groups is markedly affected by the geographic distributions of population, resources, industries, and so forth—distributions that vary markedly from state to state—whoever attempts to achieve greater equality must be prepared to make differing adjustments in differing areas.

If the Supreme Court were to be successful as democratic political theorist, it would have had to take on the chores of the political scientist, that is, the analysis of existential political relationships. It might certainly be argued that the Court is not equipped to take on such tasks of political analysis. Several elements in the situation reduce its complexity, however, and indeed the Court itself has contributed substantially to that reduction. First, the bulk of state apportionment will continue to take place where it always has, in the state legislatures. The Court has forced the legislatures into greater activity, but it has not, should not, and probably will not undertake to construct its own reapportionment schemes. The very lack of specificity in *Baker v. Carr,* of which the modest complain so bitterly, would have allowed the state legislatures to range widely in their choice of apportionment schemes while the Court prodded them a bit and set outer limits to their ingenuity. Indeed, the Court preserved considerable flexibility in assigning work to the legislatures. Depending on how well the legislatures did, the Court could have given greater or lesser weight to recent legislative reapportionments as factors in the equation of political forces to be considered in determining if the Court should intervene. If the legislatures had done fairly well, the Court could have leaned heavily on a "procedural" approach that would have found reasonable any recent legislative reapportionment to bring the representation up to date and would thus have left all or most of the substantive questions of apportionment to the legislature. If the legislatures had acted but acted badly, the Court could have de-emphasized procedure and could have itself examined the substantive merits of reapportionment more frequently.

The lack of specificity in *Baker* performed another function in lifting some of the weight of political analysis from the Court's shoulders. In a sense, the absence of rigid standards in *Baker* could have been the equivalent of the "with all deliberate speed" provision of the school-segregation cases. It might have allowed the state legislatures time to make relatively gradual adjustments in their apportionment arrangements, so that, in most instances, the Court would have had the benefit of extensive legislative tinkering before it was forced into final decisions.

What the Court would have been called upon to do would have been to make rough estimates of the over-all effects of apportionment arrangements on the general complexion of politics in certain states. It would be easy enough for any political scientist to go on *ad horrendum* and *ad nauseam* about the difficulty of this sort of thing—about how little we know about state and local government and politics in general and about the impact of electoral arrangements on politics in particular. Nevertheless, common-sense judgments about such political questions are made constantly by voters, legislators, and administrators, indeed by all political actors. Precisely because we do not have sufficient data or methods of gathering data to render "technically correct" solutions to most political problems, we must either settle for prudent, common-sense action or for total inaction. In *Baker v. Carr* the Court had taken upon itself the task of exercising its prudential judgment on the outer limits of representational inequality. The approach it had taken was in harmony with American thought and practice and, but for a certain squeamishness about judicial activism, would have been applauded by nearly everyone.

¶ From Political Scientist to Populistic Political Philosopher

In so far as its decision in *Baker v. Carr* was concerned, the Supreme Court acted as a student of law, political theory, and political philosophy, accurately reflecting American developments in those disciplines. The Court's position was fundamentally a response to and expression of existing legal and political conditions.

In three opinions following *Baker v. Carr,* the Court has embarked upon a fundamentally new course. From acknowledging with the rest of us that "eighteen to one" is too much, the Court has now gone further and declared that "one to one" is just right. *Gray v. Saunders,*[117] *Westbury v. Sanders,*[118] and the *Reapportionment Cases*[119] add up to a command that "one man, one vote" is the principle to be applied to both primary and general elections for both houses of the state legislatures, for state executive offices, for the United States House of Representatives, and (within each state) for United States senators. Only the districting of the United States Senate and the Electoral College have survived this assault.

A great hue and cry will be raised over these decisions, and they will be characterized as judicial invasion of the policy-making sphere and of states' rights and the federal system. In assessing this outcry, it should be remembered, however, that the Court did not act in the apportionment area until long after the states had shown themselves totally incapable of doing the job. In effect, the states, by their inaction, invited the Court into the apportionment field, and the Court responded to the invitation in *Baker*. Once inside the door, the Court may now have gone too far, but that does not invalidate its original entry. I do not think the objection to the new decisions is that the Court has made policy but that it has made bad policy. Significant criticism of the Court must rest not on the old yearning for judicial apoliticism but on an essentially political analysis of the Court's necessarily political stance.

I have argued that a real appreciation of the current state of American political philosophy and democratic theory would require that the Court accept the role of political scientist, analyzing actual political conditions in each state in order to determine when the electoral system *in conjunction with the rest of the political system* yielded gross underrepresentation for certain groups. The Court has now refused to accept this admittedly difficult task and has masked its refusal behind the neutral principle of "one man, one vote," a ringing Constitutional principle that exempts it from the hard political work of actually increasing the degree of equality in our political system. Here the reapportionment cases illustrate the final difficulty of neutral principles. A Court bent on action and seeking a neutral principle to protect it from the "arbitrariness" of day-to-day political choice, may solve its problems with a sledge hammer rather than with the scalpel that is actually required. Neutral principles may be fine for the supposedly rationally ordered edifice of the law, but they often lead to wildly irrational results when applied to a political structure that is something of a geometric nightmare.

By adopting the neutral principle of "one man, one vote," the Court avoids the "arbitrary" and "immodest" accusations that would arise if it were to decide in one instance that "five to one" is all right and in another that "three to one" is not. It achieves this tidying-up of its legal position, however, only at the cost of defaulting in its duties in the key sphere of its activities, the political sphere.

For the post-*Baker* decisions mean that the Court has given up its role of reflecting the American balance between Madisonian and populistic democracy and has chosen to become a leader in the populistic faction. This movement from student of American political philosophy to active American political philosopher is symbolized by the change from *Baker*'s "eighteen to one is too much" to the present "only one to one is acceptable." Such a philosophical stance is undoubtedly defensible on many grounds, but attempting to implement it by a blanket "one man, one vote" command not only ignores our solid tradition of Madisonianism but poorly serves the cause of egalitarian democracy.

The new decisions fundamentally ignore all that we have learned about the group nature of politics. By adopting the most simplistic view of the political process, and particularly of the process of representation, the Court equates the electoral and the political processes and thinks to assure each citizen "equal protection of the laws" in the political sphere by giving each citizen a vote equal to every other's. I have tried to show earlier that such a position glosses over or ignores the basic paradox hidden behind the notion of government by the people and mistakes an imperfect expedient, majority voting, for the essence of democracy. Such arguments may, however, simply be tantamount to a confession that I am a Madisonian attacking an excessively populistic Court—a good reason for attack but not the main point here. A vision of the political process as no more than the electoral process and of each citizen as exercising his whole political power in the individual act of voting cannot properly serve even the most populistic philosophy. For in the complex politics of group bargaining and shifting temporary majorities that we actually have in the United States, inequalities in voting strength may contribute in the over-all equality of all participants in the political process as a whole. Blanket and blind enforcement of electoral equality will only decrease the political inequalities in some states at the cost of increasing them in others. The result of the Court's new rulings in terms of real political equality will be largely random. In the end they may achieve somewhat greater over-all equality but only because the sum of new equalities will exceed the sum of new inequalities. Viewed as an attempt actually to contribute to greater political equality in the United States, rather than simply as a philosophical editorial, the Court's new position is little more than a random stab.

In the light of the extreme inequalities in current state districting practices, it is undoubtedly true that the immediate effects of the new decisions will probably be to decrease many grave political inequalities. But the Court's new declarations, framed as they are in terms of neutral principles, are probably irreversible. The decisions must thus be assessed on the basis not only of the immediate electoral inequities that they eliminate but also of the permanent inequities they will create, particularly in states like Michigan and California, where one geographically concentrated set of interest groups may form the permanent majority and another the permanent minority.

If it had been necessary to choose between the present inequities and the long-range ones to be anticipated from the "one man, one vote" standard, one might have chosen one of two bases: preferring to clean up present inequalities, while leaving future ones to take care of themselves, or preferring the current fluid inequalities to the future rigid ones that the new standard is likely to create. The whole point, however, is that such a cruel choice was not really necessary. If the Court had been willing to become an active political scientist, as well an an active populistic political philosopher, it could have removed the present inequities and still avoided the future ones. Its refusal to do the hard political work required to assess just what level of electoral inequality is permissable in each state, in the light of other countervailing political inequalities, left us with a Hobson's choice that need never have been faced. The Court's failure to grapple with the complex philosophical and theoretical issues that lie behind the notion of constitutional democracy led it away from the delicate and tentative adjustments that our peculiar form of democracy requires and into the formulation of appealing slogans. The "one man, one vote" slogan, in equating the whole of democracy with majority-rule elections represents naive political philosophy, bad political theory, and no political science. It remains that the *Reapportionment Cases* are, in one important sense, imprudent political action. One of the first rules of politics at any level is that a politician must keep his word. Great tactical advantage may occasionally be gained from breaking promises, but a politician who earns a reputation for breaking promises cannot survive very long. Courts are not immune to this rule. One of the principal tactics of the Supreme Court's opponents has always been to seize upon a narrowly circumscribed opinion, to inflate it to its logical extreme, and then to attack the extreme rather than the actual opinion. Defenders of the Court have traditionally replied by pointing to the limited nature of the opinions and by insisting that the Court really means only what it says and nothing more. The Court, in its two most important postwar decisions, has obviously meant more than it said, and its subsequent actions have justified those who attacked the most extreme interpretation of its decisions. The Court has, in a sense, not kept its word to those of its defenders who have relied on the initially limited arguments.

The opinion in the school segregation cases was strictly limited to education and rested upon a rationale narrowly drawn to cover only public education. Yet we learned from the subsequent *per curiam* opinions that, at the time the school cases were decided, the Court had already made up its mind that segregation, not only in schools but also in all public facilities, was unconstitutional.

In *Baker v. Carr,* the Court said, as far as the jurisdictional niceties would allow, that patently unreasonable districting was unconstitutional, but it carefully avoided the "one man, one vote" rule and hinted strongly in other directions. In *Gray v. Saunders,* the Court did use the "one man, one vote" rule but stressed that it was being applied only to nominations for statewide offices. *Gray* involved the Georgia County unit rule as applied to elections for governor and United States Senator. The Court's rejection of the system, therefore, seemed an intervention against a peculiarly invidious form of inequity unconnected with the traditional districting of state legislatures. Then in *Westbury v. Sanders,* the Court applied the "one man, one vote" rule to the United States House of Representatives but again used carefully circumscribed language that stuck to interpreting Article I of the Constitution and refused to reach the Fourteenth Amendment. *Westbury's* version of "one man, one vote" is thus strictly limited to the lower house of Congress, for Article XIV and not Article I is applicable to the states. Finally, the *Reapportionment Cases* made it perfectly clear that what the Court had really meant, although it had not said so, in *Baker* was that "one man, one vote" is the universal rule applicable to both upper and lower houses of the state legislatures.

The advantage to the Court of such an approach in both the segregation and apportionment cases is obvious. The first and greatest battle rages around the relatively narrow and therefore most easily defended opinion. Then, when the shouting has died down somewhat and the position is solidified by widespread public acceptance, the Court goes on to what it really intended all along, the broadest and most extreme application of its initial decision.

Such tactics are politically clever, but they may be too clever. It will hardly be possible in the immediate future to defend any Supreme Court position by pointing to its limited scope. Attackers of the Court will be perfectly safe in painting the most wildly exaggerated pictures of the Court's intentions in any field it enters. It remains to be seen whether or not the tactical advantage gained by its "delayed action" approach will compensate for the Court's loss of that precious political asset, a reputation for candor.

¶ Conclusion

The Court's previous decisions in the "political questions" cases did not bind it to inactivity. *Baker v. Carr,* in its very tentativeness and lack of standards, was in harmony with the current state of American political thought. The Court had intervened to assist certain powerful group interests that no other agency of government seemed capable of satisfying. Indeed, it had performed a governmental service or at least had put itself forward as initiator and overseer of a service that the public desired and that no other agency of government seemed capable of initiating. In doing so, it left plenty of room for free political play and for day-to-day adjustment. It helped to bring a crucial political question back into the arena of political negotiation from the limbo created by an institutional short circuit. It did all these things only after a long series of deliberations that allowed all groups to state their positions. And it promised by its general approach, to adjust its future actions to actual political situations as they arose rather than to hew to any rigid or unrealistic line. This seems to me to have been a creditable record for any political agency.

The Court has now taken another tack. It has ceased to be a student of law and political theory. It has refused to take up the role of political scientist. It has become the crusading political philosopher of populism. I believe this philosophy to be simplistic and the methods employed to implement it inappropriate to the achievement of real political equality. Nevertheless, it is evident that, whether the Court has succeeded or failed, its success or failure is political and must be analyzed in political terms. The Supreme Court's involvement in apportionment is surely a political question in the broadest sense of that expression.

6

The Supreme Court as Political Economist: Antitrust Law

NEARLY EVERY STUDENT of the Supreme Court has spent some time with *United States v. E. C. Knight,*[1] the famous sugar-trust case. Relatively few have devoted more than a passing glance to *United States v. Du Pont.*[2] Students of public law trained in political science departments, if asked to pick cases to illustrate Congress's power to regulate the economy, are much more likely to respond with *Gibbons v. Ogden,*[3] *Cooley v. Board of Wardens,*[4] and *Wickard v. Fillburn*[5] than with the latest antitrust decisions. Yet in widespread business and legal circles where *Gibbons* and *Cooley*—if they were ever mentioned—would evoke memories of ivy-covered walls and long-forgotten professors, the *Du Pont* decision is a fact of everyday life whose impact on the stock market and the tax structure is still being felt. Why do Constitutional scholars keep the flame of an unsuccessful 1896 antitrust prosecution and a New Deal marketing restriction alive while hiding *Du Pont* under a bushel? Because they are Constitutional scholars. The antitrust cases do not raise Constitutional questions. Indeed we owe the one incursion of antitrust questions into traditional courses and texts on the Supreme Court, the *E. C. Knight* case, to the by now fortuitous circumstance that the opinion formulated the since repudiated rule that production is not commerce. Study of the Constitutional Supreme Court thus often leads us to either legal archaeology or triviality, while major areas of the Court's activity escape us.

Of course antitrust law is hardly a neglected field. It is given major attention by political scientists interested in government regulation of industry, by economists involved in the public-policy aspects of economics, and by the many lawyers who specialize in antitrust work. Nor is there much question that lawyers, who control the antitrust machinery, and economists, who provide increasing amounts of the ammunition for antitrust litigation, should be the principal participants in the field. But in the process of scholarly division of labor, we again find extreme fragmentation. Those interested in antitrust policy are only coincidentally and peripherally interested in the Supreme Court, and those who should reintegrate antitrust materials into our picture of the Court are too preoccupied with the Constitution to do the job. As a result, although a considerable body of knowledge about antitrust law and its administration exists, that knowledge has not been properly tapped to fill out the picture of the Supreme Court as a political institution.

¶ Antitrust Policy and the Discretion of the Supreme Court

It is particularly unfortunate that the antitrust field is so frequently omitted from assessments of the role of the Supreme Court because this area of law is peculiarly policy oriented and provides exceptional opportunities for judicial policy-making. Several factors combine in this area to allow the courts, including the Supreme Court, a much more broadly discretionary role than is usually available in the enforcement of Congressional statutes.

The first of these factors is the very nature of antitrust regulation as opposed to other modes of government regulation of business. In the twentieth century, a large number of alternative methods for adjusting the relationship between government and the economy have been developed. In one sense, the simplest of these methods is government ownership of all facilities that provide economic goods and services. The government then makes nearly all economic-policy decisions through the mélange of bureaucratic and statistical devices that we label central economic planning. The problem of the relation between government and business is virtually eliminated because the government *is* business. Nearly all economic problems become internal problems of governmental administration.

The opposite and equally simple solution is complete governmental abstention from economic affairs. The government neither owns nor regulates any segment of the economy, and all economic decisions are made by private individuals. The problem of the relation between government and business is virtually eliminated because there are no such relations. The first of these two solutions seems feasible in the modern world and is now being tried in some countries. The second does not seem feasible and is not being tried. It retains, however, a certain degree of romantic attraction, just as its more practical rival inspires a certain repugnance on political grounds even among those who are inclined toward vesting economic decision-making in the public sphere.

The result is that most nations have settled for intermediate stages between the two simple solutions. These stages can be ranged along a continuum from government ownership of the major means of production to completely private ownership accompanied by some measure of government regulation. As we move along this continuum from total government ownership toward total private ownership, the problems of government *vis à vis* the economy become more and more difficult, in the sense that the government makes fewer and fewer economic decisions itself and must increasingly depend on indirectly influencing the independent policy decisions of private individuals.

While it is not possible to draw absolutely clear boundaries between positive and negative regulation, it is true that some sorts of regulation tell a business man what he must do, while others leave him free to do as he pleases as long as he does not do certain forbidden things. In terms of getting the economy to behave in ways the government wants it to behave, regulation is more complicated than government ownership and negative more complicated than positive regulation. When the government owns, it must perforce make the basic decisions. When the government regulates private owners, even when its regulations are positive commands, the regulations are simply imposed on the substructure of private decisions. It is true that regulation can become so extensive and detailed that it in effect takes over the decisional functions of private ownership, but usually it creates an interaction of private and public decisions. Moreover, unless the government takes the initiative in economic planning, regulation tends to be remedial, attempting to undo what private decision-makers are doing or have already done. Negative regulation is, of course, the most indirect and unstable of all forms of government control. In effect, it attempts to make the economy behave by forbidding it to misbehave. It attempts to tell the businessman what to do by telling him what not to do. Almost all initiative in decision-making is then left in private hands.

Antitrust laws are thus among the most cumbersome, indirect forms of government control over the economy. Because they are so indirect and indefinite, because they fail firmly to invest initiative in the government planner, and because they involve problems of command and communication that extend far beyond regularized bureaucratic channels, the government's antitrust activities create a very high level of dispersion of policy initiative, modification, and evasion among the many political actors concerned. The Supreme Court is one of these actors.

A second factor in antitrust regulation also allows the Court more scope than it often possesses in other fields. Antitrust regulation is built upon and assumes the model of free competition. A *laissez-faire,* free market economy is taken as the rule, and antitrust laws are designed to meet occasional aberrations from that model and so to maintain competition in its "normal" condition. Actually, of course the American economy differs very extensively from the model largely because *laissez-faire* itself rests on a model of economic man that is out of line with reality. That model of economic man is endowed with three characteristics. First, his sole motivation is maximization of his own profits. Second, he is rational, that is, he seeks his profit by means appropriate to the capitalistic system and recognizes and corrects past errors. The shopkeeper who murders his competitor to get his trade is not economic man. Nor is the farmer who persists each year in trying to grow oranges in Massachusetts. Third, he is basically no more skillful or intelligent than his fellows. This factor is not so obvious nor so often stressed as the other two, but it is equally important. The competitive system requires rapid shifts of resources into high profit areas, that is, those areas in which demand exceeds supply. Such shifts are only possible when outside entrepreneurs can rapidly undertake the same operations as the existing suppliers. The model assumes that new capital attracted into new areas by high profits will automatically be properly employed. Such an assumption is possible only if it is further assumed that any new capitalist or entrepreneur can quickly learn to perform the same tasks as efficiently as those who are already on the scene or can hire someone else to do so. If entrepreneur A is the only man in the world who has the skill and intelligence to fashion coffee tables out of papier-mâché and if the demand for papier-mâché coffee tables exceeds his production, the price of such tables will be high, no matter how many other entrepreneurs pour how many capital units into papier-mâché-coffee-table-producing facilities. The price system requires a high level of interchangeability among parcels of the same commodity in order to bring about "normal" prices. Human beings, executives or entrepreneurs, are a commodity, more particularly a capital good. They must therefore be relatively interchangeable if severe distortions in competition are not to occur.

In short, the model of the competitive free-enterprise system presupposes the competitive free-enterprise man. And he is a very peculiar man indeed. He thinks of and wants nothing but profit. Yet he will seek that profit only by a single approved means, competition with his fellows in the open market. He lives and breathes competition and takes his joy in constant struggle with his equally competitive and equally skillful opponents. Economic life is a kind of continuous international chess game with no winner or loser.

All these assumptions and the competitive man they define deviate considerably from the actual behavior of man in the real economic world. First, and most important, observation of business behavior over a considerable period of time shows that businessmen are not solely concerned with maximizing profits by unceasing competition. Let us admit that there is no systematic data but that anyone who looks at the history of American or European business would have to be an absolute fool to find an unswerving record of competition. Instead, we find constant attempts by business leaders to reduce the tensions and uncertainties of competition by agreements that stabilize prices or markets or by mergers and cartels that eliminate competition altogether. The desire to eliminate competition seems to be as much a part of the motivation of real economic man as his desire to compete.

Indeed, antipathy toward competition is often so great that it even overcomes the desire to maximize profits. It has not been unusual for more efficient firms to forgo the larger shares of the market and the larger profits that their greater efficiency would have assured them in order to join together with less efficient rivals in stabilizing the market. The *laissez-faire* model indicates that the desire to maximize profits leads to maximum competition. In the real world, the desire to minimize competition may well undercut the desire to maximize profit.

Moreover, the free-enterprise model incorporates a peculiarly short-sighted brand of rationality. Entrepreneur A is not only supposed to resist thoughts of murder but is supposed to believe that the best way to deal with B's competition is to compete more. It is never, for some reason, to occur to him that both he and his competitor might maximize their profits by getting together to split the market and to stabilize prices. In reality, of course, the history of American business is riddled with attempts by entrepreneurs to co-operate rather than to compete. Where competitive urges have tended to abort this co-operation, as with the early pools, businessmen have striven to create stronger and stronger co-operative institutions that could successfully resist competition.

It is not possible to make a precise quantitative statement about levels of competition and co-operation or of profit maximization and stabilization to be found in the history of American business.[6] But it is surely impossible to contend that competition has been the rule and co-operation the rare exception. Instead we find competitive and co-operative forces both constantly at work. The desire to maximize profits coexists with the desire to decrease risk and uncertainty. Action according to the rules of competition is constantly accompanied by violation of the rules in the expectation of profit or peace of mind.

Similarly, it is not historically true that economic man is interchangeable man. While there may initially be an interchangeable pool of executive talent, some entrepreneurs and their attendant technicians, having arrived in a given field, develop such outstanding skills that their would-be rivals shy away, even though the lure of profits exerts strong tugs on their capital. These skills may be either in the managerial and technological spheres or even in the realm of anticompetitive maneuvering. In this sense, the whole recent series of business histories that purport to take the "robber" out of "robber baron"[7] only lead us from the frying pan into the fire. For, if they prove that the great oligopolies were created and maintained not by breaking the rules of competition but by skillfully following them, then they prove that even within the framework of *laissez-faire,* differential skills in real economic men betray the whole intellectual framework built upon fictional economic man.

In short, real economic man does not basically correspond to the economic man of the *laissez-faire* model. He does not basically correspond because he does not meet the requirements of any pure model. He is a mixture of competitive and anticompetitive urges. He values profit maximization but not necessarily more than he values stability and peace of mind. He abides by the rules of capitalism sometimes, and sometimes he does not. He is often interchangeable with his fellows, and often he is not. And if American economic man is basically not *laissez-faire* economic man, then the American economy cannot be basically a *laissez-faire* economy.

Because real economic men are not standard competitive units and for a series of other reasons connected with the impact of modern technology on business and industrial organization, the *laissez-faire* assumption that a competitive economy will remain competitive has proven as unrealistic as its assumptions about individual human behavior. Indeed, American experience has been that a market opening in a state of nearly perfect competition ends in oligopoly. We have seen it happen most dramatically in the automobile and oil industries, but similar phenomena have occurred in such contrasting fields as grocery retailing and shoe manufacturing. The same thing may be happening right now in the electronics industry—and our newest industry, scientific research, seems to be headed in the same direction. Other markets where competition was less than perfect to begin with have become even more imperfect as time goes on. The experience of the aluminum and synthetics industries suggests that it may be equally natural for certain sectors of the economy to begin life as monopolies and remain such until government interference occurs than to begin or remain spontaneously competitive.

The economists cannot tell us exactly how much competition exists today or whether or not more exists now than fifty years ago. But this uncertainty results largely from disagreement about the extent to which oligopolistic situations are competitive. There is certainly no question that very few of the leading sectors of our economy exhibit the "many buyers, many sellers" image of the *laissez-faire* model. In this sense, the competitive system is not a self-sustaining or equilibrium one. Contrary to the *laissez-faire* image, the result of competition may be less competition. Neoclassical liberals may argue that these noncompetitive results are not caused by initial competition but by contamination from noncompetitive sectors. But whatever the reason, the history of American business is one of frequent spontaneous (in the sense of nongovernmentally inspired) movements away from pure competition toward monopolistic or oligopolistic market structures. In short neither the structure of the market nor the behavior of its participants is naturally, routinely, or overwhelmingly what the *laissez-faire* model assumes they will be spontaneously, constantly, and completely. There lies the problem of antitrust regulation.

Antitrust regulation is negative regulation. Unlike government ownership or extensive positive rule-making, antitrust regulation assigns nearly all basic decision-making and everyday practice to the private sector. It aims only to provide an occasional corrective for occasional aberrations in a business system that is basically self-correcting because it is basically *laissez-faire*. In other words, the assumptions of antitrust law are the same as those of the *laissez-faire* economic model. Antitrust policy is therefore largely incompatible with the American economic system as it actually exists. The administration of antitrust policy thus becomes a nightmare in which tools designed for one kind of machinery must be employed to repair another. In such a situation, makeshifts, *ad hoc* expedients, and the use of one tool to do a job that requires another that has not yet been invented become common place. The image of administrative and judicial agencies that simply enforce legislative commands is most nearly approximated when the legislative goal is realistic and when the statutory provisions are practical and realistic means of reaching that goal.

Because the administrative agencies and courts that enforce antitrust law must make use of statutes that are basically unrealistic in order to achieve Congressional goals of pure competition that are basically unattainable, they enjoy an extremely wide range of discretion. To a very great extent, save for occasional Congressional correction, the enforcement agencies must shape their own goals and their own tools to replace those that Congress, engrossed in the *laissez-faire* fiction, has failed to provide.

The third element of antitrust law that broadens the discretion of the Supreme Court involves the present state of economic knowledge. For all the squabbling about whether courts should hear more or less economic evidence, there is no question that economic analysis must play a crucial role in antitrust decision-making. Yet until quite recently economists could provide us with only two models for analysis, those of pure competition and monopoly. Neither of course was applicable to the real American economic world. More recently, models of oligopoly and theories of "imperfect" and "workable" competition have been developed, but too little empirical research has been done to verify the applicability of these abstractions to the real world. Indeed, there are grave doubts about even the theoretical content and soundness of the latter two approaches.[8] More specifically, economists are unable at present to "make a complete analytical chain from market structure (including conduct) to processes to performance."[9] That is, given the observed numbers, size, pricing policies, and so on of a given market, economists are unable to estimate the degree to which competitive processes are at work or the effects of those processes on the efficiency and progressiveness of the participant firms. They cannot therefore perform precisely the task that antitrust decision-makers require of them, the prediction of precisely how changes in the structure of the market or the conduct of its participants would affect levels of competition and performance. For antitrust decrees cannot directly order competition. They can only prohibit certain kinds of conduct (cease-and-desist orders, injunctions) or act on the structure of the market (dissolutions).

Generally speaking, economics as a discipline has concentrated on model building and macroanalysis of such topics as the business cycle. The relative scarcity of institutional research has resulted in some very marked gaps in the economics of antitrust regulation. We have at the moment no agreed-upon scale for measuring competition and no systematic description of how much competition or concentration exists where in the American economy. Nor has the relation of price competition to less visible forms of competitive behavior been established.[10] There are currently no single or simple economic standards for defining levels of competition or even the dimensions of the various individual markets in which levels of competition must be determined.[11] Too often seemingly technical and precise economic terms like "cross-elasticity of demand," which promise to make antitrust analysis more precise, melt away when applied to actual market situations.[12] Finally, there has been almost no study of the actual economic effects of past antitrust decisions. Failure in this area must, of course, be assigned not only to academic economists but to the administrative agencies and indirectly to Congress, which holds such a tight rein on enforcement budgets.

Not that economists have nothing to contribute or have contributed nothing in the antitrust area. Quite the contrary. Economists have provided the courts and administrative agencies with a wide range of analytical tools and descriptive data. But as these contributions have not been made within the framework of a fully articulated and empirically verified theoretical framework and have consequently been combined with large doses of rough estimates and common sense, the economist has not been able to claim a dominant expertise. The result is that the economist is considered at best a helpful adviser and at worst a confusing influence. An undercurrent of antagonism between economists and lawyers who resent the complexity of an economics that does not yield quick, convenient answers in the courtroom runs through nearly all antitrust writing and litigation. The honest attempts of economists to acknowledge their own shortcomings and to adopt an eclectic rather than a dogmatic approach to overcoming them tends to weaken their position further.

While economic analysis is becoming increasingly important in antitrust litigation, the economist has not been able to achieve the standing of the physicist, for example. The self-acknowledged incompleteness of his expertise constantly reminds all parties that antitrust decisions are policy decisions rather than purely technical ones. The Supreme Court and other antitrust agencies then preserve a very wide-ranging discretion relatively unhampered by the compelling advice of experts that marks many policy-making fields.

The final factor affecting the scope of the Supreme Court's discretion in antitrust policy is the role Congress has assigned to the courts in this area. The Sherman Act seems to have used the old common-law expression "conspiracy in restraint of trade" specifically to invite judicial initiative. The legislative history of the Act clearly shows that Congress did not know precisely what it wanted to do and therefore passed a general statute to be filled out by court interpretation and subsequently revised in the light of judicial experience. While a few sections of the Clayton and Robinson-Patman Acts are relatively detailed and precise, it has been widely remarked that the antitrust laws in general employ "Constitutional" language. The heart of the Sherman Act consists of two simple commandments:

> Every contract, combination in the form of trust or otherwise, or conspiracy, in restraint of trade or commerce among the several States or with foreign nations, is hereby declared to be illegal. . . .
>
> Every person who shall monopolize, or attempt to monopolize, or combine or conspire with any other person or persons, to monopolize any part of the trade or commerce among the several States, or with foreign nations, shall be deemed guilty of a misdemeanor. . . .[13]

The antimerger provision of the Clayton Act reads:

> That no corporation engaged in commerce shall acquire, directly or indirectly, the whole or any part of the stock or other share capital of another corporation engaged also in commerce, where the effect of such acquisition may be to substantially lessen competition between the corporation whose stock is so acquired and the corporation making the acquisition, or to restrain such commerce in any section or community, or tend to create a monopoly of any line of commerce . . .[14]

This kind of language derives partly from Congress's real desire to invite judicial policy-making and partly from Congress's inability to use any other. Since antitrust policy is designed only as negative regulation at the edges of the great body of positive initiative vested in the private sector, it cannot serve as a specific and detailed code of what business should do. Nor can it even serve as a specific and detailed code of what business should not do. The complexity of our mixed competitive and noncompetitive economy is so great that nearly any business action that Congress might specifically proscribe would, in certain circumstances, contribute a net gain to competition. Furthermore, no statute consisting only of specific negatives could be revised fast enough to keep up with new anti-competitive maneuvers. The tremendous anticompetitive pressures of our business system plus the imagination of countless business executives and the skill of their legal advisers devise new ones every hour to avoid existing prohibitions. The Congress must thus write general negatives and leave day-to-day application to others.

Why the courts? Again, basically because antitrust law is negative. As antitrust laws were designed only to keep men from undesirable economic behavior, it was natural to assign their enforcement to the routine channels for punishing undesirable acts—prosecutors and courts. Moreover, the statutes consist of a set of limitations on private property-owners. For the same ideological reasons that Americans prefer negative economic regulation to more "socialistic" measures, they prefer that judges rather than bureaucrats have the final word on restrictions on private property. Regulation by independent regulatory commission has frequently been attempted as a compromise between administrative expertise and judicial impartiality, but the commissions have not been so successful as to encourage an extension of their role. Moreover, the regulatory agencies deal largely with industries that have semi-public or utility status. Antitrust regulation involves the very *sanctum sanctorum* of private enterprise. The F.T.C. has indeed been vested with a considerable role in antitrust enforcement, but in this area of government regulation, unlike most, the courts have remained primary decision-makers rather than reviewers of administrative agencies.[15]

The Supreme Court's discretion is thus not restricted by the tenets of judicial modesty that apply in so many other fields. Congress, by the wording of its statutes, definitely invites judicial interpretation rather than judicial deference to detailed Congressional commands. The Sherman and Clayton Acts require direct litigation before the courts without the intermediary of an administrative agency to whose expertise and rulings the Court might feel bound to defer. And, although the language of the statute may be "Constitutional," the courts' decisions are statutory. The Court is thus freed of the mythical weight of finality that seems to burden it in making Constitutional judgments. The Justices may interpret the statutes with relative boldness, for Congress can quickly correct errors in judicial interpretation of its fictional intentions.

Not that we have finally found a field of law in which the Supreme Court joyously seizes and lightly wears the mantle of philosopher king. The Court in fact often feels highly constrained by the very factors that give it so much latitude. The complexity and indecisiveness of economic evidence, the necessity of negative and sporadic interference in complex business and industrial structures, the failure of Congress to state specifically what it does not want, the necessity for criminal prosecution of pillars of the community who seem to be following the normal mores of their professions, or for assault on companies that seem caught up in the basic contradictions between inappropriate and normatively loaded theories and the immediate demands of reality—all combine to give any judge pause. Nevertheless, it is clearer in this area than in most that the judges are specifically charged to act, that if they do not act no one else will, that judicial inaction cannot be neutral or self-effacing, and that, in either acting or not acting against alleged violators, the Courts must exercise considerable discretion.

In the light of these comments, I propose to investigate the antitrust decisions of the Warren Court in order to suggest the range of problems and alternative solutions facing the modern Court and the general position of the Court *vis à vis* other agencies of government and the business community. I have chosen to date the Warren Court from the 1956 term, largely for the reasons of personnel that led me to choose this boundary in considering the tax cases. Moreover, the *Du Pont* case was decided in that term, and it serves as a convenient anchor for a discussion of contemporary Court behavior.

¶ *Alcoa* and *United Shoe Machinery:* Prelude to the Warren Court

Ideally, before proceeding to the activities of the Warren Court, we should survey the historical structure and evolution of antitrust law. I forebear to do so far reasons of space and because the material is readily available elsewhere. Indeed, one of those rare finds, a full-scale study of the Supreme Court's specific contributions to one area of non-Constitutional law, covers the period up to 1940.[16] It should suffice for the moment to present the relatively familiar outlines of the antitrust statutes that we have already touched upon. The Sherman Act prohibits conspiracies in restraint of trade (Sec. 1) and monopolizing (Sec. 2). The Clayton Act, as amended by the Robinson-Patman[17] and Celler-Kefauver[18] Acts, condemns price discrimination (Sec. 2 and Robinson-Patman), exclusive dealing and tying contracts (Sec. 3), mergers (Sec. 7 and Celler-Kefauver) and interlocking directorates (Sec. 8) when any of these practices might substantially lessen competition or tend to create a monopoly. Finally, the Federal Trade Commission Act[19] declares unfair methods of competition illegal (Sec. 5), and the courts have ruled that violations of the Sherman and Clayton Acts may also be considered unfair practices under this Act.

Before turning to the Supreme Court cases, however, it is necessary to examine two lower-court decisions, *United States v. United Shoe Machinery*[20] and *United States v. Aluminum Company of America.*[21] These decisions have probably caused more comment than any of the Supreme Court's decisions in recent years, except for *Du Pont* itself. Many of the crucial issues with which the Court must deal are in effect questions of whether or not the Court will adopt these opinions as its own. Indeed, the interpretation of Sec. 2 of the Sherman Act, which, together with Sec. 7 of the Clayton Act, forms the real heart of antitrust legislation, turns largely on whether these cases are to be considered good law or obsolete deviations. *Alcoa* and *United Shoe* are then two brooding presences that loom behind much of what the Supreme Court has done in recent years. In addition, each has a rather special significance of its own. The *Alcoa* opinion was written by Learned Hand, whose credentials for judicial modesty were unimpeachable and whose influence on the Supreme Court in many areas of its jurisdiction has been so marked that his decisions have frequently been diagnostic of the eventual reaction of the Court itself. *Alcoa* thus allows us a rather unique opportunity to examine the relation of the philosophy of self-restraint to judicial decision-making in the antitrust field. It is as if we could have plucked the single factor of judicial modesty out of the complexity of Supreme Court personalities and issues and set it to work in isolation in the antitrust field. The *United Shoe* case is unusual for quite a different reason. There, Judge Wyzanski in effect made an open declaration that antitrust cases cannot be treated in a purely legal manner, by appointing an economist, Carl Kaysen, as his law clerk.

The *Alcoa* case was decided in 1945. It was brought under Sec. 2 of the Sherman Act, the section forbidding monopolizing, and a brief review of Judge Hand's opinion will serve as an outline of antitrust problems. First, monopolizing involves questions of power in the market rather than in the abstract. In order to determine how much power a firm has, the market in question must first be delimited. The basic aluminum market is made up of domestic virgin aluminum, secondary aluminum obtained from scrap, and imported aluminum. Alcoa produced 90% of the virgin ingot and 64% of the combined virgin and secondary supply. Judge Hand disposed of the 10% imports by arguing that the availability of overseas supplies simply set a ceiling on Alcoa's prices, which left the company free to set prices anywhere between its own production costs and the production costs of foreign producers plus their tariff and transportation costs. He also dismissed the secondary supplies, arguing that, as Alcoa produced nearly all the virgin aluminum, it could indirectly determine how much secondary metal would be available by its decisions on how much new ingot to produce. Hand thus took virgin ingot as the actual market, and possession of 90% of that market surely generates power to control prices in that market.

Alcoa then argued that in fact it had not taken unreasonable profits. There still lurks both in the case law and in the administrative practice of antitrust law the notion that a monopolist who charges the same prices as he would have charged if competition existed, a "good" monopolist, is not violating the Sherman Act. This notion reflects a very basic confusion in antitrust policy that we might have mentioned earlier among its fundamental contradictions. We have never really decided whether the antitrust laws are intended to preserve and to create competition, that is, to serve as economic planning devices, or are designed to punish violators of the economic mores of our society, that is, to serve as criminal statutes.

If the law is aimed at the economy *per se* and at maintaining competition, questions of "goodness" and "badness" or even of intent do not seem to apply. The public-health laws are not designed to punish bad restaurant owners but to ensure a social condition, clean food. For purposes of determining violations, we simply find whether the restaurant was or was not dirty, not whether or not the restaurant owner knew it was dirty or made an excessive profit by keeping it dirty or intended to serve dirty food.[22] It is a cliche of antitrust law that Sec. 2 is not aimed at an economic condition, monopoly, but at a personal action, monopolizing. Issues of "goodness" and "badness" and, as we shall presently see, of intent thus repeatedly arise. On the other hand, there is no question that the sentiment behind the antitrust acts was based not only on moral abhorrence of monopolizing as an activity but also on a conviction that, as a matter of economic policy, the American economy should be competitive. Moreover, precisely because we want to shape our economy principally by negative regulation, the antitrust laws are one of the very few means available for carrying out that policy.

Over and over the courts face the huge fire-breathing dragons that are incessantly dragged up before them. But then each dragon sits down, sticks its thumb in its mouth, and says, "It is true that you people don't want dragons roaming your streets, but I couldn't help being a dragon, and I am really a very nice dragon. The crime is dragonizing—not being a dragon—and while I admit being a dragon, you can't prove I have been acting like one. In fact, I have always acted like a little woolly lamb." The Court is then asked to pet the dragon on the head and to admit that it has not really violated the antidragon law. It it does so, it looks patently ridiculous to a community unversed in the niceties of legal logic. If it does not, it violates the consciences of those who are versed in the niceties of legal logic, and they are a powerful group.

Courts are caught in this contradiction because of the basic unreality of the *laissez-faire* model. Because competition was incorrectly assumed to be self-sustaining unless someone broke the rules, punishing the rule-breakers was thought to be synonymous with maintaining competition. Condemning the violation automatically ensured the preservation of the economic policy. When the economic policy was actually endangered without the criminal rules' having been broken, judges could not choose to pursue either the policy or the criminal-law tradition without seeming to violate some part of the spirit of the act. As a result, judges have for years played various games with the concepts of reasonableness, fair price, and intent (real, constructive, presumed, implied, and otherwise), in the course of which they have at different times decided that the dragon was not really a dragon at all, that he was but could not help it and had tried to behave, that he looked so awful a dragon that he certainly must have been acting like one even though nothing could be clearly proved, or that the evidence assured that he had really been a very bad dragon indeed.

Judge Hand disposed of Alcoa's reluctant-dragon act in two ways. First, he suggested that it was impossible to tell whether or not Alcoa's 10% profit, which itself seemed reasonable, was indicative of fair pricing because a fair profit might also have been made at lower prices. This paradox is one of many in antitrust policy. A fair price is, by *laissez-faire* definition, the price set by competition. Where no competition has existed, it is impossible to determine what a fair price would have been. The notion of a monopolistic fair price presents not so much a contradiction in terms as an empirical dilemma. A very inefficient monopoly might succeed in realizing only a small profit out of an exorbitant price, with the remainder of the revenue swallowed by excessive production costs. The firm's monopoly position would protect its inefficiency. Moreover, the economic analyist is unable to spot the inefficiency readily because inefficiencies are normally diagnosed through comparative cost data, and there is no other firm with whom to compare the monopolist.

Hand went on to argue that, even if prices and profits were reasonable, reasonableness was no defense. It was the creation of market power that was the offense, not the manner in which it was employed after having been created. This argument is a neat twist that turns the action standard on its head. Unlike many earlier courts, Hand refused to say, "It does not matter whether you are a monopoly if you act nicely now." Instead, he insisted, "It does not matter how nicely you act now if you actively sought to become a monopoly."

Judge Hand then reached the heart of his opinion—his definition of "monopolizing."

> It does not follow because ALCOA had such a monopoly that it monopolized the ingot market. It may not have achieved monopoly: monopoly may have been thrust upon it. . . . Persons may unwittingly find themselves in possession of a monopoly, automatically so to say; that is, without having intended either to put an end to existing competition, or to prevent competition from arising when none had existed; they may become monopolists by force of accident. . . . A market may, for example, be so limited that it is impossible to produce at all and meet the cost of production except by a plant large enough to supply the whole demand. Or there may be changes in taste or in cost which drive out all but one purveyor. A single producer may be the survivor out of a group of active competitors, merely by virtue of his superior skill, foresight and industry. . . . In such cases a strong argument can be made that, although the result may expose the public to the evils of monopoly, the Act does not mean to condemn the resultant of those very forces which it is its prime object to foster: . . . The successful competitor must not be turned upon when he wins.[23]

He finishes by disposing of the intent problem.

> We need charge it with no moral derelictions after 1912; we may assume that all it claims for itself is true. The only question is whether it falls within the exception established in favor of those who do not seek, but cannot avoid, the control of a market. It seems to us that that question scarcely survives its statement. It was not inevitable that it should always anticipate increases in the demand for ingot and be prepared to supply them. Nothing compelled it to keep doubling and redoubling its capacity before others entered the field. It insists that it never excluded competitors; but we can think of no more effective exclusion than progressively to embrace each new opportunity as it opened, and to face every newcomer with new capacity already geared into a great organization, having the advantage of experience, trade

> connections and the elite of personnel. Only in case we interpret "exclusion" as limited to maneuvers not honestly industrial, but actuated solely by a desire to prevent competition, can such a course, indefatigably pursued, be seemed not "exclusionary." So to limit it would in our judgment emasculate the Act; would permit just such consolidations as it was designed to prevent. . . . In order to fall within section 2, the monopolist must have both the power to monopolize and the intent to monopolize. To read the passage as demanding any "specific" intent makes nonsense of it, for no monopolist monopolizes unconscious of what he is doing. So here, ALCOA meant to keep, and did keep, that complete and exclusive hold upon the ingot market with which it started. That was to monopolize that market, however innocently it otherwise proceeded.[24]

These passages go very far toward defining monopolies as *ipso facto* monopolizers. It states that the condition implies the action and that the action implies the condition, so that, except in very unusual circumstances, there is no need to distinguish between the two.

To be sure, Hand remains aware of one of the basic dilemmas of American *laissez-faire*. Given differences in ability, which always exist but which the *laissez-faire* model will not admit, competition leads not to more competition but to monopoly. He excuses deviation from competition arising from this unreality of the model. But he construes the antitrust laws as directly remedial of the greatest unreality of the model. Where, in the real world, as opposed to that of the model, technological developments plus normal business practices plus the normal motivations of businessmen to reduce uncertainty lead to monopoly, the antitrust laws will intervene to restore competition even when there is no villain.

Much of the criticism of Judge Hand's opinion is really the result of the ambiguity inherent in attempting economic regulation through criminal statute. For the principal complaint is that Judge Hand branded as criminal not an overt antisocial action but routine behavior, that he punished a firm for not going out of its way and against its own best interests actively to foster the creation and growth of competitors. Criminal law usually punishes "bad" actions but not the failure to perform "good" ones.

Actually, Hand attempted to bridge the gap between monopolizing and monopoly. In effect, he declared that, if a court can find a firm that controls 90% of the production of a basic metal not guilty of violating the antitrust laws, it makes itself and the law ridiculous and destroys one of our few restraints on abuses of economic power. There is a limit to the number of times and circumstances in which the courts can call a dragon a "woolly lamb." But in order to call a dragon a "dragon" under a statute that technically forbids only dragonizing, Judge Hand had to strain the notion of criminal actions to and perhaps beyond the breaking point. He had to claim that failure to encourage competition is criminal when he meant that antitrust laws are meant to stop monopoly. It is because the antitrust laws are really aimed at stopping businessmen from doing what comes naturally, while their *laissez-faire* ideology obscures this fact, that Hand must brand natural behavior "criminal."

There is a final aspect of the *Alcoa* opinion that is characteristic of antitrust decisions and adds to their generally unsatisfactory quality as legal exercises. Under the antitrust statutes, the prosecution must prove that the monopoly has been monopolizing. As business decisions tend to be buried in a tight web of secrecy and as the most decisive actions are frequently informal and verbal, we have repeatedly been treated to the spectacle of trial judges finding that there is no evidence that an obviously monopolistic firm has done anything wrong. It has thus not violated the statute, for the statute does not make monopoly criminal but only deliberate steps to become one. Under these circumstances, some appellate judges are likely to seize upon whatever evidence is available to convict while the whole thrust of their opinions is informed by the belief that, given the great power and human weaknesses of monopoly executives, some dirty work must have been afoot even if no one can prove it. In *Alcoa,* Hand noted that the company had engaged in considerable maneuvering in its early history to discourage competitors who might have threatened its sole control over aluminum production first gained through patent rights. After the lion has eaten the lamb, do we allow him to plead that his digestive processes are simply routine and allow him to grow fat on the kill? He also suggested that some of the trial court's findings in relation to Alcoa's later maneuvers were a bit naive. While his opinion does not rest on either of these points, it is fairly obvious that he did not believe that Alcoa had been as pure as it claimed, and his formal condemnation of its "honestly industrial" maneuvers must be read in the context of his obvious belief that Alcoa had not acted with complete honesty.

Alcoa can in one sense be read as follows: It is practically impossible to prove directly that monopolistic actions have occurred because modern corporate practice can effectively hide such actions. If the antitrust laws are to be more than a hollow shell, they must be construed to reach allegedly "innocent" practices at least when the structure and past history of a firm strongly suggest nefarious practices that, but for the impossibility of proof, would have clearly justified conviction. Given the ease with which corporations can hide the truth, Judge Hand simply shifts the burden of proof. When all evidence points to monopoly, the monopolist is left with the burden of proving that monopoly was thrust upon him, that he did not do what monopolists so often do and so often succeed in hiding. The trouble is, of course, that, as the Sherman Act is a criminal statute, there are some understandable qualms about requiring the defendant to prove himself innocent simply because it is so hard to prove him guilty. But again, Alcoa is not a poor wretch charged with burglary.

The *United Shoe Machinery* case is in many ways similar to *Alcoa*. United Shoe was, in common-sense terms, obviously stifling competition. It supplied between 75% and 85% of the machines used in making shoes. It leased rather than sold these machines, and the leases required that the machines be worked to capacity. The user payed a special charge if he returned a machine before the end of the ten-year lease term, but that charge was lower if he took another U.S.M. machine than if he went to another firm. Service was included in the leasing charges, so that there were no outside servicers, and other companies entering the field would have had to provide similar full-scale service. U.S.M. collected higher charges on machines for which there were no competitive alternatives than on those varieties produced by other firms as well.

Like Alcoa, U.S.M. had had a shady past. Hand had mentioned Alcoa's past, but then, for various technical reasons that we need not go into here, he had relied entirely on more recent circumstances. Wyzanski, unlike Hand, could not mention the past directly because of the rules of *res judicata,* but his opinion, like Hand's obviously was informed by a realistic assessment of long-term developments. The Supreme Court, in one of the most laughable of a long line of laughable antitrust decisions, had held in 1919 that the original merger that formed U.S.M. had not violated the antitrust statutes.[25] In 1922, U.S.M. was found guilty of tying-clause violations under the Clayton Act.[26] For years, U.S.M. had required the lessee of any one of its machines to lease related machines from it as well. Since U.S.M. was the sole producer of some key machines, such agreements effectively excluded competitors. By one of the incredible stupidities that haunt antitrust law, Wyzanski was forced to assume that the company had indeed ended its tying practices.[27]

Wyzanski, again like Hand, was faced with a firm wearing a pious face as it fattened off a position orginally acquired by anti-competitive practices. Moreover, because of the usual difficulty of proof, there was little to indicate that U.S.M. had recently engaged in any of the practices condemned by the statutes—little that is but a privileged situation that was obviously intended to be abused and a management that had historically engaged in such abuse.

Again the judge had before him a dragon—but insufficient proof of dragonizing. Wyzanski used an approach very similar to Hand's. A dragon would be convicted of dragonizing even without proof unless *it* could show that it was truly a reluctant dragon—that it had had its monopoly position thrust upon it or earned it only by superior competitive and technical skill. Wyzanski spoke of

> . . . the intermediate case where the causes of an enterprise's success were neither common law restraints of trade, nor the skill with which the business was conducted, but rather some practice which without being predatory, abusive, or coercive was in economic effect exclusionary. . . . It is a violation of section 2 for one having effective control of the market to use, or plan to use, any exclusionary practice, even though it is not a technical restraint of trade. . . . They are not practices which can be properly described as the inevitable consequences of ability, natural forces, or law. . . . They are contracts, arrangements and policies which, instead of encouraging competition based on pure merit, further the dominance of a particular firm. In this

sense they are unnatural barriers: they unnecessarily exclude actual and potential competition: they restrict a free market.[28]

The same problem exists here as in *Alcoa.* Wyzanski admitted that the leases were normal methods of industrial development.[29] A firm could thus technically be convicted of violating a criminal statute for engaging in normal business practices when what the court really intended to imply was that the firm almost certainly did engage in dirty doings that could not be proved and that it was a monopoly of such grand proportions that, unless the court could somehow find it guilty under the antimonopoly statutes, they would simply be a joke. Again, a statute predicated on the notion that prohibiting anticompetitive actions and ending anti-competitive conditions are practically synonymous leads the court into grave difficulties when the condition is obviously there to be ended but the actions are not so obviously there to be condemned.

¶ The Warren Court

United States v. Du Pont,[30] the earliest of the Warren Court's major antitrust decisions, is in many ways strikingly similar to the *Alcoa* and *United Shoe Machinery* cases. In 1917–19, Du Pont acquired 20% of the stock of General Motors Corporation. By 1947, G.M., which had roughly half the new-car market, was buying 68% of its paints and fabrics from Du Pont. The government brought suit under Sec. 1 and Sec. 2 of the Sherman Act and under Sec. 7 of the Clayton Act. The Supreme Court found Du Pont guilty of a violation of Sec. 7.

The district court had concluded from the facts that the initial merger was neither the result of conspiracy nor an act of monopolizing, apparently accepting Du Pont's argument that it had been intended as a simple business investment. It also found that Du Pont had not used its stock interest to restrain trade between 1919 and the time of the suit and that there was therefore no reason to believe it would do so in the future.

The Supreme Court in effect rejected the trial court's conclusions about the initial acquisition and found that control of the G.M. market for paints was one of the factors motivating the stock purchase. While its decision does not directly or technically rest on this conclusion, it obviously is a decisive factor in the Court's mind. Just as in *Alcoa* and *United Shoe,* judges who for one reason or another feel they cannot rest their decisions on early "dirty work" are unwilling to let the firm off on the plea that it has merely been growing by natural processes since the original kill.

Also as in the earlier cases, the Court is seriously embarrassed by previous judicial findings of fact, which it is required to follow. In *Alcoa,* Hand, as appellate judge, quite obviously did not agree with the factual conclusions of the trial court. In *United Shoe,* in a rather bizarre twist, Wyzanski, a trial judge, did not agree with the past findings of fact of the Supreme Court in the first *Shoe Machinery* case. Yet in neither could the judges directly challenge the earlier findings, the one because of the respect due from a lower court to a higher, the other because appeals courts are not lightly to overturn trial courts' findings of fact. In *Du Pont,* the Supreme Court did not agree with the trial court's factual finding that Du Pont had not used its stock interest to influence G.M.'s paint-purchase policies, and it is upon this disagreement that the Supreme Court's reversal of the district court directly rests. Yet the Federal Rules clearly require that appellate courts shall not set aside findings of fact made by trial courts unless they are clearly erroneous.[31] The Supreme Court did not follow the example that Hand and Wyzanski had set when they, despite mock bows to the controlling fact-finding, decided the cases on other grounds guided by their own sense of the facts. It attacked the problem more directly by distinguishing in effect between findings of raw fact and factual conclusions drawn from the raw data. As for who said what to whom and who did what particular thing on what particular day, the trial court's findings were final. But the Supreme Court felt itself free to draw its own conclusions from the facts about whether or not restraint, influence, conspiracy, and so forth existed. In *Du Pont,* none of the raw facts in the record was contested, so that the Court could make a good case for its ability to draw factual conclusions from the record equaling those of the trial court. The situation might have been different had the raw facts been in dispute so that conclusions would have necessarily depended on assessments of the veracity of testimony, a job at which trial courts are supposed to be peculiarly adept.

The Supreme Court seized upon the uncontested nature of the evidence to evade unwanted trial-court conclusions of fact.

Aside from the facts, there were three principal legal issues in the case. First, did the Clayton Act apply to vertical as well as to horizontal mergers? Second, if it did, was the Court, in determining whether the "effect of such acquisition may be to substantially lessen competition . . . or tend to create a monopoly," to base its decision on the conditions at the time of the merger (1917–19) or at the time suit was brought (1949)? Third, did the behavior of the parties and the conditions of the market at the time chosen support the conclusion that violation of Sec. 7 had occurred?

In its long history, the Clayton Act had never previously been applied to vertical mergers. Its language, like that of nearly all the antitrust provisions, is very general. The Court, in a relatively unexceptionable piece of statutory interpretation found that Congress had not intended to distinguish between horizontal and vertical mergers and concluded that the statute applied to both. Every finding in the *Du Pont* case has given rise to dispute, and, of course, there can always be dispute over what Congress intended, especially when, as here, it probably had no intent, not having foreseen the problem. On the whole, however, the holding on vertical mergers seems to be the kind of judicial lawmaking to fill in the gaps that is a traditional function of the courts under the antitrust "constitution." It is the least controversial feature of the *Du Pont* opinion.

The most controversial feature is probably the question of timing. Is the tendency to create a monopoly to be calculated as of the time of the merger itself or of the suit? The Supreme Court chose the time of suit. Although the Clayton Act, unlike the Sherman Act, is not a criminal statute, punishment for violation in terms of disruption of business, forced divestment of stock, and so forth can be—and was in this case—very great. To many, it therefore seemed fundamentally unfair that Du Pont was punished for something it had done in 1919 simply because it turned out to be wrong thirty years later. It will be remembered that the Supreme Court denied that the merger was originally innocent. But because it chose technically to rest its findings on the situation in 1949, the general impression left and diligently fostered by opponents of the decision was that Du Pont was being punished retroactively because it had made a simple investment in a struggling company in 1917, when such an investment could not have been anticipated as tending toward monopoly, and was being condemned because G.M. later happened to become, through no fault of Du Pont, the largest producer of automobiles in the country. In short, it seemed that Du Pont was being punished for success or simple bigness and indeed not even for its own success but for that of the firm in which it had invested. Again the parallel with *Alcoa* is striking. Both firms were punished for what they claimed were natural business growth and practices, practices that the judges did not believe were pure but that, for various reasons, they did or could not find sufficiently anticompetitive to constitute traditional violations of the Sherman Act. In both instances, the firms can pretend that they were punished not for criminal acts but for natural business behavior that they could not have known would result in violations of the statute.

More disturbing for the antitrust community than the alleged retroactivity of the punishment was a more technical point. The standard of proof under Sec. 7 is much looser than that under Secs. 1 and 2 of the Sherman Act, which require actual restraint to be proven. This difference arises because the Clayton Act was aimed at nipping monopoly in the bud before it occurred. The Act was intended for application before the fact not after it, and a looser standard of proof was the only way to make it effective. It is impossible to prove absolutely in advance that a given merger will restrict competition. The only absolute proof would be the restriction itself. Once that had occurred, the Sherman Act, would apply. The Clayton Act, therefore requires only enough evidence to support a reasonable belief that the merger, if it occurs, is likely to restrict competition in the future.

In the *Du Pont* case, this lesser standard was used to condemn not a merger that was about to take place but one that had taken place more than thirty years earlier. Given that thirty years of past available evidence, why should not the government be held to the stricter standard of proof, which was relaxed in the Clayton Act only because of the difficulty of using the future as evidence? If the Court had chosen conditions in 1919 as determinant, then the choice of the prospective standard of proof would have seemed appropriate, but the combination of "after the fact" evidence and "before the fact" standard seemed to allow the prosecution to have its cake and eat it too.

The Court's line of argument fell into three parts: (1) The merger had been intended to restrict and had succeeded in restricting G.M.'s paint market; (2) Du Pont had used its stock interest to restrict competition in the postmerger period; (3) There was a reasonable probability therefore that the merger would tend to restrict competition in the future, and so the Clayton Act could be declared violated. But if (1) and (2) are true, why not convict under the Sherman Act? And if they are not true, then there is not sufficient evidence of the future likelihood of restraint to convict under the Clayton Act.

Just as in *Alcoa* and *United Shoe,* we encounter here the problem of the inherent and extreme difficulty of proving the punishable actions. The Supreme Court, while maneuvering around it, obviously remained much troubled by the trial court's finding that no restriction had occurred. The Court's sense of the facts, like those of Hand and Wyzanski, was clearly that restriction had occurred. But elementary standards of due process indicate that the restriction had not been proven in the strict sense that courts normally require. The Court's real position seems to have been that, while anyone could plainly see that there had been dirty work afoot, he could also plainly see that, short of abysmal stupidity, mental breakdown, or sudden and highly unlikely attacks of conscience on the part of Du Pont or G.M. executives, it could never be proved by judicial standards that the evil had been done. The availability of the loose Clayton Act standard of proof provided a convenient way of expressing this truth in "legalese." By using the trial date rather than the merger date as the point at which the Clayton standard can be applied and then using merger-to-trial conduct as evidence of future conduct, the Court can actually use the Clayton standard on past conduct. In effect, the Court declares that, while it cannot prove past misconduct sufficiently to satisfy the normal criminal-law standards of the Sherman Act, it can prove past misconduct sufficiently to imply future misconduct within the standards of the Clayton Act. In English, it means, "We can't prove it, but we know you did it; at least we can keep you from doing it again." The Court is sure enough of (1) and (2) to wish to convict Du Pont. It does not have sufficient evidence to invoke the Sherman Act, and that is why it goes to (3). The Clayton Act is used in *Du Pont* just as the "those who do not seek but cannot avoid" test is used in *Alcoa* and *United Shoe* to escape the problem of proof, which is otherwise an almost insurmountable obstacle to antitrust enforcement.

Once a reasonable probability of restriction has been established, violation of the antitrust statutes has still not been established until it is shown that the restriction has the effect of reducing competition in some section or community and of creating a monopoly in a line of commerce. In order to do so, the Court must first define the "market." In an earlier Du Pont litigation, usually referred to as the *Cellophane* case, the Court had shown that a sufficiently broad definition of "market" could take even a total monopolist off the hook. Du Pont was being prosecuted because it produced all the cellophane used in the country. But the Court, using a "cross-elasticity" approach, defined the market as "flexible wrapping materials." The theory was that, if the price of cellophane became excessive, users could switch to paper or other products, so that in fact Du Pont did not have power in the market, that is, power to fix noncompetitive prices. The fact that, for many firms and purposes, there was no practical alternative to cellophane and that Du Pont therefore exercised monopoly power *vis à vis* certain segments of wrapping users had not impressed the Court. Actually the *Cellophane* case seems to be one in which the Court really decided that Du Pont had had the monopoly of clear flexible wrappings thrust upon it through its progressive research and development programs. Unfortunately, it chose an excessively liberal market definition as the way of letting Du Pont off instead of admitting that it simply did not think Du Pont was a "bad guy." Antitrust lawyers gleefully seized upon this market approach as their defense in future cases.

One can imagine then the screams of horror when, in the new *Du Pont* case, the market was not limited to paint or even to metal-finish paint but to auto paint. The critics have hammered at the fact that an identical kind of paint is used on appliances and for many other purposes—that the Court defined the market not even as a single-commodity market but as that part of a single-commodity market used for a single purpose. There have been grave warnings of the dire consequences that would follow the application of such a rigid definition in the future, complaints of its break from the *Cellophane* precedent, and exposures of its lack of economic sophistication.

In fact, most of the criticism rests on the notion that the market approaches in both *Cellophane* and *Du Pont* were attempts at setting general standards or guidelines for all future cases. We have already noted that the *Cellophane* market definition was largely tactical. The *Du Pont* definition is even more clearly designed not to be used as a general test but to be applied only to the particular case and perhaps to future very similar ones. For lurking just below the surface of *Du Pont* is an even narrower definition than the one complained of—based not on auto paint but on G.M.'s auto paint. Du Pont was convicted of tying up G.M.'s paint market. This kind of definition of "market" is obviously closely related to the fact that *Du Pont* involves a vertical merger. When a horizontal merger is involved, when two paint firms merge, for example, the only problem is to determine how the merger affects suppliers and consumers of paint as a whole, for all consumers are able to buy from all the remaining producers, and all the remaining producers are able to sell to all the consumers. When vertical merger occurs, one producer in effect seals off one consumer from the remainder of the producers and establishes a reserved market. Where that reserved market is as large as General Motors, there is good reason for treating it as a market unto itself when vertical merger is involved. The market standard in *Du Pont* is not a general one but is rather a specific function of vertical integration between industrial giants.

The advantage of defining markets differently in different sorts of antitrust situation is very great. A generalized approach based on cross-elasticity and applied blindly to all cases is simply unrealistic. The *laissez-faire* economic model assumes uniformity and interchangeability among buyers so that all buyers can choose among all sellers of a given product and reasonable substitutes. In the real world, however, some buyers do not have that freedom of choice even when the market as a whole is operating relatively freely. The Court found that G.M., for instance, did not. Moreover, even when cross-elasticity of demand or interchangeability between products is, as a whole, very great, some buyers cannot choose between products. The cigarette companies can no more substitute tinfoil or wrapping paper for cellophane than they can choose sheet metal. If the antitrust laws are aimed at preventing noncompetitive pricing, then they cannot be effective unless they protect segments of a market that, for one reason or another, are isolated from the normal competition of that market. The question is, of course, always one of degree. Du Pont cannot be labeled a monopoly simply because Smith's Paint Store in Oskaloosa finds that, for some reason, it can buy its paint only from Du Pont. But General Motors is not Smith's Paint Store. The delimitation of the market in the *Du Pont* case takes account of a real situation in the real world.

In connection with market definition, one other factor must be mentioned. Once the market is defined and once restriction has been established, the Court must still discover whether or not the restriction actually reduced or, in Clayton Act cases, whether or not it is likely to reduce competition in the market. In *Du Pont,* the Court employed the "quantitative substantiality" test of *Standard Stations*. Once the Court found that Du Pont had a substantial share of the auto paint market and was engaging in restrictive practices, it presumed that a reduction in competition had occurred. This test has been much criticized because it does not seek to determine whether or not competition has really been reduced but simply assumes that restrictive practices by one large firm always reduce competition. But until the economists become much more expert at quantifying competition than they presently are, it is difficult to see what other approach the Court can take without getting into a quagmire of contradictory economic evidence.

Finally, there has been a good deal of comment on the impact of the Du Pont decision. The Clayton Act, before it was amended in 1950, applied only to stock not asset acquisitions, and it was the unamended Act that was applied in *Du Pont*. The actions of the Court in holding that the act applied to vertical as well as to horizontal mergers and in choosing the time of the suit and not that of the merger as the point for market analysis, therefore affected only pre-1950 stock acquisitions. As the Supreme Court had held that asset acquisition subsequent to stock acquisition and indeed even subsequent to the commencement of antitrust action was sufficient to save a merger from the operation of Sec. 7 and as most mergers in the period had involved asset acquisitions, *Du Pont* did not open a Pandora's box of potential government action against pre-1950 mergers. At the time of the decision, many commentators viewed it as the signal for a new antitrust campaign and a more vigorous antitrust attitude on the Supreme Court. Others felt that the case was *sui generis* because of the enormous sizes of Du Pont and G.M. and because the decision was rendered by a four-man majority, two of whom were "new" Justices, whose excessively liberal enthusiasm might be tempered by time.[32] In reviewing the Warren Court's subsequent record on antitrust cases, we shall see how *Du Pont* has fared.

The only other important case of the 1956 term was *Radovich v. National Football League.*[33] In 1922, the Court had held that professional baseball was not trade or commerce among the several states and was thus exempt from the Sherman Act.[34] By 1953, the Court was ready to admit that it had made a mistake but was unwilling to reverse itself because the whole structure of professional baseball had been created in reliance on its earlier decision.[35] Subsequently, it made clear that it would severely limit the precedential value of its early opinon. It held both professional boxing and theatrical roadshows to be subject to the Sherman Act.[36] Finally, in *Radovich,* the Court limited the 1922 precedent to baseball alone and held that pro football does fall under the Sherman Act. There are some interesting theoretical problems of *stare decisis* involved in *Radovich,* but the decision itself is relatively routine. Only an extremely "antiantitrust" court could have found that pro football, with teams flying from state to state each week and its national television hookup, was not interstate commerce.

In the next term's only major antitrust case,[37] the Court seemed to signal a continuation of the activist bent exhibited in *Du Pont.* Early judicial interpretations of the Sherman Act had excluded tying agreements from its reach. Congress had responded by inserting a condemnation of such agreements in the Clayton Act, but that Act applied only to commodities and not to services. Subsequent Court decisions, culminating in the *International Salt* case,[38] seemed to reverse the early trend and to extend the Sherman Act to tying agreements. In *International Salt,* in which the lessee of patented vending machines was required to buy salt from the patent holder, the Court refused to hear economic evidence on the impact of the arrangement on competition and seemed to hold tie-ins illegal *per se*. At the time, however, it was not clear whether the Court had read a general and *per se* condemnation of tie-ins into the Sherman Act or was simply extending the doctrine of patent misuse.

Subsequently, in the *Times-Picayune* case[39] the Court purported to synthesize its earlier findings. It held that a tie-in is unreasonable *per se* under Sec. 1 only when it is established that the seller has monopoly power over the tying product and that a substantial amount of trade in the tied product has been restrained in the particular case. In short, the Court preserved little more than the form of the *per se* approach and demanded proof at least of market conditions from which a reduction of competition could be inferred. Since the Times-Picayune papers had in fact been engaged in clearly anticompetitive practices, their acquittal plus practical rejection of the *per se* approach in favor of requirements of monopoly and substantial restriction, which are not normally necessary for Sec. 1 convictions, seemed largely to cripple Sec. 1 as a weapon against tie-ins.

The vote in *Times-Picayune* had been 5–4 and, by 1958, the lineup had changed. *Northern Pacific Railway Co. v. United States* registered this change. The railroad, in selling the huge tracts of land originally granted it by the government, had required all purchasers to agree to ship via Northern Pacific unless they could get lower rates on other railroads. As only services and not commodities were involved, the Clayton Act was not applicable, and prosecution was brought under the Sherman Act. The Court interpreted the *Times-Picayune* requirement of "monopoly power" or "dominance" to mean "sufficient" economic power to impose an appreciable restraint on the tied product. Then it reasoned that the existence of the tying arrangement itself proved the economic power, as no other reason had been offered for the purchasers' entering into such a restrictive agreement. The Court thus came very close to establishing a *per se* rule against tie-ins. Moreover, as there had been considerable argument in *Northern Pacific* analogizing the unique nature of land to the uniqueness of patented items *à la* the *International Salt* case, the Court went out of its way to say that neither case had been decided on this special factor, so that the nearly *per se* condemnation of tie-ins in Northern Pacific is a general rule applicable to all tie-ins and not merely to those involving unique items.

In short, faced with a hiatus in control over service tie-ins created by its own early Sherman Act decisions and the narrow wording of the Clayton Act, the Court had two alternatives. It might have extended the "commodity language" of the Clayton Act to include services as well. Instead it included both service and commodity tie-ins under the Sherman Act. The problem is that standards of proof in terms of evidence of the actual effect on the market are much higher under the Sherman Act than under the Clayton Act, so that when the evidence is minimal or incomplete, commodity tie-ins that escaped the Sherman Act could be caught under the Clayton Act, while service tie-ins could not. The introduction of the *per se* approach, which obviates the necessity of really examining evidence and thus of really meeting Sherman Act standards of proof, solves this problem and creates a symmetry of restrictions on commodity- and service-tying arrangements. The *per se* approach imports the more lenient Clayton Act standards of proof into the Sherman Act when either commodity or service tie-ins are involved and thus achieves exactly the same goal as the alternative of reading service tie-ins into Clayton Act coverage. Just as in *Alcoa, United Shoe,* and *Du Pont,* the judges were faced with obviously anticompetitive situations and adopted an approach that allowed them to see clearly without blinding legal and economic quibbles.

There was also a series of less important decisions in the 1958 term. In *United States v. Radio Corporation of America,*[40] the Court held for the first time that an F.C.C. approval of a license transfer does not exempt the transaction from subsequent antitrust prosecution. This decision seems to be in line with both Congressional intention and F.C.C. practice. While the F.C.C. considers antitrust policy among the many factors involved in its "public interest" standard for transfers, it has specifically disavowed the power to make antitrust determinations as such.

In *Melrose Distillers v. United States,*[41] Melrose and Dant, two wholly owned subsidiaries of Schenley were indicted for criminal violation of the Sherman Act. While proceedings were under way, the two subsidiary corporations were dissolved and recreated as divisions of the parent company. They then asked for an abatement of criminal penalties on the ground that the original corporate offenders had ceased to exist. As might be expected, the Supreme Court refused to play such games and found that, under the laws of the states in which the two firms had been incorporated, they continued to exist sufficiently after dissolution to be subject to Sherman Act penalties.

In *Kelly v. Kosuga*,[42] a purchaser repudiated his contract and offered as a defense against breach-of-contract action the argument that the entire transaction had violated the Sherman Act. Judges face a dilemma in such cases. They dislike being parties to contract-breaking. On the other hand, they do not wish to put themselves in the position of ordering direct violations of the Sherman Act by insisting that such contracts be completed. Courts therefore usually consider several factors. Was the purchase price reasonable? How much unjust enrichment will the contract-breaker enjoy if he does not have to complete the transaction? Was the contract itself the vehicle of antitrust violation, or was it a separable transaction merely incidental to the violation? In this case, the price was reasonable, potential unjust enrichment very great, and the transaction, while motivated by, was separable from, the actual violation. The Supreme Court accordingly would not allow a Sherman Act defense.

International Boxing Club v. United States,[43] not a particularly important case in itself, does shed some light on the problem of defining the market. In a suit charging violation of Secs. 1 and 2 of the Sherman Act in connection with its control over championship boxing events, International argued that the appropriate market was all professional boxing, as a championship fight was physically no different from any other. The trial court, which held for the government, stressed such economic aspects as differences in total revenue, returns from television, and so forth.

In affirming the trial court's definition of the market in terms of championships, the Supreme Court specifically approved the *Cellophane* test of reasonable interchangeability. By affirming it in this context, however, the Court showed that the *Cellophane* test could not be considered an automatic device for getting the culprit off or an essentially "antiantitrust" formula. Justice Clark insisted that, while the test would remain the same, the definition of market would vary with the facts. On one side then, we have *International Boxing, Du Pont* (in which the market was defined as auto paint), and *Alcoa* (in which Judge Hand refused to consider the substitutability of other metals or even of imported aluminum). On the other, there are *Cellophane* (in which the Court was willing to consider wax paper interchangeable with cellophane) and *Times-Picayune* (in which morning newspaper advertising was considered interchangeable with afternoon advertising). It can only be concluded that the definition of "market" is less a separable, preliminary operation than a function of the judges' general sense of the facts. The Court seems perfectly capable of using the market formulas of *Cellophane* and *Times-Picayune* to reach the antitrust conclusions of *International Boxing* and *Du Pont*.

In *Klor's Inc. v. Broadway-Hale Stores, Inc.,*[44] Broadway, a chain store next to one of whose San Francisco branches Klor's operated a single store, had allegedly used its superior buying power to convince ten appliance manufacturers to refuse to sell to Klor's or to sell only at highly unfavorable prices. This kind of case would be simple enough except for some of the theoretical exegesis that surrounds the Sherman Act. The argument is that the purpose of the Act was to preserve competition. "Competition" is then often defined in the sense that economists use the term, so that the purpose of the Sherman Act becomes preservation of a competitive market according to the criteria of economics. This theory is frequently expressed in the notion that the Sherman Act only applies to public not to private injury.

Broadway-Hale was able to show that, while its practice might seriously hamper its neighbor, it did not reduce competition as a whole in the sale of appliances in the San Francisco area. Because of the very large total number of retailers, the appliance market remained substantively as competitive with or without the presence of Klor's. While there may be a private injury to Klor's, no public injury in the economic sense occurs.

Underlying the Sherman Act, and made explicit in the Clayton Act, however, is a second purpose. Antitrust law is aimed not only at maintaining an economically competitive market but also at preventing or punishing certain anticompetitive practices or "dirty tricks." As we noted earlier, because of the false notion that competition was self-perpetuating as long as everyone played by the rules, the two purposes of antitrust policy were initially seen as inseparable. This case neatly shows their separability.

The Court might simply have rejected the public-injury theory. Instead it chose to sidestep the problem by arguing that the common law had condemned group refusals to deal, that is, boycotts, and that Congress had intended to incorporate the common law of restraint of trade into the Sherman Act. Congress had therefore made boycotts *per se* violations of the Sherman Act, even though it had not mentioned them. Because violation of a statute is itself a public injury, there is no need to determine whether or not this offense created a particular public injury in the sense of reducing competition as defined economically. Put another way, Congress has already determined that all boycotts result in public injury, so that courts will not concern themselves about the results of any particular boycott.

As there had previously been considerable uncertainty about the antitrust status of group refusals to deal and as some authorities thought that certain of them were legitimate, this blanket condemnation makes *Klor's* a leading case. It has been subject to much criticism on the grounds that such a *per se* rule is too inflexible and fails to anticipate those instances in which group refusals to deal may not harm competition and may serve some useful purpose. The *per se* rule on boycotts is, of course, a piece of judicial legislation. But the Court follows Congress's long tradition of labeling certain practices "immoral" under the code of *laissez-faire,* no matter what their particular effects. This decision does not represent a use of *per se* rules to avoid the evidential problem when it is clear that a certain practice is reducing competition but impossible to prove it. The *per se* approach in *Klor's* is simply the Court's way of saying that antitrust law condemns this kind of "dirty trick," no matter what its general economic consequences.

The Court adds a common-sense economic argument to bolster its *per se* approach. The boycott has, by its "nature" and "character," a "monopolistic tendency,"

> As such it is not to be tolerated merely because the victim is just one merchant whose business is so small that his destruction makes little difference to the economy. Monopoly can as surely

> thrive by the elimination of such small businessmen, one at a time, as it can by driving them out in large groups.[45]

This argument could not, of course, have been used independently, for there was no evidence to suggest that Broadway-Hale was engaged in plotting creeping monopoly. It does, however, suggest an important facet of American antitrust sentiment, one that seeks to enforce competition not only in the sense of an economist's diagram but in the behavior between man and man.

In a curious way, *Klor's,* combined with *Alcoa* and *Du Pont,* shows the unending dialetic of an antitrust policy that seeks to avoid a certain economic structure by condemning certain economic behavior rather than by acting directly on the structure. In *Alcoa* and *Du Pont,* the supposed legitimacy of the business conduct is outweighed by the resulting monopolistic condition of the market. In *Klor's,* the continuous competitive condition of the market does not save the illegitimate conduct. Meanwhile the "antiantitrust" forces plead that the courts cannot punish innocent conduct or at least conduct that cannot be proved guilty simply because they dislike the condition of the market. And when the conduct is clearly guilty, the same critics argue that the courts cannot punish the conduct unless they dislike the condition of the market as well.

Two cases in the 1959 term dealt with exceptions to the antitrust laws. In *Minneapolis and St. Louis Railway Co. v. United States,*[46] the Court held that Sec. 5 (11) of the I.C.C. Act, which required the I.C.C. to apply the standard of "public interest" to railroad mergers, had been intended to allow the I.C.C. to deviate from the results that an antitrust standard would have required. The antitrust decision was incidental to the principal issue in the case, and the Court relied heavily on a routine application of *McLean Trucking Co. v. United States,*[47] in which it had earlier held that the national transportation policy of Congress provided for certain exemptions from antitrust policy in the transportation industry. In both this case and R.C.A., the Court indicates that antitrust considerations enter into but are not decisive in commission decisions under the "public interest" standard. Although the Court in effect reads such I.C.C. decisions as granting exemptions from antitrust prosecution, while refusing to give the F.C.C. this power, the two cases reflect less a judicial appraisal of the two agencies than a routine enforcement of relatively clearly stated Congressional intent and long administrative practice.

Maryland and Virginia Milk Producers v. United States[48] shows the Court in a more positive role. Agricultural co-operatives enjoy certain exemptions from antitrust laws under the Capper-Volstead and Clayton Acts. In *United States v. Borden,*[49] however, the Supreme Court ruled that, when a co-operative is engaged in antitrust activities in conjunction with "other persons," those activities are not exempt from prosecution. At the time of *Borden,* it was not clear whether the Court had intended a definitive holding that co-ops lose their exemptions only when they conspire with outsiders or had simply held that this situation was one in which the co-ops lost it, leaving others to be defined in the future. In the *Maryland and Virginia* case, the facts would have allowed the Court simply to apply the "other persons" rule. Instead, the Court chose to enunciate a far broader standard. It held that agricultural co-operatives were to be treated as analogous to corporations and that any trade practices or methods of competition forbidden to corporations were forbidden to them as well. In effect, the Court said that the antitrust exemption had been created strictly for purposes of allowing co-ops to organize themselves without being subject to the charges of conspiracy and price-fixing that might normally have greeted the co-operation of individual producers to pool their products and sell them at uniform prices. Once the farmers have formed themselves into a business unit, however, that unit is to be treated for antitrust purposes just like any other business unit.

United States v. Parke, Davis and Company,[50] which involved resale-price maintenance, was the leading case of the 1959 term. The question of whether or not a manufacturer should be allowed to require all wholesalers or retailers of his product to sell it at a uniform price involves many of the basic problems and dilemmas of American economic thought. First, the vision of a prospective buyer's going from store to store and being confronted in each with exactly the same predetermined price for the same piece of merchandise is at odds with the most fundamental concept of *laissez-faire,* the free market of independent buyers and sellers, bargaining to set prices by supply and demand. Second, price maintenance almost invariably arises in the context of brand-name goods and enforces the distortions in supply and demand adjustments and reductions in competition inherent in the brand system. On the other hand, if resale-price maintenance is viewed as simply the refusal of a manufacturer to sell to a trader unless he agrees to meet the manufacturer's conditions, then interfering by law with that refusal would seem to contravene the whole set of values for which the "private" in private enterprise serves as a vehicle. Every businessman should have the right to sell or not to sell to whom he pleases for whatever reason he pleases. A ban on resale-price maintenance as part of a program of antitrust regulation would thus violate the very values of private economic decision-making that led us initially to solve our problems by government regulation rather than by government ownership.

Finally, resale-price maintenance is in many instances intimately connected with a basic paradox of the American economy —that initial competition frequently leads to oligopoly rather than to continued competition. Cut-rate chain drug stores have posed a serious threat to small independent drugstores. The Parke, Davis policy was designed to reduce the price competition that the chains had brought into the drug business. It was thus designed either to stifle competition or to preserve a competitive market by preventing the chains from using their competitive advantage to force out independents and create oligopolistic control, depending on whether the focus is on the initial competitive situation or its anticipated results.

Faced with all these problems, the Supreme Court, before *Parke, Davis,* had come up with some answers or at least with some outer boundaries.[51] When price maintenance is achieved by a conspiracy in the form of a contract mutually and multilaterally binding on a manufacturer and his dealers, it violates Sec. 1 of the Sherman Act. When price maintenance is nothing more than the unilateral refusal of the manufacturer to sell to a dealer because the dealer is not selling at the price the manufacturer desires, then there is no violation of the Sherman Act, for Sec. 1 requires either conspiracy or combination. Thus the two poles. The Court has also moved inward one step from each pole. When the manufacturer has in fact entered into a conspiracy or coerced a combination with his dealers, a violation of the Sherman Act may be found even if the conspiracy or combination is not embodied in a formal contract. Near the other pole, a manufacturer does not violate the Act if he announces in advance his intention to refuse unilaterally to deal with those who do not abide by his suggested price list. The grey area, of course, exists where the manufacturer has more than simply announced his intentions in advance and has done less than conspire with or coerce his suppliers.[52] It is this grey area that is before the Court in *Parke, Davis.*

Before beginning an analysis of *Parke, Davis,* the conventional thing to do would be to trace the precedents leading up to that decision in detail rather than to content ourselves with the general propositions just stated. I shall not do so for two reasons. First, Professor Levi has done the job admirably in a piece in the *Supreme Court Review.*[53] Second, he shows fairly conclusively that, for various reasons, the earlier decisions were not very precise at the times they were formulated and have been further obscured by passage of time and later developments in related areas of law. While the opinions in *Parke, Davis* devote a good deal of space to limiting, distinguishing, and interpreting precedents, the net result sheds little light on the problem precisely because the precedents are so unenlightening.

It is, however, necessary to take the next conventional step and to describe the facts in *Parke, Davis.*

Parke, Davis sold both to wholesalers and to retailers directly. When an outbreak of price-cutting from its announced lists occurred, it instructed its salesmen to inform their customers that Parke, Davis would not sell to retailers who did not maintain the suggested prices and would also refuse to sell to wholesalers who sold to such retailers. When price-cutting broke out anew, Parke, Davis refused to sell to five retailers in the District of Columbia and Virginia and informed wholesalers that it would refuse to do business with them if they continued to sell to these retailers. Three wholesalers thereupon stopped selling Parke, Davis products to those retailers.

The trial court found

> . . . there is no coercion by defendant and no agreement with coconspirators. . . . representatives of defendant notified retailers concerning the policy under which its goods must be sold, but the retailers were free either to do without such goods or sell them in accordance with the defendant's policy. . . . Wholesalers were likewise free to refuse to comply and thus risk being cut off by the defendant. . . . every visit made by the representatives to the retailers and wholesalers was, to each of them, separate and apart from all others.[54]

In short, it treated a concerted effort, by one of the half-dozen manufacturing chemists who dominate the American drug business, to control prices by manipulating both the wholesale and retail markets as if the corner buggy-whip maker had refused to sell to the Pottsville Hardware Store one day and the Humbolt Harness Supply Company the next because the cranky old man thought the quality of his workmanship was being insulted by the low prices these two outfits were charging for his product.

The Supreme Court did not see the case that way. It found that the actions of Parke, Davis constituted a conspiracy and a coerced combination within the meaning of the Sherman Act. Again, as so frequently, we find that the fact sense of the appellate court runs contrary to that of the trier of fact. Of course, it may be that we are only running across recurrent instances of trial-court judges who are more probusiness or "antiantitrust" than their higher-court colleagues. But there is probably an institutional as well as a personal factor at play. The trial court operates in a legal world that revolves around personal guilt and innocence. The whole traditional procedure and rules of the trial court are designed to prohibit the trial judge from making decisions, as decisions are made every day, on the basis of hearsay, common knowledge, surmise, experience, and estimated probabilities.

The trial judge deals with categories like "best evidence," "proved beyond a reasonable doubt," and "not proved" because we will not allow judicial decisions adverse to the individual to be made in the same way that we make most other governmental decisions. In short, for various historical and philosophic reasons, when the defendant stands at the bar of justice, we do not encourage his judge to convict him on the basis of what can be plainly seen but on the basis of what the prosecutor can prove.

Trial court findings therefore often seem unrealistic or naive, not because the trial judge is basically unknowledgeable, but because he refuses to know what the prosecutor has not proved.

The appellate court, on the other hand, and particularly the Supreme Court in the field of antitrust law, is less a determiner of individual and particular guilt or innocence than a formulator of social policy. The Court as political economist must make decisions on a basis similar to that of any other political economist. And policy-making would surely come to a complete standstill if it had to await the certainty that trial courts require. If the policy initiator had to face the same burden of proof as the prosecutor, no public policy could ever be made. The Supreme Court is therefore likely to rest its decisions on its over-all sense of the facts, including healthy doses of technically irrelevant, hearsay, and unsupportable evidence rather than to limit itself to the rigorous standards of trial courts. Otherwise, it could not perform its policy-making role successfully. This fact is particularly clear in antitrust cases, in most of which it is obviously impossible to prove conclusively the points that huge corporate entities with vast resources take infinite care to obscure. If it seems wrong that the Supreme Court should determine individual guilt and innocence by standards less exacting than those used by the trial courts because it reaches such decisions only as incidents to policy-making, that is one of the prices we pay for choosing to make economic policy by punitive statute. It is a difficulty inherent in choosing negative regulation as a principal means of adjusting the relations between business and government.

Of course, in *Parke, Davis,* the Supreme Court was caught in the usual problem it faces when it wishes to reverse a trial court's findings of fact. Appellate courts are supposed to grant the greatest respect to fact-finding below. Within the federal court system, this tradition is, as we saw in the *Du Pont* case, embodied in a "clearly erroneous" rule. It will be remembered that, in *Du Pont,* the Court overcame the problem by distinguishing in effect between findings of raw fact and conclusions drawn from those facts. In *Parke, Davis* the Court holds that the trial Court's basic findings of fact are not being questioned but that the trial court's conclusion as to absence of illegal coercion and combination was incorrect because it had used the wrong standard for interpreting the facts. Underlying the whole opinion is the Supreme Court's view that the trial court's appraisal of the facts was fundamentally at odds with the realities of the drug business.

The introduction of the "standards of interpretation" argument was, however, more than a dodge for reversing the factual findings of the trial court. For, in this case, the facts and the law play a curious game with one another. The Supreme Court might have meant that the situation in *Parke, Davis* was the "next to polar" illegal activity we sketched out earlier, in which the mere absence of a formal contract is not itself sufficient to ensure the legality of the multilateral activity. That is, Parke, Davis's activities might have constituted a multilateral refusal to deal, in that wholesalers conspired with the manufacturer to deny goods to certain retailers, and a coerced combination, in that the visitations of Parke, Davis representatives to wholesalers and retailers forced them into a concerted pricing policy even though no formal agreements were signed. If that were all the Court had meant, it could have contented itself with finding some means of reversing the trial court's findings of no coercion and unilateral action. Justice Stewart's cryptic concurrence may signify that he wished to go only this far.

A majority of the Justices apparently wanted to go further. For Justice Brennan introduced the rule that the Sherman Act is violated whenever the producer "secures adherence to his suggested prices by means which go beyond his mere declination to sell to a customer who will not observe his announced policy."[55] Such a rule in effect places the whole or nearly the whole grey area between the two "next to polar" situations in the illegal category and thus extends, or some would say, destroys, the categories established by previous decisions. It must be repeated that, whether or not the majority broke with precedent, as Justice Harlan insists in his dissent, depends on how much clarity and exactness one sees in the precedents, and I do not see very much. Nevertheless, the majority seemed anxious to obscure its new, if not deviant, rule by mixing it inextricably into the factual question. The decision does not quite say, "The facts of this case show the same kinds of actions that we have earlier condemned as conspiracy and coercion without contract." Nor does it quite say, "We now extend the illegal categories to include behavior which falls short of what we previously would have viewed as conspiracy and coercion, leaving only simple unilateral refusal safe." Instead, it says that if the trial court had applied the proper standard, presumably the "means which go beyond his mere declination to sell" test, it would have found conspiracy and coercion. The Court thus bolsters its new standard with the strong suggestion that the facts really justified conviction under the old standard anyway and bolsters its challenge to the trial court's fact finding by the introduction of its new standard.

What is perfectly clear, however, is that *Parke, Davis* joins *Du Pont* and *Klor's* as representative of the Warren Court's reaction to such "antiantitrust" decisions as the *Cellophane* and *Times-Picayune* opinions, a reaction that is closely akin to those in the *Alcoa* and *United Shoe* decisions.

The *Du Pont* decision of 1957 had remanded the problem of enforcement to the district court. It returned to the Supreme Court in the 1960 term as another *United States v. Du Pont.*[56] In enforcing the antitrust laws, American courts have shown a very strong tendency to choose divestiture when stock mergers have been involved but to bar dissolution of physically integrated concerns. Quite obviously, the courts view the Clayton Act provisions as remedial rather than punitive and wish to eliminate anticompetitive situations with as little damage to the firms involved as possible. Stock transfers have little effect on the actual operation of an industry, but actual dissolution may be highly disruptive.

Indeed, the Supreme Court has long held that antitrust decrees must consider the public interest, and industrial upheaval is not in the public interest, so that in a sense the interests of the antitrust violator and the public are partially parallel. Courts have generally considered losses to the firms involved as one factor in the public-interest criterion. But should the projected losses include, not only production losses or inefficiencies that obviously affect the whole public, but also financial losses to stockholders from tax liabilities and depressed stock-market prices encountered in the forced sale of stock when divestiture is ordered?

In *Du Pont,* the district court did take these factors into account and ordered that the voting rights be "passed through" to the Du Pont stockholders, while the G.M. stock itself might remain in the hands of the Du Pont Company. The Supreme Court reversed, holding that considerations of public interest or economic consequences could come into play only when a choice was available between alternative remedies. Since divestiture was an effective remedy and the "pass through" device was not, no such choice was available in this case.

The Court thus avoided confrontation with the problem of whether or not tax and stock-market losses to participants in illegal mergers are to be considered public-interest factors. It also denied the government's claim that Sec. 7 requires divestiture in all instances. On the other hand, it came very close to adopting an automatic divestiture rule, for it held that economic consequences were not to be considered when divestiture was the only appropriate remedy and then almost, but not quite, held that divestiture was the only appropriate remedy in stock acquisition cases.

The second *Du Pont* may thus be read—but not with absolute certainty—as furnishing a *per se* rule for divestiture. Its precedential value on this point is weakened, however, not only by the indecisiveness of the language but also by two other factors. The opinion was announced by the same shaky majority that rendered the initial decision, and it may also be argued here, as it was argued there, that the sizes of the firms involved render the decision *sui generis*. In any event, the opinion marks a continued reluctance on the part of the Court to frame its decisions in terms of a legal "never-never land" in which the corporate executive meticulously lives up to the letter and spirit of the law, in spite of vast potentials for coercion, yet always remains the very model of a modern, competitive economic man.

In *Eastern Rail Road Presidents v. Noerr Motor Freight Lines,*[57] the Court held that lobbying activity was so different from those activities normally considered economic conspiracies that it was excluded from Sec. 1 of the Sherman Act. The Court said in effect that when businesses or individuals co-operate in publicity campaigns designed to yield legislation favorable to their economic interests, their activity is political and thus outside the Sherman Act. The Court reserved judgment on publicity campaigns, ostensibly directed at government activity, that might actually be direct attempts to interfere with competition.

Radiant Burners v. Peoples Gas Co.[58] was a little noticed *per curiam* of the 1960 term but an important decision nonetheless. The American Gas Association operates a laboratory that grants a "seal of approval" to gas appliances that meet its standards. A Gas Association member will not supply gas to unapproved appliances. Radiant Burners had been refused a seal for the conversion burner it manufactured, although it claimed that the burner was safer and more efficient than several that had been approved. Member gas companies had refused to supply gas to the purchasers of these burners.

The Court of Appeals applied the "public injury" criterion and found that no public injury had occurred because there had been no "appreciable lessening" in competition. Many rival lines of conversion burners remained available. The Supreme Court reiterated the position it had taken in *Klor's* and *Radovich:* Group refusal to deal is a *per se* violation of the Sherman Act. As Congress had condemned such activity *per se,* it had determined the extent of public injury for itself, and it was not for the courts to redetermine it case by case. Of course, just as in *Klor's,* this argument is a bit circular. The Court reads the *per se* violation into Sec. 1, thus creating the Congressional declaration that group refusal itself constitutes a public injury. It then modestly bows to the Congressional determination that it itself has created. What the Court is actually saying is that it will not approve conspiratorial, anticompetitive activity simply because it results in the elimination of only one small competitor and thus does not affect the general level of competition.

This case is significant for two reasons. First, it unanimously and specifically reaffirms the *per se* doctrine of *Klor's* in the face of considerable academic sniping at the "inflexibility" of that decision.[59] Second, because *Klor's* had involved a boycott aimed solely and specifically at eliminating competition, it had left unclear the Court's position toward "ethical" group refusals to deal. Here where a more proper motive, protection of public safety, is possibly involved, the Court sticks to its *per se* rule, strongly suggesting that it will not give weight to such factors or at least that its *per se* rule had not been devised simply to stop the obviously "dirty pool" involved in *Klor's*.[60]

So far in our survey of the Warren Court, we have seen a

rather consistent hostility to anticompetitive devices and a movement toward *per se* rules to facilitate antitrust convictions. *Tampa Electric Co. v. Nashville Coal Co.*[61] deviates from those patterns. As the vote was seven to two and did not follow any radical shift in Court personnel, it cannot be explained in convenient personal terms.

Tampa Electric, a public utility in the process of constructing the first major generating plant in Florida to burn coal, had entered into a "twenty-year requirements" contract with the Nashville Coal Company. Nashville Coal later refused to perform on the grounds that the contract constituted a violation of the Clayton Act.

In the *Standard Stations* case,[62] requirements contracts were lumped together with tying arrangements as violations of the "exclusive dealing" clause (Sec. 3) of the Clayton Act. It was also *Standard Stations* that established the "quantitative substantiality" test, which is itself a kind of *per se* rule. That is, when an exclusive-dealing scheme involves a substantial portion of the market, the Court will not examine its actual effects on competition but will assume sufficient effect to constitute a Clayton Act violation. Technically and by itself *Tampa Electric* does not deviate from *Standard Stations.* The district court in Tampa had defined the market as peninsular Florida and, on that basis, found Nashville to have a quantitatively substantial share. The Supreme Court defined it as the entire Appalachian coal region. As the requirements contract involved less than 1% of this market, the Court held that it did not constitute a substantial quantity. The case was thus reduced to a problem in market definition rather than a challenge to the "quantitative substantiality" test.

Nevertheless, there was language in Justice Clark's opinion suggesting that the Court would examine the actual conditions of the market, impact on competition, and justification for restrictive practices in determining whether the "quantitative substantiality" test had been met. Such an approach would in effect convert the test from a *per se* approach into actual economic analysis and perhaps even to the rule of reason that allows anticompetitive practices when there is sufficient economic justification for them. Moreover, the Court approved a contract tying up the market provided by a huge buyer for twenty years when it had never previously approved a requirements contract for more than one year.[63]

What are the reasons for these changes in attitude? First, the Court may have wished to differentiate tying agreements from requirements contracts. When tying agreements and requirements contracts are lumped under Sec. 3 and when quantitative substantiality, a semi *per se* test, is applied to the whole clause, the Court declares in effect that both tying and requirements schemes are illegal *per se* as long as they affect more than insignificant portions of the market. Tying agreements seem to be obviously and patently anticompetitive and without any redeeming economic value, so that a *per se* approach makes sense for them. But requirements contracts have such economic advantages as assuring a steady supply of raw materials, eliminating the need for storage facilities, and reducing irrational fluctuations in costs. Justice Frankfurter had described some of these factors in *Standard Stations* before refusing to consider them because he found requirements contracts legally equivalent to tying agreements. Justice Clark notes his description but not his refusal. Clark may really be saying: "We do not wish directly to overrule the *Standard Stations* equation of tying and requirements contracts. Nevertheless, we see that, while tying is always bad, requirements contracts are sometimes justifiable. Because we are not willing to overrule *Standard's* inclusion of both in Sec. 3, we must apply the "quantitative substantiality" test to both. Because we think that they are really different, we shall not put so much *per se* into the "quantitative substantiality" approach when we apply it to requirements contracts as we do when we apply it to tying agreements."

The fact that a public utility was involved may be considered a second and independent factor or part of the first. To a utility, steady and predictable fixed costs are particularly advantageous because its rate structure is fixed and it must be able to anticipate changes in costs in order to bring the cumbersome process of rate renegotiation with public utilities commissions to a conclusion by the time its costs actually go up. Utilities may thus be entitled to a special exception in the area of requirements contracts, or, alternatively, they may provide a particularly good example of why requirements contracts should generally be considered different from tying agreements.

Finally, Justice Frankfurter had proposed the semi*per se* rule of *Standard Stations* specifically because he considered the Court incompetent to undertake detailed economic analysis. But we have seen that the Court favors *per se* rules not so much because of qualms over its economic abilities as because of its recognition of a basic paradox of regulation. Because negative regulation leaves the regular apparatus of business decision-making entirely in private hands, it leaves the ability to make secret decisions in private hands and creates maximum incentives for secrecy. Negative regulation tends to ensure that the government cannot get the evidence it needs to enforce the regulations by prosecution. *Per se* rules tend to reduce the government's burden of proof and thus to make the laws workable.

In another sense, *per se* rules reflect, not the weakness of the Court's economic expertise, but the weakness of economics generally. Because we still know almost nothing about how business really works, as opposed to how economic models work, the "anti-antitrust" forces can always muster a host of economic arguments to show that, in any given instance, a reduction in competition cannot be proved or can be justified. *Per se* rules or indeed any approach that allows the Court to use common sense prevents endless technical manipulation of our economic ignorance to protect anticompetitive forces. Finally, *per se* rules allow the Court to get at the dirty tricks—the violations of *laissez-faire* ethics—even when those tricks do not significantly reduce competition.

If the Court were using *per se* rules because of its institutional weakness, as suggested by Justice Frankfurter, one might expect it to use them uniformly, for its lack of economic expertise is continuous. If not, *per se* rules would be likely to appear only when the Court believed that things were going on that the government could not prove or when economic technicalities were being exploited to obscure basic reality, or when rules of the game were being violated even though no over-all reduction of competition occurred.

The Court obviously saw none of these factors in *Tampa* and so was led to de-emphasize *per se* rules. It may simply be a tautology to say that the Court decided the case as it did because it saw an honest arrangement by which a public utility was attempting to stabilize its rate structure rather than an anticompetitive conspiracy. Obviously some anticompetitive elements were present. But ultimately *Tampa* seems to deviate from the *per se* antitrust tendencies of the Court simply because the Court, for all its willingness to see through facades of respectability, simply did not find any "dirty dealing" in this case.

The Court returned more clearly to its previous antitrust policy in the 1961 term. In *United States v. Wise,*[64] it held that an individual corporate officer could be convicted of violation of Sec. 1 of the Sherman Act either for independent acts or for those performed solely for his corporation. Sec. 14 of the Clayton Act provides for the punishment of officers conspiring on behalf of their corporations, and until *Wise* it was unclear whether the Sherman Act also applied in such instances or was limited only to situations in which individuals had conspired in their own interests. This question was academic until 1955, for the penalties under both provisions were the same, but in that year Congress increased the maximum fine under the Sherman Act to $50,000, while leaving unchanged the $5000 fine for Sec. 14 violations. The Supreme Court's opinion, while raising some minor questions about the etiquette of statutory interpretation, simply applies the larger fines to corporate officers acting for their corporations. As there was no clear Congressional intent one way or the other and as no great problems of administration are involved, the decision is hardly earth-shaking but does indicate the Court's general sentiments.

In *California v. Federal Power Commission,*[65] El Paso Natural Gas Co., the largest distributor in the Southwest, sought a merger with Pacific Northwest Pipeline Co. After the Justice Department began a Clayton Act proceeding in federal district court, El Paso asked the Federal Power Commission to approve the merger. Such approval is necessary under the requirements of the Natural Gas Act. At the same time, El Paso asked the district court to stay its proceedings, and the court deferred to the Commission, which later approved the merger.

The Supreme Court reversed. The tone of the opinion is highly pragmatic. El Paso is just the sort of firm, undertaking just the sort of practice, that garners unfavorable Supreme Court opinions. El Paso had obviously been engaging in a devious maneuver to prevent the Clayton Act from being used for precisely the purpose for which it was intended, stopping mergers before they take place. The Court stressed the practical fact that, once a merger has occurred, the problems of dissolution might be so great that courts would be reluctant to order such a remedy, and the purposes of the Clayton Act would be frustrated. It also more than hinted that district courts might be unduly influenced by advance determination by a regulatory agency that no antitrust violation had occurred. In the interests of "orderly procedure," therefore it refused to allow the F.P.C. to consider the merits of a merger when an antitrust suit is pending in the courts.

This decision, particularly when considered in connection with *United States v. R.C.A.*, represents a declaration of independence by the Supreme Court. The Court refused to allow the frequently invoked "primary jurisdiction" doctrine to be used to transfer its antitrust powers to the commissions. In effect, it declares that, while radio and TV stations may be the special domain of the F.C.C. and pipelines of the F.T.C., antitrust policy is the special domain of the courts. While the commissions may have primary jurisdiction over the industries specially entrusted to their supervision, the courts have primary jurisdiction over antitrust matters no matter what the industry. To be sure, standards of "public interest" or "public convenience and necessity" are written into the regulatory acts, and the commissions are required to consider antitrust factors under these standards. The F.P.C. is required to find the nonexistence of antitrust violations before approving a merger. Nevertheless, the Court makes clear that these provisions do not in any way alter the antitrust statutes themselves. Unless the Court discovers clear Congressional intent to exempt a regulated industry from the general antitrust laws, the courts will apply those laws equally and in the light of the courts' own standards, no matter what standards the commissions choose to use in connection with their particular industries. The opinion clearly intimated to the district courts that they are to make their own independent antitrust determinations without all the bowing and scraping to administrative-agency expertise that usually marks court-commission relations. Indeed, the Supreme Court seems so suspicious of the fortitude of the district courts in the face of the commissions that it refuses them discretion in staying their proceedings once suit has been instituted, thus leaving to the Justice Department the decision as to whether to get a court decision first or to await a commission finding.

It must be added that Justice Douglas wrote this opinion for a majority of five, Justices Frankfurter and White not participating and Justices Harlan and Stewart dissenting. In a sense, it was an opportunity to let off steam after years of the deference to the commissions that the canons of judicial modesty require, and the language of the opinion may, in its broad sweep, be more indicative of Douglas's personal sentiments than of the firm position of the Court. It remains to be seen whether or not the tone of the opinion will be preserved in future decisions, but it does seem clear that the Court intends to maintain a pre-eminent position in antitrust matters.

The leading antitrust case of the 1961 term was *Brown Shoe Co. v. United States.*[66] Brown and Kinney shoe companies, each of which controlled both manufacturing and retailing facilities, sought to merge. The government contended that such a merger would constitute a multiple violation of Sec. 7 of the Clayton Act, for it would create a vertical combination of Brown's producing plants with Kinney's retail outlets and horizontal combinations of the two companies' manufacturing and retailing operations. The shoe industry is relatively fragmented, so that the combined manufacturing capacity of the two firms would have been only 4.5% of the total. Nevertheless, Brown was the fourth and Kinney the twelfth largest manufacturer, and combined they would have become the third largest. Moreover, Brown was the nation's third largest seller of shoes, and Kinney, with 350 stores, accounted for more than 1% of total sales.

Brown was the first Supreme Court interpretation of the new Sec. 7, as amended to cover assets as well as stock acquisitions. This factor, together with the presence of both vertical and horizontal mergers and the positions of the two firms as relatively large participants in something less than an oligopolistic market, made of this case a peculiarly good opportunity for the Supreme Court to enunciate its views on antitrust policy.

As we have already seen the definition of "market" is frequently crucial in antitrust cases. Here the Court attempted to arrive at a synthesis of its approaches in the *Cellophane* and *Du Pont* cases. It argued that the outer boundaries of a market were to be determined by reasonable interchangeability or cross-elasticity of demand but that, within such broadly bounded markets, well defined submarkets might exist that would themselves be crucial for findings of antitrust violation. It will be remembered that *Du Pont,* which might be interpreted as a rejection of the cross-elasticity or *Cellophane* test, is more precisely a definition in terms of a single firm's market because of the special circumstances of a vertical merger between two industrial giants. Indeed the difficulty with the *Cellophane* decision itself was its failure to acknowledge that, for certain key consumers, other materials simply were not reasonably interchangeable with cellophane, no matter what the cross-elasticity of demand in the wrapping-materials market as a whole.

In *Brown,* the Court held that, when such factors as distinct customers, specialized vendors, and unique production facilities create, for practical purposes, a distinct market within a market, the submarket will be the focus of antitrust attention. The same functional and specific approach is used in defining geographic and product markets. As the vertical merger in question created in effect a nationwide tie between manufacturing and retail facilities, the relevant geographic market in considering the vertical merger was the national market. In analyzing the merger of Brown and Kinney retail outlets, however, the Court considered a series of submarkets, each of which was determined by the distance a normal family might reasonably consider traveling to buy shoes, as the key factor here was not the national relationship between manufacturer and retailer but the local relationship between retailer and everyday consumer.

Having determined the market, the Court moved on to assessing the economic impact in that market of the business behavior at issue. The Court had, of course, been using the "quantitative substantiality" test of *Standard Stations* in Sherman Act cases. That is, when the anticompetitive behavior was that of a firm controlling a substantial share of the market, the behavior was assumed to have reduced competition without analysis of purposes or actual impact. The Court had used this *per se* approach in connection with the old Sec. 7 in the *Du Pont* case, but, in administering the amended Sec. 7, the F.T.C. had rejected quantitative substantiality in favor of complete historical and economic analysis.

Brown is not entirely clear on what test is to be used. Justice Warren indicates that *de minimus* mergers would not violate the statute. But he also insisted that, because the Clayton Act was intended to nip incipient monopoly in the bud, violation would be found without showing as much foreclosure of competition as would be necessary to sustain a Sherman Act conviction. This criterion certainly looks like a quantitative substantiality test. The Chief Justice goes on to say, however, that, in the area between *de minimus* and Sherman Act levels, quantity is not of itself decisive but must be viewed in the light of such factors as the nature and purpose of the merger, the trend toward concentration in the industry, the peculiarities of national chain-store developments, the integration of manufacture with retailing, and mitigating factors like the "failing firm" defense.[67] The Court then engages in a rather rambling functional and economic analysis of Brown's and Kinney's places in the shoe business and concludes that their merger would indeed tend to lessen competition substantially in violation of the Clayton Act.

This argument looks like rejection of the *per se* "quantitative substantiality" approach in favor of full economic analysis. But it is not what it seems. The "quantitative substantiality" test was originated for oligopolistic sectors of the economy. When the Court was dealing with Standard Oil, it was self-evident that Standard controlled a substantial quantity of its market. There was no need to quibble about how much "substantial" was. The shoe industry is different. Although Brown and Kinney were two of the largest firms in the market, their quantitative shares were relatively small, down near the 1% line that *Tampa* had called unsubstantial. If the Court had used the simple "quantitative substantiality" test in *Brown,* it would have involved itself in the very difficult task of drawing the precise limits of "substantiality" in a fact situation that seemed to teeter on the boundary. It is not so much because the Court is dissatisfied with quantitative substantiality but because it would have so much difficulty in arguing that the "quantitative substantiality" test was met in this case that it turns to analysis of actual market conditions. In effect, *Brown* says that, when quantitative substantiality is in doubt, other factors may show violation of Sec. 7. These other factors are used to keep the merger from falling into the "less than substantial" category and thus slipping from the Court's grasp. This fact becomes perfectly clear when we see that Justice Warren's first exercise in market analysis is to treat the vertical-merger aspects of the transaction as analogous to a tying agreement. Since tying agreements are illegal *per se,* which means that the quantities involved are immaterial, the analogy shows that, in judging vertical mergers, the Court need not give much weight to the quantities involved. *Brown* does make clear that, when quantitative substantiality is in doubt, market factors will be considered in order to condemn mergers that the Court feels are threatening to competition, even though relatively small market shares are involved. It does not preclude the Court from using the *per se* "quantitative substantiality" test of *Standard Stations* when the test is clearly met. Of course, the *Standard Stations* case could not itself be cited as a precedent, for its "quantitative substantiality" test was designed for administration of antitrust provisions aimed at specifically anticompetitive devices rather than at mergers, which unlike tie-ins, for instance, are not condemned in themselves. But there is no doubt that the spirit of the test could be applied by a similar verbal formulation.

Brown is inconclusive not only on the question of whether or not the Court will substitute real market analysis for *per se* rules but also on the question of what sort of economic analysis it will provide when it chooses to provide any. The Court has obviously not followed the advice of Professor Bok, who, afraid of involving the Court in a morass of inconclusive economic analysis, counseled that it limit itself to the consideration of a few relatively simple factors.[68] Justice Warren insists on considering every possible facet of the economic problem. On the other hand, the Court obviously has not heeded the advice of those who counsel systematic economic analysis. The Court's use of statistics is extremely haphazard and its analysis sporadic and incomplete. Its approach is again the crude one of the general policy-maker rather than the more sophisticated one of the economic technician. It is, however, difficult to defend an opinion that promises, indeed requires, complete economic analysis and then provides the "hit-or-miss" treatment that is provided here.

The most important feature of *Brown* is its open and explicit acknowledgment of the Court's antitrust philosophy, a kind of summary of the inclinations that have consistently lurked behind antitrust decisions since 1956. This philosophy is presented, as judicial philosophies often are, in terms of Congressional rather than of Court intent:

> The dominant theme pervading congressional consideration of the 1950 amendments was a fear of what was considered to be a rising tide of economic concentration in the American economy. . . . the danger to the American economy in unchecked corporate expansions through mergers. Other considerations cited in support of the bill were the desirability of retaining local control over industry and the protection of small businesses.
>
> . . . we must consider its probable effects upon the economic way of life sought to be preserved by Congress. Congress was desirous of preventing the formation of further oligopolies with their attendant adverse effects upon local control of industry and upon small business. Where an industry was composed of numerous independent units, Congress appeared anxious to preserve this structure.
>
> If a merger achieving 5% control were approved, we might be required to approve future merger efforts by Brown's competitors seeking similar market shares. The oligopoly Congress sought to avoid would then be furthered and it would be difficult to dissovle combinations previously approved.[69]
>
> But we cannot fail to recognize Congress' desire to promote competition through the protection of viable, small, locally owned businesses. Congress appreciated that occasional higher costs and prices might result from the maintenance of fragmented industries and markets. It resolved these competing considerations in favor of decentralization.
>
> We cannot avoid the mandate of Congress that tendencies toward concentration in industry are to be curbed in their incipiency, particularly when those tendencies are being accelerated through giant steps striding across a hundred cities at a time.

Quite obviously, the Court is declaring in *Brown* that, in spite of the many modern apologies for bigness, the Justices still prefer competition to oligopoly and small business to big business, even when increase in firm size does not create an obvious and immediate threat to competition. The Court in *Brown* is grappling with one of the paradoxes of antitrust legislation. In an industry where concentration is just beginning, each individual merger or expansion will be labeled a response to similar movements by competitors—an attempt to improve the firm's competitive position—and thus a contribution to competition or at least a movement that will not have a substantial adverse effect on competition. But the end result of all these "competitive" moves is likely to be an oligopoly in which competition, at least in the traditional *laissez-faire* sense, has disappeared. It is this sort of occurrence that the Court tried to prevent in the shoe industry by stressing the merits of smallness *per se,* rather than using a standard of competition that might approve each individual increment in size until nothing was left but a few giants.

It should be remembered that Kinney has been a pioneer in the chain-store, supermarket type of operation that transformed the food-retailing industry some years ago. The chain store brought more price competition to its sector of the economy than had previously existed. To meet the competitive advantage of one chain, others had to be formed. At each stage of the process, it might have been strongly argued that increase in size resulted in more competition, but the end result was the transformation of a "many buyer, many seller" market into an increasingly oligopolistic structure focused on such giants as A & P. It was obviously fear of similar developments in another marketing structure initially based on the neighborhood store that led the Court to its outspoken pronouncements in favor of small business in the *Brown* case.

Sunkist Growers, Inc. v. Winckler and Smith Citrus Products Company[70] serves as a warning against anticipating too much on the basis of projecting a tendency in the Court's opinions to its logical extreme. *Maryland and Virginia Milk Producers Assn. v. United States,* when combined with the earlier *United States v. Borden,* suggested an inclination on the part of the Court to narrow progressively the antitrust exemption of agricultural co-operatives by confining them purely to matters of internal organization while finding all relations between any given co-operative and any outsider subject to normal antitrust policy. *Sunkist* seemed tailor-made to continue the narrowing process for it involved the interrelations of three separately organized co-ops, and the trial court had cast the case in the light of a conspiracy in restraint of trade among these three co-ops, rather than as a matter of internal co-operative organization.

The Supreme Court reversed, stressing the fact that the three co-operatives were actually the same growers organized under three separate names for administrative convenience. The Court argued that the exemptions of the Clayton and Capper-Volstead Acts were specifically designed to allow growers to band together free of risk of antitrust conspiracy charges. The activities of the three co-operatives were nothing more than co-operation among the same growers under different names in the marketing of their crops. The Court thus viewed the case as one involving the specially protected right of internal organization and operation of a co-operative, rather than a conspiratorial relationship between firms. Just as this case serves warning that it is a mistake to exaggerate the trend of earlier cases, however, it is equally a mistake to infer a more benevolent attitude toward co-operatives on the part of the Court. *Sunkist* seems to maintain the distinction between protected internal organization and prohibited conspiracy with outsiders and suggests that the Court will trust its sense of the facts to determine whether any given conduct falls in one sphere or the other.

In the 1961 term, the Court handled two appeals from summary judgments against plaintiffs in private, treble-damage antitrust suits. In both it returned the cases to the trial courts for further exposition of the facts and eventual decisions by juries, which the summary judgments had prevented. Yet one of the decisions was five to four, and the other was unanimous. The dissenters in *Poller v. Columbia Broadcasting*[71] argued that treble-damage actions were frequently a harassing and vexatious technique for attempting to recover losses incurred in the routine course of business. A businessman who has suffered any one of the many kinds of setbacks normal in a competitive market puts on the mask of an aggrieved victim of conspiracy and goes to the courts to achieve the results that his business acumen had failed to accomplish. They saw the *Poller* case in this light and, therefore, supported summary judgment as a useful device of judicial economy to reduce the excessive demands on the district courts entailed by such tactics.

The majority stressed two factors in calling upon district courts to be cautious in their use of summary judgments in antitrust cases. First, the issues in such cases are exceedingly complex and usually require full airing before accurate conclusions can be reached. Second, and here again we return to the basic problem of proof in antitrust law, it is inevitable that nearly all proof of an antitrust conspiracy will be in the hands of the conspirators and the minds of hostile witnesses. The alleger of such a conspiracy must therefore be given the maximum opportunity to develop his proofs if the anticonspiracy provisions are to remain more than formalities.

The majority and dissenting opinions do reveal some differences in outlook. One side is readier to believe the worst of a large and potentially oppressive firm, even when the facts are rather thin. The other is somewhat more cautious about judicial intervention and more sensitive to matters of judicial economy. Nevertheless, the unanimous decision reversing a summary judgment in the very similar case of *Continental Ore Company v. Union Carbon and Carbide Corporation*[72] indicates that the fact situations were the decisive factors. The facts in *Poller* were indeed ambiguous and might well have suggested to anyone a normal business loss dressed up as a deeply laid conspiracy. In *Union Carbide,* the Court was confronted with an obvious monopoly and a set of circumstances that very strongly suggested monopolizing. Whether or not monopolizing could be proved was, of course, another story, but the Court had heard enough to want the story told in full.

The decisions in *Union Carbide* and *Poller,* even when offset by the dissent in the latter, indicate that the Justices are conscious of the extreme difficulties of proof and the subsequent need for fairly wide inference on the part of trial judges and juries. They want antitrust stories told in full and not stifled by summary judgments based on technicalities that might thwart the effective administration of antitrust policy.

The 1962 term also offered a summary judgment case, although the real issue was *per se* rules. The district court, declaring the vertical territorial limitations by which White Motor Company confined each of its dealers to sales in a specified geographic area illegal *per se,* granted summary judgment without full examination of the economic situation. The Supreme Court, in *White Motor*

Company v. United States,[73] decided that it could not determine whether or not vertical territorial limitations were illegal *per se* until it had examined the actual impact of such arrangements on competition. It reversed the summary judgment and remanded the case to the district court for a full examination of the facts.

So far, we have seen *per se* rules employed basically to avoid the problem of proving reduction in competition. When the Court deals with a fundamentally anticompetitive practice, it may anticipate great difficulties in proving by economic analysis that competition has been significantly reduced even when it obviously has been. Or, as in the *Klor's* case, it may know that competition has not been reduced but may wish to condemn the practice anyway. In either instance, it may hold that the practice constitutes a violation of the Sherman or Clayton Act *per se* and may thus relieve itself of the necessity for examining economic consequences. In this sense, a *per se* rule is a presumption of the anticompetitive economic consequences of actions that are inherently anticompetitive.

It can be argued that *per se* rules also serve another purpose. Generally speaking, the "rule of reason" applies in Sherman Act cases, that is, the Act is held to condemn only unreasonable restraints of trade. Under the rule of reason, a firm may seek to explain or to mitigate its behavior by showing that the restriction on competition is necessitated by legitimate business or economic considerations. If an action is a *per se* violation, its matrix of business and economic relations is not examined. In this sense, *per se* rules may be considered as devices for eliminating the rule of reason from certain sectors of antitrust law.

In *White,* the majority attempts to clear up the relation of *per se* rules to the rule of reason. It catalogues certain kinds of behavior that are always *per se* violations and thus never entail examination of surrounding circumstances. In this category, the rule of reason does not apply. It then describes a second category of practices that are *per se* violations under certain circumstances. These practices are generally so inherently anticompetitive as to be automatically condemned but are not always *per se* violations. In this category, the Court first applies the rule of reason and, if mitigating circumstances are not found, then presumes significant reduction of competition. The Court thus declares that, in connection with some kinds of behavior, it uses the *per se* rule both to abrogate the rule of reason and also to avoid the problem of proving reduction of competition, while in others it uses the *per se* approach only for the latter and not for the former purpose. The majority argues that it needs the experience that an examination of a complete trial record would give, to decide (a) whether the action in question in *White Motors* belongs in the first or second or in neither of the *per se* categories; (b) if it belongs in the second, what mitigating circumstances would abrogate the normal finding of *per se* violation.

Justice Brennan's opinion suggests that the Court may not find vertical territorial limitations *per se* violations at all, but that does not mean that the Court will necessarily approve the practice, even if it finds that it is not a *per se* violation.

The dissenting Justices, Warren, Clark, and Black, went to the substance of the case and, in doing so, exposed another of those paradoxes that haunt antitrust law. The crux of the matter was that White had eliminated sales competition among its dealers by assigning each an exclusive sales area and forbidding each to sell to customers from outside his own area. White argued that, as a struggling independent, fighting the powerful big three, the only way it could compete successfully was by insuring that its dealers were given every incentive to take sales away from the big three rather than from one another. It is typical of oligopolistic markets that relatively small firms may better their competitive positions *vis à vis* the giants by developing anticompetitive practices and that they excuse those practices by claiming necessity for the firm's survival, without which over-all competition in the industry will decrease.

Justice Clark wrote ". . . its actions may be good for White Motor but they are disastrous for free competitive enterprise. . . ."[74] But, assuming for the moment that White's arguments are correct, does the Court serve the Sherman Act best by forbidding an anticompetitive practice or by preserving another competitor in an already highly concentrated market. Oligopoly plays hob with the *laissez-faire* logic of competition that is the intellectual baggage of the antitrust laws.

The position of tie-ins as a *per se* category becomes clearer when *White* is considered together with *Loew's Inc. v. United*

States.[75] It will be remembered that, at the time of *Northern Pacific,* it had been argued that what made the tie-ins involved there and in the leading previous precedent (*International Salt*) *per se* violations was the unique nature of the tying products, land and patented devices. It will also be remembered that the Court went out of its way to indicate that it was not simply the uniqueness of the tying products in these particular cases that had led the Court to find tie-ins *per se* violations.

In *White Motor,* the Court used tie-ins as the principal example in distinguishing between arrangements that are always illegal *per se* and those that are only sometimes illegal *per se*. Tie-ins built on patented products are always illegal *per se*. Others are illegal only if the firm "has sufficient economic power with respect to the tying product to appreciably restrain free competition in the market for the tied product."[76] There is also an aside in *White* that quotes an aside in *Brown:*

> Thus, unless the tying device is employed by a small company in an attempt to break into a market, the use of a tying device can rarely be harmonized with the structures of the anti-trust laws, which are intended primarily to preserve and stimulate competition.[77]

This comment may indicate that the rule of reason may sometimes apply in this *per se* area, although the question is not yet resolved.

In *Loew's,* the Court makes clear just what "sufficient economic" means and what significance it has for the *per se* approach to tie-ins. Once "sufficient economic power" is shown, the tie-in is illegal *per se,* in the sense that no economic analysis of its actual impact on competition is necessary (unless perhaps under such special circumstances as those suggested in *Brown*). But is detailed economic analysis necessary to determine whether or not a firm has sufficient economic power? The Court stresses that "sufficient economic power" does not mean market dominance, that is, "some power to control prices and exclude competition in the normal sense of the Sherman Act." Sufficient economic power is a lesser degree of power, and it can be inferred from the tying products' desirability to consumers or their uniqueness.

If we envision the *per se* approach as entering the tie-in cases twice—once at the stage of determining whether or not sufficient economic power exists and again at the stage of determining whether or not the tie-ins restrict competition, three categories emerge. First, where an item is patented, the patent is taken by the Court as conclusive proof of the uniqueness of the item and therefore as conclusive proof of both market power and restriction of competition. This approach is the *per se-per se* approach in the sense that at neither stage is there any economic analysis of actual market conditions.

Second, for unpatented items, since the test is not market dominance but simply uniqueness or consumer demand, the Court says it will seldom be necessary to embark on full-scale market analysis. Indeed, as the incentive for and effectiveness of a tying agreement almost inevitably arise from the uniqueness of or demand for the tying item, it seems clear that in most instances the Court will almost automatically find "sufficient market power." For most unpatented items there is therefore a semi*per se-per se* approach. At the first stage, there is cursory examination of business facts. At the second, there is no examination of the facts.

Third, in those peculiar instance in which there appears to be no market dominance and no uniqueness or special demand, the Court will apparently engage in economic analysis to show insufficient market power, so that the approach can be characterized as non *per se* in the first stage and *per se* in the second. Indeed, as suggested by the aside in *Brown Shoe,* the Court may on occasion use a non*per se*-non*per se* or even a non*per se*-"rule of reason" approach.

The result of all these distinctions seems to be simply that, when the Court does not like a tie-in, it can sweep away all economic analysis designed to protect it by adopting *per se* and semi*per se* approaches at either or both stages of analysis. On the rare occasions when it finds tie-ins innocuous or desirable, it can resort to economic analysis to assert their legality. The Court thus places itself in a perfect position to use whatever tools it pleases to arrive at whatever conclusions it pleases. Again, this position may seem unsuitable for the Supreme Court as court of law, but it has a certain attractiveness for the Court as economic policy-maker.

As to the specific holding in *Loew's,* it drew an anology between copyright and patent, thus using the *per se-per se* approach to condemn block booking of copyrighted feature films to television stations. As the Court had previously condemned block booking to motion-picture theatres, the decision as such is little more than a routine extension of an earlier holding. It might be added that seven Justices indicated their relatively strong antitrust sentiments by granting the government's request to the Court to strengthen the district court's enforcement decree, although, as Justice Harlan pointed out, normal juridical etiquette would have left the matter entirely to the district court.

In several earlier cases, we have noted that the Supreme Court has trodden a wary path with the regulatory agencies *vis à vis* the antitrust laws, insisting on its own predominance but occasionally granting the agencies certain special reserves of power.

In *Pan American World Airways Incorporated* v. *United States,*[78] the Court held that the Civil Aeronautics Act[79] granted immunity from the antitrust laws in matters of division of territories, allocation of routes among American carriers, and combinations between common and air carriers, these issues to be decided by the C.A.B. under its public-interest criteria. It therefore found the case unsuited for judicial decision. While retaining general antitrust jurisdiction, the Court actually amended the Act by putting Sec. 411, which concerns such matters, in the same category as Secs. 408, 409, and 412, in which Congress had specifically included antitrust exemptions. Since Congress's intent is unclear, the Court's action is in fact judicial legislation, granting an antitrust exemption to Sec. 411 matters.

Justice Brennan in dissent complained that, if the Court were concerned with premature antitrust litigations upsetting the necessarily delicate adjustments of regulatory practice, it might have resorted to the primary-jurisdiction technique. But that is precisely what the Court could not do. It has long insisted that the courts are the pre-eminent power and the agency of special expertise in the antitrust area. To grant primary jurisdiction over any antitrust matter to a regulatory agency would undermine that claim. When, therefore, the Court, for whatever reason, does wish to defer to a regulatory agency, it is likely to insist that the regulatory statute has created an exemption from the antitrust laws. The argument is, not that the regulatory agency is a more appropriate decision-maker on this kind of antitrust matter than the

Court, but that this matter is not an antitrust matter at all and thus falls to the regulatory agency. In this way, the Court, by divesting certain problems of the antitrust label, can turn them over to the regulatory agencies without compromising its own primary and final jurisdiction over all problems that do bear that label.

It is relatively easy to see what leads the Court to its conclusion in this case. The problem of air routes and the control of one type of carrier by another is a peculiar one. Past experience has made it fairly obvious that maximum competition is not necessarily the best solution. Route regulation is at the very core of C.A.B. activity and an essential feature of a regulatory policy whose purpose is maximum transportation efficiency rather than maximum competition. While granting antitrust exemptions to Sec. 411 matters, the Court retains general antitrust jurisdiction over all matters not exempted. The justices thus leave to the C.A.B. the routing problem, which is an integral part of a scheme of regulation not primarily directed at maintaining competition, while retaining for themselves jurisdiction over anticompetitive maneuvers of the "dirty trick" variety. The Court will give the C.A.B. a free hand at routing but can still intervene when carriers conspire or resort to other monopolistic practices outside the regulatory scheme.

Nevertheless, on the common-sense grounds so frequently invoked in antitrust analysis, the *Pan Am* decision is far from satisfactory. The case is the latest episode in Pan Am's long fight to keep Panagra out of competition with it in the United States-South American traffic. Justice Brennan summed up neatly:

> By its decision today the Court brings to naught nine years of litigation. Yet these nine years actually represent only the most recent phase of a continuing problem first placed before the Civil Aeronautics Board 22 years ago. For 22 years Pan American World Airways has staved off the day of reckoning in respect to the tactics which, Judge Murphy found below, violated Sec. 2 of the Sherman Act. Today's decision vindicates these tactics beyond Pan American's fondest expectations, for the problem is now back with the C.A.B. which has from the outset protested its inability to deal with it. . . . repeatedly over a period of many years, the Board has adverted to its felt

helplessness in the face of the divided control of Panagra by two powerful corporations, one the dominant United States company in the field of foreign transportation.[80]

Moreover, as Justice Brennan also pointed out, while C.A.B.'s "public interest," "unfair methods of competition," and "unfair practices" criteria would allow it to engage in something very like antitrust administration, the Agency has not in fact done so. In shifting antitrust administration to the C.A.B. in the guise of an antitrust exemption for C.A.B.-regulated activity, the Court has shifted the job from an expert, the Court itself, to an amateur and an amateur whose internal structure and external constituency do not promise the development of vigorous antitrust enforcement.

The last two antitrust cases of the 1962 term are particularly well placed for examination of the Supreme Court as political economist. Between them they offer a kind of summary of present antitrust policies and tactics of the Court, a summary that indicates the extremely wide-ranging policy-making inclinations of the Justices. Indeed, *United States v. Philadelphia National Bank*[81] contains an open and direct essay on political economy, of which the major thrust is the subordination of both economics and law to the general policy goals of antitrust regulation.

It will be remembered that in the *Brown* case the Court moved away from semi*per se* tests toward full-scale, albeit haphazard, economic analysis of the effects of a merger. I have argued that this movement in *Brown* was not the result of dissatisfaction with *per se* approaches as a device for penetrating smoke screens of economic analysis thrown up by monopolists but a tactical move inspired by the difficulty of showing quantitative substantially in that case. The decision in *United States v. Philadelphia National Bank* seems to confirm that argument in a concise and strikingly frank analysis that deserves to be quoted at some length.

> [W]e come to the ultimate question under Sec. 7: whether the effect of the merger may be substantially to lessen competition in the relevant market. Clearly, this is not the kind of question which is susceptible of a ready and precise answer in most cases. It requires not merely an appraisal of the immediate impact of the

merger upon competition, but a prediction of its impact upon competitive conditions in the future; . . . Such a prediction is sound only if it is based upon a firm understanding of the structure of the relevant market; yet the relevent economic data are both complex and elusive . . . [W]e must be alert to the danger of subverting congressional intent by permitting a too-broad economic investigation. And so in any case in which it is possible, without doing violence to the congressional objective embodied in Sec. 7, to simplify the test of illegality, the courts ought to do so in the interest of sound and practical judicial administration. . . . [I]ntense congressional concern with the trend toward concentration warrants dispensing, in certain cases, with elaborate proof of market structure, market behavior, or probable anti-competitive effects. Specifically, we think that a merger which produces a firm controlling an undue percentage share of the relevant market, and results in a significant increase in the concentration of firms in that market is so inherently likely to lessen competition substantially that it must be enjoined in the absence of evidence clearly showing that the merger is not likely to have such anti-competitive effects.

Such a test lightens the burden of proving illegality only with respect to mergers whose size makes them inherently suspect in light of Congress' design in Sec. 7 to prevent undue concentration. . . . The merger of appellees will result in a single bank's controlling at least 30% of the commercial banking business in the four-county Philadelphia metropolitan area. Without attempting to specify the smallest market share which would still be considered to threaten undue concentration, we are clear that 30% presents that threat. Kaysen and Turner suggest that 20% should be the line of prima facie unlawfulness; Stigler suggests that any acquisition by a firm controlling 20% of the market after the merger is presumptively unlawful; Markham mentions 25%. Bok's principal test is increase in market concentration, and he suggests a figure of 7% or 8%. We intimate no view on the validity of such tests for we have no need to consider percentages smaller than those in the case at bar, but we note that such tests are more rigorous than is required to dispose of the instant case. Needless to say, the fact that a merger results in a less-than-30% market share, or in a less substantial increase in concentration than in the instant case, does not raise an inference that the merger is *not* violative of Sec. 7.

Further, whereas presently the two largest banks in the area

> . . . control between them approximately 44% of the area's commercial banking business, the two largest after the merger . . . will control 59%. Plainly, we think this increase of more than 33% in concentration must be regarded as significant. . . . There is nothing in the record of this case to rebut the inherently anti-competitive tendency manifested by these percentages.[82]

This argument embodies, of course, not a *per se* but a presumption approach. It remains to be seen how close the presumption is to irrebuttability, but the whole tone of the opinion suggests that it is very strong indeed. Moreover, as the presumption is created in order to keep the Court out of complex economic analysis and as serious consideration of rebuttal evidence would put the Court right back into such analysis, the presumption must be very strong if it is to achieve the Court's purposes.

Combining *Philadelphia National Bank* with *Brown,* the following rules emerge: Where the percentage of concentration is high (although the Court now refuses to commit itself as to how high), the Court will avoid real economic analysis that might obstruct the enforcement of Sec. 7 by suggesting an anticompetitive tendency. The Justices thus go even further than those who wish the Court to simplify its economic tasks by concentrating on a few factors. When it can, the Court will rely on a single factor, introducing other considerations only in the loaded context of dealing with rebuttals to a strong presumption. When the percentages, as in *Brown,* are not high enough to allow this simplification, the Court will apparently engage in broad market analysis, although, if *Brown* is any indication, not the sort of analysis that the "antiantitrust" forces would relish.

Finally, when the general policy statements against mergers in *Brown* are combined with the similar statements in *Philadelphia Bank* that we shall note presently, it becomes clear that, in the Court's view, mergers as a category are moving closer and closer to tie-ins and other inherently anticompetitive devices. We may therefore, anticipate that the Court is likely to use something like the "quantitative substantiality" test—itself a kind of *per se* device—for cases that fall below the high percentages of *Philadelphia Bank* but are above the low percentages of *Brown.* In general, *Philadelphia Bank* marks a high point in the Court's movement toward *per se* and similar tests as devices for avoiding extended economic analysis in order to facilitate vigorous antitrust policies.

Like *Brown, Philadelphia Bank* contains a considerable number of statements that indicate the extent to which the Court has become the champion of antitrust policy.

> It is no answer that among the three presently largest firms . . . there will be no increase in concentration. If this argument were valid, then once a market had become unduly concentrated, further concentration would be legally privileged. On the contrary, if concentration is already great, the importance of preventing even slight increases in concentration and so preserving the possibility of eventual deconcentration is correspondingly great.[83]

> . . . it is suggested that the increased lending of the resulting bank will enable it to compete with the large out-of-state bank, particularly the New York banks, for very large loans. We reject this application of the concept of countervailing power. If anticompetitive effects in one market could be justified by procompetitive consequences in another, the logical upshot would be that every firm in an industry could, without violating Sec. 7, embark on a series of mergers that would make it in the end as large as the industry leader.[84]

> We are clear, however, that a merger the effect of which may be substantially to lessen competition is not saved because, on some ultimate reckoning of social or economic debits and credits it may be deemed beneficial. A value choice of such magnitude is beyond the ordinary limits of judicial competence, and in any event has been made for us already by Congress when it enacted the amended Sec. 7. Congress determined to preserve our traditionally competitive economy. It therefore proscribed anti-competitive mergers, the benign and the malignant alike, fully aware, We must assume, that some price might have to be paid.[85]

This general antitrust attitude is also evident in the technique used for delimiting the market. The rule that the Court announces "is not where the parties to the merger do business or even where they compete, but where, within the area of competitive overlap, the effect of the merger on competition will be direct and immediate." Such a rule of course is tantamount to saying that the market definition will always be that most favorable to a finding against the merger. The Court was careful in its language to limit the rule to this specific case, but it is unlikely to stay limited. The Court also relied heavily on the submarket device of *Brown,* in order to narrow the scope of the relevant market sufficiently to put real teeth in Sec. 7.

The *Philadelphia Bank* case also provides the latest episode in the exemption and regulatory-agency story. After having gone out of its way to read an exemption from antitrust prosecution into the Civil Aeronautics Act, the Court, in *Philadelphia Bank,* goes out of its way to maintain the dominance of Sec. 7 over bank mergers. The original Sec. 7 and its 1950 amendments were so obviously unclear on the question of whether or not they applied to bank mergers that Congress passed a special bank-merger statute in 1960. As a result, it is possible to engage in endless ratiocinations over whether Sec. 7 did or did not initially apply to bank mergers and whether or not, if it did, it still does, now that Congress has passed a new statute. All that can be said conclusively is that the whole situation is so mixed up that the Justices are free to do what they please, and they used that freedom to assume antitrust jurisdiction over bank mergers in the first such case ever to reach the Supreme Court.[86] Several considerations seem decisive in this regard. First, banking is not a fully regulated industry like transportation, and such regulation as does exist is highly fragmented. Second, unlike *Minneapolis and St. Louis Railway Company* and *Pan American,* this case offers no specific exemption from antitrust proceedings anywhere in the regulatory statutes. Third, banking is one of those sectors of the economy in which there is now relatively high dispersion but in which the tempo of concentration is rapidly increasing through mergers and other devices. While some state agencies have been hostile to this development, most of the federal agencies have not, and the Court's opinion quite obviously reflects its desire to enlist the powers of the federal government against increasing concentration.

United States v. Singer Manufacturing Company[87] was the last antitrust decision of the 1962 term, and it provides a suitable conclusion to this survey of the Warren Court's antitrust work because it returns us to a key problem, the problem of proof. For *Singer* is in effect a catalogue of the devices that the Supreme

Court uses to overturn trial-court findings of fact favorable to antitrust violators. The government alleged that arrangements for cross-licensing and purchase of patent rights between Singer and certain European firms was a conspiracy designed to prevent the sale of Japanese sewing machines in the United States. The district court dismissed the suit because it found that the "dominant and sole purpose" of the arrangement was not the exclusion of Japanese competition but the settlement of a potential conflict of patent rights between United States and European patent holders.

Singer is, of course, the largest American manufacturer of sewing machines. The American manufacturers had suffered heavily from Japanese competition, so heavily that Singer was the single American firm left in the market and was engaged in a constant struggle with the Japanese imports. Singer's arrangements with the European firms would have avoided a few minor infringement suits between Singer and two minor European competitors, but it would also have allowed Singer to enforce the pooled patent rights of all three in the United States, thus providing a good chance that Singer could stop the influx of Japanese machines into this country by a series of patent-infringement suits. The district court's findings amounted to a decision that a "secondary" purpose of the agreement was to protect against Japanese machines. A conflict thus seems to exist among the various findings of the district court, and the Supreme Court seizes upon the conflict to justify making its own findings. Then the Court invoked the *Du Pont* distinction between findings of fact and conclusions from fact, arguing that the trial court's findings of who said what to whom, how, when, and where were undisputed but that an appellate court was free to accept or reject its conclusions from those findings as to whether a conspiracy did or did not exist. Then the Court invoked a doctrine of mixed factual and legal questions that allowed it to reverse a finding of fact, as if it were a finding of law. "Likewise we reject, as a question of law, the court's inference that the attitude of suspicion, wariness and self-preservation of the parties negated a conspiracy."

The Court's main ploy, however, was to adopt the technique of *Parke, Davis,* in which the Justices had claimed that the trial court was reversible on its findings, even though they rested on undisputed facts because it had applied the wrong evidential standard to the facts.

> Given the court's own findings and the clear import of the record it is apparent that its conclusions were predicted upon "an erroneous interpretation of the standard to be applied . . ." Thus, "because of the nature of the District Court's error we are reviewing a question of law, namely, whether the District Court applied the proper standard to essentially undisputed facts."[88]

In connection with this ploy, the Court read its subordinates a lesson in the ways of the world, in effect instructing district courts to begin recognizing what any one can see, instead of sticking to what is in the narrow records before them.

> . . . the influence of an agreement in violation of the Sherman Act is not merely limited to particular fact complexes. . . . judicial inquiry is not to stop with a search of the record for evidence of purely contractual arrangements. . . . Whether the conspiracy was achieved by agreement, by tacit understanding, or by acquiescence. . . . coupled with assistance in effectuating its purpose is immaterial. . . . whether an unlawful combination or conspiracy is proved is to be judged by what the parties actually did rather than by the words they used."[89]

This passage is to my knowledge the clearest acknowledgment yet of the crucial institutional conflict between trial courts, using rigorous and circumscribed rules of evidence to determine personal guilt, and appellate courts, using wide ranging and inferential knowledge to determine broad social policies.

Finally when the Justices come up against a solid factual finding by the trial court that the dealings of the three firms "were characterized by an absence of unity or identity of any common purpose or motive," they had to admit that such a finding could not be entirely overcome by talk of "conclusions" and "standards." Having made the admission that this finding fell under the "clearly erroneous" rule (that is, the rule that allows an appellate court to reverse a trial court's finding of fact only when it is clearly erroneous and not simply different from the one the appellate court would have made on its own), the Court simply concluded that the finding was clearly erroneous on the basis of an independent analysis of the record.

The Supreme Court, therefore, found that Singer's arrangements constituted a conspiracy and combination in violation of the Sherman Act. There is, as Justice Harlan suggests in dissent, no clearer instance of the Supreme Court's reversing a trial court not because of its legal errors but because of its naive and narrow findings of fact.

In the 1963 term, the Court handed down four major antitrust decisions, all exhibiting a strong anti-bigness policy. In the *Penn-Olin* case,[90] the Court held for the first time that Sec. 7 of the Clayton Act was applicable not only to mergers but also to joint ventures. In reversing the findings of fact of the trial court by saying that it had used the wrong criteria for evaluating the facts, the Court warned that, in spite of the near impossibility of proving the facts, the trial judge must nevertheless find a violation if a reduction of competition was really to be anticipated. The Court also went out of its way to see the threat of such a reduction. In *United States v. Alcoa,*[91] the Court again reversed the findings of fact of the trial court, defined the market in the way most damaging to the defendant, and, although the decrease in competition resulting from the merger would be very small, held that, where a market was already oligopolistic, even a very small decrease in competition could not be tolerated. In *United States v. First National Bank,*[92] the Court undermines one of the last of the old pro-big business decisions and comes very close to holding that, where a substantial level of competition has previously existed between two firms, their merger is a *per se* violation of the Sherman Act without need of economic analysis of its actual consequences. In *United States v. El Paso Natural Gas,*[93] the Court was willing to go far out on the limb of prediction in order to anticipate a future threat to competition in view of El Paso's presently monopolistic position in the California gas market.

¶ Conclusion

It has become a cliche of antitrust analysis that the courts have a good record of arriving at common-sense, case-by-case conclusions but have been unable to formulate a clear and consistent doctrinal basis for their individual decisions. What this statement usually means in practice is that commentators are unable to find any principles or standards uniting the decisions into a coherent whole or any adequate legal rationales even in particular opinions. I see no reason to cover this problem with the vague umbrella of common sense.

It is better to acknowledge openly that, pending a revolutionary change in the relations of government to business, the Supreme Court has arrived and will continue to arrive at decisions that are strikingly unsatisfactory in terms of the formal logic of law or economics. What other result is possible when the Court is asked to apply an unrealistic economic philosophy full of unresolvable paradoxes and dilemmas and an economic science full of gaps at the crucial level of institutional analysis to an increasingly complex economic system? In a quite fundamental way, criticism of the Supreme Court's performance in terms of logical consistency and precedential stability is futile. For the level of Court performance is inextricably linked with the level of logic and consistency in the general line of policy within which it must operate, and there is very little logic or consistency there. It is the policy and not the Court that is at fault, if fault there be.

As long as we continue to rely on antitrust regulation as a principal mode of adjusting the relationship between government and business, we must be satisfied with less than perfection. Basically, the Supreme Court has two choices. It may stress the traditional safeguards of criminal law and the conventional legal virtues of stability, consistency, clarity, logic, and equality of treatment for all litigants. If it takes this tack, it can expect to play no important role in antitrust regulation, for the basic incompatibilities between the *laissez-faire* model and the real economic world mean that antitrust enforcement cannot be effective if it is fair (by criminal-law standards), stable, consistent, clear, logical, and equitable.

On the other hand, the Court may choose to make policy day by day on the same rough basis that other political agencies use, with due regard to fairness, logic, and consistency but only as factors to be considered along with other policy goals and political preferences. One thing the Court cannot do is fairly and equitably to administer existing statutory law, for there is almost no such existing law, and what there is, if administered routinely and inflexibly without large dollops of judicial lawmaking, would be ineffectual and meaningless.

It may well be that the real test of Supreme Court performance in every area of its jurisdiction is whether or not one likes the results it achieves. However that may be in general, it is certainly true in antitrust law. If we are asked whether a given act of Congress is a good one or a bad one, we do not normally engage in long discussions about the role of Congress or the sublimity of logical consistency. A law is either "good" or "bad" as it does or does not conform to our own notions of social desirability or our particular visions of the good life. This criterion is precisely that for judging the antitrust decisions of the Supreme Court, for they are not basically judicial decisions, in the sense of individual applications of existing statutes, but lawmaking decisions based both immediately and ultimately on the Court's vision of what the economy is and should be. Because the Court is willy-nilly a political economist in the antitrust area, its decisions must be judged, like all political and economic decisions, on the basis of political and economic values.

The Warren Court has acted with a rather high degree of consistency against anticompetitive forces. It has been engaged in developing techniques for disposing of problems of proof and economic complexity that would otherwise stand in the way of vigorous antitrust enforcement. It has clearly enunciated a philosophy favorable to small business and unfavorable to concentration and has indicated its belief that antitrust regulation can contribute to the realization of that philosophy. It has developed the political and economic outlook embodied in the *Alcoa, United Shoe,* and *Du Pont* decisions. Whether one approves this judicial stance or not must ultimately depend on whether or not one approves the economic philosophy and the commitment to techniques of negative regulation that underlie it. Just as the work of the Court in the antitrust area can best be described in terms of its role as political economist, an evaluation of its role can only be derived from the realms of political, social, and economic philosophy and not from traditional categories of law. The Antitrust jurisdiction of the Supreme Court thus shows clearly what its Constitutional jurisdiction often may not—that the Court is a political agency doing a job fundamentally similar to that of other political agencies and subject to the same modes of evaluation.

Conclusion

IDEALLY, THE CONCLUSION to a book, particularly one with a point of view or line of argument, would be a simple *Q.E.D.* Unfortunately, things are not always quite so simple. Indeed, in one sense, that is precisely what I have been trying to demonstrate. In fact, the Supreme Court plays a wide variety of roles in the various areas of its jurisdiction. It may be policy leader, as in the antitrust area, or it may retreat from policy-making, as it does in the tax field. It may face such a relatively simple task in political analysis as assessing the function of Congressional investigations or the immensely complex one of deciding how to alter the geographic bases of representation. It may brush aside other agencies' findings of fact as it tends to do in antitrust cases, or it may seek to leave fact-finding entirely to another agency like the N.L.R.B. In some instances, it develops strong doctrinal positions like those of legislative purpose and presumption. In others, the gift cases in the tax area, for instance, it resolutely refuses to have any doctrine at all. All this variation might seem rather strange in an isolated and insulated court administering The Law by processes of rigorous legal logic. It hardly seems unusual in a political agency faced with a wide range of problems, each entailing a different constellation of political forces.

In this respect, the debate over judicial modesty and judicial activism has been too generalized. What we must actually decide is, not how much we want the Supreme Court to do, but how much we want it to do in each area of its jurisdiction. The circumstances or criteria on which such individual decisions should be based vary considerably from area to area. In antitrust cases, where power has been clearly delegated by the font of popular authority, Congress, there is no issue of democracy. What determines the desired level of judicial activity is likely to be one's attitudes toward government regulation of business. In the tax field, the crucial issue may be the relative merits of generalists *versus* technicians. In reapportionment, it may be the inability of other agencies to perform the desired service or the inability of the Court to formulate the desired standards. Here again it might be better to give up our world historical perspective and, accepting the Court as a fact of political life, simply to ask in each instance, what do we want the government to do for us? and, Will the Court do as good or better a job than other government agencies?

Of course, there is the danger that, in the course of area-by-area judgments on the proper level of judicial activity, we shall arrive at a sum that exceeds the working capacity of nine men with relatively little staff help. At some point, the total must surely be considered. But the issue should not be predecided by the preliminary application of criteria that ignore the range and variety of the Supreme Court's functions in favor of some pat formula about *the* role of *the* Court.

In the first chapter of this book, I suggested that if we are ever to know about *the* Court, that knowledge will have to be built up from studies of the individual areas of the Court's work. Unfortunately, at the end of this book, I am not ready for many generalizations. The few studies presented here are partial and highly incomplete. The fact is, for all the scholarly resources expended on the Supreme Court, we still know very little of its real relations with such other government agencies as the Interstate Commerce Commission and the Bureau of Immigration or the scope and impact of its own policy-making. We know equally little of the relative distribution of policy-making powers even within the judicial sphere, that is, between the Supreme Court and its subordinate courts. Does the Fifth Circuit make whatever oil and gas law the courts make, or does the Supreme Court? That question remains even more obscure than the usual question—What are the relative shares of Congress and the Court in law-making?

It is the better part of valor but the poorer part of scholarship to suggest that what one has done is only preliminary. Nevertheless, with the dearth of real and specific findings on what the Court does to whom, where, and when and on what others do to it, it must be admitted that we simply do not yet know enough about the Court to assess finally its place in American politics. We must leave the vast questions aside long enough to discover whether or not the Court gives the I.C.C. a free hand in rate-making while withholding it in issuing certificates of convenience and necessity to truckers. Or to ask whether or not the Court has assigned the shaping of admiralty law to the Second Circuit rather than retaining that responsibility for itself. Political jurisprudence, using both traditional and new techniques, has a long way to go even toward finding the pieces to the puzzle, let alone fitting them together to reveal a complete picture of the whole Supreme Court.

We can say with a considerable degree of certainty, however, that, if we are to learn about the Court, we must deal with it in the context of politics. At the very minimum, the Court is a student of politics, required in many areas of its jurisdiction to develop its own analyses of how the political system operates. The Court is political, in the sense of having to deal with political materials. To be sure, a simple observer or describer of politics does not become a particularly significant political figure. But judges are notorious mixers of "is" and "ought," and a political analyst whose analysis contributes to the legitimation and alteration of the political process he observes is something more than a student of politics.

Probably the most important political analysis undertaken by the Supreme Court is the examination of its own role *vis à vis* other government agencies. In several areas of its jurisdiction, we have seen that the Court's conclusions about the proper distribution of decisional power between itself and other agencies is a decisive factor in shaping its doctrines. To the extent that the Court constructs a body of law not by logical deduction from statutory language or legal premise but by considerations of its own place in a complex decisional structure that is indisputably "political," the Court is engaged in politics. The Supreme Court itself is undoubtedly our foremost political jurist. For many of its decisions show that the Justices are highly aware of the constant and intimate relationships between themselves and other government agencies and that they create both substantive and procedural law that seeks to acknowledge the complex patterns of power and capacity in which the Court operates. Much of the legal performance of the Supreme Court that seems unclear, illogical, or contradictory when examined in strictly legal terms comes into focus under political analysis.

The politics of the Court, in the sense of its position *vis à vis* other government agencies, thus becomes an important influence in certain areas of the substantive law it administers. But these elements are not the only political considerations that enter into the Court's work. The antitrust and reapportionment cases clearly show that the Court is also political in the sense of making and enforcing government policies on the basis of its own vision of what the politico-economic structure of the nation should be. Typically enough, one of these areas is Constitutional, the other statutory. In one, the Court has seized the initiative, while in the other, initiative was forced upon it by Congress and by the very nature of the governmental function involved. Yet it is in the statutory area that the Court serves as continuous leader and in the Constitutional area that it began to lead only after leadership was made necessary by the default of the other participants.

While the grand policy-making areas like antitrust law and reapportionment are the most dramatic symbols of the Court's politicism, it is the "little" areas that finally confirm the Court's political role by showing how firmly the Justices are involved in the routine processes of government and how much they act like other governmental decision-makers. When the question is one of reserved-gate picketing or ordinary and necessary business expenditures, Congress makes decisions, administrative agencies make decisions, the lower courts make decisions, and the Supreme Court makes decisions. Few of these decisions are grand, none is final, and it is only their collective impact that makes law. Interested citizens and the agency participants themselves attempt to persuade each of the agencies to decide in their favor. Each decision does benefit some persons at the expense of others. Each is a policy decision, in that it determines the impact of government activities not only on a specific individual but on large classes of persons.

When the Supreme Court decides that a subcontractor doing routine maintenance is not entitled to reserved-gate protection from picketing, how is the result different from that of a similar decision by the N.L.R.B.? Or from that of the Congressional committee that had added such a proviso as Sec. 17b 2 (A) of a new labor-relations act? The decision of the Court is purportedly based on the general intent of Congress to encourage collective bargaining and to maintain a fair parity between management and labor. But, by a marvel of coincidence, the purposes imputed to Congress are precisely those at which the Court has arrived on its own. The Court's decision is final and binding and will in reality immediately stimulate evasion and alteration tactics by all the other political participants, tactics that may eventually totally change the policy. The Court's decision is the exalted mandate of the highest tribunal in the land and may have less impact than the next finding of an N.L.R.B. hearing officer as to whether a certain kind of operation is or is not routine maintenance. The Court's subordinates may ignore or circumvent the decision. The Court's colleagues may join to overcome it. The interests it regulates may campaign against the decision and, through a variety of such tactics as creating conflicts on the circuits, force it to make new decisions. If it wishes to maintain its position, the Court will have to exert fairly constant pressure on other participants. Like other agencies, when attacked it must decide whether to give in gracefully or to seek new channels to carry on the fight. Like other agencies, it feels more institutional loyalty to some of its colleagues than to others. Like the rest, it operates within certain rules and conventions about the legislative process and knows that no agency can extend its particular powers to their logical extremes without wrecking the whole arrangement. In wide areas of its jurisdiction, the Supreme Court engages in the very stuff of routine politics: changes, adjustments, and accommodations of governmental activity in constant co-operation and rivalry with other governmental agencies, all designed to meet the demands of the citizenry. From the heights of the First Amendment to the depths of the Internal Revenue Code, the Supreme Court is deeply committed to activities that we would unhesitantly label "political" if any other agency of government were involved.

In commenting on some developments in political theory, a colleague of mine once titled his remarks, "What Ever Happened to the Great Issues?" The great issues seem too much with us in the study of the Supreme Court. Is judicial review compatible with democracy? Can the Supreme Court successfully oppose the Congress? Should the Justices seek the moral decision or excise their own values from the decisional process as much as possible? Can the Court find happiness without eternal legal principles? The soap-opera debate over the Supreme Court runs continuously. Like its counterpart in the entertainment world, the dramatic dialogue deals with vital questions but frequently within a frame of reference created by convention rather than an appreciation of the full length and breadth of reality. Those questions can only be answered successfully when we have built up such a reality from the whole range of Supreme Court activity and have placed that activity firmly in the matrix of the governmental process.

Notes

¶ Chapter 1

1. I have used the rather cumbersome "power or importance or function" in order to avoid the elaborate debate over the definition of power, which seems to have become a permanent feature of political science but is tangential to my point here. In general, of course, my statements are in harmony with Dahl's. See Dahl, *The Concept of Power,* 2 BEHAVIORAL SCIENCE 201 (1957).

2. YOUNG, APPROACHES TO THE STUDY OF POLITICS (1958).

3. Morganthau, *Power as a Political Concept,* in *op. cit* note 2 *supra.*

4. Sherwood, *The Role of Public Law in Political Science,* in *op. cit* note 2 *supra.*

5. For instance, such works as SCHMIDHAUSER, CONSTITUTIONAL LAW IN THE POLITICAL PROCESS (1960); BERNS, CONSTITUTIONAL CASES IN AMERICAN GOVERNMENT (1963); SCHUBERT, CONSTITUTIONAL POLITICS (1960); and BETH, POLITICS, THE CONSTITUTION AND THE SUPREME COURT (1962) are attempts by political scientists to fit the traditional subject of "Constitutional law" into the mainstream of political science curricula. The core chapters of Beth's book are entitled *The Courts as Political Agencies.* See also Jacob, *The Courts as Political Agencies—An Historical Analysis,* 8 TULANE STUDIES IN POLITICAL SCIENCE 9 (1963).

6. See Schubert, *Behavioral Research in Public Law,* 57 AMERICAN POLITICAL SCIENCE REVIEW 433 (1963); and Shapiro, *Political Jurisprudence,* KENTUCKY LAW JOURNAL (1963).

7. (1951).

8. For instance, SCHATTSCHNEIDER, THE SEMI-SOVEREIGN PEOPLE (1961), an attack on group theory, argues that group struggle is not the only facet of politics. He indicates that groups finding themselves outnumbered initially struggle to broaden the arena of combat by appealing to broader and broader interests. In this process, the final descision is often brought to the broadest arena, general public sentiment. Using this model of politics, trial-court proceedings may be viewed as the initial group struggle and appeal as the attempt to broaden the arena. The broadest arena is reached when litigation is brought to the Supreme Court, which tends to reflect general public sentiment. Indeed, the whole process of litigation may be a device for finding new support by groups that are initially at a disadvantage.

9. See VOSE, CAUCASIANS ONLY—THE SUPREME COURT, THE N.A.A.C.P. AND THE RESTRICTIVE COVENANT CASES (1959); Vose, *The National Consumers League and the Brandeis Brief,* 1 MIDWESTERN JOURNAL OF POLITICAL SCIENCE 267 (1957); Vose, *Litigation as A Form of Pressure Group Activity,* 319 ANNALS 20 (1958); Vose, *Comment, Outside Influences on the Supreme Court of the United States—How Effective Are These?* 39 CANADIAN BAR REVIEW 631 (1961); and JACOBS, LAW WRITERS AND THE COURTS (1954).

10. TWISS, LAWYERS AND THE CONSTITUTION: HOW LAISSEZ FAIRE CAME TO THE SUPREME COURT (1942); Schu-

bert, *Politics and the Constitution: The Bricker Amendment During 1953,* 16 JOURNAL OF POLITICS 257 (1954); and SCHMIDHAUSER, THE SUPREME COURT—POLITICS, PERSONALITIES, AND PROCEDURES, Part 2 (1960).

11. Dahl, *Decision-Making in a Democracy: The Supreme Court as a National Policy-Maker,* 6 JOURNAL OF PUBLIC LAW 275 (1957).

12. MURPHY, CONGRESS AND THE COURT (1962); and BICKEL, THE LEAST DANGEROUS BRANCH—THE SUPREME COURT AT THE BAR OF POLITICS (1962).

13. MASON (1953).

14. WESTIN (1962).

15. Hacker, *Pressure Politics in Pennsylvania: The Truckers* vs. *the Railroads,* WESTIN, THE USES OF POWER (1962).

16. AUERBACH, GARRISON, HURST & MERMIN (1961).

17. 1955.

18. 1955.

19. 6 JOURNAL OF PUBLIC LAW 275 (1957).

20. See WESTIN, ANATOMY OF A CONSTITUTIONAL CASE (1958); and PRITCHETT & WESTIN, THE THIRD BRANCH OF GOVERNMENT—EIGHT CASES IN CONSTITUTIONAL POLITICS (1963).

21. See, for example, Barker, *The Supreme Court as Policy Maker: The Tidelands Oil Controversy,* 24 JOURNAL OF POLITICS 350 (1962); and Schubert, *Policy Without Law: An Extension of the Certiorari Game,* 14 STANFORD LAW REVIEW 284 (1962).

22. Murphy, *Chief Justice Taft and the Lower Court Bureaucracy: A Study in Judicial Administration,* 24 JOURNAL OF POLITICS 453 (1962); and Murphy, *Lower Court Checks on Supreme Court Power,* 53 AMERICAN POLITICAL SCIENCE REVIEW 1017 (1959).

23. For two quite different "term" approaches, see McCloskey, *Deeds Without Doctrines: Civil Rights in the 1960 Term of the Supreme Court,* and Schubert, *The 1960 Term: A Psychological Analysis,* both in 56 AMERICAN POLITICAL SCIENCE REVIEW.

24. See particularly PRITCHETT, THE ROOSEVELT COURT—A STUDY IN JUDICIAL POLITICS AND VALUES, 1937–1947 (1948); and PRITCHETT, CIVIL LIBERTIES AND THE VINSON COURT (1954). These two works are pioneering efforts in the political analysis of the Supreme Court.

25. See Kort, *Predicting Supreme Court Decisions Mathematically: A Quantitative Analysis of the "Right to Counsel" Cases,* 51 AMERICAN POLITICAL SCIENCE REVIEW 1 (1957); and Kort, *Content Analysis of Judicial Opinions and Rules of Law,* SCHUBERT, JUDICIAL DECISION-MAKING (1963).

26. See works cited note 24 *supra.*

27. The techniques of both group and scale analysis are fully explained in Schubert, *The Study of Judicial Decision Making as an Aspect of Political Behavior,* 52 AMERICAN POLITICAL SCIENCE REVIEW 1007 (1958). A closely related technique, factor analysis, is explained in Schubert, *A Solution to the Indeterminate Factorial Resolution of Thurstone and Degan's Study of the Supreme Court,* 7 BEHAVIORAL SCIENCE, 448 (1962).

28. See Ulmer, *Supreme Court Behavior and Civil Rights,* 13 WESTERN POLITICAL QUARTERLY 288 (1960); Spaeth, *Warren Court Attitudes Toward Business: The "B" Scale,* SCHUBERT, JUDICIAL DECISION-MAKING (1963); and Spaeth, *An Analysis of Judicial Attitudes in the Labor Relations Decisions of the Warren Court,* 25 JOURNAL OF POLITICS 290 (1963).

29. Tannenhaus, *Supreme Court Attitudes Toward Regulatory Agencies,* 14 VANDERBILT LAW REVIEW 473 (1961); Grossman, *Role-Playing and the Analysis of Judicial Behavior: The Case of Mr. Justice Frankfurter,* 11 JOURNAL OF PUBLIC LAW 285 (1962); and Spaeth, *Judicial Power as a Variable Motivating Supreme Court Behavior,* 6 MIDWEST JOURNAL OF POLITICAL SCIENCE 54 (1962).

30. See, for example, TRESOLINI, JUSTICE AND THE SUPREME COURT (1963).

31. Schmidhauser, *The Justices of the Supreme Court: A Collective Portrait,* MIDWEST JOURNAL OF POLITICAL SCIENCE 1 (1959).

32. See Schmidhauser, *State Decisis, Dissent and the Background of the Justices of the Supreme Court,* 14 UNIVERSITY OF TORONTO LAW JOURNAL 194 (1962); Nagel, *Testing Relations Between Judicial Characteristics and Judicial Decision-Making,* 15 WESTERN POLITICAL QUARTERLY 425 (1962); Na-

gel, *Ethnic Affiliations and Judicial Propensities,* 24 JOURNAL OF POLITICS 92 (1962); Nagel, *Political Party Affiliation and Judges' Decisions,* 55 AMERICAN POLITICAL SCIENCE REVIEW 843 (1961); and Ulmer, *Public Office in the Social Background of Supreme Court Justices,* 21 AMERICAN JOURNAL OF ECONOMICS AND SOCIOLOGY 57 (1962).

33. See Snyder, *The Supreme Court as a Small Group,* 36 SOCIAL FORCES 232 (1958); and Ulmer, *Homeostatic Tendencies in the United States Supreme Court,* ULMER, INTRODUCTORY READINGS IN POLITICAL BEHAVIOR (1961).

34. Murphy, *Marshalling the Court: Leadership, Bargaining and the Judicial Process,* 29 UNIVERSITY OF CHICAGO LAW REVIEW 640 (1962); and Danelsky, *The Influence of the Chief Justice in the Decisional Process,* MURPHY & PRICHETT, COURTS, JUDGES AND POLITICS (1961).

35. See Schubert, *The 1960 Term: A Psychological Analysis,* 56 AMERICAN POLITICAL SCIENCE REVIEW 90 (1962).

36. See Nagel, *Off-the-Bench Attitudes,* SCHUBERT, JUDICIAL DECISION-MAKING (1963).

37. The principal contributions are BICKEL, note 12 *supra* at 49–65 and *passim;* Pollak, *Constitutional Adjudication: Relative or Absolute Neutrality?,* 11 JOURNAL OF PUBLIC LAW 48 (1962); Rostow, *American Legal Realism and the Sense of Profession,* 34 ROCKY MOUNTAIN LAW REVIEW 123, 136–46 (1962); Henkin, *Some Reflections on Current Constitutional Controversy,* 109 UNIVERSITY OF PENNSYLVANIA LAW REVIEW 637 (1961); Henson, *A Criticism of Criticism: In re Meaning,* 29 FORDHAM LAW REVIEW 553 (1961); Miller, *A Note on Criticism of Supreme Court Decisions,* 10 JOURNAL OF PUBLIC LAW 139 (1961); Wright, *The Supreme Court Cannot Be Neutral,* 40 TEXAS LAW REVIEW 599 (1961); Arnold, *Professor Hart's Theology,* 73 HARVARD LAW REVIEW 1298 (1960); Black, *The Lawfulness of the Segregation Decisions,* 69 YALE LAW JOURNAL 421 (1960); Givens, *The Impartial Principles Supporting Brown v. Board of Education,* 6 HOWARD LAW JOURNAL 179 (1960); Griswold, *Of Times and Attitudes: Professor Hart and Judge Arnold,* 74 HARVARD LAW REVIEW 81 (1960); Karst, *Legislative Facts in Constitutional Litigation,* 1960 SUPREME COURT REVIEW 75; Miller & Howell, *The Myth of Neutrality in Constitutional Adjudication,* 27 UNIVERSITY OF CHICAGO LAW REVIEW 661 (1960); Mueller & Schwartz, *The Principle of Neutral Principles,* 7 UNISITY OF CALIFORNIA, LOS ANGELES, LAW REVIEW 571 (1960); Hart, *Forward, The Time Chart of the Justices,* 73 HARVARD LAW REVIEW 84 (1959); Pollak, *Racial Discrimination and Judicial Integrity: A Reply to Professor Wechsler,* 108 UNIVERSITY OF PENNSYLVANIA LAW REVIEW 1 (1959); Wechsler, *Toward Neutral Principles of Constitutional Law,* 73 HARVARD LAW REVIEW 1 (1959); Brown, *Forward, Process of Law,* 72 HARVARD LAW REVIEW 77 (1958); Bickel & Wellington, *Legislative Purpose and the Judicial Process: The Lincoln Mills Case,* 71 HARVARD LAW REVIEW 1 (1957); and Braden, *The Search for Objectivity in Constitutional Law,* 57 YALE LAW JOURNAL 571, 594 (1948).

38. Wechsler, note 37 *supra* at 11, 15; Brown, note 37 *supra* at 82; Hart, note 37 *supra* at 98; and Henkin, note 37 *supra* at 654.

39. Wechsler, note 37 *supra* at 19, 23; and Bickel & Wellington, note 37 *supra* at 3.

40. Wechsler, note 37 *supra* at 19; Brown, note 37 *supra* at 82; Bickel & Wellington, note 37 *supra* at 3; and Hart, note 37 *supra* at 124.

41. Griswold, note 37 *supra* at 85; and Hart, note 37 *supra* at 95.

42. Wechsler, note 37 *supra* at 26–34; Bickel & Wellington, note 37 *supra* at 3–6; and Hart, note 37 *supra* at 100, 121.

43. Wechsler, note 37 *supra* at 14–15; and Griswold, note 37 *supra* at 92.

44. Wechsler, note 37 *supra* at 15–19; and Griswold, note 37 *supra* at 92.

45. Wechsler, note 37 *supra* at 11–13, 19; Griswold, note 37 *supra* at 91; and Henkin, note 37 *supra* at 653.

46. Wechsler, note 37 *supra* at 11–12; and Griswold, note 37 *supra* at 91.

47. Wechsler, note 37 *supra* at 15.

48. WECHSLER, PRINCIPLES, POLITICS AND FUNDAMENTAL LAW XIII–XIV (1961).

49. See Henkin, note 37 *supra* at 653. Wechsler has subsequently written:

> I surely cannot have afforded any basis for the view that I posed an antithesis between "making an enduring contribution to the quality of our society" and resting on "neutral principles." By no possible reading did I say that the Supreme Court "should have cast out of its reckoning the likelihood that, a decision one way rather than another would effect 'an enduring contribution to the quality of our society.'" What I did say is that it is not enough that a decision makes such a contribution unless it also rests on neutral principles, i.e., was not merely an ad hoc disposition of its immediate problems unrationalized by a generalization susceptible of application across the board.

Quoted in Pollak, note 37 *supra* at 60–61. But, as Professor Pollak says immediately following the quotation:

> [Wechsler] apparently would permit his model judge to consider the "contribution to the quality of our society" which might ensue from one or another constitutional choice. But his judge's estimate of the likely impact on American life of a proposed constitutional decision remains a thing apart from the competing constitutional principles whose neutral accommodation yields one or another constitutional result.

Ibid. I myself cannot see how Professor Wechsler can have his cake and eat it too. If the "enduring contribution" happens to correspond to the neutral solution, then no problem exists. But what if the two are in conflict? Everything Professor Wechsler has written suggests that it must be the enduring contribution that gives way. The decision will thus always fall where the neutral principle leads it, and the enduring contribution will be at best a fortuitous dividend and at worst a sacrificial lamb to jurisprudential sanctity.

50. Wechsler, note 37 *supra* at 15; and Griswold, note 37 *supra* at 93.

51. See Mavrinac, *From Lochner to Brown v. Topeka, The Court and Conflicting Concepts of the Political Process,* 53 AMERICAN POLITICAL SCIENCE REVIEW, 641 (1958).

52. Wechsler, note 37 *supra* at 11.

53. LLEWELLYN, THE COMMON LAW TRADITION—DECIDING APPEALS (1960).

54. *Id.* at 122, quoting Goldschmidt, Preface to *Kritik des Entwurfs eines Handelsgesetzbuchs,* 4 KRIT. ZEITSCHR. F.D. GES. RECHTSWISSENSCHAFT.

55. Wechsler, note 37 *supra* at 12 (emphasis added); see also Henkin, note 37 *supra* at 654.

56. Miller & Howell, note 37 *supra* at 686; Miller, note 37 *supra* at 146; Mueller & Schwartz, note 37 *supra* at 585; Wright, note 37 *supra* at 616–18; and Clark, *Federal Procedural Reform and States' Rights; to a More Perfect Union,* 40 TEXAS LAW REVIEW 211, 227 (1961), following Braden, note 37 *supra.*

57. Wechsler, note 37 *supra* at 15–16; and Griswold, note 37 *supra* at 93.

58. Miller & Howell, note 37 *supra* at 691; and Miller, note 37 *supra* at 147.

59. See Pollak, note 37 *supra* at 55–60.

60. Miller & Howell, note 37 *supra* at 689.

61. *Id.* at 678.

62. Arnold, note 37 *supra.*

63. Griswold, note 37 *supra* at 85.

64. Miller & Howell, note 37 *supra* at 686.

65. Mueller & Schwartz, note 37 *supra* at 585.

66. Miller & Howell, note 37 *supra* at 689.

67. *Id.* at 683–84.

68. BICKEL, THE LEAST DANGEROUS BRANCH—THE SUPREME COURT AT THE BAR OF POLITICS 235–40 (1962).

69. See Wright, note 37 *supra;* Henson, note 37 *supra;* and WECHSLER, note 48 *supra.*

70. HAND, THE BILL OF RIGHTS 1–30 (1958).

71. Hart, note 37 *supra* at 96–99.

72. LLEWELLYN, note 53 *supra* at 17–18.

73. HAND, note 70 *supra* at 71–72.

74. Wechsler, note 37 *supra* at 12–14; and Hart, note 37 *supra* at 98–99.

75. Miller, note 37 *supra* at 150.

76. Professor Wright acknowledges this propagandistic value of "neutral" modes of judicial expression (and seems to favor this sort of neutrality), but he feels that Wechsler must have meant much more and attacks him for not making clear what more he meant. Wright, note 37 *supra* at 617–18.

77. See Miller & Howell, note 37 *supra* at 664–86; and Rostow, note 37 *supra* at 140, n.37, 145.

78. Mueller & Schwartz, note 37 *supra* at 585–86; and Bickel, note 68 *supra* at 63–64, 69.

79. *Id.* at 582–83.

80. See Rostow, note 37 *supra* at 138.

81. Arnold, note 37 *supra* at 1310.

82. Professor Bickel, from a somewhat different point of view, puts the the matter this way: ". . . the Court should declare as law only such principles as will—in time, but in a rather foreseeable future—gain general assent . . . The Court is a leader of opinion, not a mere register of it, but it must lead opinion, not merely impose its own; and—the short of it is—it labors under the obligation to succeed." Note 68 *supra* at 239.

83. TRUMAN, THE GOVERNMENTAL PROCESS 498 (1948).

84. See WECHSLER, note 48 *supra.*

85. See Bickel, *Foreward, the Passive Virtues,* 75 HARVARD LAW REVIEW 40, 48 (1961).

86. See Wright, note 37 *supra* at 617.

87. See Wechsler, note 37 *supra* at 15.

88. Henkin, *Some Reflections on Current Constitutional Controversy,* 109 UNIVERSITY OF PENNSYLVANIA LAW REVIEW 637 (1961).

89. Since these words were first written, another philosophical article, Golding, *Principled Decision Making and the Supreme Court,* 63 COLUMBIA LAW REVIEW 35 (1963), has appeared. It seems to me to confirm my point that nothing further, at least about the Supreme Court, can be learned from this type of approach.

90. Schubert, *From Public Law to Judicial Behavior,* SCHUBERT, JUDICIAL DECISION-MAKING (1963).

91. See Spaeth, *Judicial Power as a Variable Motivating Supreme Court Behavior,* 6 MIDWEST JOURNAL OF POLITICAL SCIENCE 54 (1962); and Grossman, *Role Playing and the Analysis of Judicial Behavior: The Case of Mr. Justice Frankfurter,* 11 JOURNAL OF PUBLIC LAW 285 (1962).

92. Joel Grossman's criteria for choosing cases to scale for his research are "questions of jurisdiction, federalism, deference to some other governing unit within the system or any question involving the right or propriety of the Supreme Court deciding the case . . . where . . . the issue of judicial responsibility was raised." *Id.* at 298. Spaeth uses three criteria: 1) cases in which the fact situations, issues requiring resolution, and points emphasized in the opinions clearly indicate the dominance of considerations of Supreme Court power as the basis for the Court's decision; 2) those cases that do not scale on certain social-attitude (civil rights, business, labor, and so forth) indices; and 3) comity and Federal Rules of Civil Procedure cases. Note 91 *supra* at 56–57. Obviously, all these criteria depend basically on traditional doctrinal analysis.

93. Indeed, even in the Constitutional areas, there is often one group of four or five with a strongly defined common attitude and another group of four or five that can be called a "group" only by virtue of its opposition to the first and not because of a commonly held value.

94. See Yntema, *American Legal Realism in Retrospect,* 14 VANDERBILT LAW REVIEW 317 (1960).

95. Technicians will note that the tax burden would not be lost but only shifted to the wife, but she would normally be in a much lower tax bracket than her ex-spouse. As the parties to the divorce could split the tax windfall by arranging slightly

higher alimony payments than would otherwise be paid, there would be a strong incentive for them to co-operate in drafting this part of the decree.

96. See Kort, *Content Analysis of Judicial Opinions and Rules of Law*, SCHUBERT, JUDICIAL DECISION-MAKING (1963); and Kort, *Predicting Supreme Court Decisions Mathematically: A Quantitative Analysis of the "Right to Counsel Cases*, 51 AMERICAN POLITICAL SCIENCE REVIEW 1 (1957). Both these pieces are basically attempts at traditional analytical jurisprudence, that is, precise explication of judicial holdings, using new techniques.

97. The *Du Pont* case is, of course, the exception. See pp. 275–83.

98. The reader will note that I myself have not offered a rigorous definition of "politics" or "political." I have contented myself with arguing that, as the courts perform the same functions and act within the same decisional matrices as do other agencies that all agree are political, they too are rightly labeled "political." Nevertheless, I challenge the reader to find any definition of politics from the time of Aristotle on, that is *not consciously designed by its author to exclude courts*, that is not applicable to what courts do. My point is that the only definitions of "politics" that would exclude courts are those shaped by a precommitment to judicial apoliticism.

99. Professor Hyneman grappled with these problems when he wrote that "the political process in the United States . . . stands in sharpest contrast to the judicial process. . . . I think no one will deny that the Supreme Court is a nonpolitical organ of government, if the word 'political' is given the meaning I attach to it here. 'Political' can be given a meaning which makes everything connected with government a political fact or one which makes every decision that fixes policy a political decision whether related to government or not. In these uses of the word, every significant act of a judge is political. I have used the word both ways in earlier parts of this book, calling certain decisions of the Supreme Court political and calling the Supreme Court a political institution. But when I call an office, institution, or process 'political' in this chapter, I refer to a relationship with a sizable population which makes it legitimate and customary for the population to control or influence that office, institution, or process. In this sense, the Supreme Court and its action on the cases that come before it are removed from politics." His book also illustrates the danger of finally assigning the banners of politics to the legislature and executive and of law to the courts. For, in the end, he too lapses into treating all we have discovered of the politics of courts as addenda to the basic vision of a neutral, law-finding rather than lawmaking judiciary. HYNEMAN, THE SUPREME COURT ON TRIAL 241 (1963).

100. Indeed, Professor Hyneman's attempt to restrict the term "political" so as to exclude courts is not really based on any systematic theoretical definition but on his desire to allow policy-making only to "democratic" agencies.

101. DAHL, A PREFACE TO DEMOCRATIC THEORY 34–62 (1956).

102. See McCloskey, *Economic Due Process and the Supreme Court: An Exhumation and Reburial*, 1962 SUPREME COURT REVIEW 34.

¶ Chapter 2

1. 103 U.S. 168 (1880).
2. 103 U.S. 168, 191 (1880).
3. 103 U.S. 168, 193 (1880).
4. 103 U.S. 168, 195 (1880).
5. 103 U.S. 168, 190 (1880).
6. 273 U.S. 135 (1927).
7. Dimock, *Congressional Investigation Committees*, 47 JOHNS HOPKINS UNIVERSITY STUDIES IN HISTORICAL AND POLITICAL SCIENCE 9, 138 (1929).
8. See Landis, *Constitutional Limitations on the Congressional Powers of Investigation*, 40 HARVARD LAW REVIEW 153 (1926); Potts, *Power of Legislative Bodies to Punish for Contempt*, 74 UNIVERSITY OF PENNSYL-

VANIA LAW REVIEW 691 (1926); and Frankfurter, *Hands Off the Investigations,* 38 NEW REPUBLIC 329 (1924).

9. The issue had been deliberately left open in *Kilbourn.*

10. McGrain v. Daugherty, 273 U.S. 135, 174–75 (1927).

11. 273 U.S. 135, 178 (1927).

12. 279 U.S. 263 (1929).

13. 72 F. Supp. 58 (1947), rev'd *per curiam* on other grounds, 174 F.2d 525 (1949), rev'd on other grounds, 339 U.S. 323 (1950). The court of appeals did not consider the issue, and the Supreme Court specifically refused to decide this and other questions not passed on by the court of appeals.

14. 165 F.2d 82, 89 (1947), *cert.* denied, 333 U.S. 838 (1948).

15. 167 F.2d 241, *cert.* denied, 334 U.S. 843 (1948).

16. 167 F.2d 241, 252 (1948).

17. 345 U.S. 41 (1953).

18. 60 Stat. 839, 2 *U.S.C.* §§ 261–70 (1958).

19. 140 F. Supp. 383 (1956).

20. 354 U.S. 178 (1957). But the Chief Justice does support the requirement of legislative purpose. 354 U.S. 178, 199 (1957); Quinn v. United States, 349 U.S. 155, 161 (1955).

21. 360 U.S. 109 (1959).

22. 365 U.S. 399 (1961).

23. 365 U.S. 431 (1961).

24. See CHAMBERLAIN, DOWLING & HAYS, THE JUDICIAL FUNCTION IN FEDERAL ADMINISTRATIVE AGENCIES (1942).

25. See pp. 59–61.

26. See the series of articles by Louis Jaffe, 67 HARVARD LAW REVIEW 1105 (1954); 69 HARVARD LAW REVIEW 239 (1955); 69 HARVARD LAW REVIEW 1020 (1956); and 70 HARVARD LAW REVIEW 953 (1957).

27. See WILLOUGHBY, PRINCIPLES OF PUBLIC ADMINISTRATION 9–35 (1927).

28. See Cooper, *The Legislative Veto: Its Promise and Its Perils,* 7 PUBLIC POLICY 128 (1957); and Schauffer, *The Legislative Veto Revisited,* 8 PUBLIC POLICY 296 (1958).

29. See GRIFFITH, CONGRESS, ITS CONTEMPORARY ROLE 50, 59, 158 (3rd ed. 1961); and FREEMAN, THE POLITICAL PROCESS: EXECUTIVE BUREAU-LEGISLATIVE COMMITTEE RELATIONS (1955).

30. See pp. 58–9.

31. See ROSSITER, THE AMERICAN PRESIDENCY 28 (Rev. ed. 1960).

32. See BINKLEY, THE MAN IN THE WHITE HOUSE 161–84 (1958); CORWIN, THE PRESIDENT, OFFICE AND POWERS 263 (1957); and NEUSTADT, PRESIDENTIAL POWER 5–6, 103 (1960).

33. See HAND, THE BILL OF RIGHTS 39 (1958).

34. FRIEDRICH, CONSTITUTIONAL GOVERNMENT AND DEMOCRACY 297 (Rev. ed. 1950).

35. ROSSITER, note 31 *supra.*

36. See BECK, CONTEMPT OF CONGRESS 66, 181 (1959); GRIFFITH, note 29 *supra* at 100–01, 108; and WHITE, CITADEL 232–33 (1956).

37. See BAILEY & SAMUEL, CONGRESS AT WORK 305 (1952); BURNHAM, CONGRESS AND THE AMERICAN TRADITION 233–34, 247 (1959); BURNS, CONGRESS ON TRIAL 101 (1949); Dimock, note 7 *supra* at 85–116; EBERLING, CONGRESSIONAL INVESTIGATIONS 277 (1928); GRIFFITH, note 29 *supra* at 42–44, 49, 101–02, 114–15; GROSS, THE LEGISLATIVE STRUGGLE 136–39 (1953); RIDDICK, THE UNITED STATES CONGRESS, ORGANIZATION AND PROCEDURE 25 (1949); and YOUNG, THE AMERICAN CONGRESS 187–88 (1958).

38. Both *McGrain* and *Sinclair* involved investigations of the executive branch.

39. 354 U.S. 178, 187 (1957).

40. Dimock, note 7 *supra* at 27–29.

41. See FRIEDRICH, note 34 *supra* at 37–58; and HYNEMAN, BUREAUCRACY IN A DEMOCRACY (1951).

42. The extended and bitter polemic over surrender of executive papers to Congress, in which so many Presidents have played a leading part, indicates recognition by both sides that administrative investigations are a key factor in the continuing struggle between Congress and the President.

43. Woodrow Wilson somewhat overstated the case: "Congress cannot control the officers of the executive without disgracing them. Its only whip is investigation, semi-judicial examination into corners suspected to be dirty." WILSON, CONGRESSIONAL GOVERNMENT 183 (Meridian ed. 1956). Bailey's case study of the Truman Committee is particularly enlightening in this regard. See BAILEY & SAMUEL, note 37 *supra* at 294–321.

See also YOUNG, note 37 *supra* at 187–88.

44. The first Congressional investigation, that of the St. Clair fiasco, served to uncover the administrative failures of the War Department. EBERLING, note 37 *supra* at 36–37. The *McGrain* case resulted from an investigation of suspected malfeasance in the Justice Department. Two of the most famous investigating groups, the Committee on the Conduct of the War and the Truman Committee, were primarily concerned with discovering shortcomings in executive direction of the war effort.

45. TAYLOR, GRAND INQUEST (1955).

46. WILSON, note 43 *supra* at 198.

47. Wilson, like the original American users of the "Grand Inquest" tag, was probably referring only to control of administration and not to general investigative power over all public affairs. Furthermore, both were undoubtedly leaning heavily on British practice with all the attendant risks of borrowing one country's experience for use in another. Nevertheless, these tags have survived and grown familiar precisely because Congress has in fact always carried on this "general information" type of investigation.

48. BURNHAM, note 37 *supra* at 223–24.

49. The Nye Committee. See MCGEARY, DEVELOPMENT OF CONGRESSIONAL INVESTIGATIVE POWER 57–60, 83–84 (1940).

50. The O'Mahoney Committee (T.N.E.C.). See *id.*, 146–48.

51. The Kefauver Crime and Juvenile Delinquency Committees.

52. The investigation of subversion is not new. Spanish bribery of General Wilkerson (1810), the Burr conspiracy (1808), and John Brown's raid (1859) have all been investigated.

53. GRIFFITH, note 29 *supra* at 102–03.

54. GALLOWAY, THE LEGISLATIVE PROCESS IN CONGRESS 316 (1953); and BURNHAM, note 37 *supra* at 234.

55. The proceedings of the House Un-American Activities Committee provide the most obvious example of one kind of judicial investigation. What particular individuals are or are not, or were or were not, Communists is a key question in the Committee hearings, and those labeled Communist are subject to social sanctions, sanctions whose severity is at least in part due to the success of the Committee's own public-education campaign. The first Congressional investigation, that of General St. Clair, illustrates the same phenomenon. Although the investigation in part concerned itself with administrative failings, it also examined charges of incompetence, insubordination, and conduct unbecoming an officer on the part of the General. The Committee thus acted in lieu of a military court and substituted the sanction of public condemnation for the normal sanctions of military law.

56. See WERNER & STARR, TEAPOT DOME (1959).

57. See BURNHAM, note 37 *supra* at 221, 223 (n. 3), 230–31, 244; GRIFFITH, note 29 *supra* at 12, 108; and YOUNG, note 37 *supra* at 245–46.

58. Wilson, note 43 *supra* at 62–76.

59. See BURNS, note 37 *supra* at 54–55; GRIFFITH, CONGRESS, ITS CONTEMPORARY ROLE 50, 158 (2d ed. 1956); GROSS, note 37 *supra* at 265–336; and MATHEWS, THE U.S. SENATOR AND HIS WORLD 147–76 (1960).

60. 2 *U.S.C.* §190b (1958).

61. 354 U.S. 178 (1957).

62. 354 U.S. 178, 197–98 (1957).

63. 354 U.S. 178, 198 (citing United States v. Rumely 345 U.S. 41 [1953]).

64. 354 U.S. 178, 201 (1957).

65. 354 U.S. 178, 203–04 (1957).

66. 354 U.S. 178, 205 (1957).

67. 354 U.S. 178, 205 (1957).

68. 354 U.S. 178, 198 (1957).

69. 354 U.S. 178, 204 (1957).

70. 354 U.S. 178, 187 (1957).

71. 354 U.S. 178, 187 (1957).

72. 354 U.S. 178, 200. But, unlike that in *Josephson*, this decision includes a hint that they might vitiate the committee's legislative purpose.

73. The criminal contempt statute specifies punishment for failure to answer pertinent questions. To avoid unconstitutional vagueness in the application of a criminal statute, the witness must be able to judge whether he is refusing to answer a pertinent or nonpertinent question.

74. On the Court's general tendency to decide cases on procedural rather than Constitutional grounds, see

PRITCHETT, THE POLITICAL OFFENDER AND THE WARREN COURT (1958); and the series of articles by McCloskey, 42 VIRGINIA LAW REVIEW 735 (1956); 43 VIRGINIA LAW REVIEW 803 (1957); and 44 VIRGINIA LAW REVIEW 1029 (1958). Kalven, in *Mr. Alexander Meiklejohn and the Barenblatt Opinion,* 27 UNIVERSITY OF CHICAGO LAW REVIEW 315, 329 (1960), speculates that the two parts of the *Watkins* decision when read together constitute a plea to Congress to rein in its committees and a threat to act if Congress does not do so. But he concludes that Congress paid no attention to the plea and that the Court has backed down on its threat.

75. 306 U.S. 109 (1959).

76. 360 U.S. 109, 117–20 (1959).

77. Standing Rule XI of the House

78. 360 U.S. 109, 127–29 (1959). The court first stated the presumption

79. 360 U.S. 109, 132–33 (1959).

80. 360 U.S. 109, 134. See also Black's dissent at 144–45.

81. 360 U.S. 109, 111, 127 (1959).

82. 360 U.S. 109, 111–12 (1959).

83. 360 U.S. 109, 127 (1959).

84. 360 U.S. 109, 132 (1959).

85. 360 U.S. 109, 133 (1959).

86. Indeed, it is worth pausing briefly to examine just how the circuit court in this case examined the record. The court first stated the presumption doctrine. Then it examined activity of Congress in the area of subversion legislation, the committee authorization, its annual reports (which make legislative recommendations), the statements of the chairman, and so forth. From these records, it concluded that the primary purpose of the investigation was legislative. Then it refused to give weight to any contrary evidence because, once a legislative purpose had been established, other purposes could not vitiate the investigation's legitimacy. Having thus rigorously excluded any evidence that could rebut it, the court could triumphantly conclude that the presumption had not been successfully rebutted. As some pretense of legislative purpose can be dreamed up by any committee member who was not an absolute fool, this approach in fact establishes an irrebuttable presumption.

87. 365 U.S. 399 (1961).

88. 365 U.S. 431 (1961).

89. See 365 U.S. 431, 432–35; 365 U.S. 399, 407–10, 413–15.

90. 365 U.S. 431, 433; 365 U.S. 399, 413.

91. 365 U.S. 399, 408–10.

92. 365 U.S. 431, 435.

93. 365 U.S. 399, 411.

94. 365 U.S. 399, 412.

95. 365 U.S. 431, 435.

96. Similar techniques that purport to look at the record have been used in several circuit-court cases since *Barenblatt*. See United States v. Yellin, 287, F.2d 292 (1961); Liveright v. United States, 280 F.2d 708 (1960); Gojack v. United States, 280 F.2d 678 (1960); Grumman v. United States, 294 F.2d 708 (1961); Hartman v. United States, 290 F.2d 460 (1961); and Davis v. United States, 269 F.2d 357 (1959).

97. The bible of the modest has become HAND, THE BILL OF RIGHTS (1958) in which the position is clearly and forcibly stated.

98. The "preferred position" doctrine, which would deny this presumption to laws touching on Bill of Rights freedoms, is currently in hibernation. It may be found sleeping in the dissents of the "liberal" four, Black, Douglas, Brennan and Warren. See MASON, THE SUPREME COURT FROM TAFT TO WARREN 146–47, 183 (1958).

99. See HAND, note 97 *supra* at 14–15, 29–30.

100. The Court has recognized the danger of exposure in other areas. See Talley v. California, 362 U.S. 60 (1960); and NAACP v. Alabama *ex. rel.* Patterson, 357 U.S. 449 (1958).

101. United States v. Rumely, 345 U.S. 41 (1953).

102. Readers will undoubtedly sense the ghost of Courts past in this passage. The technique suggested here is, of course, modeled on that of Marbury v. Madison, 1 Cranch 137 (1803), in which the very large pill of judicial review was sweetened by the Court's self-denial of certain powers that it could not, in terms of political reality, hope to exercise anyway.

103. See Elkins v. United States, 364 U.S. 206 (1960); and Mapp v. Ohio, 367 U.S. 643 (1961). The Court

could then derive Congress's power of investigation from its power to organize itself or from the historically sanctioned inherent powers of legislative bodies transmitted to Congress by the general grant of legislative power in Article I.

104. "Careless" because the opinions themselves are actually grounded on the "nothing-but-the-law" approach.

105. United States v. Rumely, 345 U.S. 41, 43 (1953).

106. Watkins v. United States, 354 U.S. 178, 187 (1957).

107. See United States v. Rumely, 345 U.S. 41 (1953); the dissents in Barenblatt v. United States, 360 U.S. 109 (1959), Wilkinson v. United States, 365 U.S. 399 (1961), and Braden v. United States, 365 U.S. 431 (1961); and the majority opinion in Deutsch v. United States, 365 U.S. 456 (1961).

108. 83 Sup. Ct. 1828 (1963).

109. 369 U.S. 749 (1962).

110. 83 Sup. Ct. 889 (1963).

111. 83 Sup. Ct. 889, 894 (1963).

112. 83 Sup. Ct. 889, 899 (1963).

113. 369 U.S. 599 (1962).

114. Note that Frankfurter did go far toward abandoning at least part of the presumption doctrine in the Rumely case.

115. See, for example, Sweezy v. New Hampshire, 354 U.S. 234 (1957); and United States v. Rumely, 345 U.S. 41 (1953).

116. See Jaffe, The Judicial Universe of Mr. Justice Frankfurter, 62 HARVARD LAW REVIEW 357 (1949).

¶ Chapter 3

1. Considering only decisions with full opinions. The exact figures will vary depending on how certain borderline cases are classified. See the HARVARD LAW REVIEW's annual summary in its November issue.

2. See Spaeth, *An Analysis of Judicial Attitudes In the Labor Relations Decisions of the Warren Court,* 25 JOURNAL OF PUBLIC LAW 290 (1963).

3. See, for example, Kagel & Smith, *Chief Justice Warren and Labor Law,* 49 CALIFORNIA LAW REVIEW 126 (1961).

4. American Steel Foundries Company v. Tri-City Central Trades Council 257 U.S. 184 (1921); and Truax v. Corrigan, 257 U.S. 312 (1921).

5. Senn v. Tile Layers Protective Union, 301 U.S. 468 (1937).

6. 310 U.S. 88 (1940).

7. Milk Wagon Drivers Union of Chicago, Local 753 v. Meadowmoor Dairies, Inc., 312 U.S. 287 (1941).

8. American Federation of Labor v. Swing, 312 U.S. 321 (1941).

9. Carpenters and Joiners Union of America v. Ritter's Cafe, 315 U.S. 722 (1942).

10. Bakery and Pastry Drivers v. Wohl, 315 U.S. 769 (1942).

11. 336 U.S. 490 (1949).

12. Hughes v. Superior Court of California, 339 U.S. 460 (1950).

13. International Brotherhood of Teamsters Unions v. Hanhe, 339 U.S. 470 (1950).

14. Local 262, Building Service Employees Union, v. Gazzam, 339 U.S. 532 (1950).

15. Local 695, International Brotherhood of Teamsters v. Vogt, 354 U.S. 284 (1957).

16. 354 U.S. 284 (1957).

17. American Federation of Labor v. Swing, 312 U.S. 321 (1941).

18. The Court was thus in tune with Congress, which had passed the Taft-Hartley Act in 1947.

19. Local 10, United Association of Journeymen, Plumbers and Steamfitters v. Graham, 345 U.S. 192 (1953).

20. See Tanenhaus, *Picketing-Free Speech: the Growth of the New Law of Picketing from 1940 to 1952,* 38 CORNELL LAW QUARTERLY 1 (1952).

21. 364 U.S. 485 (1953).

22. See National Labor Relations Board v. Reliance Fuel Oil Corporation, 83 Sup. Ct. 312 (1962); and Innes Steam Ship Company v. International Maritime Workers Union, 83 Sup. Ct. 611 (1962).

23. 325 U.S. 538 (1945).

24. International Union, United Auto Workers v. Wisconsin Employ-

ment Relations Board 336 U.S. 245 (1949).

25. International Union, United Auto Workers v. O'Brien, 339 U.S. 454 (1950); and Amalgamated Association of Street Employees v. Wisconsin Employment Relations Board, 340 U.S. 383 (1951).

26. 364 U.S. 485 (1953).

27. 347 U.S. 656 (1954).

28. Weber v. Anheuser-Busch, Inc., 348 U.S. 468 (1955).

29. United Automobile, Aircraft and Agricultural Implement Workers of America v. Wisconsin Employment Relations Board, 351 U.S. 266 (1956).

30. 355 U.S. 131 (1957).

31. 353 U.S. 969 (1957).

32. International Union, United Automobile, Aircraft and Agricultural Implement Workers of America v. Russell, 356 U.S. 634 (1958).

33. International Association of Machinists v. Gonzales, 356 U.S. 617 (1958).

34. 359 U.S. 236 (1959).

35. 355 U.S. 131 (1957).

36. 312 U.S. 569 (1941).

37. It was precise because there was only the threat of violence in *Youngdahl,* so that the union could argue that no violence had occurred and make some sort of plausible case for federal protection, that the First Amendment had to be dragged in to bolster the Court's position.

38. National Labor Relations Board v. Drivers, Chauffeurs, Helpers, Local 639, 362 U.S. 274 (1960).

39. Subsequent legislation prohibited minority picketing (Labor Management and Reporting Act of 1959), but its passage has no bearing on the Court's general tactical problem with the "neither protected nor prohibited" area.

40. 359 U.S. 236, 250, 1959).

41. 359 U.S. 236, 254 (1959).

42. 359 U.S. 236 (1959).

43. See Campbell v. Hussey, 368 U.S. 297, 315 n. 29 (1961); and *in re* Green, 369 U.S. 689, 693 (1962).

44. Bogle v. Jakes Foundry Co., 326 U.S. 401 (1960) (*per curiam*); McMahon v. Milam Manufacturing Co., 359 U.S. 236 (1961) (*per curiam*); *In re* Green, 369 U.S. 689 (1962); and Superior Court v. State *ex rel.* Yellow Cab Service Inc., 361 U.S. 373 (1960).

45. 370 U.S. 173 (1962).

46. 83 Sup. Ct. 1429 (1963).

47. Cf. Innes S.S. Co. v. International Maritime Workers Union 83 Sup. Ct. 611 (1963), in which the Court invokes the "arguable" doctrine but leaves the state jurisdiction because the N.L.R.B. had no jurisdiction in the area at all.

48. See pp. 129–30.

49. 83 Sup. Ct. 1423 (1963).

50. Local 438, Construction and General Laborers' Union, AFL-CIO v. Curry, 83 Sup. Ct. 531 (1963). See also Liner v. Jafco, Inc., 84 Sup. Ct. 391 (1964); Hattiesburg Building and Trades Council v. Broome, 84 Sup. Ct. 1156 (1964). The violence exception remains. See United Steel Workers v. N.L.R.B., 12 L. Ed.2d 899 (1964).

51. National Labor Relations Board v. General Motors Corp. 83 Sup. Ct. 1453 (1963); Retail Clerks International Association, Local 1625, AFL-CIO v. Schermerhorn, 83 Sup. Ct. 1461 (1963).

52. 361 U.S. 477 (1960).

53. 29 U.S.C.A. Sec. 185(a) (1958).

54. Charles Dowd Box Co. v. Courtney, 368 U.S. 502 (1962); and Local 174, Teamsters, Chauffeurs, Warehousemen and Helpers of America v. Lucas Flour Co., 369 U.S. 95 (1962).

55. I have omitted another area of federalism, the so-called "no man's land" problem, because there the Court did not so much make policy as render a set of opinions intended to be so unsatisfactory that Congress would be forced to make policy. In this aim the Court succeeded. See Rothman, *Federal-State Relationships as Affected by the Landrum-Griffin Provisions,* 40 UNIVERSITY OF DETROIT LAW JOURNAL 228 (1962).

56. 346 U.S. 464 (1953).

57. See Frankfurter's dissent, 346 U.S. 464, 478 (1953).

58. National Labor Relations Board v. Wooster Division of Borg-Warner Corp., 356 U.S. 342 (1958).

59. National Labor Relations Board v. Truck Drivers Local 449, International Brotherhood of Teamsters, Chauffeurs, Warehousemen and Helpers, AFL, 353 U.S. 87 (1957).

60. 366 U.S. 731 (1961). See also N.L.R.B. v. Exchange Parts Co., 84 Sup. Ct. 457 (1964).

61. 353 U.S. 313 (1957).

62. Sec. 8(b)(4)(A); and 29 U.S.C.A. 158(b)(4)(A) 1958.
63. National Labor Relations Board v. International Rice Milling Co., 341 U.S. 665 (1951).
64. 366 U.S. 667 (1961). See also United Steel Workers v. N.L.R.B., 12 L. Ed.2d 899 (1964).
65. Local 1976, United Brotherhood of Carpenters and Joiners AFL v. National Labor Relations Board, 357 U.S. 93 (1958). See also N.L.R.B. v. Fruit Packers, Local 760, 84 Sup. Ct. 1063 (1964); N.L.R.B. v. Servette, 84 Sup. Ct. 1099 (1964).
66. Sec. 8(b)(4)(A); and 29 U.S.C.A. 158(b)(4)(A) (1958).
67. See *Note,* 57 MICHIGAN LAW REVIEW 291 (1958).
68. In the Labor Management Reporting and Disclosure Act of 1959, Congress made hot-cargo contracts an unfair labor practice and declared such provisions unenforceable and void, thus closing the door left open by the Court.
69. 351 U.S. 105 (1956).
70. Mastro Plastics Corp. v. National Labor Relations Board, 350 U.S. 270 (1956).
71. 352 U.S. 282 (1957).
72. 210 F.2d 325 (1954).
73. See Universal Camera Corporation v. National Labor Relations Board 340 U.S. 474 (1951).
74. National Labor Relations Board v. Drivers, Chauffeurs, Helpers Local 639, 362 U.S. 274 (1960).
75. International Ladies' Garment Workers Union, AFL-CIO v. National Labor Relations Board, 366 U.S. 731 (1961).
76. Labor-Management Reporting and Disclosure Act of 1959, Sec. 704(c) 29 U.S.C.A. Sec. 158 (1958).
77. Fourth Local Lodge 1424 v. National Labor Relations Board, 362 U.S. 411 (1960).
78. 347 U.S. 17 (1954).
79. 29 U.S.C.A. Sec. 158(a)(3) (1958).
80. 351 U.S. 149 (1956).
81. Cox *The Duty to Bargain In Good Faith,* 71 HARVARD LAW REVIEW 1401 (1958).
82. National Labor Relations Board v. United Steelworkers, 357 U.S. 357 (1958).
83. 243 F.2d 593 (1956).
84. 361 U.S. 477 (1960).
85. 369 U.S. 736 (1962).
86. 369 U.S. 736, 745 (1962).
87. 365 U.S. 667 (1961).
88. See also Local 100, United Association of Journeymen and Apprentices v. Borden, 83 Sup. Ct. 1423 (1963).
89. 83 Sup. Ct. 1139 (1963).
90. 304 U.S. 333 (1938).
91. Note that the N.L.R.B. also found that the company's refusal to include the superseniority question in strike negotiations was a refusal to bargain but that the Court could not very well decide on those grounds because of its insistence on a subjective test in that area.
92. See National Labor Relations Board v. Fant Milling Company, 360 U.S. 301 (1959), in addition to the cases discussed above.
93. Bickel, *Forward: The Passive Virtues,* 75 HARVARD LAW REVIEW 40 (1961).
94. Charles Dowd Box Co. v. Courtney, 368 U.S. 502 (1962).
95. Local 174, Teamsters, Chauffeurs, Warehousemen and Helpers v. Lucas Flour Co., 369 U.S. 95 (1962).
96. In Erie Railroad v. Tompkins, 304 U.S. 64 (1938), it was held that, in cases reaching the Supreme Court because of the diversity of citizenships of the litigants, the law of the state in which the action arose, rather than federal common law, would apply.
97. United States v. Warrior and Gulf Navigation Co., 363 U.S. 593 (1960).
98. 370 U.S. 254 (1962).
99. See also United Steelworkers v. American Manufacturing Co., 363 U.S. 564 (1960), which carries the doctrine so far that arbitration clauses in the future will have to be very carefully worded. For a treatment of the Sec. 301 arbitration cases from the point of view of the relations between both state and federal courts and arbitrators see Kovarsky, *Labor Arbitration and Federal Preemption: The Overruling of Black v. Cutter Laboratories,* 47 MINNESOTA LAW REVIEW 531 (1963).
100. Atkinson v. Sinclair Refining Company, 370 U.S. 238 (1962).
101. Drake Bakeries, Inc. v. Local 50, American Bakery Workers, 370 U.S. 254 (1962). See also Local Union

721, United Packinghouse Workers v. Needham Packing Co., 84 Sup. Ct. 773 (1964).

102. Sinclair Refining Co. v. Atkinson, 370 U.S. 195 (1962).

103. Of course, the Norris-LaGuardia Act as modified by the Wagner Act did provide for injunctions in the form of N.L.R.B. orders enforceable by the circuit courts. The Act was principally aimed at privately sought injunctions. The labor law of several states permits an arbitrator to issue injunctions or injunction-like orders as part of his disposition of a dispute. The Supreme Court may then find that the common law of Sec. 301 will allow injunctions by federal courts aimed at strikes that violate the orders of arbitrators. The Court could reason that these orders are more analogous to "public" than to "private" injunctions.

104. The point has been repeatedly made that labor contracts cannot be treated by strict analogy to regular commercial contracts and that past judicial attempts to do so have led to unsatisfactory results. The argument is obviously a reaction to courts that, in the early days of the labor movement, treated contracts of employment as if they had been entered into voluntarily by two equal and independent parties, when in fact they had not. Nevertheless, it does not necessarily follow that labor contracts need now be interpreted as if they had been entered into by an overwhelmingly strong management and a weak union that requires exceptionally favorable judicial treatment in order to survive.

105. 369 U.S. 689 (1962).

106. 83 Sup. Ct. 267 (1962). General Drivers, Local Union 89 v. Moore, 84 Sup. Ct. 363 (1964).

107. National Labor Relations Board v. General Motors Corp., 83 Sup. Ct. 1453 (1963).

108. Lincoln Federal Labor Union v. Northwestern Iron and Metal Co., 335 U.S. 525, 536 (1949).

109. Algoma Plywood and Veneer Co. v. Wisconsin Employment Relations Board, 336 U.S. 301, 313–14 (1949).

110. 156 F. Supp. 89, 262 F.2d 359, *cert.* denied 359 U.S. 935 (1959); 351 U.S. 225 (1956); and Wellington, *The Constitution, The Labor Union and Government Action,* 70 YALE LAW JOURNAL 345 (1961).

111. 45 U.S.C.A. Sec. 152 (1958).

112. 334 U.S. 1 (1948).

113. Nixon v. Herndon 273 U.S. 536 (1927); Nixon v. Condon, 286 U.S. 73 (1932); Grovey v. Townsend, 295 U.S. 45 (1935); Smith v. Allwright, 321 U.S. 649 (1944); and Terry v. Adams, 345 U.S. 461 (1953).

114. 323 U.S. 192 (1944).

115. 359 U.S. 935 (1959).

116. 351 U.S. 225 (1956).

117. 351 U.S. 225, 238 (1956).

118. 351 U.S. 225, 235 (1956).

119. 367 U.S. 740 (1961).

120. In Brotherhood of Railway Clerks v. Allen, 83 Sup. Ct. 1158 (1963), the Court has attempted to shift the burden of making the bookkeeping calculations to the unions and suggested various modes by which the *Street* decision could be implemented either by court order or voluntary union action. In addition, this decision indicates that the court is not going to be prodded into an antiunion crusade on the basis of *Street.*

121. Wellington, *Machinists v. Street: Statutory Interpretation and the Avoidance of Constitutional Issues,* 1961 SUPREME COURT REVIEW 49 (1961).

¶ Chapter 4

1. For an important exception, see Lowndes, *Federal Taxation and the Supreme Court,* 1960 SUPREME COURT REVIEW 222.

2. I have taken the 1957 term as the beginning of the "Warren Court." In that term, Justices Brennan and Whittaker succeeded Justices Minton and Reed. Justice Harlan had participated in none of the 1955 term tax decisions, in only one, and there indecisively, during the 1956 term. It was not until 1957 that decisions can be considered even roughly indicative

of present Court attitudes.

3. See *Note,* 1960 UNIVERSITY OF ILLINOIS LAW FORUM 585.

4. This article deals only with the former. Cases involving collection rather than assessment, like United States v. Price, 361 U.S. 304 (1960) (ninety-day letters) and United States v. Massie, 355 U.S. 595 (1958) (burden of proof in tax-evasion prosecution), and the very extensive litigation over federal tax liens have not been treated.

5. See, for example, Putnam v. C.I.R., 352 U.S. 82 (1956); Peurifoy v. C.I.R., 358 U.S. 59 (1958); Tank Truck Rentals, Inc., v. C.I.R., 356 U.S. 30 (1958); C.I.R. v. Sullivan, 356 U.S. 27 (1958); C.I.R. v. P.G. Lake, Inc. 356 U.S. 260 (1958); Parsons v. Smith, 359 U.S. 215 (1959); C.I.R. v. Hansen, 360 U.S. 446 (1959); Hanover Bank v. C.I.R., 369 U.S. 672 (1962); United States v. Davis, 370 U.S. 65 (1962); Turnbow v. C.I.R., 368 U.S. 337 (1961); C.I.R. v. Bilder, 369 U.S. 499 (1962); United States v. Gilmore, 83 Sup. Ct. 623 (1963); Maximov v. United States, 83 Sup. Ct. 1054 (1963); and Braunstein v. C.I.R., 83 Sup. Ct. 1663 (1963).

6. Cary, *Reflections Upon the American Law Institute Tax Project and the Internal Revenue Code: A Plea for a Moratorium and Reappraisal,* 60 COLUMBIA LAW REVIEW 259, 281.

7. 364 U.S. 361 (1960).

8. 353 U.S. 382 (1957).

9. *Id.* at 385. The Code refers to "the tax payer (who) has a net operating loss." Sec. 122 (b) (2) (C) 64 Stat. 937, 938, 65 Stat. 505, 26 U.S.C.A. Sec. 122 (b) (2) (C) (1954).

10. 352 U.S. 82 (1956).

11. The guarantor had been the principal organizer and eventually sole stockholder of the corporation whose loans he had guaranteed. The Court concluded that "There is no real or economic difference between the loss of an investment made in the form of a direct loan to a corporation and one made indirectly in the form of a guaranteed bank loan." 352 U.S. 82, 92 (1956).

12. 368 U.S. 337 (1961).

13. 356 U.S. 274 (1958).

14. One could argue that this position is realistic, for the annuity and the policy could be sold or otherwise disposed of separately. But the actual fact situation is one in which the purchaser reaps his intended benefits by maintaining the two in combination.

15. 364 U.S. 410 (1960).

16. 366 U.S. 299 (1961).

17. 370 U.S. 65 (1962).

18. 83 Sup. Ct. 1054 (1963).

19. 60 Stat. 1377, 1384 (1945).

20. This case is of interest in the tax field largely because of the simplification technique used. It is basically a treaty rather than a tax case, and the Court's analysis of the treaty is not excessively formal but quite realistic.

21. 83 Sup. Ct. 1168 (1963).

22. See, for example, Whipple v. C.I.R., 301 F.2d 108 (1962); Maytag v. United States, 289 F.2d 647 (1961); Mays v. C.I.R., 272 F.2d 788 (1959); C.I.R. v. Stokes Estate, 200 F.2d 637 (1953).

23. A glance at the facts in this case as described by the Court will convince the reader of this complexity. *Whipple* was not actually decided against the taxpayer but remanded for consideration of one of the relationships between the taxpayer as individual and his corporation that had escaped the attention of the lower courts. It might be argued that the decision is essentially realistic in the sense that, if an individual adopts the corporate form, he does so to reap the advantages of a formal distinction between himself and his business, and he ought to reap the disadvantages as well. But the Court does not use this argument or hint that it is the basis of its position.

24. 353 U.S. 180 (1957).

25. See *Note,* 1957 UNIVERSITY OF ILLINOIS LAW FORUM 517, 520–21 (1957).

26. 353 U.S. 180, 189 (1957).

27. American Automobile Association v. United States, 367 U.S. 687 (1961).

28. 83 Sup. Ct. 601 (1963).

29. As in the gift cases discussed immediately below, it is possible, by elaborate interpretation, to derive some tentative rules from these three

cases, but such rules would lie entirely in the eye of the beholder and not in the mouth of the Court.

30. 363 U.S. 278 (1960).

31. 363 U.S. 299 (1960).

32. 363 U.S. 278 (1960).

33. 302 U.S. 34 (1937).

34. By elaborate inference, some new rules or at least approaches can be derived. See Hauser, *Business Gifts and the Supreme Court,* 38 TAXES 942 (1960). But the point is that it is only by a kind of guessing game that such rules emerge. The Court has not committed itself to anything.

35. It reversed *Duberstein* because the Tax Court findings were not "clearly erroneous," remanded *Stanton* for further finding of facts, and upheld a jury's finding of fact in *Kaiser.*

36. This point undoubtedly shows why the majority felt that Justice Black's fears were excessive. The case does not commit the Court to applying case-by-case a rule that distinguishes tax avoidance from "legitimate" transactions. It only requires that lower courts make factual determinations of whether or not loans in which interest deductions are claimed actually occurred.

37. 359 U.S. 215 (1959).

38. It is not clear in this case whether the Court is rejecting all the tests in favor of a "realistic" examination of the actual economic situation or marshalling a series of black and white tests and declaring that the taxpayer flunks them all, thus obviating the need to determine which test is decisive.

39. 358 U.S. 59 (1958).

40. It ruled that the decision of the Tax Court (27 T.C. 149 [1957]) hinged on a finding of fact (that the employee's job was "temporary" rather than "indefinite"), that the circuit found the Tax Court finding "clearly erroneous" (254 F.2d 483 [4th Cir. 1957]), and that in doing so the Circuit made a "fair assessment of the record," so that Supreme Court intervention was not required. See also Rudolph v. United States (370 U.S. 269 [1962]), in which, although three of the Justices wanted to provide some guidance to the lower courts on the tax treatment of expense-paid trips, the majority, using the "clearly erroneous" rule, dismissed a previously granted writ of *certiorari* in order to avoid dealing with the problem.

41. C.I.R. v. Flowers, 326 U.S. 465 (1946). See *Note,* 44 CORNELL LAW QUORUM 270 (1959).

42. 356 U.S. 30 (1958).

43. 356 U.S. 38 (1958).

44. 356 U.S. 27 (1958).

45. Deputy v. DuPont, 308 U.S. 488 (1940), particularly Roberts's dissent at 499; and Welch v. Helvering, 290 U.S. 111 (1933).

46. C.I.R. v. Lester, 366 U.S. 299 (1961).

47. See C.I.R. v. Weil, 353 U.S. 958 (1957) (*cert.* denied), and Eisinger v. C.I.R. 356 U.S. 913 (1950) (*cert.* denied).

48. See *Note,* 45 MARQUETTE LAW REVIEW 123 (1961).

49. Justice Clark based his opinion on the supposed Congressional intent that child-support portions were to be expressly specified before they became taxable. The whole opinion is a clear declaration to Congress that if it wants something done in this field it must do it itself.

50. 83 Sup. Ct. 623 (1963).

51. 26 U.S.C.A. Sec. 23 (a)(2) (1958).

52. 343 U.S. 118 (1952).

53. 343 U.S. 118, 123, 125–6 (1952).

54. 276 U.S. 145 (1928).

55. 83 Sup. Ct. 618 (1963).

56. 83 Sup. Ct. 623, 629 (1963).

57. 83 Sup. Ct. 1168 (1963).

58. See NEALE, THE ANTITRUST LAWS OF THE U.S.A. (1960).

59. The Court sometimes draws a distinction between Treasury Regulations and Service Rulings, viewing only the former as authoritative. See Higgins v. C.I.R., 312 U.S. 212 (1941); Biddle v. C.I.R., 302 U.S. 573 (1938); and Helvering v. New York Trust Co., 292 U.S. 455 (1934). But the stronger tendency seems to have been to ignore the distinction. See Corn Products Refining Co. v. C.I.R., 350 U.S. 46 (1955); Helvering v. Wilshire Oil Co., 308 U.S. 90 (1939); and Estate of Sanford v.

C.I.R. 308 U.S. 39 (1939). The Warren Court seems to be following the latter course. See Cory Corp. v. Sauber, 363 U.S. 709 (1960); and Hanover Bank v. C.I.R. 369 U.S. 672, 686 (1962).

60. 358 U.S. 498 (1959).

61. 358 U.S. 508, 510 (1959).

62. See Brown, *Regulations, Re-enactment and the Revenue Acts,* 54 HARVARD LAW REVIEW 377 (1941); Griswold, *A Summary of the Regulations Problem,* 54 HARVARD LAW REVIEW 398 (1941); and Paul, *Use and Abuse of Tax Regulations in Statutory Construction,* 49 YALE LAW JOURNAL 660 (1940).

63. See *Comment,* 69 YALE LAW JOURNAL 1017 (1960); and Spiefel, *Deductibility of Lobbying Initiative and Referendum Expenses: A Problem for Congressional Consideration,* 45 CALIFORNIA LAW REVIEW 1 (1957).

64. 364 U.S. 92 (1960). The Court again relies on a combination of long-standing practice and re-enactment in United States v. Davis, 370 U.S. 65, 71 (1962). See also Maximov v. United States 83 Sup. Ct. 1054 (1963).

65. 353 U.S. 81 (1957).

66. Hanover Bank v. C.I.R., 369 U.S. 672, 687 n.21 (1962); and see Cory Corp. v. Sauber, 363 U.S. 709 (1960). The Court again combines re-enactment with long-standing practice: "Congress did not change the statute though it was specifically advised in 1956 that that was the test which was being applied" (at 712).

67. See *Comment,* 28 UNIVERSITY OF CHICAGO LAW REVIEW 380 (1961).

68. See Tank Truck Rentals, Inc. v. C.I.R. 356 U.S. 30 (ruling 1942, rescinded 1950, case 1958); C.I.R. v. P.G. Lake, Inv., 356 U.S. 260 (service reversed self 1946, case (1958); and Automobile Club of Michigan v. C.I.R., 353 U.S. 180 (original rulings 1934 and 38, reversed 1945, case 1956). In the last named case, taxpayer argued unsuccessfuly that previous ruling estopped C.I.R. from making retroactive assessments. In general, the doctrines of collateral estoppel, *res judicata,* and *stare decisis* have been severely limited in connection with Service and Treasury decisions. See *Note,* 56 COLUMBIA LAW REVIEW 1115, 1115–17 (1956).

69. The problem of retroactivity in both its legal and moral aspects hovers over all these cases. See *Comment,* 28 UNIVERSITY OF CHICAGO LAW REVIEW 380 (1961). From this point of view, the Court's general attraction to consistency may be a good thing. We are concerned here, however, with the impact of such an approach on the Court's relation with the Service.

70. 364 U.S. 122 (1960).

71. Yellon, *Depreciation Development in Congress and the Courts,* 38 TAXES 952, 952–53 (1960); and *Note,* 107 UNIVERSITY OF PENNSYLVANIA LAW REVIEW 865, 866 (1959), and cases cited there.

72. *Id.,* pp. 865, 869–70 (1959).

73. *Cf.* Evans v. C.I.R., 264, F.2d 502 (9th Cir. 1959) revised 364 U.S. 92 (1960), with United States v. Massey Motors, Inc., 264 F.2d 552 (5th Cir. 1959), aff'd 364 U.S. 92 (1960).

74. 360 U.S. 446 (1959).

75. See *Note,* 7 UNIVERSITY CALIFORNIA AT LOS ANGELES LAW REVIEW 154, 155–6 (1960).

76. Internal Revenue Code of 1954, Sec. 462. See *Finance Reserves of Small Installment Sales Dealers,* 97 *Journal of Accountancy* 201 (1954).

77. 69 Stat. 134 (1955); and 26 U.S.C.A. 462 (1958).

78. The cases are collected in *Note,* 1959 UNIVERSITY OF ILLINOIS LAW FORUM 878, 880 (1959).

79. Another example of Service persistence in the face of Congressional dissatisfaction may be seen in the scholarship and fellowship area. The Service has always attempted to narrow the tax exemptions for such payments as much as possible. In the 1954 Code, Congress voiced specific discontent with the old I.R.S. rule and passed a new provision calculated to give scholars more liberal treatment (Sec. 117). But the Service for some years continued to use its old rule in interpreting the new statute. See Mansfield, *Income from Prizes and Awards and from Scholarships,* 19 NEW YORK UNIVERSITY INSTITUTE ON FEDERAL TAXATION 129, 137–39 (1961).

80. Internal Revenue Code of 1954, Sec. 452.

81. 69 Stat. 134 (1955).
82. Beacon Publishing Co. v. C.I.R., 218 F.2d 697 (1955).
83. 367 U.S. 687 (1961).
84. 83 Sup. Ct. 601 (1963).
85. 26 U.S.C.A. Sec. 41, Sec. 446 (1958).
86. In the year of the switch, a taxpayer could take his full nonaccrual deductions but then also defer part of his income to future years under the accrual principle that receipts are not income until the time that the services entailed in those payments are performed.
87. It should be noted that *Schulde* is one of the rare cases that reached the Court without conflicts on the circuits, apparently because it is one of those rare cases that has stirred conflict on the Supreme Court. As the decision was five to four, it may be assumed that *certiorari* was granted under the rule of four because the dissenters wished to reopen the issue.
88. See S. Rep. No. 141, 82nd Congress 1st Session 31 (1951).
89 A.L.I. Federal Income Tax Stat., Sec. X 165 (i) (1) (Feb. 1954 draft).
90. Brownel, *Address to A.B.A. Annual Meeting*, Aug. 27 (1953), 78 A.B.A REP. 334, 337–38 (1953).
91. 356 U.S. 27 (1958).
92. 358 U.S. 59 (1958).
93. Internal Revenue Code of 1939, Sec. 23 (a) (1) (A).
94. Sec. 162 (a) (2).
95. *Cf.* Barnhill v. C.I.R., 148 F.2d 913 (4th Cir. 1945), with Flowers v. C.I.R. 148 F.2d 163 (5th Cir. 1945) rev'd on other grounds 326 U.S. 465 (1946); and see Wallace v. C.I.R., 144 F.2d 407 (9th Cir. 1944).
96. 326 U.S. 465 (1946).
97. 27 T.C. 149 (1957); and 254 F.2d 483 (1957).
98. See *Note,* 107 UNIVERSITY OF PENNSYLVANIA LAW REVIEW 871, 873 (1959).
99. 83 Sup. Ct. 1663 (1963).
100. 26 U.S.C.A. Sec. 117 (m).
101. R. C. Nail, 27 B.T.A. 333 (1932), acq. XII–1 Cum. Bull. 9, acq. withdrawn and non-acq. 1949–1 Cum. Bull. 6.
102. Benjamin & Currier, *The Supreme Court and the Taxation of Oil, Gas and Production Payments; The Lake Cases,* 19 LOUISIANA LAW REVIEW 579, 582–3 (1959).
103. G.C.M. 24849, 1946–1 Cum. Bull. 66; I.T. 3935 (1949–1 Cum. Bull. 39); and I.T. 4003 (1950–1 Cum. Bull. 10).
104. John D. Hawn, 23 T.C. 516 (1954); and Lester A. Nordan, 22 T.C. 1132 (1954).
105. The cases are described in Benjamin & Currier, note 102 *supra* at 579, 586–89. See also *Note,* 37 TEXAS LAW REVIEW 100 (1958).
106. C.I.R. v. Hawn, 231 F.2d 340 (1956).
107. See note 105 *supra.*
108. C.I.R. v. Slagter, 238 F.2d 901 (1956).
109. S.R. No. 2375, 81st Congress 2d. Sess. 66, 91 (1950).
110. H.R. No. 9559, 84th Congress, 2d. Sess. (1956).
111. 356 U.S. 260 (1958).
112. For instance, after *Cammarano,* in which the Court refused authoritatively to interpret the "ordinary and necessary" clause, the Service issued a new set of regulations and stepped up enforcement. *Comment: Deducting Business Expenses Designed to Influence Governmental Policy as 'Ordinary and Necessary': Cammarano v. United States and a Bit Beyond,* 69 YALE LAW JOURNAL 1017 (1960).
113. See *Note,* 46 CORNELL LAW QUARTERLY 359, 362–3 (1961). The Service actually won the cases but did not get the judicial legislation it was after.
114. 369 U.S. 672, 681–682 (1962).
115. 366 U.S. 299 (1961).
116. 356 U.S. 274 (1958).
117. 26 U.S.C.A. Sec. 23 (m) 114 (b) (I.R.C. 1939); and Sec. 613 (I.R.C. 1954).
118. See *Note,* 59 MICHIGAN LAW REVIEW 649, 650 (1961) and cases cited there.
119. See Riddell v. Monolith Portland Cement Co., 301 F.2d. 488 (1962), which collects the earlier cases at 493–4.
120. 364 U.S. 76 (1960).
121. 364 U.S. 76, 88–89 (1960).
122. 364 U.S. 76, 86 (1960).
123. 364 U.S. 76, 86 (1960).
124. 74 Sts. 1018 (1960). In the same year, the Congress gave some support to the Service's position on

clay processing in *Cannelton.* 74 Stat. 292 (1960).

125. Riddell v. Monolith Portland Cement Co., 301 F.2d 488 (1962).

126. 83 Sup. Ct. 379 (1963).

127. See C.I.R. v. Duberstein, 363 U.S. 278 (1960); Peurifoy v. C.I.R., 358 U.S. 59 (1958); Rudolph v. United States, 370 U.S. 269 (1962); and Whipple v. C.I.R., 83 Sup. Ct. 1168 (1963).

128. Gregory v. Helvering, 293 U.S. 465, 469 (1935), cited with approval in Knetsch v. United States 364 U.S. 361, 365 (1960).

129. Knetsch v. United States, 364 U.S. 361 (1960).

130. Libsom Shops v. Koehler, 353 U.S. 382 (1957) (loss carry-over); Automobile Club of Michigan v. C.I.R., 352 U.S. 180 (1957) (accrual); C.I.R. v. P. G. Lake, Inc., 356 U.S. 260 (1958) (capital gains); Hoover Motor Express Co. v. United States, 356 U.S. 38 (1958) (business deductions); Tank Truck Rentals, Inc. v. C.I.R. 356, U.S. 30 (1958) (business deductions); Parsons v. Smith, 359 U.S. 215 (1959) (depletion); Cammarano v. United States, 358 U.S. 498 (1959) (business deductions); C.I.R. v. Gillette, 364 U.S. 130 (1960) (capital gains); Hertz Corp. v. United States 364 U.S. 122 (1960) (depreciation and capital gains); C.I.R. v. Duberstein, 363 U.S. 278 (1960) (gifts); United States v. Kaiser, 363 U.S. 299 (1960) (gifts); Stanton v. United States, 363 U.S. 278 (1960) (gifts); Knetsch v. United States, 364 U.S. 361 (1960) (interest); United States v. Cannelton Sewer Pipe Co., 364 U.S. 76 (1960) (depreciation); C.I.R. v. Bilder, 369 U.S. 499 (1962) (medical deductions); Schulde v. C.I.R., 83 Sup Ct. 601 (1963) (accrual); and Riddell v. Monolith Portland Cement Co., 83 Sup. Ct. 378 (1963) (depletion).

131. Eustice & Lyon, *Federal Income Taxation,* 36 NEW YORK UNIVERSITY LAW REVIEW 642, 649–53 (1961).

132. See Shapiro, *Morals and the Courts: The Reluctant Crusaders,* 45 MINNEAPOLIS LAW REVIEW 897 (1961).

133. Lowndes, *Federal Taxation and the Supreme Court,* 1960 SUPREME COURT REVIEW 222.

134. Citing Griswold, *The Need for a Court of Tax Appeals,* 57 HARVARD LAW REVIEW 1153 (1944); and Pope, *A Court of Tax Appeals: A Call for Re-examination,* 39 AMERICAN BAR ASSOCIATION JOURNAL 275 (1953).

135. House Ways and Means and Senate Finance Committees.

136. Cary, *Reflections on the American Law Institutes Tax Program,* 60 COLUMBIA LAW REVIEW 259, 260 (1960). The obvious counterploy by the friends of the Service is the old routine that runs "Congress ought to handle general policy and leave details to the administrators" (see *id.*).

137. I do not mean that Congress always listens to its committees and to its committees only but that an unfavorable committee report or lack of committee action almost invariably blocks Congressional action, no matter how much information individual Congressmen have independently received. See GROSS, THE LEGISLATIVE STRUGGLE 265–353 (1953); and GRIFFITH, CONGRESS, IT'S CONTEMPORARY ROLE 75 (3rd ed. 1961).

138. See, for example, Surrey, *The Congress and the Tax Lobbyist—How Special Tax Provisions Get Enacted,* 70 HARVARD LAW REVIEW 1145 (1957), in which Professor Surrey seems actually to express dislike for nasty old politics that keep smudging up the nice neat tax schemes devised by the bureaucratic "good guys."

¶ Chapter 5

1. 369 U.S. 186 (1962).

2. POST, THE SUPREME COURT AND POLITICAL QUESTIONS (1936); Weston, *Political Questions,* 38 HARVARD LAW REVIEW 296 (1925); Field, *The Doctrine of Political Questions in the Federal Courts,* 8 MINNESOTA LAW REVIEW 485 (1924); and Finkelstein, *Judicial Self-Limitation,* 37 HARVARD LAW REVIEW 338 (1924). See also

Lewis, *Legislative Apportionment and the Federal Courts*, 71 HARVARD LAW REVIEW 1057 (1958); and CAHN, SUPREME COURT AND SUPREME LAW 36–47 (1954).

3. Hart & Wechsler, THE FEDERAL COURTS IN THE FEDERAL SYSTEM 192 (1953).

4. Rose v. Himely, 4 Cranch 241 (1808); and Gelston v. Hoyt, 3 Wheat. 246 (1818).

5. United States v. Ortega, Fed. Cas. 15,971 (1825); *Ex parte* Hitz, 111 U.S. 766 (1884); and Doe v. Borden, 16 How. 635 (1853).

6. Foster v. Neilson, 2 Peters 253 (1829).

7. See POST, note 1 *supra* at 36–50.

8. 12 Wall. 700 (1871).

9. Post, note 1 *supra at* 64, 67–81.

10. 5 Peters 1 (1831).

11. 7 How. 1 (1849).

12. Pacific States Telephone and Telegraph Co. v. Oregon, 223 U.S. 118 (1912).

13. 6 Wall. 50 (1867).

14. 7 Wall. 700 (1869).

15. Phillips v. Payne, 92 U.S. 130 (1876).

16. 12 Peters 657 (1838).

17. 143 U.S. 649 (1891).

18. Coleman v. Miller, 307 U.S. 433 (1939).

19. The National Prohibition Cases, 253 U.S. 350 (1920).

20. Dillon v. Gloss, 256 U.S. 368 (1921).

21. United States v. Sprague, 282 U.S. 716 (1931).

22. Conflicts between state and federal laws, which the Court routinely handles, do not fall in this category because the Constitution creates a single system within which state and nation operate *vis à vis* one another.

23. (1952).

24. 6 Peters 515 (1832).

25. The Cherokee Nation v. Georgia, 5 Peters 1, 20 (1831).

26. 7 How. (1849).

27. 328 U.S. 549 (1946).

28. It should be noted, however, that the whole "political questions" discussion in *Luther* is *obiter dictum*. The state courts had held that the Dorr movement had never been the government of Rhode Island. Taney's actual decision rests on the point that the legitimacy of a given state government is a question of state law on which the findings of the state courts are binding on the Supreme Court.

29. 7 How. 1, 41 (1849).

30. 7 How. 1, 44 (1849).

31. 328 U.S. 549 (1946).

32. 328 U. S. 549, 552 (1946).

33. See p. 192.

34. 328 U.S. 549, 552 (1946).

35. 328 U.S. 549, 553 (1946).

36. 328 U.S. 549, 572–3 (1946).

37. 328 U.S. 549, 553–4, 556 (1946).

38. 328 U.S. 549, 554 (1946).

39. 328 U.S. 549 553–4, 556 (1946).

40. Guinn v. United States 238 U.S. 347 (1915); Lane v. Wilson, 307 U.S. 268 (1939); United States v. Classic, 313 U.S. 299 (1941); Nixon v. Herndon, 273 U.S. 536 (1927); Nixon v. Condon, 286 U.S. 73 (1932); Grovey v. Townsend, 295 U.S. 45 (1935); Smith v. Allwright, 321 U.S. 649 (1944); and Terry v. Adams, 345 U.S. 461 (1953).

41. United States v. Classic, 313 U.S. 299, 314 (1941).

42. United States v. Saylore 322 U.S. 385 (1944); and *Ex parte* Siebold, 100 U.S. 371 (1880).

43. 285 U.S. 355 (1932).

44. 287 U.S. 1 (1932).

45. 328 U.S. 549, 564 (1946).

46. Cook v. Fortson, 329 U.S. 675 (1946); Turman v. Duckworth, 329 U.S. 675 (1946); Colegrove v. Barrett, 330 U.S. 804 (1946); MacDougall v. Green, 335 U.S. 281 (1946); South v. Peters 339 U.S. 276 (1950); Tedesco v. Board of Supervisors of Elections of New Orleans, 339 U.S. 940 (1950); Remmy v. Smith, 342 U.S. 916 (1952); Cox v. Peters, 342 U.S. 936 (1952); Anderson v. Jordan, 343 U.S. 912 (1952); Kidd v. McCanless, 352 U.S. 920 (1956); Radford v. Gary, 352 U.S. 991 (1957); Hartsfield v. Sloan, 357 U.S. 916 (1958); and Matthews v. Handley, 361 U.S. 127 (1959).

47. 335 U.S. 281 (1948).

48. 335 U.S. 281, 284 (1948).

49. 330 U.S. 804 (1947).

50. 287 U.S. 1, 8 (1932).

51. 339 U.S. 276, 277 (1950).

52. This statement is much oversimplified and is useful only for our purpose here. In fact, the "balancing of equities" doctrine is full of subrules and qualifications. See CHAFEE & POUND, CASES ON EQUITABLE RELIEF AGAINST TORTS 313–14 (1933); and DE FUNIAK,

HANDBOOK OF MODERN EQUITY, 44 (1956).

53. South v. Peters, 339 U.S. 276, 277 (1950).

54. 364 U.S. 339 (1960).

55. 364 U.S. 339, 342 (1960).

56. 369 U.S. 186, 196 (1962).

57. 369 U.S. 186, 196 (1962).

58. 369 U.S. 186, 217 (1962).

59. 369 U.S. 186, 211 (1962).

60. 369 U.S. 186, 213 (1962).

61. 369 U.S. 186, 217 (1962).

62. 343 U.S. 579 (1952).

63. 369 U.S. 186, 210–17 (1962).

64. 369 U.S. 186, 210 (1962).

65. 369 U.S. 186, 211 (1962).

66. 369 U.S. 186, 214 (1962).

67. 369 U.S. 186, 214 (1962).

68. 369 U.S. 186, 220 (1962).

69. 369 U.S. 186, 222 (1962).

70. 369 U.S. 186, 217 (1962).

71. 369 U.S. 186, 211 (1962).

72. 369 U.S. 186, 220 (1962).

73. 369 U.S. 186, 226 (1962).

74. 347 U.S. 438 (1954).

75. 369 U.S. 186, 278 (1962).

76. 369 U.S. 186, 280–81 (1962).

77. 369 U.S. 186, 289 (1962).

78. 369 U.S. 186, 297–98, 301 (1962).

79. 369 U.S. 186, 299–301, 321–24 (1962).

80. See MACREDIS, THE STUDY OF COMPARATIVE GOVERNMENT (1955); and ALMOND & COLEMAN, THE POLITICS OF DEVELOPING AREAS (1960).

81. See RANNEY & KENDALL, DEMOCRACY AND THE AMERICAN PARTY SYSTEM 14 (1956).

82. This example is not entirely satisfactory, but I do not wish to pursue at great length what is, for purposes of my argument here, a minor point. See Riker, *Voting and the Summation of Preferences,* 55 AMERICAN POLITICAL SCIENCE REVIEW 900 (1961).

83. BARKER, THE SOCIAL CONTRACT XLVI (1947).

84. See MILLS, THE POWER ELITE (1956).

85. See KORNHAUSER, THE POLITICS OF MASS SOCIETY (1959).

86. See DE GRAZIA, PUBLIC AND REPUBLIC (1950).

87. See especially THE AMERICAN POLITICAL SCIENCE ASSOCIATION, TOWARD A MORE RESPONSIBLE TWO PARTY SYSTEM (1950); and BURNS, DEADLOCK OF DEMOCRACY (1963).

88. See e.g. KEY POLITICS, PARTIES AND PRESSURE GROUPS 218–49 (1958).

89. See DAHL, PREFACE TO DEMOCRATIC THEORY 63–89 (1956); and SARTORI, DEMOCRATIC THEORY 124–28 (1962).

90. SCHUMPETER, CAPITALISM, SOCIALISM, AND DEMOCRACY 282–83 (1942); HERRING, THE POLITICS OF DEMOCRACY 203–305 (1940).

91. DAHL, WHO GOVERNS (1961).

92. See BENTLEY, THE PROCESS OF GOVERNMENT (1935); TRUMAN, THE GOVERNMENTAL PROCESS (1958); and LATHAM, THE GROUP BASIS OF POLITICS (1952). The notions of the British pluralists are similar. See LINDSAY, THE MODERN DEMOCRATIC STATE (1943); and BARKER, REFLECTIONS ON GOVERNMENT (1942).

93. See KEY, note 88 *supra.*

94. See Riker & Niemi, *The Stability of Coalitions on Roll Calls in the House of Representatives,* 56 AMERICAN POLITICAL SCIENCE REVIEW 58 (1962).

95. SCHATTSCHNEIDER, THE SEMISOVEREIGN PEOPLE (1962).

96. DAHL, note 89 *supra.*

97. See SCHUBERT, THE PUBLIC INTEREST (1960).

98. It should be evident by this stage that many of the points I have been making are held in common with Professor De Grazia. (See especially his *Apportionment and Representative Government,* 1963). I hesitate to adopt his position as my own, however, for several reasons. First, his work is more wide ranging than mine, treating geographic apportionment itself as only one among several alternative forms of apportionment and, therefore, suggesting that inequality of population in geographic districts is only one factor that must be balanced off against other inequalities inherent in geographical, as opposed to other, modes of apportionment. I accept geographic apportionment as given, at least in the context of factors the Supreme Court should have considered in Baker, and am, therefore, more willing to accept the notion that, given geographic apportionment, extreme inequality is undesirable. Second, De Grazia's basis for evaluation is a vision of the United States as a constitutional state with some democratic features. I have preferred to argue that, even within an essentially demo-

cratic framework, absolute equality in voting is not called for. Third, I am not entirely in accord with De Grazia on issues of Constitutionalism and federalism so that I am not concerned, as he is, with the danger of Supreme Court attack on these hallowed institutions or at least his version of them. My views are, of course, quite opposed to his on the nature of courts and judging. For this reason and also I suspect because he is more "traditional organic" than I, I am not prepared to follow his implication that courts should wait until political science can provide them with more answers. Courts are political actors, and, if political actors were to wait for political science to provide them with precise information, very little would get done in politics.

99. 369 U.S. 186, 270 (1962).

100. The doctrine is fully described in Mason, *The Core of Free Government, 1938–40; Mr. Justice Stone and "Preferred Freedoms,"* 65 YALE LAW JOURNAL 597 (1956).

101. 369 U.S. 186, 198 (1962).

102. It would be possible here, as well as at several other points, to examine state judicial experience on these questions, but I forgo doing so because it is not conclusive. The state courts have felt themselves severely limited by *Colegrove*. Those that have struck down or have threatened to strike down apportionments, however, have generally elicited positive legislative response, but it is usually not clear whether the response was caused by or only coincidental to court action or whether or not the new apportionment was much more satisfactory than the old. See Lewis, *Legislative Apportionment and the Federal Courts,* 71 HARVARD LAW REVIEW 1057 (1958); and Dixon *Legislative Apportionment and the Federal Constitution,* 27 LAW AND CONTEMPORARY PROBLEMS 329 (1962).

103. See Tyler, *Court Versus Legislature,* 27 LAW AND CONTEMPORARY PROBLEMS 390 (1962).

104. See JEWELL, THE POLITICS OF REAPPORTIONMENT (1962), for an examination of the problem from many angles. The bibliographical note at the end of the volume provides the necessary sources for statistical analysis.

105. Dixon, note 102 *supra* at 329, 332–38 (1962).

106. Justice Douglas asks but does not answer the question, ". . . may a state weight the vote of one county or district more heavily than it weighs the vote in another?" 369 U.S. 186, 724 (1962). He does not answer the question directly, but, to the extent that he does, his answer seems to be "yes."

107. 369 U.S. 186, 192 (1962) (quoting from the complaint).

108. 369 U.S. 186, 193 n.13 (1962 (quoting from the complaint).

109. 369 U.S. 186, 207–08 (1963) (paraphrasing the complaint).

110. 369 U.S. 186, 208 (1963).

111. 369 U.S. 186, 226–27 (1963).

112. 369 U.S. 186, 244–45 (1963) (Justice Douglas concurring).

113. 369 U.S. 186, 251–54 (1963) (Justice Douglas concurring).

114. 369 U.S. 186, 265–66 (1963) (Justice Stewart concurring).

115. 355 U.S. 281 (1948).

116. THE VOCABULARY OF POLITICS (1953).

117. 83 Sup. Ct. 801 (1963).

118. 84 Sup. Ct. 526 (1964).

119. 84 Sup. Ct. 1363–1518.

¶ Chapter 6

1. 156 U.S. 1 (1895).
2. 353 U.S. 586 (1957).
3. 9 Wheat. 1 (1824).
4. 12 How. 299 (1851).
5. 317 U.S. 111 (1942).
6. See MASON, ECONOMICS CONCENTRATION AND THE MONOPOLY PROBLEM 16–54 (1957).
7. See e.g. NEVINS, JOHN D. ROCKEFELLER (1940); and HIDY, HIDY, GIBB & KNOWLTON, HISTORY OF THE STANDARD OIL COMPANY (NEW JERSEY) (1955).
8. Stocking, *Economic Change and the Sherman Act: Some Reflections on "Workable Competition,"* 44 VIR-

GINIA LAW REVIEW 537 (1958); and Stigler, *Report of the Attorney General's Committee on Antitrust Policy, Discussion,* 46 AMERICAN ECONOMIC REVIEW, SUPPLEMENT, 504ff. (1956).

9. KAYSEN & TURNER, ANTITRUST POLICY 60 (1959).

10. MASSEL, COMPETITION AND MONOPOLY, 87–88 (1962).

11 *Id.,* 271.

12. HALE & HALE, MARKET POWER: SIZE AND SHAPE UNDER THE SHERMAN ACT 109 n.9 (1958).

13. 15 *U.S.C.A.* Secs 1 and 2 (1958).

14. 15 *U.S.C.A.* Sec. 18 (1958).

15. I have omitted Supreme Court review of F.T.C. orders from this chapter because they raise many problems of interagency relations peripheral to the main issues of antitrust policy.

16. HODGES, THE ANTI-TRUST ACT AND THE SUPREME COURT (1941).

17. 15 *U.S.C.A.* Sec. 13(c) (1958).

18. *U.S.C.A.* Sec. 18 (1958.)

19. *U.S.C.A.* Sec. 45 (1958).

20. 110 F. Supp. 295 (1953).

21. 148 F.2d 416 (1945).

22. See Sayre, *Public Welfare Offenses,* 33 COLUMBIA LAW REVIEW 55 (1933); and Levitt, *The Extent and Functions of the Doctrine of Mens Rea,* 17 ILLINOIS LAW REVIEW 578 (1922).

23. 148 F.2d 416, 429–30 (1945).

24. 148 F.2d 416, 431–32 (1945).

25. United States v. United Shoe Machinery Company of New Jersey, 247 U.S. 32 (1918).

26. United Shoe Machinery Corporation v. United States, 258 U.S. 451 (1922).

27. No government agency polices the carrying out of antitrust decrees. Such policing would of course look like positive regulation, a step beyond the negative regulation that is as far as we have been willing to go down the slippery slope to socialism.

28. 110 F. Supp. 295, 341–2, 344–5 (1953).

29. 110 F. Supp. 295, 344 (1953).

30. 353 U.S. 586 (1957).

31. Fed. Rules Civ. Proc. 52(a).

32. Justices Brennan, Warren, Black, and Douglas composed the majority. Justices Burton and Frankfurter dissented. Justices Clark, Harlan, and Whittaker took no part in the decision.

33. 352 U.S. 445 (1957).

34. Federal Baseball Club of Baltimore v. National League, 259 U.S. 200 (1922).

35. Toolson v. New York Yankees, Incorporated, 346 U.S. 356 (1953).

36. United States v. International Boxing Club, 348 U.S. 236 (1955); and United States v. Shubert, 348 U.S. 222 (1955).

37. Northern Pacific Railway Company v. United States, 356 U.S. 1 (1958).

38. International Salt Company v. United States, 332 U.S. 392 (1947).

39. Times Picayune Publishing Company v. United States, 345 U.S. 594 (1953).

40. 358 U.S. 334 (1959).

41. 359 U.S. 271 (1959).

42. 358 U.S. 516 (1959).

43. 358 U.S. 242 (1959).

44. 359 U.S. 207 (1959).

45. 359 U.S. 207, 213 (1959).

46. 361 U.S. 173 (1959).

47. 321 U.S. 57 (1944).

48. 362 U.S. 458 (1960).

49. 308 U.S. 188 (1939).

50. 362 U.S. 29 (1960).

51. If price maintenance is an integral part of a monopolizing scheme or a conspiracy to monopolize, it falls when the more general conduct is condemned, and we are not concerned with that problem here.

52. I have not bothered with strings of citations to support these general propositions for reasons that will become clear shortly. The cases can be easily found in Professor Levi's article cited in the next note.

53. Levi, *The Parke, Davis—Colgate Doctrine: The Ban on Resale Price Maintenance,* 1960 SUPREME COURT REVIEW 258.

54. 164 Supp. 827, 829 (1958).

55. 362 U.S. 29, 43 (1960).

56. 366 U.S. 316 (1961).

57. 365 U.S. 127 (1961).

58. 364 U.S. 56 (1961).

59. See *Note,* 1961 DUKE LAW JOURNAL 302, 305.

60. Technically, the Supreme Court does nothing more than reverse the circuit's holding that no *per se* violation had been alleged and remand to the district court for trial, so that *Radiant Burners* is not absolutely conclusive on the issue of motives. For in-

stance, courts might find that, when the motives are benevolent, no conspiracy to restrain trade has in fact occurred.

61. 365 U.S. 320 (1961).

62. Standard Oil Company v. United States, 337 U.S. 293 (1949).

63. *The Supreme Court, 1960 Term,* 75 HARVARD LAW REVIEW 80, 208–09 (1961).

64. 370 U.S. 405 (1962).

65. 369 U.S. 482 (1962).

66. 370 U.S. 294 (1962).

67. Courts have usually approved mergers designed to save one of the firms from bankruptcy.

68. Bok, *Section 7 of the Clayton Act and the Merging of Law and Economics,* 74 HARVARD LAW REVIEW 226 (1960).

69. 370 U.S. 294, 315–16, 333, 343–44, 346 (1962).

70. 370 U.S. 19 (1962).

71. 368 U.S. 464 (1962).

72. 370 U.S. 690 (1962).

73. White Motor Company v. United States, 83 Sup. Ct. 696 (1963).

74. 83 Sup. Ct. 696, 710 (1963).

75. 83 Sup. Ct. 97 (1962).

76. 83 Sup. Ct. 696, 701 (1963).

77. 83 Sup. Ct. 696, 702 (1963).

78. 83 Sup. Ct. 476 (1963).

79. 49 *U.S.C.A.* Secs. 401–788 (1958).

80. 83 Sup. Ct. 476, 494 (1963).

81. 83 Sup. Ct. 1715 (1963).

82. 83 Sup. Ct. 1715, 1741–43 (1963).

83. 83 Sup. Ct. 1715, 1742 n.42 (1963).

84. 83 Sup. Ct. 1715, 1745 (1963).

85. 83 Sup. Ct. 1715, 1745–46 (1963).

86. The Supreme Court rejected the "primary jurisdiction" doctrine in this case, just as it had in previous antitrust cases involving regulatory agencies.

87. 83 Sup. Ct. 1773 (1963).

88. 83 Sup. Ct. 1773, 1783 (1963).

89. 83 Sup. Ct. 1773, 1783–84 (1963).

90. United States v. Penn-Olin Chemical Co., 12 L.Ed.2d 775 (1964).

91. 12 L.Ed.2d 314 (1964).

92. 84 Sup. Ct. 1033 (1964).

93. 84 Sup. Ct. 1044 (1964). See also Simpson v. Union Oil Co., 84 Sup. Ct. 1051 (1964), in which the Court strikes down one of the "dirty tricks" even though no actual lessening in competition can be shown.

Table of Cases

Index

DATE DUE
MR 10 '71
DEC - 6 1976
APR 18 '95
MAY 11 '95
IL 7365566
sent 960628
MAY 31 '98